PMI-ACP®

Study Guide

PMI-ACP®
Project Management Institute Agile Certified Practitioner Exam
Study Guide

J. Ashley Hunt

PMP, PMI-ACP, Project +, CSM, MCAS

SYBEX®
A Wiley Brand

Senior Acquisitions Editor: Kenyon Brown
Development Editor: Gary Schwartz
Senior Production Editor: Christine O'Connor
Copy Editor: Judy Flynn
Editorial Manager: Mary Beth Wakefield
Production Manager: Kathleen Wisor
Executive Editor: Jim Minatel
Book Designers: Bill Gibson and Judy Fung
Proofreader: Nancy Carrasco
Indexer: Robert Swanson
Project Coordinator, Cover: Brent Savage
Cover Designer: Wiley
Cover Image: Getty Images Inc./Jeremy Woodhouse

Copyright © 2018 by John Wiley & Sons, Inc., Indianapolis, Indiana

Published simultaneously in Canada

ISBN: 978-1-119-43445-0
ISBN: 978-1-119-43463-4 (ebk.)
ISBN: 978-1-119-43446-7 (ebk.)

Manufactured in the United States of America

For general information on our other products and services or to obtain technical support, please contact our Customer Care Department within the U.S. at (877) 762-2974, outside the U.S. at (317) 572-3993 or fax (317) 572-4002.

Wiley publishes in a variety of print and electronic formats and by print-on-demand. Some material included with standard print versions of this book may not be included in e-books or in print-on-demand. If this book refers to media such as a CD or DVD that is not included in the version you purchased, you may download this material at http://booksupport.wiley.com. For more information about Wiley products, visit www.wiley.com.

Library of Congress Control Number: 2017963889

10 9 8 7 6 5 4 3 2 1

For my husband, Chris, and my daughter, Izabella. I love you both so much.

Acknowledgments

This book would not exist were it not for the prompting of my husband, Chris, to step out of my day-to-day routine and follow a bucket list item to completion. Thanks also go to Will Panek, an accomplished author, a co-worker, and my foot in the door of publishing.

I also have to thank StormWind Studios for supporting me always and being an all-around amazing place to work and learn, as well as all of my students over the years who challenged me, learned from me, and in the end allowed me to benefit from their experience and their stories.

My thanks are also due to Gary Schwartz, for being one of the best editors in publishing to work with and for his tireless contributions to my very steep learning curve. And to all of those at Wiley who gave me a shot and who helped with this title, many thanks.

About the Author

J. Ashley Hunt is currently an instructor of project management at StormWind Studios for Waterfall and Agile project management. She has helped certify over 10,000 students around the world in the PMI-ACP® Agile certification, Project Management Professional (PMP®) certification, and CompTIA Project +® certification, with a first-time pass rate of over 90 percent. Ashley has expertise in consulting globally for best practice implementation and certification in multiple project management best practices as well as leadership skills instruction.

She has over 20 years of public speaking and project management experience. She has traveled the world teaching and consulting in many industries, including government, manufacturing, pharmaceuticals, and technology. Ashley has authored over 150 courses that have been taught by her and others around the world. She enjoys engaging people in stories and taking large amounts of information and breaking it down into fun, real-world levels. This is her first published study guide.

Contents at a Glance

Contents

Chapter 7   Effective Team Performance on Agile Projects   201

Chapter 8   Agile Execution and Tracking of Iterations   231

Preface

There have been so many times in my career when people asked me what they should do in one situation or another on their projects, and my answer usually is something like, "It depends." That is, it depends on the situation, it depends on your team, and it depends on your organizational processes. If something isn't working, then it's necessary to change it. Their response would often be that they couldn't change it because of a lack of support from senior management or stringent guidelines set in place by a project management office (PMO). This circular conversation is ever present in a Waterfall environment. Once I started becoming more ingrained in an Agile environment, the conversation shifted from "What *should* we do?" to "What *could* we do?" And that shift changed everything.

Now when I'm presented with a problem in a process or a unique direction, we can all work together to figure out the solution, knowing full well that we will make mistakes but that we will also learn from them. This is why Agile frameworks are so exciting! "What is the simplest thing we can do that works" is an Agile mantra as well as a reminder that being able to pivot and adapt to our environments is something that has not been present in our projects for years. Now the ability to tailor and learn is becoming *the* best practice.

My hope for you is that as you learn more and adapt to new best practices, you will not only have more freedom to determine what works, but you will also experience the catharsis of knowing that if it doesn't work, you will fix it in the next iteration, expand your knowledge, and work together with your team to find the best solution—not because it is dictated by rules, but because it is the best solution in the moment.

Introduction

If you're preparing to take the PMI-ACP® exam, you'll undoubtedly want to find out as much information as you can about multiple Agile frameworks. The more information you have at your disposal, and the more hands-on experience you gain, the better off you'll be when attempting the exam. This study guide is written with that in mind. The goal is to provide you with enough information to prepare you for the test, but not so much that you'll be overloaded with information that's outside the scope of the exam.

This book presents the material at an intermediate technical level. Experience with and knowledge of different Agile frameworks like Scrum, eXtreme Programming (XP), Lean, and Kanban will help you to get a full understanding of the challenges that you'll face as an Agile project management professional.

I've included review questions at the end of each chapter to give you a taste of what it's like to take the exam. If you're already working in an Agile or project management field, I recommend that you check out these questions first to gauge your level of expertise. You can then use the book primarily to fill in the gaps in your current knowledge. This study guide will help you round out your knowledge base before tackling the exam.

If you can answer 90 percent or more of the review questions correctly for a given chapter, you can feel safe moving on to the next chapter. If you're unable to answer that percentage of questions correctly, reread the chapter and try the questions again. Your score should improve.

It Pays to Get Certified

In a world that is becoming more focused on technology, project management literacy in multiple modalities is an essential survival skill. Agile certification proves that you have the knowledge and skills to solve business problems in virtually any business environment.

Certification makes you more competitive and employable. Research has shown that people who study project management best practices get hired. In the competition for entry-level jobs, applicants with high school diplomas or college degrees who included Agile project management coursework in their academic load fared consistently better in job interviews and were hired in significantly higher numbers. When considered a compulsory part of technology education, testing for certification can be an invaluable competitive distinction for Agile and project management professionals.

How Certification Helps Your Career

Obtaining certifications can be highly beneficial for your career strategy and in many cases having multiple certifications shows a wide range of abilities in your chosen careers.

Agile is one of the job categories in highest demand. According to the Project Management Institute's (PMI)® digital *Pulse of the Profession, Global Project Management Survey* (2017),

Agile is a topic of growing importance in project management, with 71 percent of organizations now reporting that they use Agile approaches to their projects sometimes or more frequently than in the past. The report states that over the past 12 months, one in five projects has used Agile approaches, whereas another one in five has used hybrid or blended approaches. Another item from the report worth mentioning is that the percentage of projects that used something other than Agile, hybrid, or plan-driven approaches, which could be a further blend or customization of other approaches, is approximately 23 percent.

Get your foot in the door.   The Project Management Institute's goal in putting together the Agile Certified Practitioner exam is to call attention to the multiple methodologies and best practices involved in projects that would utilize an Agile approach. There are many other certification types that are proprietary; for example, the Scrum Alliance (www.scrumalliance.org) has numerous certifications that are applicable to the methodology of Scrum, but this is the first certification exam of its kind to combine many best practices across multiple methodologies. The content itself is not company-specific or partial to any one methodology over another. The content is based on numerous books and best practices surrounding Agile projects.

Potential income for Agile Project Managers   Earn a national average of almost $90,000 to $151,000 per year depending on their location and specialty according to Glassdoor.

The Project Management Institute's Agile Certified Practioner (PMI-ACP®) certification enhances your project management knowledge.   Professionals who are PMI-ACP® certified are 85 percent more likely to believe that they have the knowledge and skills needed to fulfill their jobs successfully. The PMI-ACP® certification is a big step in starting your career as a certified Agile professional.

Popularity of the PMI-ACP® certification is increasing.   More than 17,000+ individuals worldwide are PMI-ACP® certified and that number is growing daily and exponentially.

Agile project management is regularly used in organizations.   Companies such as Pixar, Spotify, video gaming companies, marketing organizations, staffing companies, manufacturing companies, and many software developers are using Agile methods to complete their projects effectively.

Steps to Getting Certified and Staying Certified

While the steps for gaining your certification may seem daunting, the steps below will help guide you through the process.

Review the exam objectives.   Review the certification objectives to make sure you know what is covered in the exam:

```
www.pmi.org/-/media/pmi/documents/public/pdf/certifications/
agile-certified-exam-outline.pdf
```

Practice for the exam.   After you have studied for the exam, review and answer as many sample questions as you can to prepare for it.

Submit your application.   Fill out your application and determine your next steps for the 21 hours of education:

   www.pmi.org/certifications/types/Agile-acp

Take the test!   Once your application is approved, you will be given information on payment and scheduling options. Most exams are hosted through Prometric:

   www.prometric.com/en-us/for-test-takers/pages/schedule.aspx?Type=schedule

Stay certified through continuing education!   PMI-ACP® certifications are valid for three years from the date of certification. There are a number of ways the certification can be renewed. For more information, check the Project Management Institute's site.

How to Obtain More Information

There is a lot of information online about PMI certifications but it's always best to go directly through the contact information below first.

- Visit the Project Management Institute's website (www.pmi.org) to learn more about getting PMI-ACP certified.

- Contact PMI by calling +1 (855) 746-4849, emailing customercare@pmi.org, or using live chat directly from the website Monday through Friday, 9:00 a.m.–8:00 p.m. US EDT (GMT-4).

- Connect with PMI on LinkedIn, Facebook, Twitter, Flickr, and YouTube.

Don't just study the questions and answers! The questions on the actual exam will be different from the practice questions included in this book. The exam is designed to test your knowledge of a concept or objective, so use this book to learn about the objectives behind the questions.

Before You Begin Studying for the PMI-ACP® Certification Exam

Before you begin studying for the exam, it's imperative that you understand a few things about the PMI-ACP® certification.

There is a fine balance between doing Agile types of projects and studying and taking practice exams. *Rote memorization will not help you.* There's not a lot that I go through in this study guide that will help you pass by just memorizing.

Every single question will be situationally based. It will test your ability to *be agile, not to do Agile.*

Agile, as a term, is the umbrella over all of the different frameworks that you can absorb, use, and understand. To pass an exam like this, you have to get into that frame of mind.

The Agile mindset involves the following principles:

- Exploring, embracing, and applying Agile principles while incorporating that mindset across the team and the organization

- Value-driven delivery is primarily focused on creating high-value increments and making sure that they are produced early and often.

- Meeting and reviewing stakeholder priorities

- Gaining feedback on the increments that your team produces and then prioritizing and improving upon them

You'll see some aspects of these principles across every single one of the different domains.

When you're studying for any exam, the first step in preparation should always be to find out as much as possible about the test: The more you know up front, the better you can plan your course of study. The current exam, and the one addressed by this book, is the 2017 update. Although all variables are subject to change as this book is being written, the exam consists of 120 multiple-choice questions, there is only one correct answer for each question, and you will have three hours to complete the exam.

The exam is predominantly multiple choice with short, concise questions, usually followed by four possible answers. Don't expect lengthy scenarios and complex solutions. This is an exam of knowledge-level topics; you're expected to know a great deal about Agile topics from an overview perspective.

You're likely to see a question on the exam about what an Agile project manager does in different situations, based on servant leadership and best practices. Spend your study time learning the different frameworks and tools and techniques where they would be applicable. Don't get bogged down in step-by-step details; regardless of the framework to which you subscribe, you must be able to participate and collaborate. Those are skills that are crucial to a successful project outcome and to answering questions on the exam.

You should also know that PMI® is notorious for including vague questions on all of its exams. You might see a question for which two of the possible four answers are correct—but you can choose only one. Use your knowledge, logic, and intuition to choose the best answer and then move on.

Sometimes, the questions are worded in ways that would make English majors cringe—a typo here, an incorrect verb there. Don't let this frustrate you—answer the question, and go to the next one. Although I haven't intentionally added typos or other grammatical errors, with the questions throughout this book, I make every attempt to re-create the structure and appearance of the real exam questions.

 PMI® frequently does what is called *item seeding* or *pre-test questions*, which is the practice of including unscored questions on exams. It does so to gather psychometric data, which is then used when developing new versions of the exam. Before you take it, you are told that your exam may include unscored questions. So, if you come across a question that does not appear to map to any of the exam objectives—or for that matter, does not appear to belong in the exam—it is likely a seeded pre-test question. You never really know whether or not a question is seeded, however, so always make your best effort to answer every question correctly.

As you study, you need to know that the exam you'll be taking was created at a certain point in time. Due to the recently released Agile Practice Guide and minor updates to the PMI-ACP® exam for 2018, there may be some variations in terminology and exam structure. This is the most up-to-date version, and therefore you should be okay. Remember, you will need to take a training course to obtain your 21 hours of contact hour from a registered education provider, or REP (1 = 1 hour of training). More information on the exam itself and what you'll need to do appears later in this Introduction.

You won't see a question about the new tailored version, which was just created, but you'll see questions about concepts that existed when this exam was created. Updating the exam is a difficult process, and the exam number is incremented to reflect the new version.

Why Become PMI-ACP® Certified?

There are a number of reasons for obtaining a PMI-ACP certification:

It provides proof of professional achievement.   The certification requirements include general project management experience as well as Agile project management experience. Certification demonstrates that you have the knowledge and the experience, and it provides you with opportunities in your current industry that you may not have had before certification.

It increases your marketability.   Almost anyone can bluff their way through an interview. Once you're PMI-ACP® certified, you'll have the credentials to prove your competency. Moreover, certifications can't be taken from you when you change jobs—you can take that certification with you to any position you accept. Many project management positions these days have minimum requirements for certification in multiple areas of project management, including Agile.

It provides opportunity for advancement.   Individuals who prove themselves to be competent and dedicated are the ones who will most likely be promoted. Becoming certified is a great way to prove your skill level and to show your employer that you're committed to improving your skill set. Look around you at those who are certified: They are probably the people who receive good pay raises and promotions.

It fulfills training requirements.   Many companies have set training requirements for their staff so that they stay up-to-date on the latest project management frameworks and best practices. Having a certification program in Agile frameworks provides project managers and development teams with another certification path to follow when they have exhausted some of the other industry-standard certifications.

It raises customer confidence.   As companies discover the advantages of Agile frameworks, they will undoubtedly require qualified staff to achieve these certifications. Being proficient in Scrum or XP goes a long way to understanding other methodologies, but learning new best practices tools and techniques through the process of certification will improve your current knowledge and add new knowledge that is applicable in your day-to-day management of projects.

How to Become a PMI-ACP Certified Professional

The first place to start to get your certification is to review the specifics of education and experience needed to apply.

Education   High school diploma, associate's degree, or global equivalent at minimum

Experience in Project Management   The *2,000 hours of project management experience* can be any type of project management experience. If you are currently PMP® certified, or you have your PgMP®, PMI® will waive that 2,000 hours because it has already been proven on your PMP® application.

1,500 Hours' Additional Experience   This can be gained by working on Agile types of projects as either a team member or Scrum Master or as any other role you played on Agile projects.

21 Contact Hours of Training   The training is necessary and should be focused on Agile methodologies and practices. Self-study is one category of Contact hour, but an e-learning or live course can count for the rest and is highly recommended.

To maintain your PMI-ACP® (much like a PMP® certification), you will have to obtain 30 PDUs (basically 30 hours) every three years based on Agile topics.

If you're not familiar with the professional development or PDU process, the best thing to do is to go to www.pmi.org and look at what counts as a professional development unit and how the Project Management Institute's talent triangle works for professional development. You will also need to fill out an application in order to sit for your PMI-ACP® exam.

The PMI-ACP® Application Process

The application process is comprehensive for the PMI-ACP® exam but not impossible. There are several things to document and you may need to do some pre-work to collect the information in advance of beginning your application.

- Create an account at www.pmi.org. You could join PMI® or simply apply. Either way, you will need to log in to fill out your application.

- Be honest about your experience, and be prepared in advance with the names and addresses of the companies you worked with and for as well as the contact information for individuals who can validate your experience. Also, be aware of dates and hours spent on the projects on which you worked.

- You can start your application, save it, and continue completing it for up to 90 days, so if you are missing information, you have the time to obtain it.

- Once you submit your application, it takes about five business days for approval. Keep checking your PMI® account using your login information to see when the application is accepted. In some cases, you will get an email, but it's best to check the website after about three days.

- Once approved, you have one year to sit for the exam and three opportunities in that year to pass it. Exam pricing may fluctuate, so it's always best to check www.pmi.org for any updates on pricing.

- If you are already certified with a PMP®, CAPM®, or PgMP®, have your certification number handy so that you can forego the 2,000-hour requirement and focus only on the 1,500 hours of Agile experience needed.

- Read through the guidebook on the application found at the following address. This will give you all of the information you'll need to fill out and submit your application, as well as how the hours are calculated.

    www.pmi.org/-/media/pmi/documents/public/pdf/certifications/
    Agile-certified-practitioner-handbook.pdf

- Be prepared to write short descriptions of the projects on which you worked. Be concise and focus on the deliverables and your role on the project.

- When you submit payment, you will receive an email with instructions on how to schedule your exam plus a registration code that will allow you to arrange it through www.prometric.com. Once you are logged into the Prometric site, you can search for and find the testing location closest to your home or office.

- *One* out of *four* applications are *randomly* selected for audit, and you will know if you are being audited after you pay for the exam. Even though it sounds like an ominous process, PMI® will walk you through everything. I recommend that you send out your application to those who can validate your experience in advance of submitting it. That way, if you are indeed audited, those who can validate your experience will know how to respond to the audit. If you are properly prepared, you can submit all of the additional information quickly. Also, have a certificate of completion from the training organization who provided the exam prep training and a copy of your diploma(s). Once PMI® has all of the information they need, it will take another five days or so to process your application.

  The Project Management Institute

  www.pmi.org

  United States and Canada: 1 (855) 746-4849

When you schedule the exam, you'll receive instructions regarding the appointment and cancellation procedures, ID requirements, and information about the testing center location. In addition, you'll receive a registration and payment confirmation email.

Exams can be scheduled up to six weeks out, or as late as the next day (in some cases, even on the same day). Prometric testing centers have a variety of schedules for exams, and some even have weekend and evening schedules.

You'll be able to choose your exam date and time from the available time/date slots. Be sure that you can keep the appointment, because after a certain amount of time, you will be charged a fee for cancellation or rescheduling unless it is for a medical reason or for another covered cancellation allowance.

On Exam Day

It's easy to be a bit anxious or nervous before taking an exam so to make sure exam day goes smoothly keep these things in mind.

- Bring the authorization letter sent via email by PMI® to the testing center, as well as two forms of identification with the exact name that you put on your application.

- You will be asked to place everything into a locker prior to going into the testing room and to sign in.

- You will be given something to write on and write with. The exam is highly proctored.

- Your exam will be computer-based with one question displayed at a time.

- You can mark questions for later review and click the next or back button as needed to review your answers.

- You will get your results immediately after you click Submit, or if you choose to fill out the survey, you will get your results after you complete that. Completing the survey isn't mandatory, but you can fill out the survey based on your exam experience (should you choose to do so). The only time that this is different is in the rollout of a latest version of the exam. Usually, with the first couple of months of a new exam, the results are delayed for a couple of weeks.

- You will have access to a calculator should you need one.

- The PMI-ACP® exam is pass/fail and based on proficiency in each domain. It is best to take practice exams and focus on gaining a score of at least 90 percent to be totally prepared.

- The PMI-ACP® exam is not adaptive; your test pool is static throughout the exam. There are no points subtracted for incorrect questions, only points given for correctly answered questions.

- The exam provides level of proficiency ratings in each domain. The proficiency ratings for each domain are Proficient, Moderately Proficient, and Below Proficient.

 Exam prices and rules may vary based on the country in which the exam is administered. For detailed pricing and exam registration procedures, refer to PMI's website at www.pmi.org/certifications/types/Agile-acp.

If you pass, you will also receive a proof of certification on the day of your exam from Prometric. They will give you a certified copy of your results, which proves that you have passed the exam and shows the levels of proficiency in each domain. You can call yourself a PMI-ACP right away. It does take some time to get the official certificate from PMI, though.

The Project Management Institute will award you a formal certification. Within four to six weeks of passing the exam, you'll receive your official certification. (If you don't receive these items within eight weeks of taking the exam, contact PMI® directly using the information found in your registration packet.)

Who Should Read This Book?

If you want to acquire a solid foundation in Agile frameworks and best practices, and your goal is to prepare for the exam by learning how and why the best practices work in an Agile environment, this book is for you. You'll find clear explanations of the concepts that you need to grasp and plenty of help to achieve the high level of professional competency that you'll need in order to succeed in your chosen field.

If you want to become PMI-ACP® certified, this book is definitely what you need. However, if you just want to attempt to pass the exam without really understanding Agile, this study guide isn't for you. It's written for people who want to acquire understanding, skills, and in-depth knowledge of multiple Agile frameworks.

In addition to reading this book, you might consider downloading and reading the white papers on Agile that are scattered throughout the Internet, as well as other source materials that cover Agile concepts in depth. The suggested reading list can be found on PMI®'s website in a downloadable PDF found here:

www.pmi.org//media/pmi/documents/public/pdf/certifications/
Agile-gain-insights.pdf

What Does This Book Cover?

This book covers everything you need to know to pass the PMI-ACP exam.

Chapter 1: Agile Foundations

Chapter 2: Scrum and eXtreme Programming (XP)

Chapter 3: Key Aspects of Additional Agile Methodologies

Chapter 4: Agile Initiation and Stakeholder Engagement

Chapter 5: The Human Side of Agile Project Management

Chapter 6: Agile Estimation and Planning

Chapter 7: Effective Team Performance on Agile Projects

Chapter 8: Agile Execution and Tracking of Iterations

Chapter 9: Detecting Problems and Working Through Changes

Chapter 10: Tailoring, Quality Management, and Improving Project Processes

Appendix A: Next Steps

Tips for Taking the PMI-ACP Exam

Here are some general tips for taking your exam:

- Bring two forms of ID with you. One must be a photo ID, such as a driver's license. The other can be a major credit card or a passport. Both forms must include a signature.

- Arrive early at the exam center so that you can relax and review your study materials, particularly tables and lists of exam-related information. After you are ready to enter the testing room, you will need to put everything into a locker; you won't be able to bring any materials into the testing area.

- Read the questions carefully. Don't be tempted to jump to an early conclusion. Make sure that you know exactly what each question is asking.

- Don't leave any unanswered questions.

- The exam requires and tests on actual experience and knowledge with 120 situational questions.

- Some questions have two or more seemingly "correct" answers. There is only one correct answer, so you will need to select the best answer.

- Many questions have extra information that doesn't apply to the actual answer.

- You have the option of going through the exam several times to review your answers for correctness until you submit it or to review or answer marked questions. Most people mark about 10 to 25 questions and then go back to them after they have completed the other questions.

- Read Carefully!

- Use all of your time to review, and only change your answers if you misread the question. Don't rush through it.

- When answering multiple-choice questions about which you're unsure, use a process of elimination to get rid of the obviously incorrect answers first. Doing so will improve your odds if you need to make an educated guess.

- For the latest pricing on the exams and updates to the registration procedures, visit PMI®'s website at www.pmi.org.

This exam is pass/fail, and it's all based on knowledge work, such as, for example, developing software, IT projects, or developing apps. PMP® or Waterfall project management, on the other hand, is more focused on longer-term, tangible work efforts like building a bridge, constructing a building, or mass production of "something." Those project types need a more formal Waterfall approach that uses preplanning and formal change control systems to update work that is being executed.

Your results on an Agile project can be completely intangible, and you can expect the scope of work to change. Scope change is just part of the day-to-day process. This means continuous improvement is necessary.

With Agile (think agility), you must be malleable to improve best practices and products or services. Yes, you are self-driven, self-motivated, and self-managed. Nevertheless, you are also coached in the best practices that you choose or a hybrid approach of several.

What's Included in the Book

We've included several testing features in this book and on the companion website. These tools will help you retain vital exam content as well as prepare you to sit for the actual exam.

Assessment Test   There is an assessment test at the end of this Introduction that you can use to check your readiness for the exam. Take this test before you start reading the book;

it will help you determine the areas in which you might need to brush up. The answers to the assessment test questions appear on a separate page after the last question of the test. Each answer includes an explanation and a note telling you the chapter in which the material appears.

Objective Map and Opening List of Objectives   After this book's Introduction, I have included a detailed exam objective map showing you where each of the exam objectives is covered in this book. In addition, each chapter opens with a list of the exam objectives that it covers. Use these to see exactly where each of the exam topics is covered.

Exam Essentials   Just before the summary, each chapter includes a number of exam essentials. These are the key topics that you should take from the chapter in terms of areas to focus on when preparing for the exam.

Review Questions   To test your knowledge as you progress throughout the book, there are review questions at the end of each chapter. As you finish each chapter, answer the review questions and then check your answers. The correct answers and explanations are found in Appendix B. You can go back to reread the section that deals with each question that you got wrong in order to ensure that you answer them correctly the next time you're tested on the material.

 The Sybex Interactive Online Test Bank, flashcards, practice exam, and glossary can be accessed at www.wiley.com/go/sybextestprep.

Interactive Online Learning Environment and Test Bank

The interactive online learning environment that accompanies the *PMI-ACP® Agile Certified Practioner Exam Study Guide* provides a test bank with study tools to help you prepare for the certification exams and increase your chances of passing them the first time! The test bank includes the following elements:

Sample Tests   All of the questions in this book, including the assessment test that you'll find at the end of this Introduction and the review questions found at the end of each chapter, are provided. In addition, there is a practice exam. Use these questions to test your knowledge of the study guide material. The online test bank runs on multiple devices.

Electronic Flashcards   One set of questions is provided in digital flashcard format (a question followed by a single correct answer). You can use the flashcards to reinforce your learning and to provide last-minute test prep before the exam.

Glossary   The key terms from this book and their definitions are available as a fully searchable PDF.

How to Use This Book and the Interactive Online Learning Environment and Test Bank

If you want a solid foundation for preparing for the PMI-ACP exam, this is the book for you. Countless hours have been spent putting this book together with the sole intention of helping you prepare for the exam.

This book is loaded with valuable information, and you will get the most out of your study time if you understand how it is put together. Here's a list that describes how to approach studying:

1. Take the assessment test immediately following this Introduction. It's okay if you don't know any of the answers—that's what this book is for. Carefully read over the explanations for any question that you get wrong, and make a note of the chapters where that material is covered.

2. Study each chapter carefully, making sure you fully understand the information and the exam objectives listed at the beginning of each one. Again, pay extra-close attention to any chapter that includes material covered in the questions that you missed on the assessment test.

3. Read over the summary and exam essentials sections in each chapter. These will highlight the content from the chapter with which you need to be familiar before sitting for the exam.

4. Answer all of the review questions at the end of each chapter. Specifically note any questions that confuse you, and study those sections of the book again. Don't just skim these questions—make sure you understand each answer completely.

5. Go over the electronic flashcards. These help you to prepare for the latest PMI-ACP® exam, and they're really great study tools.

6. Take the practice exam.

General Exam Considerations

You'll see quite a few questions on the exam about self-organizing teams utilizing emotional intelligence to enhance relationships and a culture of high performance. To do that is to be adaptive in planning and have an evolving, changeable, malleable plan. From iteration to iteration and sprint to sprint, incorporate a lot of stakeholder feedback. During reviews, find out if it is working and if the result is what you thought it would be. How is risk impacting your project? Is it possible to reach fast failure where a risk event overshadows everything, resulting in a cancelled project? All of this is based on stakeholder feedback and the ability to plan (and adapt) team performance, not to mention continuously identifying problems and impediments and constantly improving quality effectiveness and the value of the product and/or service.

Another item to consider is that the Project Management Institute has a framework of ethical decision making, and I think you'll find that if you haven't taken a PMP® exam or anything like it, there are a lot of ethical types of situations. As the manager of an Agile team, it's up to you to assess the differences between what decisions you could make and what other alternatives you have analyzed. Take that information, apply it, and then act on it. It is not really something that you need to memorize; it's more about getting into PMI®'s mind frame as far as ethics are concerned. We are responsible, we respect, we are fair, and we are honest, to name just a few.

Final PMI-ACP® Exam Considerations

Honestly, to pass this exam there is a fine balance of doing Agile types of projects and studying and taking practice exams. *Rote memorization will not help you.*

Every single question will be situationally based. It will test your ability to *be agile, not to do Agile.*

Agile, as a term, is almost the umbrella over all of the different frameworks and tools and techniques that you can absorb, use, and understand. To pass an exam like this, you have got to get into that frame of mind.

The Agile principles mindset involves the following principles:

- Exploring, embracing, and applying Agile principles while incorporating that mindset across the team and the organization

- Focusing value-driven delivery on high-value increments and making sure they are produced early and often

- Meeting and reviewing stakeholder priorities

- Gaining feedback on the increments you produce and then prioritizing and improving upon them

You'll see some aspects of these principles across every single one of the different domains.

PMI-ACP® Exam Objectives

The Project Management Institute goes to great lengths to ensure that its certification programs accurately reflect the industry's best practices. They do this by establishing committees for each of its exam programs. Each committee comprises a group of IT professionals, training providers, volunteers, and publishers, who are responsible for establishing the exam's baseline competency level, and who determine the appropriate target-audience level.

The PMI-ACP® exam updates come from a collaboration with the Agile Alliance and Role Delineation Studies (RDS) that help craft the exam updates.

Once these factors are determined, PMI® shares this information with a group of hand-selected subject matter experts (SMEs). These people are the true brainpower behind the certification program. In the case of this exam, they are Agile-seasoned pros. The SMEs review the committee's findings, refine them, and shape them into the objectives that follow this section.

Even so, they have to go back to the drawing board for further refinements in many cases before the exam is ready to go live in its final state. Rest assured that the content you're about to learn will serve you long after you take the exam.

 Exam objectives are subject to change at any time without prior notice and at PMI's sole discretion. Visit the certification page of PMI's website at www.pmi.org/certifications/types/Agile-acp for the most current listing of exam objectives.

PMI® also publishes relative weightings for each of the exam's objectives. The following table lists the seven PMI-ACP® objective domains and the extent to which they are represented on the current exam. As you use this study guide, you'll find that just the right dosage of objective knowledge has been administered by tailoring coverage to mirror the percentages that PMI uses.

Domain	% of Exam
I. Agile Principles and Mindset	16%
II. Value-Driven Delivery	20%
III. Stakeholder Engagement	17%
IV. Team Performance	16%
V. Adaptive Planning	12%
VI. Problem Detection and Resolution	10%
VII. Continuous Improvement	9%
Total	100%

PMI-ACP® Certification Exam Objective Map

Objective	Chapter
Domain I: Agile Principles and Mindset	
Task 1: Advocate for Agile principles by modeling those principles and discussing Agile values in order to develop a shared mindset across the team as well as between the customer and the team.	Chapter 1, 2, 3
Task 2: Help ensure that everyone has a common understanding of the values and principles of Agile and a common knowledge around the Agile practices and terminology being used in order to work effectively.	Chapter 1, 2, 3
Task 3: Support change at the system or organization level by educating the organization and influencing processes, behaviors, and people in order to make the organization more effective and efficient.	Chapter 1, 2, 3
Task 4: Practice visualization by maintaining highly visible information radiators showing real progress and real team performance in order to enhance transparency and trust.	Chapter 1, 2, 3
Task 5: Contribute to a safe and trustful team environment by allowing everyone to experiment and make mistakes so that each can learn and continuously improve the way he or she works.	Chapter 1, 2, 3
Task 6: Enhance creativity by experimenting with new techniques and process ideas in order to discover more efficient and effective ways of working.	Chapter 1, 2, 3
Task 7: Encourage team members to share knowledge by collaborating and working together in order to lower risks around knowledge silos and reduce bottlenecks.	Chapter 1, 2, 3
Task 8: Encourage emergent leadership within the team by establishing a safe and respectful environment in which new approaches can be tried in order to make improvements and foster self-organization and empowerment.	Chapter 1, 2, 3
Task 9: Practice servant leadership by supporting and encouraging others in their endeavors so that they can perform at their highest level and continue to improve.	Chapter 1, 2, 3

Objective	Chapter
Domain II: Value-Driven Delivery	
Task 1: Define deliverables by identifying units that can be produced incrementally in order to maximize their value to stakeholders while minimizing non-value-added work.	Chapter 6
Task 2: Refine requirements by gaining consensus on the acceptance criteria for features on a just-in-time basis in order to deliver value.	Chapter 6
Task 3: Select and tailor the team's process based on project and organizational characteristics as well as team experience in order to optimize value delivery.	Chapter 6
Task 4: Plan for small releasable increments by organizing requirements into minimally marketable features/minimally viable products in order to allow for the early recognition and delivery of value.	Chapter 6
Task 5: Limit increment size and increase review frequency with appropriate stakeholders in order to identify and respond to risks early on and at minimal cost.	Chapter 6
Task 6: Solicit customer and user feedback by reviewing increments often in order to confirm and enhance business value.	Chapter 6
Task 7: Prioritize the units of work through collaboration with stakeholders in order to optimize the value of the deliverables.	Chapter 6
Task 8: Perform frequent review and maintenance of the work results by prioritizing and maintaining internal quality in order to reduce the overall cost of incremental development.	Chapter 6
Task 9: Continuously identify and prioritize the environmental, operational, and infrastructure factors in order to improve the quality and value of the deliverables.	Chapter 6
Task 10: Conduct operational reviews and/or periodic checkpoints with stakeholders in order to obtain feedback and corrections to the work in progress and planned work.	Chapter 6
Task 11: Balance development of deliverable units and risk reduction efforts by incorporating both value producing and risk reducing work into the backlog in order to maximize the total value proposition over time.	Chapter 6
Task 12: Re-prioritize requirements periodically in order to reflect changes in the environment and stakeholder needs or preferences in order to maximize the value.	Chapter 6

Objective	Chapter
Task 13: Elicit and prioritize relevant non-functional requirements (such as operations and security) by considering the environment in which the solution will be used in order to minimize the probability of failure.	Chapter 6
Task 14: Conduct frequent reviews of work products by performing inspections, reviews, and/or testing in order to identify and incorporate improvements into the overall process and product/service.	Chapter 6

Domain III: Stakeholder Engagement

Task 1: Identify and engage effective and empowered business stakeholder(s) through periodic reviews in order to ensure that the team is knowledgeable about stakeholders' interests, needs, and expectations.	Chapter 4, 5
Task 2: Identify and engage all stakeholders (current and future) by promoting knowledge sharing early and throughout the project to ensure the unimpeded flow of information and value throughout the lifespan of the project.	Chapter 4, 5
Task 3: Establish stakeholder relationships by forming a working agreement among key stakeholders in order to promote participation and effective collaboration.	Chapter 4, 5
Task 4: Maintain proper stakeholder involvement by continually assessing changes in the project and organization in order to ensure that new stakeholders are appropriately engaged.	Chapter 4, 5
Task 5: Establish collaborative behaviors among the members of the organization by fostering group decision making and conflict resolution in order to improve decision quality and reduce the time required to make decisions.	Chapter 4, 5
Task 6: Establish a shared vision of the various project increments (products, deliverables, releases, iterations) by developing a high-level vision and supporting objectives in order to align stakeholders' expectations and build trust.	Chapter 4, 5
Task 7: Establish and maintain a shared understanding of success criteria, deliverables, and acceptable trade-offs by facilitating awareness among stakeholders in order to align expectations and build trust.	Chapter 4, 5
Task 8: Provide transparency regarding work status by communicating team progress, work quality, impediments, and risks in order to help the primary stakeholders make informed decisions.	Chapter 4, 5
Task 9: Provide forecasts at a level of detail that balances the need for certainty and the benefits of adaptability in order to allow stakeholders to plan effectively.	Chapter 4, 5

Objective	Chapter
Domain IV: Team Performance	
Task 1: Cooperate with the other team members to devise ground rules and internal processes in order to foster team coherence and strengthen team members' commitment to shared outcomes.	Chapter 7
Task 2: Help create a team that has the interpersonal and technical skills needed to achieve all known project objectives in order to create business value with minimal delay.	Chapter 7
Task 3: Encourage team members to become generalizing specialists in order to reduce team size and bottlenecks, and to create a high performing cross-functional team.	Chapter 7
Task 4: Contribute to self-organizing the work by empowering others and encouraging emerging leadership in order to produce effective solutions and manage complexity.	Chapter 7
Task 5: Continuously discover team and personal motivators and demotivators in order to ensure that team morale is high and team members are motivated and productive throughout the project.	Chapter 7
Task 6: Facilitate close communication within the team and with appropriate external stakeholders through co-location or the use of collaboration tools in order to reduce miscommunication and rework.	Chapter 7
Task 7: Reduce distractions in order to establish a predictable outcome and optimize the value delivered.	Chapter 7
Task 8: Participate in aligning project and team goals by sharing project vision in order to ensure the team understands how their objectives fit into the overall goals of the project.	Chapter 7
Task 9: Encourage the team to measure its velocity by tracking and measuring actual performance in previous iterations or releases in order for members to gain a better understanding of their capacity and create more accurate forecasts.	Chapter 7
Domain V: Adaptive Planning	
Task 1: Plan at multiple levels (strategic, release, iteration, daily) creating appropriate detail by using rolling wave planning and progressive elaboration to balance predictability of outcomes with ability to exploit opportunities.	Chapter 8

Objective	Chapter
Task 2: Make planning activities visible and transparent by encouraging participation of key stakeholders and publishing planning results in order to increase commitment level and reduce uncertainty.	Chapter 8
Task 3: As the project unfolds, set and manage stakeholder expectations by making increasingly specific levels of commitments in order to ensure common understanding of the expected deliverables.	Chapter 8
Task 4: Adapt the cadence and the planning process based on results of periodic retrospectives about characteristics and/or the size/complexity/criticality of the project deliverables in order to maximize the value.	Chapter 8
Task 5: Inspect and adapt the project plan to reflect changes in requirements, schedule, budget, and shifting priorities based on team learning, delivery experience, stakeholder feedback, and defects in order to maximize business value delivered.	Chapter 8
Task 6: Size items by using progressive elaboration techniques in order to determine the likely project size independent of team velocity and external variables.	Chapter 8
Task 7: Adjust capacity by incorporating maintenance and operations demands and other factors in order to create or update the range estimate.	Chapter 8
Task 8: Create initial scope, schedule, and cost range estimates that reflect current high-level understanding of the effort necessary to deliver the project in order to develop a starting point for managing the project.	Chapter 8
Task 9: Refine scope, schedule, and cost range estimates that reflect the latest understanding of the effort necessary to deliver the project in order to manage the project.	Chapter 8
Task 10: Continuously use data from changes in resource capacity, project size, and velocity metrics in order to evaluate the estimate to complete.	Chapter 8

Domain VI: Problem Detection and Resolution

Task 1: Create an open and safe environment by encouraging conversation and experimentation, in order to surface problems and impediments that are slowing the team down or preventing its ability to deliver value.	Chapter 9
Task 2: Identify threats and issues by educating and engaging the team at various points in the project in order to resolve them at the appropriate time and improve processes that caused issues.	Chapter 9

Objective	Chapter
Task 3: Ensure issues are resolved by appropriate team members and/or reset expectations in light of issues that cannot be resolved in order to maximize the value delivered.	Chapter 9
Task 4: Maintain a visible, monitored, and prioritized list of threats and issues in order to elevate accountability, encourage action, and track ownership and resolution status.	Chapter 9
Task 5: Communicate status of threats and issues by maintaining a threat list and incorporating activities into the backlog of work in order to provide transparency.	Chapter 9

Domain VII: Continuous Improvement (Product, Process, People)

Task 1: Tailor and adapt the project process by periodically reviewing and integrating team practices, organizational culture, and delivery goals in order to ensure team effectiveness within established organizational guidelines and norms.	Chapter 10
Task 2: Improve team processes by conducting frequent retrospectives and improvement experiments in order to continually enhance the effectiveness of the team, project, and organization.	Chapter 10
Task 3: Seek feedback on the product by incremental delivery and frequent demonstrations in order to improve the value of the product.	Chapter 10
Task 4: Create an environment of continued learning by providing opportunities for people to develop their skills in order to develop a more productive team of generalizing specialists.	Chapter 10
Task 5: Challenge existing process elements by performing a value stream analysis and removing waste in order to increase individual efficiency and team effectiveness.	Chapter 10
Task 6: Create systemic improvements by disseminating knowledge and practices across projects and organizational boundaries in order to avoid re-occurrence of identified problems and improve the effectiveness of the organization as a whole.	Chapter 10

Exam objectives are subject to change at any time without prior notice and at PMI's discretion. Visit PMI's website (www.pmi.org) for the most current listing of exam objectives.

Assessment Test

1. What is the last value of the Agile Manifesto?
   A. Responding to change over following a plan
   B. Individuals and interactions over processes and tools
   C. Customer collaboration over contract negotiation
   D. Working software over comprehensive documentation

2. Is Scrum an Agile methodology?
   A. Yes. One of many
   B. No. Scrum is a Waterfall method.
   C. Yes. Scrum applies to best practices or methods of Agile.
   D. No. Scrum is a framework.

3. What does MoSCoW stand for?
   A. Must Scrum Consistently Not Waterfall.
   B. More Scrum Coding Willingly.
   C. Must, Should, Could, and Won't.
   D. MoSCoW is a made-up acronym.

4. What is the difference between Waterfall/predictive project management and Agile frameworks?
   A. Waterfall is preplanned and so are Agile projects.
   B. Scope is fixed on Agile projects but not on Waterfall projects.
   C. Agile plans are just in time, and Waterfall projects are preplanned.
   D. They both are project management frameworks.

5. Bill and Juan are discussing their Scrum project and are trying to understand empirical process control. As their Scrum Master, how would you explain it?
   A. Decisions are made based on observation and experimentation rather than on detailed up-front planning.
   B. Decisions are made based on a business case rather than at the last minute.
   C. Decisions are made based on expert judgment.
   D. Decisions are made by senior management.

6. Scrum can best be described as which of the following?
   A. A methodology
   B. A philosophy
   C. A framework
   D. A method of project management

7. XP is an acronym that stands for which of the following?

   A. Extra Projects

   B. Extreme Projects

   C. Extreme Programs

   D. Extreme Programming

8. Which of the following describes the seven forms of waste on an Agile project?

   A. Kanban

   B. Lean

   C. Kaizen

   D. Crystal

9. During a sprint, which of the following describes the development team meeting to discuss what they worked on the day before, what they worked on today, and what impediments are in their way?

   A. Daily stand-up meetings

   B. Sprint planning

   C. Sprint review

   D. Daily Scrum

10. What is the difference between a Waterfall project charter and an Agile project charter?

   A. Agile projects don't use charters.

   B. Waterfall charters are comprehensive, and Agile charters are more flexible.

   C. Waterfall charters are needed for formal authorization to begin, and Agile charters are just a kickoff document.

   D. There isn't a difference.

11. In order for all stakeholders to have an idea as to what the finished product increment will be, what must be discussed and agreed upon?

   A. The final product

   B. The schedule

   C. The definition of done

   D. The scope definition

12. You are the Agile project manager for a brand-new team who is just learning about Agile frameworks. How do you explain your role on the project?

   A. You are a servant leader.

   B. You manage the product backlog.

   C. You create schedules and budgets for senior management.

   D. You have the final say on the definition of done.

13. Your newly formed team is experiencing some conflict in work styles and can't seem to agree on a direction. According to Tuckman's Ladder, what stage is your team currently in?

    A. Forming

    B. Storming

    C. Norming

    D. Mourning

14. As an Agile project manager, it is important for you to have a variety of interpersonal skills. This will enable you to better lead your team. Which of the following describes your leadership capabilities?

    A. Effective leadership

    B. Adaptive leadership

    C. Agile leadership

    D. Team leadership

15. A team that is very new to Agile decides that they will have a bit of an initiation phase to determine how to move forward. The phase will not produce an increment, but it is helpful to determine direction. What is this phase referred to?

    A. Iteration Zero

    B. Initiation phase

    C. Iteration one

    D. Kickoff phase

16. A distinct iteration length or meeting duration can best be described as which of the following?

    A. Schedule

    B. Timebox

    C. Duration estimation

    D. Epics

17. Why is planning poker an effective way to plan how much work the team will accomplish in a sprint or iteration?

    A. The team decides what to discuss.

    B. Size is easier to estimate than duration.

    C. The Agile project manager can team build.

    D. It allows for bonding on the team level.

18. Which of the following best describes how the scope of work is represented?

    A. Tasks

    B. Activities

    C. Maps

    D. User stories

19. Your customer has explained to the team that they want a software program that will help them with their sales data. After you collect requirements and build out the first increment, the customer states that it isn't anything like what they were picturing and it is going in the wrong direction. What could have happened to cause this?

    A. The gulf of misunderstanding

    B. The project manager didn't collect the right information.

    C. The customer doesn't know what they need.

    D. The customer is just being difficult because they don't understand software design.

20. In a group discussion with your stakeholders, the team suggests that they give the customer the equivalent of the total budget in fake money to see how they would spend it and on what features. This is referred to as which of the following?

    A. 100-point method

    B. Kano analysis

    C. Monopoly money

    D. Dot voting

21. You are the product owner working on the backlog, and your team identifies a risk event that could potentially be more expensive than three of the four features being built. How could the product owner address this?

    A. With a risk-adjusted backlog

    B. With a risk register

    C. With a discussion meeting

    D. With a risk response

22. Carl is working on a string of code he created several weeks ago in order to make it more efficient without changing its behavior. What is Carl doing?

    A. Tech debt

    B. Refactoring

    C. Bug fix

    D. Fixing defects

23. Right in the middle of a very important project, the entire team's computers crash due to a virus. This is an example of which of the following?

    A. A special cause

    B. A common cause

    C. A defect

    D. A risk

24. Bill is explaining to Ling that the best practice is not to take on too much work in an iteration, which creates partially done work. Which of the following is Bill talking about?

    A. Cycle time

    B. Lead time

    C. Limiting work in progress (WIP)

    D. Risk mitigation

25. Your team has a chart in its team space that depicts risk mitigation efforts. Currently, the chart shows a downward trend. What does this tell the team?

    A. Risk isn't being managed effectively.

    B. Mitigation efforts are working.

    C. What is in the risk-adjusted backlog.

    D. The team's velocity

26. Dennis and Abdul are working with their team members to reduce the time it takes to produce value. The team is examining the current state and working toward a future state in a visual manner. Which of the following will help with that?

    A. Value stream mapping

    B. Continuous improvement

    C. Shu Ha Ri

    D. Retrospective

27. You are facilitating your team through an exercise called "remember the future." Which of the following facilitated meetings are you holding?

    A. Lessons learned

    B. Intraspective

    C. Retrospective

    D. Daily Scrum

28. Your team has just wrapped up a review with the customer, and it is now meeting to discuss how the iteration went. Which of the following timeboxed meetings is your team in?

    A. Intraspective

    B. Lessons learned

    C. Retrospective

    D. Kick down

29. Your organization runs mostly Waterfall projects, but it sees the value in several Agile best practices. So, the organization adopts those practices and adds them to the project as a hybrid approach. This is referred to as which of the following?

    A. ScrumBan

    B. Enterprise Scrum

    C. Tailoring

    D. Process improvement

30. The best type of team space tooling includes having the team be set up in what way?

    A. Colocated

    B. Virtual

    C. A combination of colocated and virtual

    D. How the organization decides it should be set up

Answers to Assessment Test

1. **A.** The Agile Manifesto's last principle is responding to change over following a plan. See Chapter 1 for more information about the Agile Manifesto and its principles.

2. **B.** Scrum is considered an Agile framework rather than a methodology. See Chapter 2 for more information.

3. **C.** The mnemonic MoSCoW is used to help prioritize features into must have, should have, could have, and won't have. See Chapter 8 for more information.

4. **C.** Agile frameworks focus on making plans at the last responsible moment to accommodate changes. Waterfall projects preplan and create baselines. See Chapter 1 for more information.

5. **A.** Empirical process control is using observation and experimentation rather than detailed up-front planning. See Chapter 2 for more information.

6. **C.** Scrum is described as a framework to manage projects. For more information, see Chapter 2.

7. **D.** XP is the acronym for eXtreme Programming, which is a type of Agile project management process. For more information, see Chapter 2.

8. **B.** The seven forms of waste are part of Lean. Waste consists of areas where poor practices are slowing down production of value. For more information, see Chapter 3.

9. **D.** The daily Scrum is considered a daily stand-up meeting but specific to the Scrum environment. For more information, see Chapter 2.

10. **B.** Project charters on an Agile project focus on the who, what, where, when, and how aspects with the knowledge that items may change rather than a formal, set approach to project charters as found in Waterfall projects. For additional information, see Chapter 4.

11. **C.** All stakeholders, including the team, must understand the definition of done so that everyone knows what the increment will be at the end of the iteration. For more information, see Chapter 4.

12. **A.** As an Agile project manager, you act as a coach and servant leader to your team. For more information, see Chapter 5.

13. **B.** A team that can't manage its own conflict because it is newly formed is experiencing storming. For additional information, see Chapter 5.

14. **B.** Having good interpersonal skills allows you to practice effective adaptive leadership. For additional information, see Chapter 5.

15. **A.** Iteration Zero allows the team to create a plan for the first iteration. Typically, it is less than a full iteration length. For additional information, see Chapter 6.

16. B. A timebox is a set amount of time for a meeting or an iteration. For example, the daily Scrum is timeboxed for 15 minutes and a sprint is timeboxed for 30 days or fewer. For additional information, see Chapter 6.

17. B. Size is easier and more accurate to estimate than direction. Planning poker is a way to gain consensus on the sizing of work. For more information, see Chapter 6.

18. D. User stories are easier to understand than a list of requirements. For more information, see Chapter 6.

19. A. The gulf of misunderstanding occurs when the definition of done isn't well understood or requirements gathered were not clear enough. For additional information, see Chapter 8.

20. C. Monopoly money is an excellent exercise to see where the customer would spend their budget and on what. This allows for a better understanding of the goals for all involved. For additional information, see Chapter 8.

21. A. A risk-adjusted backlog allows the team to build in time to mitigate the risk and still work on valuable features in an iteration. For more information, see Chapter 9.

22. B. Refactoring is adapting the code without changing its behavior. For additional information, see Chapter 9.

23. A. Both common and special causes create defects or problems on a project. In this case, even though crashes are commonly known, this was a surprise and affected everyone, therefore it is a special cause. For additional information, see Chapter 9.

24. C. Limiting WIP is the best way to make sure that all work selected is completed without partially done work. For additional information, see Chapter 9.

25. B. If the risk burn down chart is trending down, it means that the team's mitigation efforts are going well. For more information, see Chapter 9.

26. A. Value stream mapping allows the team to focus on the current state and map out future states that can be improved. For additional information, see Chapter 10.

27. B. An intraspective allows the team to focus on the future, determine what could go wrong, and focus on the best ways to move forward. See Chapter 10 for more information.

28. C. A retrospective is a timeboxed meeting in which the team discusses what went well and not so well and creates plans for process improvement. For more information, see Chapter 10.

29. C. Tailoring is when value is seen in approaches outside of the normal set of best practices and a hybrid is created to suit the project. For more information, see Chapter 10.

30. A. Best practice would state that the team be colocated for the best performance. However, there are many teams that are virtual or combinations of both. For additional information, see Chapter 10.

Chapter

1

Agile Foundations

THE FOLLOWING PMI-ACP® EXAM TOPICS ARE COVERED IN THIS CHAPTER:

Agile Principles and Mindset

- Task 1: Advocate for agile principles by modeling those principles and discussing agile values in order to develop a shared mindset across the team as well as between the customer and the team.

- Task 2: Help ensure that everyone has a common understanding of the values and principles of agile and a common knowledge around the agile practices and terminology being used in order to work effectively.

- Task 3: Support change at the system or organization level by educating the organization and influencing processes, behaviors, and people in order to make the organization more effective and efficient.

- Task 4: Practice visualization by maintaining highly visible information radiators showing real progress and real team performance in order to enhance transparency and trust.

- Task 5: Contribute to a safe and trustful team environment by allowing everyone to experiment and make mistakes so that each can learn and continuously improve the way he or she works.

- Task 6: Enhance creativity by experimenting with new techniques and process ideas in order to discover more efficient and effective ways of working.

- Task 7: Encourage team members to share knowledge by collaborating and working together in order to lower risks around knowledge silos and reduce bottlenecks.

- Task 8: Encourage emergent leadership within the team by establishing a safe and respectful environment in which new approaches can be tried in order to make improvements and foster self-organization and empowerment.

- Task 9: Practice servant leadership by supporting and encouraging others in their endeavors so that they can perform at their highest level and continue to improve.

In this chapter, we will go through some of the information found in *Agile Principles and Mindset* of the PMI-ACP exam as an overview of how Agile began. We will continue in Chapter 2 and Chapter 3 as we get into greater depth on frameworks and the tasks of Agile.

History and the Agile Manifesto

When most people think of *Agile*, they see it as a recent development of a new kind of *methodology*. In fact, in the age of technology and software development, there are a lot of buzzwords out there revolving around continuous delivery and software production. The history of Agile spans a decade or more. As early as the 1990s, it became necessary for organizations to keep up with the rapid pace of enterprise software development. Technology went from answering machines to dial-up modems and "You've got mail" to the types of technology that we're using today. Due to the proliferation of software programs, apps, and other cutting-edge technologies, it became necessary for organizations to find a better way to manage and adapt.

Most organizations had trouble keeping up with changes in requirements, computer systems, and software, and many were using outdated modalities and best practices. In some industries, it took much longer than expected to create the technology necessary to run the organization or to get certain projects off the ground. The industries that were affected were not necessarily companies that produce software or computer technologies; rather, it was the companies that were using those technologies to get their projects off the ground that felt the greatest impact. Industries like government, telecommunications, automotive, and others that were dependent on software and processing technologies being totally up-to-date were finding that the technologies that they were using were outdated and not effective for the projects they were working on currently.

Organizations were also figuring out that heavier project management methodologies, which focused more on long-term planning, were not as effective for the types of projects they were working on now. Due to a highly changing environment and constant demands to stay current on innovative technologies, it was imperative to find newer and better ways of doing things.

The Agile Alliance

The frustration of heavy methodologies that didn't work for the industry and attempting to find a more "lightweight" model of project management led 17 software developers to meet and discuss new methods or ways to embrace changes and to provide enhanced on-time feedback.

When most people hear about these software developers getting together, they think about the well-known *Agile Alliance*, which created the Agile Manifesto. While it wasn't the first time this group got together to discuss a variety of methodologies and best practices, the most famous meeting was in Snowbird, Utah, in February 2001.

The goal of this meeting was to discuss ways to simplify or create a lightweight type of practice or practices that could fluctuate depending upon the project's needs. The ability to build working software quickly by understanding what the customer needs with very little front-end planning and documentation formed a large part of the discussions. Some of the more recognizable names that make up the Agile Alliance are Kent Beck and Ward Cunningham, who created the *eXtreme Programming* methodology, or XP, as well as Jeff Sutherland and Ken Schwaber, who created the *Scrum* process in the early 1990s.

The Agile Alliance determined that new methods should be based on *iterative and incremental development* rather than a preplanned and well-defined scope of work right at the very beginning of the project. This would allow the result to surface organically as new features or requirements were discovered.

The second driving factor was creating *higher quality software in shorter time frames*, running short sprints or iterations and work to produce something usable at the end of each. This would allow the user to test the increment and make determinations for new requirements for the next iteration. To run quick iterations and create usable increments, it was difficult to preplan everything. Thus, the Agile Alliance determined that it was necessary to have *requirements and solutions evolve through collaboration and self-organizing, cross-functional teams*. This would allow for business value to evolve and develop a cross-pollinated understanding of what the results should be at the team level. Everyone knows the vision, even when the vision changes.

The Agile Manifesto

For those variables to work effectively, it was necessary to adapt current methods, including a Waterfall type framework to suit the needs of more technical types of projects. Based on the discussions and the need to adapt the common Waterfall types of methodologies to suit a rapid, frantic pace in technology, the *Agile Manifesto* was born.

The Agile Manifesto was designed to be a set of lightweight and guiding principles rather than set rules and formal processes. The goal of a written manifesto is for a person or persons to publicly announce something they feel strongly about or to make their views known. That doesn't mean a long statement spanning pages and pages. In fact, much like Agile methodologies in general, the manifesto is short and easy to understand and gets straight to the point without any additional noise.

> The Agile Manifesto forms the basis for most methods currently in use today, including Scrum, eXtreme Programming, Lean, Crystal Methods, and others.

The Agile Manifesto has very specific values that are stated very simply without any additional explanation. The reason for this is so that each project could develop their best practices around these very simple considerations.

Individuals and Interactions over Processes and Tools　The first value puts people first over the staunch best practices found in heavier methodologies. Without interactions and collaboration, the processes and tools don't work. Instead, they hinder a project's ability to be successful in the tech space specifically. This isn't a suggestion that process and tools are unnecessary; rather, it's more that there is better value found in individuals and interactions.

Working Software over Comprehensive Documentation   Excessive documentation is seen as wasteful if the software doesn't work. Too many methodologies are focused on up-front planning, setting hard due dates and baselines, and continual updates as things change. Many Agile practices focus on documentation at the "last responsible moment." It's more important to have software that works and that meets business value and tech specs than it is to spend time putting together massive plans that will change.

Customer Collaboration over Contract Negotiation   As we go forward, you'll come to see that procurement is more flexible on Agile types of projects because it *has to be*. Having requirements that are flexible doesn't mean that external sellers or support staff via contractual relations aren't necessary—they are. However, collaboration with the customer and working toward the right solution is more important than locking down a contract that doesn't meet the needs of the customer in the end. Breach of contract is no joke, and lack of flexibility in procurement counteracts flexibility of requirements and customer needs.

Responding to Change over Following a Plan   This goes back to comprehensive documentation being a waste of time if you know that it is going to change anyway. Anyone in the project management space knows that putting together a well-thought-out plan and then finding out that things have changed is frustrating. It's a lot like planning and saving to buy what you thought was the latest, greatest piece of technology only to find out that your neighbor just bought the next version of this technology and it's way cooler than yours. Not fun! All kidding aside, preplanning something that you suspect may look and act totally different in the end won't work. The ability to pivot and be agile is the crux of all methods and frameworks. Change happens—it's expected and embraced.

A lot of people look at the Agile Manifesto and think that individuals and interactions are more important than processes and tools, or that customer collaboration takes the place of contract negotiation. That is not the case at all. The consensus was that heavier processes and an overuse of tools and documentation were not working in cutting-edge industries, and that current methods and frameworks were too heavily skewed toward items that dragged projects down rather than on areas that could enhance the overall project and customer needs.

Too many projects were focused on the project manager and team spending an exorbitant amount of time doing comprehensive documentation, and this was taking away from interacting with individuals on the team and creating working software. Add to that limited collaboration with the customer and not being able to quickly respond to changes in the scope of work.

The Agile Manifesto does not suggest that we do one over the other; rather, it advocates that while all of the mentioned items are important, some are valued more than the others. If there is a need for comprehensive documentation due to a customer or organizational request, that's fine if there is also working software. Working software, though, is valued more than excessive or comprehensive documentation that may change soon after you have completed it. Any methods that fall under the Agile umbrella are based on iterative and incremental development by producing higher quality software in shorter time frames. As you will see, requirements and solutions can evolve with a team that is able to collaborate freely, self-organize, and be cross functional.

> For the PMI-ACP exam, be very aware of the Agile Manifesto and its values because that will enable you to answer more questions correctly. If you are unsure of the correct answer, or you are deciding between two answers, always revert to the Agile Manifesto and ask yourself if the answer you are leaning toward is describing processes and tools, comprehensive documentation, contract negotiation, and following a plan; if so, then the best answer is the one that best reflects the Agile Manifeso rather than answers that are more focused on processes, tools, and documentation. It's tempting because of your own individual experiences on the job to zero in on an answer that seems to match your experience. Make sure that you read the other answers, and use the Agile Manifesto as your guide to the correct choice.

The 12 Principles of the Agile Manifesto

The 12 major principles that were developed and placed in the Agile Manifesto are also items to bear in mind as you are reading questions on the exam. This goes further than an exam situation though, as it also addresses organizations who are trying to implement an Agile methodology and may be used to a heavier set of processes. Organizations may have to adapt their current organizational culture to embrace the 12 principles of the Agile Manifesto. Although the methodologies are lightweight and the manifesto is brief, trying to implement new methodologies is easier said than done. The Agile Manifesto and its values and principles are easy to talk about but very hard to implement.

The 12 principles are the guiding force in all methodologies that we will cover, and they are very heavily represented on the exam.

1. Our highest priority is to satisfy the customer through early and continuous delivery of valuable software.

2. Welcome changing requirements, even late in development. Agile processes harness change for the customer's competitive advantage.

3. Deliver working software frequently, from a couple of weeks to a couple of months, with a preference for the shorter timescale.

4. Business people and developers must work together daily throughout the project.

5. Build projects around motivated individuals. Give them the environment and support they need, and trust them to get the job done.

6. The most efficient and effective method of conveying information to and within a development team is face-to-face conversation.

7. Working software is the primary measure of progress.

8. Agile processes promote sustainable development. The sponsors, developers, and users should be able to maintain a constant pace indefinitely.

9. Continuous attention to technical excellence and good design enhances agility.

10. Simplicity—the art of maximizing the amount of work not done—is essential.

11. The best architectures, requirements, and designs emerge from self-organizing teams.

12. At regular intervals, the team reflects on how to become more effective and then tunes and adjusts its behavior accordingly.

The 12 Principles Simplified

Even though the 12 principles make sense as their own entities, it's always a good idea to break them down to how they apply to keeping that Agile mindset on the exam and in your work environments. Remember that all of these principles are easier said than done in the real world, and mastering all of them takes time and dedication to the craft of Agile.

1. **Customer Satisfaction:** All Agile methodologies are looking for ways to bring value to the customer on a regular basis by communicating and adapting to changing customer needs.

2. **Welcome Changes:** This keeps the team on top of new requirements and allows for some flexibility in the design rather than preplan and go through a formal change control system every time there is an update to the scope of work.

3. **Frequent Delivery:** Like many methodologies and frameworks that deal with short iterations, the goal is to produce something usable early and often. Frequent delivery is about producing a usable increment in a short time span that the customer finds valuable.

4. **Collocated Teams:** Many best practices in Agile project management have collocated teams. If team members are located remotely or are virtual, the best practice is to collocate them for at least one iteration if possible.

5. **Motivated Individuals:** Teams are self-managed and self-organizing, and they are there because they want to be there. Demotivation doesn't produce good working increments or keep the team focused on providing value.

6. **Face to Face Contact:** Communication is a large part of Agile project management, and face-to-face contact is the best way to communicate. It ties into collocation as well as open and honest communication across the team dynamic.

7. **Working Software:** Focus is on a usable increment that works, and not spending a lot of time on creating software that doesn't work. This is done by getting frequent feedback, utilizing frequent testing and reviews, and looking back to see what changes for the better are necessary.

8. **Constant/Sustainable Pace:** Try to achieve a 40-hour work week and no overtime if possible.

9. **Continuous Attention:** The entire team looks for ways to improve quality, the design, and the overall process on a regular basis.

10. **Simplicity:** Keep it simple. Don't add extra features that are unnecessary.

11. **Self-Organization:** The team decides for itself what it can and can't do, and it works together on solutions.

12. **Regular Reflection:** The team keeps a constant focus on looking back to move forward more successfully.

The Declaration of Interdependence

The Agile Manifesto gained traction in the knowledge work arena, but many believed additional input was necessary to provide principles that could be utilized in other situations outside of software development. Several of the original authors of the Agile Manifesto, as well as other experts in the field, put together the *Declaration of Interdependence* in 2005. The concept behind the Declaration of Interdependence was to develop modern management principles essential to project management and management in general. Since the Agile Manifesto was specific to software development, more clarification was needed to apply the mindset to other projects.

The six principles are based on what might be required to achieve the mindset of an Agile-type project, regardless of the industry. The Declaration of Interdependence begins with a statement that provides the philosophy of the creators and is followed by six principles.

> Agile and adaptive approaches for linking people, projects, and value. We are a community of project leaders that are highly successful at delivering results.
>
> To achieve these results:
>
> 1. We increase return on investment by making continuous flow of value our focus.
>
> 2. We deliver reliable results by engaging customers in frequent interactions and shared ownership.
>
> 3. We expect uncertainty and manage for it through iterations, anticipation, and adaptation.
>
> 4. We unleash creativity and innovation by recognizing that individuals are the ultimate source of value and creating an environment where they can make a difference.
>
> 5. We boost performance through group accountability for results and shared responsibility for team effectiveness.
>
> 6. We improve effectiveness and reliability through situationally specific strategies, processes, and practices.
>
> Citation: [©2005 David Anderson, Sanjiv Augustine, Christopher Avery, Alistair Cockburn, Mike Cohn, Doug DeCarlo, Donna Fitzgerald, Jim Highsmith, Ole Jepsen, Lowell Lindstrom, Todd Little, Kent McDonald, Pollyanna Pixton, Preston Smith, and Robert Wysocki.] http://pmdoi.org/

The Declaration of Interdependence Simplified

The Declaration of Interdependence is a guide to the importance of an Agile mindset, and it is an excellent way to absorb that mindset for the exam. As we go further you will see a lot of frameworks and methodologies that build on both the Agile Manifesto and the Declaration of Interdependence and have led to the creation of many of today's Agile best practices.

We increase return on investment by making continuous flow of value our focus.   Many projects don't reach expected return on investment (ROI) due to scope creep and lack of a clear requirements definition, which in turn bogs down the schedule and the budget and results in defect repair or added scope costs. The goal is to produce something of value by collecting requirements as current information is gathered. Requirements are collected on a continuous basis, with quick turn-around of results so that value is returned and ROI is achieved.

We deliver reliable results by engaging customers in frequent interactions and shared ownership.   Many times, the customer isn't involved in the planning or review of items produced on a project until the very end, and only then do you find out it wasn't what they thought they wanted. The results are dependent on interacting with the customers on a regular basis to find out what is new, what has changed, and what they find valuable today. Then and only then can we produce what they want or need. The customer is part of owning the result and therefore is more invested in how they communicate and interact.

We expect uncertainty and manage for it through iterations, anticipation, and adaptation. All projects carry risk, changes, and uncertainty. We can't control everything, but we can accept that we must be ready at any time for whatever happens. By carrying the expectation that we don't have an *if* situation but instead a *when situation*, we can adapt and pivot as needed.

We unleash creativity and innovation by recognizing that individuals are the ultimate source of value and creating an environment where they can make a difference.   Think of the many organizations that are on the cutting edge, such as Amazon, Facebook, Apple, Microsoft, Cisco, Tesla, or the many more out there who are leading the charge for creativity and innovation. Those organizations recognize the value of innovative ideas, trying out new things, and creating an environment where their people can flex their creative muscles and produce the newest ways to influence the world. It is because these organizations set it up that way that it works.

We boost performance through group accountability for results and shared responsibility for team effectiveness.   This is a far cry from the hierarchical, functional organizations that were prevalent during the industrial revolution. While those organizations still exist and are necessary for some industries, the Agile world is more equal in the distribution of the work, the accountability, and the glory. It is a shift in focus to a team dynamic rather than a top-down hierarchy.

We improve effectiveness and reliability through situationally specific strategies, processes, and practices.   The crux of Agile frameworks and best practices is being just that: agile. We must shift, pivot, change, and adapt as required by the situation. We can't cram one set of rules onto every single project and expect it to work every time. What works for one project will not work for another. Knowing this leaves a more fluid focus on solutions rather than on rules, and with that comes ROI, reliable results, managed risk, creativity, and boosted performance. Everything is interdependent on the rest.

> It is typical to adopt the defined (theoretical) modeling approach when the underlying mechanisms by which a process operates are reasonably well understood. When the process is too complicated for the defined approach, the empirical approach is the appropriate choice.
>
> Process Dynamics, Modeling and Control *by Babtunde Ogunnaike and W. Harmon Ray*

Empirical Process Control

Ken Schwaber and Jeff Sutherland are the creators of the *Scrum methodology*. They adapted and used empirical process control to develop the best practices of Scrum along with the Agile Manifesto as the guiding principle. The three key aspects of *empirical process control* are also the three pillars of Scrum.

Empirical process controls focus on the following:

Transparency: This encompasses not just the process itself but all communications.

Inspection: Frequent inspection and the utilization of frequent reviews of the product service or results is essential.

Adaptation: None of the above will work fully without adaptation, which is the ability to embrace uncertainty and changes and manage risks accordingly.

Many of the questions on the PMI-ACP exam are based on your ability to place yourself into the mindset of the Agile team and how to function in an Agile environment. Empirical process control embraces the Agile Manifesto, but when you think of the definition of *empirical* (using your own experiences and knowledge rather than buying into a set of processes based on theory or even known logic at the time), it's easy to see that when we find better ways of doing things, we embrace them rather than being stuck in a process or processes that simply do not work. Empiricism involves learning and adapting as needed.

 **Real World Scenario**

There Is a Better Way...

Most of my experience has been working with some kind of technology or another either as a consultant or running my own projects. I've worked with red tape and slow-moving wheels of change and I know how frustrating it is to be accountable for over-budget, behind-schedule projects due to heavy expectations of process, scope creep, or excessive documentation. Many times in my career, I would be asked to do something a "certain way," and my response was, "Yeah but...there is a better way." In my experience, this wasn't taken very well because the process was set in stone. Change is painful for organizations, and the thought that they have always done it "this way" is hard to circumvent. That is the beauty of Agile; it is based on observation and conversation. Don't confuse that with a free-for-all though. Many of the frameworks and methods that we'll discuss have specific timeboxing rules and best practices. However, if someone says, "Yeah but there is a better way," then everyone listens and they decide to move forward with it as a team. If they fail, they dust themselves off and try again.

The following are great guiding principles to know that get you into the mindset of empirical process control:

- Iterative

- Incremental

- Frequent reviews

- Adaptation

- Uncertainty and risks during execution

- It isn't a "defined" process; it's a way of being and doing

Agile vs. Waterfall Project Management

Regardless of the methodologies you choose, in both Agile and Waterfall types of project management, the goal is to produce a result that meets spec and customer requirements. But what exactly is the difference between Agile and *Waterfall project management*? We know based on the Agile Manifesto that software development got a bit of a facelift once the decision was made to embrace frequent changes, frequent reviews, and adaptation, and also by putting certain aspects first, like people over formal process. That wasn't always the case with software development projects (or other projects). The Waterfall method was created in the 1970s, and it was utilized in many large projects, including those within the United States Department of Defense. Many standards and books of knowledge were created from the Waterfall philosophy, including *A Guide to the Project Management Body of Knowledge (PMBOK® Guide), Fifth Edition* (Project Management Institute, 2013).

Waterfall and its model are attributed to an article written by Winston W. Royce, and even though he didn't specifically use the term "Waterfall," and he looked at the model as flawed in general, he is often the one credited with creating the Waterfall model.

In Royce's original model, work flows from top to bottom, as does a Waterfall. In software development, the project begins with a collection of requirements and the documentation of those requirements. Once those requirements are collected, you can then move into the design phase of software architecture. Only after the architecture has been designed can you move forward to project implementation. Once the product is complete, verification can take place. Approval of the final deliverable is needed before moving into the maintenance phase and/or operations and support.

While there are many opinions on the Waterfall model being ineffective for software development, the fact of the matter is that all projects can benefit from Waterfall best practices. Many of the best practices for Waterfall project management are found in the *PMBOK® Guide*. The Project Management Institute recognizes the need for tailoring projects and potentially having a combined approach between Waterfall and Agile project management (when needed) for the effective delivery of a result that meets requirements. It is important to note that if an organization is building a skyscraper, a bridge, or a highway system, Agile methods may not be the best way to manage those projects. It's inherently better to have preapproved requirements, a plan in place, formal change control, and validation that the project requirements for scope, time, and cost are met and are monitored and controlled. In some cases, there is room for both.

The *PMBOK® Guide* embraces best practices of a formal life cycle much like the Waterfall approach where many things are preplanned before execution, and it follows a very formal change control system not found in many Agile approaches. Because technology and software development is a very large part of the project management industry globally, it is relevant to compare different best practices and have a flexible approach to producing the result for the best interests of the customer and the organization. It may also be relevant to mention that projects are unique and therefore one project might need a formal Waterfall type of approach and yet another might benefit strictly from Agile types of approaches like Scrum or XP. Still another project may need a more *tailored project management approach with a combination of some Waterfall best practices and some Agile best practices.*

The Benefits of Using Agile in Any industry

The benefits of using Agile in other industries beyond software development are many. In order to tailor approaches that better meet the rapid pace of projects today, it is important for organizations to be able to respond to the swift changes in technology, competition for products, services, results, and changing requirements. That, however, is easier said than done.

For an organization to practice agility at the true organizational level, it must start with an understanding and internalization of Agile principles. Not until recently has there been much of a collective understanding of Agile methodologies across the board. It's been something of a well-guarded secret for only software development projects or Scrum aficionados. Some organizations attempt to implement Agile best practices but are not using them effectively. It is important for effective implementation of any Agile methodology to practice the steps until proficient and to encourage others not only to internalize Agile best practices but to practice them regularly. The hard part is that a lot of organizations are used to their current process flow, and even though it may not be working sufficiently, change is always a bit painful.

Agile, as a term, is the umbrella over all of the different methodologies that you can absorb, use, and understand. To pass the PMI-ACP exam, you have got to get into that frame of mind. The Agile principles mindset involves the following:

- Exploring, embracing, and applying Agile principles while incorporating that mindset across the team and the organization

- Focusing value driven delivery on high-value increments and making sure that they are produced early and often

- Meeting and reviewing stakeholder priorities

- Gaining feedback on the increments you produce and then prioritizing and improving upon them

> You'll see some aspects of these principles across every single one of the different domains.

Regardless of the methodology to which you subscribe, you must be able to participate and collaborate. Those are the skills that are crucial to a successful project outcome.

You must make effective decisions and meet expectations and, at the same time, practice agility. There is a continually changing landscape requiring updates or changes to the value of what you're trying to accomplish.

You can't do that without team performance, and that is dependent on trust, learning, collaboration, and conflict resolution.

> You'll see quite a few questions on the exam about self-organizing teams utilizing emotional intelligence to enhance relationships, and how that helps to help create a culture of high performance. To do that is to be adaptive in your planning and have an evolving, changeable, and malleable plan from initiation all the way through closure.
>
> From iteration to iteration and sprint to sprint, incorporate a lot of stakeholder feedback. During reviews, you'll find out if it is working and if the result is what you thought it would be. How is risk impacting your project? Is it possible to reach fast failure where a risk event overshadows everything, resulting in a cancelled project?
>
> All of this is based on stakeholder feedback and the ability to plan (but adapt) team performance, not to mention continuously identifying problems and impediments and continuously improving quality effectiveness and value of the product and/or service.

You also may have to go through an analysis and design process to get the organization on board. This can be a more difficult aspect than learning the ins and outs of Agile yourself and guiding your team to the understanding of what that methodology looks like. Some good questions to ask yourself and your teams are as follows:

- What are the guidelines?
- What are the processes that you can utilize to estimate how long things will take or how much work you can accomplish in a sprint or iteration?
- What interpersonal skills can you utilize to manage your team of individuals who are also self-managed? What different metrics should you follow closely and how do you plan, monitor, and adapt?

The big dance is "Agile," and part of that dance is incorporating continuous improvement in the process:

- Making sure that you're producing something to quality spec
- Managing risk
- Having the backlog or the work that you're performing be of value to the customer
- Prioritizing the work in such a way that you are providing value consistently through each sprint/iteration of the project

 Whatever works for you is cool, and that's the beauty of agility.

Scope change is just our day-to-day routine. We try to get over that or get through it, but we know that change is going to occur, so we prepare ourselves for it. This means that continuous improvement is necessary. With Agile (think agility), you must be malleable to improve your best practices and products or services. You are self-driven, self-motivated, and self-managed, yes, but you are also coached in the best practices of the methodologies that you choose or a hybrid approach of several methodologies.

Work is planned at the last responsible moment with the expectation that things will change, which is completely the reverse of The *PMBOK® Guide* mentality of project management. What is interesting is that more Waterfall types of projects are now incorporating some of that Agile methodology, and even the PMI-ACP exam is adapted to accommodate more Agile types of approaches. The *PMBOK® Guide* is inclusive of Agile and tailoring approaches. This will make the *PMI-ACP* certification more relevant than ever. Soon more people will get certified, and more people will be implementing the many best practices available. Agile will improve knowledge work globally.

 **Real World Scenario**

Satir Model

We will call our fictitious organization the ABC Company. ABC determined that an Agile approach to its projects was necessary. So it hired an Agile coach and sent its staff to a training program to learn the latest and greatest best practices in Agile project management. The team came back from training and was looking forward to implementing the best practices that they had learned.

The Agile coach worked on a regular basis to help them become more proficient in the practices they were using. Every day the team had a 10-minute stand-up meeting, and the team members would update their progress in a highly visible, low-tech, high-touch way of information radiating. At the same time, executive management was constantly asking for formal documentation, constant updates in the form of long meetings, and long-term projections of the schedule and the costs as well as demanding all of the updates that they were used to getting on other projects prior to the implementation of Agile.

Over time, the project team went back to the habits they had created prior to the training and implementation of Agile practices; the Agile coach became increasingly frustrated with the lack of support from senior management, and senior management deemed that Agile project management simply doesn't work.

This is not a unique situation. Anytime an organization updates its processes, it is important for all levels to understand the best practices and to embrace the changes that will inevitably improve business exponentially. The hard part is the actual change.

The Satir model, created by Virginia Satir during her work as a family counselor, correctly depicts how organizations go from the status quo to the introduction of a foreign element and then resist the changes. Once resistance begins, chaos ensues. Most organizations throw away the best practices of Agile because of the chaos instead of realizing that chaos is necessary for the transformation of ideas and the integration of those innovative ideas in order to move forward to a new status quo.

ABC Company determined that chaos was the new norm and never got to the point where the entire organization engaged in the transforming ideas and integration of new best practices, and therefore it went back to the old status quo. Millions of dollars were spent and lost because chaos won.

Satir Model

The Satir model was created by Virginia Satir for changes in family dynamics during counseling. It applies to implementing change organizationally. In Figure 1.1 you will see the Satir model visually represented.

FIGURE 1.1   The Satir model

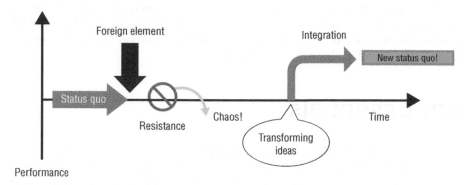

Organizational Agility Tips

To implement Agile methodologies successfully, your organization will need to do the following:

- If your team or organization is new to Agile, it is best to use a proven method of best practices and then to try to create a hybrid approach.

- Implement Agile on the organizational level starting with an understanding and internalization of Agile principles.

- Practice the steps of a chosen Agile methodology until proficient.

- Encourage others to internalize and practice Agile.

- Learn the techniques before throwing a methodology out as not working.

- Embrace the higher criticality and weight of method based on team size and project length.

Summary

This chapter started with a discussion of the roots of Agile's history, which served as the springboard for the Agile Manifesto and multiple types of frameworks and methodologies.

Next, we reviewed the 12 principles of Agile that influence every aspect of Agile project management regardless of type. The Agile Manifesto and its principles are excellent to keep in mind whether you are implementing some type of process on your projects or answering questions on your exams.

While Agile differs from a Waterfall type of project management, it is relevant to mention again that it is possible to have best practices come from each as needed on your unique projects. All of what we will discuss in this book are best practices, and they can be adapted as needed for your organization.

Even though Agile has been around in some way since the early 1990s, it is just now becoming more relevant across multiple modalities, project types, and organizations due to the technology age and cutting-edge knowledge work taking place in all industries globally. All can benefit from either an Agile approach to projects or a tailored approach between aspects of Waterfall and Agile project management.

Exam Essentials

Be able to understand and embrace the Agile Manifesto.   Know how Individuals and Interactions over Processes and Tools, Working Software over Comprehensive Documentation, Customer Collaboration over Contract Negotiation, and Responding to Change over Following a Plan are important aspects of all Agile methodologies. Know that the Agile Manifesto will help you answer many questions on the exam.

Be able to embrace the principles of the Agile Manifesto.   The principles include customer satisfaction, welcome changes, frequent delivery, collocated teams, motivated individuals, face-face contact, working software, constant/sustainable pace, continuous attention, simplicity, self-organization, and regular reflection. These principles will be excellent reminders of Agile, and you will see them reflected many times throughout all domains.

Be able to understand the Declaration of Interdependence and empirical process control. Know how both aspects led to better definition of the principles and the development of Agile frameworks/methodologies like Scrum and XP.

Understand the differences between Agile and Waterfall.   Agile is focused on rapid production of a working increment in an iterative fashion. Iterations are run for abbreviated time spans, which allow continuous feedback and reflection with a focus on continuous improvements.

Waterfall project management is more involved with long-term planning and making sure that the plan is in place and approved before execution of work begins. Changes are embraced, but they follow a strict change control system throughout the life cycle. Heavier documentation, larger teams, and more tangible products, services, or results are created. Hybrid methods of Agile/Waterfall are becoming more popular today.

Be able to place yourself in an Agile type of environment and get into the Agile mindset. If you are new to Agile or specialize on one type of framework, then it is important to keep an open mind about diverse ways of running an Agile project. You must always keep in mind the influencers and their desire for a better way of producing valuable results.

Be able to utilize the Agile Manifesto in order to answer questions appropriately.   This is probably the most important aspect outside of memorizing the manifesto for the exam. Every question will relate to your ability to be in the mindset of best practices and determine the *best* answer based on the principles of Agile.

Review Questions

You can find the answers to the review questions in Appendix B.

1. What is the first value in the Agile Manifesto?
    A. Contract Negotiations over Working Plans
    B. Working Software over Comprehensive Documentation
    C. Individuals and Interactions over Processes and Tools
    D. Comprehensive Documentation over Customer Interaction

2. Who were the creators of the Agile Manifesto?
    A. PMI
    B. The Agile Alliance
    C. Ken Beck
    D. The Scrum Alliance

3. In the Agile Manifesto, it is more important to respond to changes than to do which of the following?
    A. Comprehensively document
    B. Use processes and tools
    C. Negotiate contracts
    D. Follow a plan

4. Which of the following is the highest priority of the 12 major principles?
    A. Face-to-face conversation
    B. Motivated individuals
    C. Working software
    D. Customer satisfaction

5. You are working to implement Agile in your organization, and a key stakeholder asks you to explain Agile to them. What would be the best answer to explain Agile to someone who doesn't know anything about it?
    A. Agile is a way to produce software without change control.
    B. Agile is a framework for better project management.
    C. Agile is a mindset that allows an organization to focus on better ways to produce value for the customer and practice continuous improvement.
    D. Agile is the opposite of Waterfall.

6. Bill is a key stakeholder in your organization and has recently learned about your usage of an Agile framework on your current project. You've invited Bill to a planning meeting, and he says, "I thought you didn't do formal planning in Agile." How should you respond?

   A. "We do plan our projects, but we keep our focus on the immediate items and we value working software over comprehensive documentation during planning."

   B. "We plan as much as anyone working on projects and try to incorporate the opinions of many stakeholders to help us do it."

   C. "We don't plan normally, but since you are new to Agile we thought we would plan as much as possible until you get comfortable with Agile."

   D. "We build plans that we know won't work to meet stakeholder requirements."

7. Empirical process control has three main aspects to it. What would those three be?

   A. Transparency, inspection, and adaptation

   B. Iterative, incremental, and uncertainty

   C. Transparency, iterative, reliability

   D. Inspection, incremental, adaptable

8. In the past, your team has run projects using a more formal Waterfall method and now is incorporating Agile methodologies. What will be the biggest difference in how you manage your projects?

   A. Waterfall preplans the entire project before execution, and Agile only plans out just far enough to create a workable increment that is valuable to the customer.

   B. Agile is much more flexible in how the best practices work. As long as your team creates something usable, it doesn't matter how you accomplish it.

   C. The Waterfall method has many books of knowledge and best practices, but Agile only has the Manifesto.

   D. Agile plans less, and Waterfall plans more.

9. The Satir model correctly predicts why some organizations have a challenging time changing methodologies. What is the reason for that based on the model?

   A. Organizations don't spend enough time training their people and that causes chaos.

   B. Organizations often determine that the new method isn't working because they have not reached the integration stage and have only seen the chaos.

   C. Organizations are used to doing things a certain way and nobody likes to change.

   D. Organizations don't allow enough time for the chaos, which in turn doesn't allow things to level out in integration.

10. What is the main reason organizations should not jump into a hybrid method if they are new to Agile approaches?

   A. It takes practice to implement Agile effectively on an organizational level. It's better to practice one method and become proficient before trying to combine two.

   B. Organizations that have used both should determine which one works the best individually before creating a hybrid option.

   C. Hybrids are not recommended for large software organizations.

   D. It can get very confusing as to which frameworks to follow if it is a combination of two types.

11. Seventeen developers met in Snowbird, Utah, in February 2001 to discuss better ways of managing software projects. What was the result of that meeting?

   A. The Declaration of Interdependence

   B. The Agile Manifesto

   C. The Scrum Theory

   D. The *PMBOK® Guide*

12. What does the Agile Manifesto mean by "individuals and interactions over processes and tools"?

   A. It means that processes and tools aren't needed on Agile projects.

   B. It means that without processes and tools, the individuals and interactions will not be effective.

   C. It means that individuals and interactions are valued more than processes and tools.

   D. It means that both are necessary and work together to produce working software.

13. Which of the following best describes why Waterfall project management isn't the most effective way to manage software development projects?

   A. The rapid pace and constant changes make it difficult to preplan and create baselines.

   B. The Agile life cycles are different and therefore incompatible with Waterfall.

   C. Waterfall is for construction, and Agile is for software.

   D. Waterfall is an effective way to manage software projects as long as you have the scope of work up front.

14. Complete the rest of this statement from the Agile Manifesto: Individuals and interactions over _____.

   A. Following a plan

   B. Comprehensive documentation

   C. Contract negotiation

   D. Processes and tools

15. Complete the rest of this statement from the Agile Manifesto: Responding to change over _____.

   A. Following a plan

   B. Comprehensive documentation

   C. Contract negotiation

   D. Processes and tools

16. Complete the rest of this statement from the Agile Manifesto: Working software over _____.

    A. Following a plan

    B. Comprehensive documentation

    C. Contract negotiation

    D. Processes and tools

17. Complete the rest of this statement from the Agile Manifesto: Customer collaboration over _____.

    A. Following a plan

    B. Comprehensive documentation

    C. Contract negotiation

    D. Processes and tools

18. In the Declaration of Interdependence, which of the following increases by making continuous flow of value the focus?

    A. Reliable results

    B. Creativity and innovation

    C. ROI

    D. A boost in performance

19. What is the best way to explain Agile project teams based on the values of the Agile Manifesto?

    A. Managed by a project manager

    B. Managed by an Agile project manager

    C. Not managed by anyone

    D. Self-directed and self-managed

20. Agile project teams work best in what dynamic?

    A. Collocated

    B. Virtual

    C. A combination of collocated and virtual

    D. A cross-functional dynamic

Chapter

2

Scrum and eXtreme Programming (XP)

THE FOLLOWING PMI-ACP® EXAM TOPICS ARE COVERED IN THIS CHAPTER:

✓ **Domain I: Agile Principles and Mindset**

- Task 1: Advocate for Agile principles by modeling those principles and discussing Agile values in order to develop a shared mindset across the team as well as between the customer and the team.

- Task 2: Help ensure that everyone has a common understanding of the values and principles of Agile and a common knowledge around the Agile practices and terminology being used in order to work effectively.

- Task 3: Support change at the system or organization level by educating the organization and influencing processes, behaviors, and people in order to make the organization more effective and efficient.

- Task 4: Practice visualization by maintaining highly visible information radiators showing real progress and real team performance in order to enhance transparency and trust.

- Task 5: Contribute to a safe and trustful team environment by allowing everyone to experiment and make mistakes so that each can learn and continuously improve the way he or she works.

- Task 6: Enhance creativity by experimenting with new techniques and process ideas in order to discover more efficient and effective ways of working.

- Task 7: Encourage team members to share knowledge by collaborating and working together in order to lower risks around knowledge silos and reduce bottlenecks.

- Task 8: Encourage emergent leadership within the team by establishing a safe and respectful environment in which new approaches can be tried in order to make improvements and foster self-organization and empowerment.

- Task 9: Practice servant leadership by supporting and encouraging others in their endeavors so that they can perform at their highest level and continue to improve.

In this chapter, you will continue going through Domain I on the PMI-ACP exam content outline about the mindset of Agile. Understanding different best practices and applying them, regardless of your choice of method, is a large part of absorbing Agile. In Chapter 1, you covered the beginnings of Agile and the reasons it was necessary to find better ways to manage technology projects. This chapter and the next chapter, will move through all of the principles and mindsets that cover all nine tasks found on the exam content outline under Domain I.

It is unnecessary to memorize the exam content outline, as you won't get questions that ask, "Which of the following is Task 1 in Domain I?" What you will get asked are situational questions that test your ability to be in the mindset of the tasks and domains and to understand what our roles are as Agile practitioners. It's good to read and absorb the outline to know what are the best practices upon which you will be tested.

What Is Scrum?

Ken Schwaber and Jeff Sutherland first co-presented Scrum at the *Object-Oriented Programming, Systems, Languages & Applications (OOPSLA)* conference in 1995. Their definition of Scrum is as follows:

> A framework within which people can address complex adaptive problems, while productively and creatively delivering products of the highest possible value.

Scrum was designed to be a *framework*, not a process. This framework is lightweight, very simple to understand but inherently difficult to master. It takes years of practice and continuous improvement to truly master Scrum, but this doesn't mean that you can't use it daily on your projects and work hard to master all aspects of it.

Scrum theory was founded or based upon the *empirical process control theory*, or *empiricism*. Much as with many other Agile methodologies, knowledge comes from experience and making decisions based on what is currently known about features, the customer value, and what being done looks like today. At a very basic level, utilizing Scrum allows us to review, adapt, and improve on an iterative level while producing value incrementally and optimizing predictability. This will then reduce risk exponentially. Since the Scrum methodology was created based on empirical process control, the three pillars of Scrum theory are *transparency, inspection*, and *adaptation*. Let's break down these three pillars as they are attributed to Scrum theory and focus on some of the items to bear in mind while answering questions on your exam.

Transparency

Transparency, or even transparent communication, creates a mutual understanding of standards, a common language so that the process can be shared and understood, and most important, a transparent understanding of the definition of done. As you go forward through many of the various aspects of Agile project management, you will see a common theme of openness and communication about value, processes, techniques, and even how to manage risks and issues. The entire focus is based on the understanding that everyone knows what everyone else is doing and how they are doing it. If someone makes a mistake, they own it and work as a team to fix it. Transparent and clear communication across all aspects of the Scrum framework sets the stage for effective production of "done" increments and a team atmosphere of unity.

Inspection

As with many Agile methodologies, frequent *inspection* of the increments is a highly important aspect of producing to spec and being "done." In the Scrum framework, frequent inspection also allows progress toward the overarching Scrum goal and allows for identification of variances that would keep the result from being accepted. While frequent inspection is a crucial aspect of Scrum theory, performing inspections too frequently will do the opposite and actually can hinder progress. Too frequent inspections will disrupt the work rather than promote effective execution of it. It is usually a promising idea to have a skilled inspector review the results and work with the team to improve them, but not all organizations have inspectors on hand to do so. Therefore, continuous improvement in those practices would need to be the focus. It makes sense if you are creating something, or if you are the customer, to inspect the results to make sure that you are doing things right and building the right thing.

 Design Scenario

Inspect and Adapt

Imagine that you are creating an app that stores all of your passwords securely. It's important to inspect often to make sure that the app is functioning and protecting your customers from hackers. Thus you would test again and again, every step of the way. Your customers are also going to check and inspect with a different set of eyes—those of an end user. They may not understand the code or the inner workings of the app, so they are going to inspect it with their knowledge of what they want the app to do in mind, and they will provide you with feedback on what is working and what is not. This cycle of transparent communication and inspection allows you to adapt as needed.

Adaptation

The final pillar in Scrum theory is *adaptation*. Think of the word *agile* or *agility*, which describes the ability to adapt and change directions as needed. In Scrum, if inspection shows a result that is not acceptable or that is undesirable, this then points to a problem in the process and the execution of the process. If the process is deemed to be not working and affecting the result or increment, the process itself must be adjusted.

This does not mean that you switch from Scrum to something else like XP. It simply means that the process is not being effectively executed, and it's necessary for the team to adapt or revisit best practices of Scrum and constantly check to make sure the process is working. Adaptation also points to the way the process is being used and whether the customer is getting the value they expected. The further you go without adapting, the worse it can get. You open yourself to risks and issues and deviate further from the value that you were supposed to create. This doesn't mean that you don't have creative license in software design, because it is very much both a science and an art form. The bottom line, however, is if the process isn't working, it's time to adapt. Much like the definition of insanity is doing things the same way and expecting a different result, the adaptation pillar is there to make sure that you can adjust your direction and provide a better process to produce the result. Always Practice Agility!

Scrum Values

Even though Scrum is a lightweight framework, there are very specific events that are used for inspection and adaptation. If they are not done correctly, it could lead to the need to review the execution of the framework and to determine if changes are necessary.

The Five Values of Scrum

The five values of Scrum are commitment, courage, focus, openness, respect. That is why Scrum is easy to understand but very difficult to put into practice. The entire Scrum team must be committed to the goals and to the process. Have the courage to try new things and to make mistakes. Stay focused on building value, be open to new thoughts, opinions, and even criticisms all the while showing respect to each other, to the customer, and to the process. Therefore, Scrum is set up with very specific responsibilities across the team dynamic. All the values support the pillars of Scrum and empirical process control.

These values, again, are as follows:

- Commitment
- Focus
- Openness
- Respect
- Courage

The Five Values of Scrum Explained

Even though the five values are daily words that are easy to explain, the importance they play in Scrum sets the stage for effectively implementing the framework.

Commitment: The first value of Scrum is commitment, which is easier said than done. The group needs to commit to the goal, the process, and the team. They need to make sure that they don't take on too much but that they commit to what they do take on. Remember that Scrum is easy to talk about but very hard to do. The wonderful thing about this framework is that is gives the team the ability to be self-directed and self-managed. With that comes the need to be focused on the team and the goal. Meeting commitments is an important aspect of Scrum. This is why, as you go forward, you'll see that work is broken down in such a way so that the team decides what to commit to and what to work toward in order to meet the end goal.

Focus: If you've ever tried multitasking, or doing many things at once, but not being completely successful at any one task, you know that multitasking really is a myth in terms of productivity. If you focus on a few things at a time, you will get more done.

If you focus on just a few things, then you know your goals and roles and responsibilities. You can then zero in on the work that needs to be done. The beauty of the Scrum framework is the team's ability to choose what they can commit to. That will then allow them to focus exclusively on the work that needs to be done and to know with some degree of certainty that they will be able to accomplish it.

Openness: Nobody likes surprises, least of all project sponsors, customers, and project managers! That is why openness is one of the five values of Scrum. Remember that one of the pillars of Scrum is transparency, which means having everything out in the open. As you move forward through the exam content outline, you'll discover the best practices of using information radiators and big visible charts and graphs that show precisely how the project is progressing in a simple visual way. Openness also applies to the team dynamic— openness in communication, challenging the status quo, and updating the project status daily. This may be very different from your organization's current way of doing things.

 Real World Scenario

A Frustrating Project

During a very large project, many of my team members were grumbling about how the process that we were using wasn't working, and they were upset that nobody seemed to care that they were getting blamed for mediocre performance when the process created the problems in the first place. I was feeling the pressure too, and I attempted to be the buffer for my team with upper management. A meeting was called to get everyone in a room and everything out on the table. Most of the team members were afraid to speak up because the "powers that be" were in the room. Because of the lack of transparent communication, management was unaware that a better way was out there. We managed not to get much done, and the status quo returned. This was very frustrating indeed!

This is not the case with Scrum or Agile methods in general. Everyone from the higher-ups to the team are open about progress, concerns, and innovative ways of doing things.

You can't commit and focus if you don't know the real inner workings of the team and the project's progress.

Respect: Accountability on the team level is a major aspect of Scrum, but let's not forget the individuals. Everyone makes mistakes, and a key aspect of many Agile methodologies is the rule of no finger pointing. Respect is earned, but it is also given. The team lifts each other up and helps where needed. Team accountability also means that if one team member needs help, it is given without question.

Most professionals express respect to their team members, but occasionally there is a dynamic of drama or one-upmanship. That is simply not one of the tenants of Scrum. Respect is expected, given, and received on a regular basis. If there is a problem, everyone is open and consensus is reached to solve it. This allows the team to make a commitment to the work, focus on their work, and be open about the work and their successes and challenges. Respect for the team and each other is paramount to all of the rest of the values working correctly.

Courage: For the previous four values to work, the team must be courageous. You expect change, and change can be uncomfortable. You are in very cutting-edge industries, so you must be courageous to push the boundaries. You must be courageous to speak up when you have challenges or make mistakes and to push the status quo.

Organizations who practice Scrum probably feel the chaos of this change in the beginning. Nobody likes being challenged, especially those in power positions. For Scrum to work across the organization, there must be people who are courageous enough to speak up and say, "Always doing it this way isn't working, and we need to step out of our comfort zone and practice agility." Much as with a tightrope walker stepping from the safe, solid platform and onto the rope, courage is needed to make changes to a less solid and rigid footing of old, worn-out practices.

 In the sport of rugby, a scrum is a banding together of certain players on the team working toward a common goal—they are stronger working together than they are when working apart. As in most sports, there are distinct positions that are played, and Scrum in the Agile world is no different.

The Scrum Team

There are very specific roles on the Scrum team, and each of those roles has its own focus, responsibilities, and abilities. Scrum teams are self-organizing and cross functional. That might sound vastly different from the thought process of a hierarchical organizational dynamic, but self-organizing doesn't mean team members doing whatever they want, whenever they want. The self-organization model is truly designed to optimize the flexibility of decision making and the courage to be creative. Believe it or not, productivity increases if self-organization is done correctly!

The ability to have cross-functional team members also allows for more experience in a lot of different avenues, which in turn amps up the courage, focus, and respect aspects. To function effectively, the Scrum team is made up of three roles: the product owner, the development team, and the Scrum Master.

Even though the PMI-ACP exam is not 100 percent Scrum focused, the Scrum is one of the most popular frameworks, and therefore you will see questions about the distinct roles and responsibilities of Scrum team members. You will read the questions from the perspective of some (if not all) of the roles, and you will need to have a good understanding of what each role does and why it is so important. It is also the methodology on which you will spend the most time, as the mindset of Agile is important to know for the exam, and Scrum is a terrific way to depict that mindset. Scrum isn't more or less important than the other methodologies, but the framework is a great way to set the stage for the other types of Agile best practices.

The Product Owner

You'll start with the *product owner*, whose main job is to maximize the value of the product and the value of the work of the development team.

The product owner's sole responsibility is to manage the product backlog.

The *product backlog* contains all of the possible items that could go into a result or increment requested by the customer. Because the product owner is the sole party responsible for managing the product backlog, it is their job to express clearly what items are in the backlog and, at the same time, reorganize and reorder work items in the best way to achieve the goals and mission of the project while balancing the requirements set by the customer. The main reason for this is to optimize value so that whatever the development team is working on will produce a valuable, usable increment.

That doesn't mean that the development team and Scrum Master have no idea what's in the backlog. The backlog is transparent and visible, so it is clear to all involved what work is next on the list. Because the product owner is accountable for the product backlog, they are also accountable for making sure that the development team understands the items in the backlog to whatever level is necessary to accomplish the work. This means that the product owner is constantly in contact with the customer, other stakeholders, the development team, and the Scrum Master.

The backlog itself is constantly changing and updated to push what is valuable to the front of the line based on the information gathered from the customer and stakeholders. It is important to note that the product owner is also able to say "no" when they feel that the customer is asking for items that may not be able to be done, or may inherently affect the result they're trying to obtain. It is also important to note that the product owner's decisions and accountability for the product backlog is respected by the entire organization. The development team will not be allowed to act on other work or requirements outside of the product owner's decisions. This is partially why implementation on the organizational level can be painful for high-level executives.

The Development Team

Once the product owner decides which items in the backlog are the most valuable, the *development team* will do the work of producing a potentially releasable increment at the end of each 30-day sprint, which is a typical length of a Scrum sprint. We will discuss sprints in depth later in this chapter. The development team itself is designed to be small enough to adapt quickly to changes and risks, and to be Agile but also large enough as well to complete the work. In a perfect world, the Scrum team would be somewhere between seven and nine members. This is so that the team is structured correctly and empowered to organize and manage its own work.

A Scrum development team is self-organizing and cross functional.

What is interesting about a Scrum development team is there are no distinct titles other than "developer," regardless of the work being done—*no* exceptions. That may be very different for your organization, where there are some team members, such as testers or business analysts, outside of the development team. On a Scrum development team, they are all developers with different skill levels and different knowledge, but the entire team is accountable for the work they do.

Scrum Master

That brings us to the *Scrum Master*, who is described as a servant leader. A Scrum Master is responsible for making sure Scrum is understood, making sure the Scrum team adheres to the Scrum framework's practices and rules, and keeping the ball rolling in general. You might think, isn't that just describing a project manager? In its truest generic sense, you could call a Scrum Master an Agile project manager.

You may see *Agile project manager* as a term on the PMI-ACP exam used as a general descriptor of a servant leader no matter what methodology is the focus of the questions.

Because organizations tend to try to implement Scrum without seeing the value of a Scrum Master, often Scrum is blamed for not working. Notice that the Scrum Master is described as a servant first and a leader second, not a manager, nor a business analyst, and not a senior stakeholder.

The goal of the Scrum Master is to maximize value in all interactions with the product owner, the development team, and the entire organization. Their role in the organization is to make sure that Scrum is effectively implemented from the top down and from the bottom up.

Let's look at some of the interactions that the Scrum Master might have on a regular basis and why those interactions are important for effective implementation of Scrum as well as for effectively answering exam questions.

Scrum Master and the Product Owner

You know that the product owner is solely responsible for the product backlog, and that in and of itself is a big job. Thus the Scrum Master will provide servant leadership to the product owner in a variety of ways. For example, the Scrum Master will help find newer and better techniques for effectively managing the backlog. The Scrum Master will also help the product owner inform the team about backlog items as well as assist with the understanding of the need to keep backlog items concise. The Scrum Master is also there to help the product owner understand product planning in an empirical environment, which can be difficult when first implemented. They may also serve as a coach to make sure that the product owner knows how to maximize value, understand and practice agility, and help facilitate some of the Scrum events, which we will cover a bit later in this chapter. Keep in mind that the Scrum Master is not the boss of the product owner or of the development team. They all work together to achieve a common goal. The Scrum Master is the glue that holds it all together.

Scrum Master and the Development Team

The Scrum Master's interactions with the development team are very much on the coaching level, but not in the way that you might think. The coaching is about how to self-organize and be cross functional while utilizing both principles effectively. The goal of any project is to produce high-value products, and occasionally the development team will need some help in doing that. The Scrum Master is there to remove any impediments to the development team's progress. If you've ever had key stakeholders interrupt your work by asking too many questions, sending too many emails, or scheduling too many meetings, you know that it can impede or disrupt your progress. The Scrum Master is there to stop those things from happening while coaching the organization in diverse ways to interact with the team without impeding progress. The Scrum Master is also poised to take on administrative work for the team if it is hindering their work. Sometimes you'll see this characterized as carrying the food and water.

> Many exam questions may refer to servant leadership as taking on administrative tasks when the team becomes overwhelmed so that the team can focus on producing a valuable increment.

Scrum Artifacts

Now that you have a basic understanding of the distinct roles and responsibilities on the Scrum team, as well as the value that a Scrum Master provides, let's take a deeper dive into the artifacts with which the Scrum team works. There are three distinct artifacts utilized in Scrum methodology: the product backlog, the *sprint* backlog, and the increment. You know that the product owner oversees the product backlog, but what exactly is it?

The Product Backlog

The *product backlog* is a list of all features, functions, requirements, enhancements, and fixes. The backlog is dynamic, and it is constantly changing as value is recognized and new decisions are made by the product owner. It encompasses descriptions, the order in which work will be accomplished, and the items that are of most value to produce in the moment. Because all Agile methodologies are based around the ability to adapt, the backlog will evolve as the product evolves. Also, the environment in which the product will be used is evolving as well. That is the dynamic nature of providing value and how it can change on a regular basis. In that respect, *a product backlog is never complete*.

Another key element of Agile methodologies, including Scrum, is that the customer doesn't necessarily need to know every single thing that they want and need in the increment or finished product right at the beginning of the project, or even halfway through it. The customer may only know what they want the end result to do.

Design Scenario

Backlog Adjustments

Your client might want a software program that allows them to collect money from their customers online after sending them an electronic bill. They may not know anything about which features and functions will allow them to do that. The product owner will collect some of those requirements and figure out what they need today—what's a must-have and what would be nice to have. This can change as the increment is getting built, and therefore the product backlog needs to be malleable, dynamic, and transparent. The product backlog exists as long as the product exists.

Grooming the Backlog

The product owner and the development team are working together to provide value, so it is important to refine the product backlog constantly in a process called *grooming*. Grooming the product backlog is an ongoing process where items are reviewed and revised to add detailed estimates and a semblance of order to the backlog itself. Even though the product owner is solely responsible for the product backlog, it is important to work together as a Scrum team to decide how and when this will occur in order to make sure that it doesn't consume too much time or capacity of the development team. The process of reviewing and revising items in the backlog happens on a regular basis.

A key aspect of Scrum and product backlog grooming or refinements is that the grooming should take place at the same time, same place, and have the same duration for each iteration or sprint. When the team takes the time to groom the backlog, it will help to streamline sprint planning meetings and ensure that the preliminary planning is discussed before an actual plan is created for the sprint.

An uncomplicated way to simplify the understanding of this process is to look at it as a way of prioritizing what will be worked on first, like main functions or features:

- Ask questions about what in the backlog could be ranked as more of a medium priority that could be worked on later. The answer is dependent upon backlog dynamics and changes. If it does change, it is possible that those features may move up in priority.

- Low-priority items may never be built, and as higher-priority items show up as determined by the product owner, the lower in priority ranking these items will go.

Design Scenario

Prioritizing Value

Imagine if somebody asks you what are your three favorite flavors of ice cream, and you say, "Vanilla, chocolate, and strawberry" in that order. Clearly vanilla is your first choice and a priority now. Now when you get to the ice cream shop and they tell you that they are out of vanilla, chocolate moves up in priority. The strawberry ice cream won't ever get served because the favorite ice cream flavor goal has been accomplished by higher-priority items. What initially makes the product owner's job so difficult is determining what the priority is based on delivering value to the customer. Also difficult is having to say no to some of the items that may be requested. Ordering the backlog in an effective manner takes a collective work effort on the part of the development team and the Scrum Master. Let's face it, most customers want all three flavors if given the choice, but sometimes telling them no is for the good of both their waistline and their product.

Let's assume that a new customer approaches your organization and asks it to create a software program that allows them to manage online customer payments better. The new customer wants your organization to produce a new version of this program to replace the software they are currently using. The product owner collects the requirements, and based on conversations with the customer determines what is most valuable to the customer today. The product owner gathers information about what the customer likes about their current software, what they would like to change or add, and what would be removed completely. The product owner would then work with the development team on backlog grooming to push to the front the items needed to produce an increment that is usable.

 Design Scenario

Grooming the Backlog

This is a good spot to stop and reflect on what an actual usable increment is and why backlog grooming is so important. Even though most of what we are discussing is "knowledge work," like creating a software program, it can also be attributed to tangible items. Let's say that you approached an organization and said, "I would like a beach chair that has an insulated cup holder and an umbrella with SPF material." In your mind, you know what that looks like, or at least you *think* you do. The product owner asks you what the most valuable features are and what that looks like today?

All of the wish list items would go into the product backlog. The product owner uses transparent communication to help determine what is valuable or necessary right now. To prioritize the work and create a usable increment at the end of the sprint, the backlog might include work to produce just the seat of the beach chair and four legs. Then you would review and inspect that increment and discuss moving on to adding other things that you, the customer, find valuable. Should the cup holder be on the left or the right? Should the umbrella have SPF 50 or 15?

As we learn more, the backlog gets adjusted based on what is valuable today. The final result may very well be a beach chair with a small cooler attached and an umbrella that has different levels of SPF depending on how it is placed. We don't need to know everything right now, we just need to know what is valuable today. We groom the backlog as the wish list or high- to low-priority items change.

The Sprint Backlog

Because the product backlog is constantly changing and being updated, it is necessary to set goals and to forecast what the increment might look like at the end of an iteration called the *sprint*. That is why there is a *sprint backlog*. Basically, a *sprint backlog* is just an itemized version of the overarching product backlog, but it is based on the backlog items that have been selected to be accomplished right now.

It is also important to put together a plan for delivering the product increment as well as realizing the goal of the sprint itself. This is not done in a vacuum, however. It's done with transparent communication between what the product owner discovers is valuable today and by the development team forecasting the work that is needed and that can be accomplished. This is necessary in order to deliver the chosen functionality into an increment that can be called "done" at the end of the sprint. It is also important to know that the sprint backlog provides visibility into all of the work that the development team identifies as necessary to meet the sprint goal. The Scrum Master perpetuates the vision on a regular basis.

 Remember when I said that rote memorization probably won't help you when answering questions on the PMI-ACP exam? There are some things, though, that you can memorize to help you get into the mindset of some of the concepts that we are discussing in this book. A good mnemonic for Agile software projects is the INVEST acronym created by Bill Wake in 2003 to determine what items make up an effective product backlog item (PBI).

INVEST

The *INVEST* acronym applies to having superior quality in the actual product backlog and serves as a way to check ourselves and not to produce defects or waste in the process flow. A good-quality backlog equals good-quality user stories, which in turn produce good-quality increments. It is a way of replacing or adapting the SMART acronym (specific, measurable, accurate, realistic, and time based) to be more specific to software development. INVEST can be used in Scrum, Kanban, Lean, and XP. As you will see in Figure 2.1, using the acronym as a guide can help define what success looks like and help the team create a product backlog that is efficient and well understood.

FIGURE 2.1   INVEST

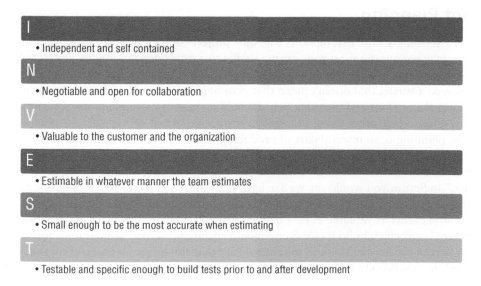

I
• Independent and self contained

N
• Negotiable and open for collaboration

V
• Valuable to the customer and the organization

E
• Estimable in whatever manner the team estimates

S
• Small enough to be the most accurate when estimating

T
• Testable and specific enough to build tests prior to and after development

This definitely doesn't mean that after the very first sprint the customer happily walks away with brand-new software that does everything that they want. What it does mean is that something usable will be created, which can be reviewed by the customer and adapted as needed. This would lead to updates in the product backlog, backlog grooming, and a refocus at the start of the next sprint.

This is where Scrum events or activities/ceremonies begin.

Scrum Events

Four formal events accompany the values of Scrum and complement the three pillars as well as building trust. It's one thing to go through the motions of sprint planning, daily Scrums, reviews, and retrospectives; it is quite another thing to build proficiency.

There are five main Scrum events:

- Sprint planning
- The Sprint
- The daily Scrum
- The Sprint review
- Sprint retrospective

The term *sprint* is unique to the methodology of Scrum, but it could be considered interchangeable with the term *iteration*. A sprint or an iteration is a timeboxed grouping of activities designed to produce a releasable product increment.

Sprint Planning

There is a seemingly false assumption that Agile projects don't have any planning at all. In fact, you may see questions on your exam relating to a misunderstanding by key stakeholders that planning is nonexistent on an Agile project. While unnecessary documentation is considered a waste, that doesn't mean that planning does not occur. In fact, frequent planning replaces front-end planning, which could prevent massive amounts of surprise changes, scope creep, other risks, and sunken costs.

Sprint planning is an integral part of producing value. The actual sprint planning meeting is timeboxed. The simplest way to describe a timebox would be a set a time frame in which certain Scrum events occur. Much as you might say, "We will have a one-hour status meeting," in Scrum you would say we are having a timeboxed status meeting of one hour. Different events in Scrum are timeboxed to benefit the sprint and make the time spent during those events as valuable as they can be. A single timebox for sprint planning falls somewhere between eight hours for a one-month sprint and shorter time frames for shorter sprints. Part of the Scrum Master's job is to ensure that the sprint planning event takes place and that everybody understands its purpose and, most important, keeps it within the timebox. Crucial planning questions will include what can be delivered in the increment at the end of the sprint and how the required deliveries will be achieved.

The entire Scrum team is helping to achieve the correct results of each sprint, but each facet is contributing in its own way. The development team's job is to forecast what functionality is to be developed during the sprint. The product owner keeps the team focused on the objectives that the sprint should achieve and the backlog priority items that are necessary to achieve it. The Scrum Master makes sure the event happens within its assigned timebox. The Scrum Master also maintains the vision and provides coaching as needed.

Eight hours may seem like a very long meeting to most, but spending eight hours to accomplish a done increment effectively at the end of 30 days takes some planning. There are key collaborations among the Scrum team so that everyone understands the work that needs to be done and exactly what the definition of *done* is. Consensus by the team is necessary so that everyone is aware of the goal and agrees to it.

Other aspects of sprint planning are reviewing the product backlog, product increments that may have been produced prior to this planning meeting, projected capacity of the development team during the sprint, and a focus on continuous improvements by looking at past performance.

Later we will cover how projected capacity is determined. Items like planning for risk, duration/velocity estimations, and cost estimating are part of the tasks found in *Domain V: Adaptive Planning* of the PMI-ACP exam content outline, and they can be applied across multiple frameworks and Agile methodologies.

It is the development team's job to take the advice of the product owner and the backlog information, but the bottom line is that there are several items to accomplish in the sprint. It is totally up to the development team to identify those items. Remember that the team is self-directed and self-managed, so the assumption is that they know the capacity that they can achieve and will select accordingly.

Typically, the first few sprints are planned based on expert judgment. There is no expectation that all is perfect right out of the gate. Teams determine the amount of work they can achieve, and they know that it will fluctuate in the beginning and plateau as more is learned. It's not unusual for teams new to Scrum, or at the beginning of the project, to over- or underestimate their capacity a bit at the start.

During the wrap of the meeting, the development team forecasts the product backlog items that it will deliver in the sprint. The team will then create their sprint goal.

In a perfect world everything will go smoothly, but there may be trade-offs or conversations and even negotiations during the sprint planning meeting. The big question is how will it all get done? The development team will decide how to build out the functionality into something that could be considered done at the end of the sprint. It is up to the development team to design a system that will work for them to produce a working product increment. You know from working on projects yourself that all work comes in a variety of sizes and levels of effort. The team will plan the first couple days of the sprint by taking bulky items and decomposing them down to the task level. If they determine that they have taken on too much or too little work, there may be a renegotiation of the selected product backlog items with the product owner.

It's important to know that, even though the development team is cross functional, they may not have all of the answers up front, especially if it is something brand-new and totally unique. They may invite other people to attend the sprint planning meeting to learn and gather information as well as technical or other types of advice.

By the end of the sprint planning meeting, the development team should be able to explain to the product owner and the Scrum Master how they intend to accomplish the result and produce the anticipated increment. This then becomes the sprint goal.

The Sprint

When you think of the word *sprint*, you might think of running very quickly but not very far. It's the same concept for an actual sprint in Scrum. The sprint itself is timeboxed to one month or less in order to have consistent durations in place for development efforts.

When the sprint backlog is created, it is formed with the assumption that whatever's been selected can be accomplished in that one-month time frame. The result will be a usable and potentially releasable product increment. That does not mean that the project is totally over and complete; in fact, a new sprint starts immediately after the previous sprint is over until such a time when it is determined that the project is "done-done," or that the product has been deployed.

Remember that Scrum is a framework, and while there is a lot of flexibility on the team level and with changes or updates, there are very distinct rules that need to be followed in order to provide structure for better understanding on an organizational level.

It would be up to the Scrum Master and the rest of the team to make sure no changes are made in the middle of a sprint that could endanger the goal or negate the production of quality increments. This doesn't mean that the scope would never be clarified and renegotiated between the product owner and development team because learning is constant and changes are always expected.

An uncomplicated way to think of a sprint is to think about it as its own small distinct project with no more than a one-month time span. Something usable by the customer will come out of it. This doesn't mean that it has all of the features and functions the customer wants; it just means that the customer will walk away with something that they can currently test, review, and use at the end of each sprint.

If you think about how much risk could be prevented by not preplanning the unknowns, you'll find another reason why sprints are limited to one calendar month. Under the Scrum framework, the scope of work is a bit more buffered from the impacts of risk, and it also protects the budget because only a certain amount has been executed and paid for in any one month time frame. Now the customer can change their mind about certain features, the product owner can shift the value in the backlog, and the team can go into another sprint, producing something valuable and usable at the end.

The Sprint Goal

Basically, the *sprint goal* is an objective that will be met with this sprint through the implementation of the product backlog items and by providing guidance on why the team is building this particular increment in this particular sprint.

I like to think of a sprint goal as the mantra or motivation behind what it is that you're trying to accomplish. You know what the specific objectives are, but you also have the ability to embrace flexibility to some extent within the sprint. Part of that flexibility is the ability to make mistakes and learn from them. A lot of times the sprint goal may just be one specific function, but it is always kept in mind by the development team and reiterated by the Scrum Master.

The Definition of Done

One key aspect of all sprint planning and sprint goals is to understand completely what the definition of done is. Each member of the team needs to have a shared understanding of what it means for the actual work to be complete. This provides transparency and guards against misinterpretations and misunderstandings. If the team truly understands what the definition of done is for each individual sprint, then it is far easier for them to determine how many product backlog items they can accomplish to produce a completed increment. This doesn't necessarily mean that everybody knows the exact results, what the result will look like, and what functionality will be available when the entire project is completed. It does mean, however, that the team understands that the purpose of the sprint is to deliver increments of potentially releasable functionality based on the Scrum team's current definition of done.

Canceling a Sprint

As you know, sometimes projects get canceled, and the same applies to Scrum projects (although it is rare). Even though a sprint can be canceled before it ends, it is only by the product owner's authority that the cancellation may occur. Generally, a sprint is canceled after the goal of the sprint is no longer needed or necessary. If in fact the sprint were to be canceled, anything that's been completed to date and is currently done would be reviewed, and if any part of the work is potentially releasable, the product owner will typically accept it. This will allow payments to be made, as needed, for the work completed. Once that happens, all incomplete product backlog items are reestimated and put back into the product backlog for potential future use. Remember, a product backlog is never complete. Sprint cancellations are very uncommon due to the consistent use of sprint planning, daily Scrums, development work, sprint reviews, and sprint retrospectives. Even if the sprint were to be canceled, you would only be less than a month into the work at any given time.

The Daily Scrum

Now that the team has determined what work they will accomplish during the sprint, the sprint goal, and the understanding of what it is that they are trying to produce, they begin the work on the sprint. Transparent communication is an important aspect of all Agile methodologies, and one of the most popular Agile best practices comes in the form of the daily stand-up meeting, or in this case the *daily Scrum*. The daily Scrum is a 15-minute timeboxed event specific to the development team so that they can synchronize their activities and determine what the next 24 hours will look like. You might be thinking to yourself, there's no way that you can discuss all that in 15 minutes! That would take at least an hour-long meeting. That's true if you only meet once a week. The daily Scrum is just that—daily. The key to the daily Scrum is not talking in circles about solutions to problems, finger pointing, or catching up about the weekend.

It is a quick update that happens in the *same location, at the same time, with the same people, answering the same questions* every day. Take, for example, the following questions:

- What did I do yesterday to help the development team meet the sprint goal?

- What will I do today to help the development team meet the sprint goal?

- Do I see any impediments that prevent me or the development team from meeting the sprint goal?

It's the Scrum Master's job to make sure that the daily Scrums occur and to set some rules to keep the focus on the answers to these three questions. It is also the Scrum Master's job to stop any brainstorming on solutions during the daily Scrum meeting, because as you know everyone has an opinion and the team would end up standing there all day. That is not the goal of the daily Scrum. Because of this, it is the Scrum Master's job to teach the development team how to keep the daily Scrum within the 15-minute timebox as well as enforcing the rule that only development team members participate. Finally, standing keeps everyone focused without anyone getting too comfortable.

The beauty of daily Scrums is that they improve communications across the board, which may eliminate the need for other meetings. Perhaps one of the most important aspects is for the team to identify any impediments in their way and to keep everyone on the development team up-to-date on what everyone else is doing. The daily Scrum is considered a key inspect and adapt meeting. You inspect what happened yesterday and today and what impediments are in your way, and then you adapt your tactics accordingly if needed.

Scrum of Scrums

Any organizations that are heavily involved in Scrum *have more than one* Scrum team, Scrum Master, and product owner. Therefore, it might be necessary to hold something called a *Scrum of Scrums*. The *Scrum of Scrums meeting* allows for larger-scale interactions between multiple Scrum teams in an organization. Each Scrum team will meet for their daily Scrum, and at the end one member will be designated as the ambassador and will meet with other ambassadors from other teams. This will allow a specific focus on the challenges of coordination between the teams and an overarching resolution to some of the impediments that the teams are facing. The Scrum of Scrums allows for tracking of these items and impediments in a backlog of its own where each item is contributing to improvement between team coordination. This allows the organization to improve collaboration on Scrum best practices across many teams focused on different projects. This is similar to a biweekly all-hands meeting where better ways of doing daily work are discussed. The Scrum of Scrum meeting is only held once or twice a week; otherwise, there is a risk of those meetings doing the opposite of what they are designed to do by creating impediments for each individual team. The questions are similar in nature to a daily Scrum, except on a team level:

- What has your team done since the last meeting?
- What will your team do before the next meeting?
- Is anything getting in your team's way?
- Are you about to put something in another team's way?

The Sprint Review

Let's assume that you are nearing the end of the sprint and you believe that a functional increment has been created, so you want to get together with the customer and determine whether the increment is done. This all sounds like a very formal event, but the bottom line is that the sprint review is an informal meeting and not a status meeting. This informal meeting is utilized to inspect the increments and adapt the product backlog as needed. The major goal of the *sprint review* is to present the increment to the customer in order to gain their feedback and to encourage collaboration. While much of the sprint review looks at the things that have been done, it is also looking forward to determining the next things that could be done to optimize value.

Remember that changes are encouraged and expected, so what was valuable to the customer a month ago may very well have changed since then. This happens a lot, especially after the customer has the ability to inspect the increment that was produced and use that information to focus forward.

 Design Scenario

The Expectation of Value

My daughter has always wanted a Camaro because she likes the look of the car. The first time she drove it, she found numerous things that didn't fit her needs (or mine since I foresaw a lot of speeding tickets in her future!). It was too low to the ground, and it had a lot of blind spots. She realized that, for her needs, she wanted something that looked cool but that was functional for day-to-day driving. Now she wants to buy a Jeep instead.

The point of my story is that taking the increment for a "test drive" could very well change the direction of the project. This is key because, otherwise, you would present the Camaro of software at the end of the project and find out that what the customer really wanted was a Jeep.

The best practice for the sprint review would be a four-hour timeboxed meeting for the typical one-month sprint. Of course if the sprint was shorter, the event would be shorter as well. Either way, it is up to the Scrum Master to make sure that the sprint review takes place, and if the organization is new to Scrum, it is very important that the Scrum Master ensure that all in attendance understand its purpose.

Elements of the Sprint Review

Even though the sprint review is looked upon as a more casual informal meeting, there are still some best practices that are followed. The attendees include the entire Scrum team and key stakeholders, which could include the customer. The product owner invites participants to the review and is also in attendance. Because this is a key inspect and adapt meeting, it is the product owner's job to explain which product backlog items have been done and which have not been done. Then the development team will discuss what went well during the sprint, what problems they ran into, and how those problems were solved. The development team's job is also to demonstrate the work that has been done and to answer any questions that anyone has about the increment.

The important thing about reviews like this is that it gives the customer an opportunity to touch, use, and inspect the increment that was produced. The act of doing this may very well change the backlog going forward. The product owner will discuss the product backlog as it stands today and any likely completion dates based on progress in the current sprint and to date as needed.

Keep in mind that this is typically a four-hour time-boxed meeting, so there is plenty of time to collaborate on what to do next. This will then provide valuable input to sprint planning for the next sprint. A key factor of all Agile methodologies is to try to figure out the most valuable thing to do next. This can be totally dependent upon the marketplace, or simply what the potential use of the product is by the customer and how that might have changed before or during the review

Because you're looking at a sprint as its own singular entity or project, each sprint will have its own timeline, budget, potential capabilities, and anticipated release of the result. Once the sprint review is over, the Scrum team will have a revised product backlog that will define what could probably be done in the next sprint, and they may even have additional items that have moved up in priority or that may provide more value to the customer.

The Sprint Retrospective

You will continue to see the theme of continuous improvement both on the product level and the team level throughout all Agile methodologies. Therefore, the *sprint retrospective* is an important piece of continuous improvement in the Scrum framework as well as many other Agile best practices. Many of us view the retrospective like a lessons learned meeting, a kick-down meeting, or a postmortem. In a way, that is what it is. It is an opportunity for the Scrum team to spend three hours inspecting itself and to create a plan for improvements. Those improvements are not in some far-off project somewhere—they are to be implemented by the team right away to the best of their ability during the next sprint. The retrospective is sandwiched between the sprint review and the next sprint planning meeting, so the team can keep in mind what was talked about in the review and use that information to plan forward while improving the results. Continuous improvements, making and correcting mistakes, and learning valuable lessons are major tenants in Agile project management.

The Purpose of the Sprint Retrospective

In a lot of project management methodologies, the big focus is on the quality and the scope of the result. In Scrum and other Agile methodologies, however, the team is also looking at how the last sprint went with regards to people, relationships, and team interactions as well as processes, tools, and performance results. Once that occurs and the team has identified these items and placed them in a semblance of an order, identifying the major ones that went well and those that went not so well, it is easier to work through solutions. They have checked these items themselves for potential improvements, so it's time to put together a plan to improve the way the Scrum team does its work. It is important to note that this is a very open and honest meeting. The team is transparent about their feelings on what went well, what did not go well, and what changes they would like to see made. By the end of the sprint retrospective, the Scrum team will have identified improvements that it will implement in the next sprint.

Scrum Events

Scrum events are an important part of the Scrum framework and are time-boxed for maximum effectiveness.

In Figure 2.2 you will see a very simple version of Scrum events, including the length of time for each event.

FIGURE 2.2 Scrum Events

The Sprint Planning Meeting
- Incorporates the groomed backlog and the sprint goal determined by the development team during 8-hour sprint planning meeting.

The Sprint
- Usually a one-month sprint in where a usable increment is created.

The Sprint Retrospective
- A chance for the team to look back at the sprint and discuss what they thought went well and areas for improvements.
- Important for continuous improvement.

The Daily Scrum
- Fifteen-minute timeboxed daily meeting.
- What did we do yesterday, today, and what are impediments to progress?
- Not solution oriented just informational and helps identify risks and maintains the sprint goals.

The Sprint Review
- Informal four-hour meeting with the team and the customer.
- Work completed is demonstrated and may lead to an update to the backlog for the next sprint.

The following are great guiding principles to get you into the mindset of Scrum:

- A Team of between seven to nine members does the work.

- Team is cross functional.

- Team owns its process.

- Product owner provides the work requests.

- Product owner determines priority.

- Scrum Master provides support and coaching for the whole team.

- Scrum Master observes and helps the whole team adjust.

- Scrum Master guides the team.

- Daily Scrum reveals any adjustments needed.

- Work is done in short bursts of fewer than 30 days each (sprints).

- Work starts and stops with planning and review.

- Review demos the product.

- Retrospective allows for improvements to be identified and implemented.

As you can see, the Scrum framework has a well-rounded approach to time boxing or scheduling, transparent communication, and interactions. A large focus of the team is that it is self-managed and self-directed, and an Agile project manager/Scrum Master keeps the sprint running smoothly while promoting the reasons for it and the vision of the result. Finally, a product owner determines what is valuable to the customer today and helps the team see the vision by constantly communicating that value.

As you will come to see, there are many other Agile methodologies. Beginning with Scrum, however, really lets you see that as you move forward, practicing agility is represented in all methodologies and you can turn around and start using some of the best practices immediately. Scrum is easy to explain and difficult to implement, but the more organizations begin to embrace or improve upon Agile best practices, the better they will be.

eXtreme Programming (XP) Overview

Now that you've gone through the nuances of Scrum, it's time to shift gears and look at *eXtreme Programming (XP)*. Going back to the 1990s, the beginnings of what you know as the Internet of today and the dot-com boom, it was imperative for organizations to produce results and get them to market quickly. Requirements changed rapidly, and heavier processes simply were not working. A better, faster way was needed. Even though many of the best practices found in XP had been used in one way, shape, or form during that time frame, they needed to be taken to an *extreme* level to meet the demands of the marketplace and to keep up with the cutting edge of technologies at the time.

XP was created in 1996 by Kent Beck, who also helped to create the Agile Manifesto. Beck's contribution to the Agile Manifesto came from his experience and his work efforts on the Chrysler Comprehensive Compensation Systems (C3) payroll project. Beck determined that it was necessary to create a process for software development that incorporated methods to improve quality and accept rapid changes in requirements. Beck collaborated on the methods with Ward Cunningham and Ron Jeffries (other contributors to the Agile Manifesto) and XP was born.

Key Aspects Of XP

The key aspects of XP include the following:

- Frequent feature and functionality releases
- Short life cycles
- Test-first development

Because of this, XP is one of the most popular Agile approaches. Over time, XP has been adapted from more rigid formats into something that is more usable and flexible. XP's metamorphosis from the 1990s to what has come to be known as XP today is an excellent representation of Agile. Try something courageous, learn from it, and implement better/best practices because of lessons learned. Many times, organizations will utilize some aspects of XP with a hybrid approach, including aspects of Scrum.

Because XP is one of the most popular Agile methodologies and overlaps somewhat with Scrum in some organizations, you will see several aspects in questions about both on the PMI-ACP exam. Terms like *iterations* and *increments* and terms for similar roles and responsibilities, albeit with different titles, occur quite frequently in questions on the exam.

XP Core Values

Part of getting into the mindset of Agile methodologies is to understand that a lot of the values and best practices overlap. Nevertheless, the constant goal is that all of your focus be on producing valuable product features and functional releases.

XP has five core values, and what you'll notice is their alignment to the Agile Manifesto and much of what you learned about Scrum. The number one value of simplicity is quite crucial to much of the practice of agility, so keep it simple! The aspects of communication, feedback, and respect are transparent across all methodologies, and the ability to be courageous and try new things, make mistakes, and express your opinions is core, not just to XP but also to many of the Agile methodologies if not all of them.

- Simplicity
- Communication

- Feedback
- Courage
- Respect

XP Core Values Simplified

The core values of XP are very aligned to the Agile Manifesto as well as other Agile frameworks. In order to absorb the values into your day to day, it's important to understand the meaning behind them.

Simplicity: Keeping things simple is paramount to successful results. If things are too complicated, then miscommunication, scope creep, and risks occur. The simplest way to produce the increment is what you will do. Nothing more, nothing less. You know that if your job responsibilities become too confusing or overwhelming, the odds of you being successful are very slim indeed, and if in fact you do what you are supposed to, you know that you will make mistakes along the way. Making things too convoluted or confusing muddies the waters and opens the door for many U-turns and corrective actions.

 Design Scenario

Keeping It Simple

If you've ever been given driving directions from someone who is directionally challenged and had to turn around numerous times, you know what I'm talking about! It's probably a big reason GPS was created in the first place. Keeping it simple leaves less room for mistakes, fewer U-turns, and a more effective way to produce to spec. Start here, end here. It's as simple as that.

Communication: Having a shared understanding of requirements, common metaphors/similes to describe the work, frequent feedback, and face-to-face communication is the crux of many Agile methodologies, XP included. If everyone on the team has a shared vision of what success looks like, then the probability is high that they will reach it. That vison could change throughout the iteration, but it would be communicated and understood so that a new shared vision would be the focus.

You will see many ways Agile teams communicate above and beyond face-to-face communication as you go forward through other chapters and domain tasks in the exam content outline. Don't worry, it's not like the 8,000 emails a day you may receive. It's low-tech, high-touch information radiating that speaks louder than words.

Feedback: Giving and receiving feedback is a necessary component in fast moving Agile projects. When developing software, you are getting feedback through frequent testing of the programming and the system. The customer is giving feedback on what is working, what needs to change, and what they find valuable today. You and your team are constantly engaged in communication and feedback with each other to determine the best ways to accomplish your iteration and project goals.

In many organizations, feedback is reserved for yearly reviews, where your manager remembers the last two weeks of your life and the one stupid thing that you did all year! Alternatively, many companies I've consulted with follow a "no news is good news" policy. This is not the case with Agile methodologies, which is probably why they resonate with me so much. Giving and receiving feedback takes practice, but once everyone feels comfortable with the process, it is absolutely the best way to accomplish the goal. I believe that this policy works best: Show me the boundaries, point me in the right direction, and correct that direction as needed.

Courage: The quality of courage comes up a lot in Agile practices. It is part of the fabric of risk-taking industries like software development and technology projects. Because XP is very focused on programming, a lot of courage comes in the form of code modifications, keeping the design relevant and practical, and refactoring code as needed. Imagine spending 30 hours writing strings of code only to find out that it just isn't working or that someone decides that it is no longer necessary. It would be exceedingly difficult to look at the delete key and actually push it after all that effort. It takes courage to delete challenging work.

You will review refactoring as a process in later chapters involving continuous improvements. Basically, *refactoring* is simplifying the code without changing how it works.

Respect: Keeping an elevated level of motivation on development teams is a big focus of everything you will go through. Is everyone going to be motivated and happy-go-lucky all of the time? Of course not! But I know that it's a heck of a lot easier to swallow constructive feedback if it comes from a place of respect. If I feel underappreciated, ignored, and underdeveloped as a professional, I tend to start updating my resume. The same thing goes for an XP team or any other Agile-type team. Self-respect and team respect allows for courage, effective feedback, effective communication, and an easier definition of simplicity across the board.

XP Roles

There are roles and responsibilities for XP projects that are similar to those for Scrum projects. Even though the titles may be different, there is still some overlap in both methodologies, which is why a hybrid approach is far easier between Scrum and XP.

Coach

A straightforward way to look at the coach role on an XP project is to compare it to the Scrum Master role on a Scrum project. It's almost a better descriptor of both roles, since being a coach is helping the team, the organization, and your customers embrace and understand the methodology.

Customer

The customer role is basically the product owner's role on a Scrum project. *The customer* is a generic term, and it can be used in different project management methodologies to mean somebody from the outside asking for something to be created for them or somebody on the inside—basically internal and/or external customers. For the exam, it is important to note that the customer is very much like the product owner, meaning that they are the ones who determine value, organize and communicate the backlog, and are typically on site.

Programmers

This role is exactly what it sounds like. These are the team members who are "writing" the code and creating the initial tests for that code. Notice that on Scrum projects, everyone is just called a developer, but in XP projects, there are programmers and there are testers. Both roles are much like the combined development team on a Scrum project, but they do have very distinct roles and are much more software-development focused.

Testers

There are some who would argue that programmers and testers are interchangeable roles, and I'm sure many XP iterations are run successfully this way. Testers have more experience in quality assurance and are many times developers themselves. Testers may play a role in helping the customer determine what the test results should show and then write and run the tests. The quality assurance aspects keep a focus on quality software, quality tests, and quality releases.

Core Practices of XP

It's easy to see from the core practices of XP why it is one of the most popular Agile frameworks or methodologies because simplicity is incorporated across the board. These core practices are designed to do several things, from producing frequent features and functionality releases to keeping their iterations short (approximately two weeks versus one month). Other aspects of XP are a big focus on improving productivity, frequently testing the software and the code, incorporating *pair programming* so that one person is coding and another person is watching the code, and checking for quality. Another important aspect of XP is the focus on minimizing threats and issues while at the same time not executing any work until the team is sure that their technical approach has been proven to work utilizing something called an *architectural spike*.

You will learn about risks, issues, and spikes in depth when you review the tasks found in *Domain VI: Problem Detection and Resolution* in later chapters.

Another best practice for Agile teams is always to be *colocated*. Even though in a lot of global industries it is impossible to have everyone in the same location, it is still considered a core best practice for XP teams. In fact, location doesn't just mean in the same building—it means the entire team is no more than about 33 feet away from each other. This keeps the team very colocated and enables the members to overhear all conversations and absorb relevant information. At the same time, it allows for some elbow room to work. This does many important things to improve the team dynamic, facilitate transparent communication, and bolster constant learning from others.

You may get questions about virtual teams and colocation on your exam. Colocation is a core tenant of communication and tacit knowledge acquisition. If your team is virtual, what do you do? Colocating the team for at least one iteration is the best answer, even if the team is remote on a regular basis. You may also see the terms *caves* and *common rooms*. These are applicable to designated spaces specific to a colocated team working on the same project. It is a place where they can go for privacy or solitude. Since colocation is the norm, a team member may need some quiet space to think or work through a problem or even to make a personal phone call. That is how colocating the team works. It is very different from normal dynamics in many project-management-oriented organizations.

The 13 Core Practices of XP

Next we will review the 13 core practices of XP in depth. These 13 core practices are as follows:

- Whole team
- Planning games
- Small releases
- Customer tests
- Collective code ownership
- Code standards
- Sustainable pace
- Metaphor (similes)
- Continuous integration
- Test-driven development

- Refactoring
- Simple design
- Pair programming

It is *not* necessary to memorize all 13 for the PMI-ACP exam because, as I mentioned, rote memorization will not be a huge help to you in getting a passing score. As you go through these practices, it is more important to put yourself into their mindset and understand why they're so important to successful results.

The 13 Core Practices Simplified

The 13 core practices of XP help set the groundwork for faster iterations and continuous feedback. The main focus of XP is software development, but many of the best practices can be seen in other Agile frameworks.

Whole Team: The entire XP team is colocated in order to improve communication, learning, and structure of process.

Planning Games: During release and sprint planning estimation, it may be a bit different from the typical "How many days will it take to finish the project?" and "How much will it cost?" questions found on many Waterfall projects. XP iteration cycles are only two weeks long, and so planning is done a bit differently. In fact, in both Scrum and XP as well as other Agile methodologies, planning games are used as an effective way to determine how much work can be accomplished in the iteration. Things like planning poker, T-shirt sizing, and affinity estimating are used instead of specific duration estimations of days and weeks. Once you get further into the chapters that incorporate duration planning, you will review planning games in much greater depth, and you'll see what a cool and unique way it is to estimate.

Even though planning only lasts two weeks at a time, a lot can happen in two weeks. Think of your last 80 hours' worth of work, and I'm sure you got a lot accomplished. Perhaps you didn't accomplish as much as you did last month or last year, but isn't it nice to know that you can compartmentalize two-week chunks of time, review what was done, and plan what you need to do in the next two weeks? If only the rest of life were that simple!

Small Releases: Frequent releases and testing are important core practices in XP and Scrum. But in XP, the frequency is twice as much. Small releases over the course of two-week iterations allow the team to produce the code, test the code, release the code, and gain feedback on it quickly.

> ## ⟳ Design Scenario
>
> ### The Art of Small Releases
>
> Imagine that you are an artist and have been requisitioned to do a painting of your customer's favorite forest landscape. Every two weeks, the customer wants to check on your progress and make suggestions. In the first two weeks, you sketch out the entire scene in pencil and the customer reviews it. The next two weeks, you add some color to the trees, then sharpen and define, and so on. The bottom line is that, after each review, the customer could (if they wanted to) hang the sketch on the wall and go no further. It is a usable, reviewable increment. That is Agile. You wouldn't sketch and paint one tree and present it, because the customer can't hang that on the wall, review it in total, or see the vision of what it will become.

Customer Tests: As you can see, XP is much more focused on software development than some of the other methodologies and frameworks. To make sure that the software that is being developed really works, customer tests are necessary. It's not as you might think, though. It is not a matter of the customer physically testing the software—it is the team creating tests in advance that are automated in order to prove that the test criteria from customer requirements for working software is managed effectively. It would also be safe to say that the customer will inevitably test the finished increment as well.

Collective Code Ownership: Much as with Scrum, the entire XP development team owns their work. In XP, there is a collective code ownership that is shared, and it helps build out knowledge for everyone on the team. One of the greatest things about Agile methodologies is that you're not going to see a lot of finger-pointing when mistakes are made because if one makes a mistake, the entire team owns it and helps overcome it.

Code Standards: Because the focus of XP is software development and the actual coding that the programmers do, there has to be a consistent approach to writing the code until a better approach is determined. This makes it very easy for one person to write the code and another person to review it and then switch places. Having very specific code standards means that anyone could work on the code at any given time and produce a similar result.

Sustainable Pace: Many of us work more than 40 hours a week, and I'm sure you've experienced the burnout that comes with that when trying to wrap up a project. The beauty of XP is the concept of sustainable pace. This means no more 40+ hour workweeks and absolutely no overtime (if possible). This then becomes a sustainable pace to infinity and beyond. There is no calling in sick just to get some rest or having a disgruntled team and the inevitable mistakes that occur when people are exhausted. Organizations and customers not having to pay for overtime also helps keep the budgets where they need to be.

Metaphor (Similes): Anytime there's a difficult concept to grasp or understand, using a metaphor or a simile can help. It works by explaining the concepts in an understandable way through the use of an example that is relative to the individual's experiences. The person who is attempting to understand can clearly grasp it quickly because they can relate to the metaphor/simile.

Software programming without code standards and sustainable pace is the equivalent of squirrel wrangling—not to be attempted! User stories allow the team to understand exactly what it is that the end user needs and wants and how the software will be used. Many times, metaphors are used to help define the user stories and to achieve collective understanding.

When you think of software code, it can be a bit overwhelming for the novice or for someone who doesn't have that skill set. Metaphors or similes help to explain concepts in understandable ways to all.

 Design Scenario

Making the Metaphor

Imagine not knowing anything about computers, but you have to go buy one at a large "big box" store. You ask a salesperson for help, and they start throwing computer jargon at you like quad-core processor, 8 GB memory, and 1 TB hard drive. How confused would you be? Very!

What if instead they said something like the following? "What will you be using this computer for?" Now you say, "Storing photos, email, and Internet access." Then they tell you that the more gigabytes or terabytes you have, the more photos you can store—much like the bigger the suitcase, the more you can pack. When you think about a processor, think about it as the brain of the computer. Some people need really high-IQ computers while others just need a smaller-IQ model that does fewer things well.

If the salesperson spoke this way, you would then begin to have a better understanding of what these things do, not necessarily the technology they use to do it. Metaphors or similes take real-life examples that anyone can understand so that everyone is on the same page.

Continuous Integration: Imagine how frustrating it would be to purchase a software program that has all of the features and functions that you want but nothing is integrated or works well together. Maybe you have purchased software that does word processing, offers spell checks, and prints documents, and you think that you have everything you need. However, when you go to use the software for word processing, you have to close and reopen it. Next, when you want to spell check your document, you have to close and reopen it again! Finally, when you want to print your document, you have to close and reopen it still yet again! This would certainly get tedious after a while.

Thus continuous integration is important in order to make sure the software works together the way that you would expect. That's why continuous integration testing on a frequent basis is one of the core competencies of XP. Is the software working together, or is everything going its own direction?

I have a friend who is a professional dog walker, and watching her walk five dogs at once going in five different directions reminds me of how frustrating it is to not be continuously integrated. This is why running the tests often helps to find compatibility problems sooner rather than later. Discovering problems later in the iteration creates a lot of rework and furious coding up to the deadline.

Finally, everyone needs to be working on the most up-to-date version as well. You know this through communication. It doesn't make sense to update something that is obsolete.

Test-Driven Development: Imagine that before you began to study for the Agile exam, or even read the study guide, I handed you all of the questions in a practice exam that you were going to see on your actual Agile exam. Chances are that you would fail the practice exam the first time out of the gate and maybe even the next five times. At the same time, you would learn what the result is supposed to look like, and even though you expected to fail the practice exam numerous times, as soon as you pass, you know that you're ready for the real exam.

The same thing is true for test-driven development. The tests are written before the code. You know going in that if you do this, the initial code will fail, but as soon as it passes it is correct.

This is the opposite of many project management methodologies that produce first and test later. A lot of defect repair, scope creep, and replanning come with that mentality.

It makes sense when you are building a bridge or skyscraper to have a formal front-end plan. It's tough to test a bridge by walking on it when it only has the footers built. Because XP iterations are so short, the team knows going in what they are trying to accomplish and what the behavior of the code should be. They can then build a test first, knowing that it will fail.

This is kind of a freeing notion, isn't it? That is, I know I'm going to fail, and if at first I don't succeed—try, try again until I pass. This is a change in the paradigm of today's success-driven culture. Imagine that you're successful if you fail because you have to fail to succeed.

> Success consists of going from failure to failure without loss of enthusiasm.
> *Winston Churchill*

Refactoring: You know in life and in software that there are many ways of accomplishing the same result. A large part of the process of refactoring is to improve the code design continuously without altering functionality. This means that a customer gets the same result, but maybe it works more fluidly based on the refactoring. Most of us who use software don't really think about the factoring or design of computer code—you just want the external behavior that you're looking for to work. Peeking into the matrix isn't a typical day for many people, but everyone is an end user of software. People who write code for a living, however, may notice duplications or behaviors of code that are unnecessary, even though they don't impact the final increment.

Design Scenario

Refactoring for Simplicity

Let's say that you write a macro in Excel that will find every instance of your name in a large spreadsheet, highlight it, and boldface it. When you run the macro, it loops through that same process three times in a row—select, highlight, and boldface. You get the same result, and it "works." However, it's taking unnecessary extra steps to get to the same result, and it needs to be refactored, or in the macro's case, re-recorded or re-coded.

I think about a DVR that records my favorite shows. When I forget to select the option to *record new shows only*, I get the new shows and all the repeats that I've seen before. Annoying? Yes. Are the new shows there? Yes. But now I need to go through and delete the ones that I have seen and reset the setting for recording. I get the same new shows result, but without extra noise in the system.

Refactoring is beneficial in a lot of ways because it is a lot easier for somebody to go back and fix a bug in the source code if it is easier to read. It is also easier to expand the capabilities of an actual application if they used recognizable patterns in the design.

It is unnecessary to truly understand the coding of software for your exam, but one of the topics that you will cover in upcoming chapters is tech debt. If the team fails to perform refactoring on a regular basis, an accumulation of tech debt can occur. If that happens, it will distract the team from the work at hand. It will also add up over time, and it must be dealt with eventually. In fact, many iterations or sprints may have to accommodate some tech debt on a regular basis so that it doesn't spin out of control. Some of that tech debt could also be from prior iterations.

Simple Design: What is the simplest thing you can do that will still work? That is really the premise of simple design in XP. The goal at the end of each iteration is to produce a workable increment—the more complicated it gets, the longer it takes, and this can amp up the risk of failure.

This goes back to the philosophy of keeping things simple across all methodologies of Agile. If the customer wants a software program that word processes, spell checks, and prints documents, then what is the simplest way to get to that result? Certainly, you're not going to spend a lot of time and energy adding additional scope and functionality. You want to keep the code as simple as possible and make sure the result was what the customer requested.

Simple design reduces the risk of failure, which can be very costly in the long run. This doesn't mean that failure never happens, and it also doesn't mean that risk events don't occur. Keeping it simple, though, does minimize those risks and helps to keep them to a controllable level.

Pair Programming: One of the most discussed aspects of XP is the fact that pair programming is involved in the software design. It is exactly what it sounds like—a pair of programmers programming.

The way that it works is that one programmer will write the code while another basically looks over their shoulder and determines if the code is good quality or if it contains a mistake—basically if it is looking good to them. Then they switch.

When I first learned about this, it reminded me of highway road workers in the way that 1 person is always working while another 20 people stand around and watch. How could anything possibly get done? That misconception, as it applies to pair programming (not road work), is why a lot of organizations will push back against this philosophy. They believe that productivity is stilted by having two people work on one thing at the same time. Believe it or not, however, the opposite is true! More work is done faster, with better quality and transparent communication that leads to learning following this philosophy. It also keeps the coder accountable for a simple design, continuous integration, and test-driven development. It's a lot like having a spell check on your computers that gives you a gentle reminder by underlining words that you have misspelled so that you can go back and correct them. I'm pretty sure my editor is thankful for that particular feature. *Two heads are better than one.*

Because XP and Scrum are two of the most popular Agile methodologies, or frameworks, keep in mind that you will see questions on the PMI-ACP exam written from the perspective of the different players and the different best practices. Terms like *refactoring*, *pair programming*, *user stories*, and *planning games*, plus *sustainable pace* and *spikes*, are all highly testable. At this point, you have just gone through an overview of the core factors of XP and Scrum, but as you move forward through adaptive planning techniques and continuous improvements topics, you will take a deeper dive into what these mean for the exam.

The following are great guiding principles to get you into the mindset of XP:

- Onsite customer

- User story

- Acceptance tests

- The planning game

- Unit tests

- Test-first design

- Refactoring

- Simple design

- Pair programming

- Spike solution

- Collective ownership

- Coding standard

- Continuous integration

- Metaphor

- Forty-hour week

Summary

This chapter started with an overview of the Scrum framework from its beginnings and how it is described as a lightweight framework that is easy to learn but difficult to master.

Next, I went over the three pillars of Scrum, the Scrum roles, and the Scrum values as well as key aspects of sprints. Keep in mind that although the exam isn't strictly focused on Scrum, knowing the basics and putting yourself into its distinct roles and responsibilities goes a long way to absorbing how to *be* Agile. Understanding how the values and pillars influence Agile projects, as well as the artifacts like daily Scrums and stand-up meetings, is an important aspect of day-to-day learning and implementation of Scrum and other types of Agile methodologies.

Finally, we went through an overview of eXtreme Programming (XP) and covered the team roles and the life cycle. Then we wrapped up with the key aspects of XP iterations.

Scrum and XP will set the groundwork for many of the other methods and best practices that you will cover going forward and that you will see on the exam. Both are excellent representations of how to be Agile. They aren't the be-all and end-all, as you'll see in the next chapter, but they do set the stage for what is to come and allow us to build on that knowledge and take it to the next step.

Exam Essentials

Be able to understand and absorb Scrum theory.   Scrum is based on empirical process control. It is not a set methodology but instead is a framework. Transparency, inspection, and adaptation are the pillars of Scrum.

Be able to put yourself in the shoes of the Scrum team.   Understanding each role on the team is crucial to answering questions correctly on the PMI-ACP exam. Know that the product owner is responsible for the product backlog, that the development team executes the work, and that the Scrum Master provides servant leadership to the entire team and organization. They promote the values of Scrum and help to maintain the vision.

Understand Scrum artifacts and other aspects that are involved in the framework. Time boxing, backlog grooming, sprint planning meetings, reviews and retrospectives, and colocation are all key techniques used to provide value. These items were covered at a high level in this chapter, and they will be seen in detail as you progress through other chapters. It is always good to know, however, what to keep an eye out for as you move forward with your studies.

Know the five values of Scrum. Even though rote memorization won't help you answer questions entirely, in order to truly understand and get into the mindset, it is a good idea to memorize the values of commitment, focus, openness, respect, and courage. This will really give you the background that you need to put yourself into the right frame of mind on the exam and while practicing Scrum yourselves.

Understand XP and its life cycle. A key aspect of the XP life cycle you should be aware of is the two-week iteration (remember *sprint* and *iteration* can be interchangeable terms on the exam, though *iteration* is used more often). Keep in mind the idea of test-driven development and pair programming as well.

Know the differences and the commonalities of the team roles. For example, the product owner in Scrum is the customer in XP, and the Scrum Master in Scrum is the coach in XP. You may be asked to answer questions from one perspective or another. It's a good idea to truly understand who does what and how that supports the rest of the team. Many questions will be written from the perspective of the coach or Scrum Master, or what PMI will label as the "Agile project manager."

Review Questions

You can find the answers to the review questions in Appendix B.

1. Which of the following best describes Scrum?
   A. A process
   B. A framework
   C. An Agile method
   D. A Waterfall method

2. Which of the following is not a Scrum artifact?
   A. Retrospective
   B. Product backlog
   C. Sprint backlog
   D. Increment

3. When is it an acceptable time to cancel a sprint in the middle of a project?
   A. When the product owner says so
   B. When the customer requests it
   C. When the scope of work changes
   D. Never

4. Which of the following is *not* a core value of XP?
   A. Coaching
   B. Communication
   C. Respect
   D. Courage

5. Which of the following best practices are unique to eXtreme Programming?
   A. Scrum of Scrums
   B. MoSCoW
   C. Kanban
   D. Pair programming

6. One Scrum ceremony or activity is the team getting together to discuss what they will do today, what they did yesterday, and anything standing in their way. This is known as which of the following?
   A. Scrum of Scrums
   B. Daily Scrum
   C. Sprint review
   D. Sprint retrospective

7. You are a Scrum Master, and you hear during a daily Scrum that your team is a bit behind schedule. The impediments they mention are having to do too many updates to stakeholders and too much paperwork. What is the best thing to do?

A. Communicate with the stakeholders, and ask them not to bother your team.

B. Coach the team on Agile principles to help them get back on schedule.

C. Do nothing; the team is self-managed.

D. Take on administrative work as needed to help your team.

8. During your 15-minute stand-up meeting, two of your team members start discussing a solution to one of the issues that they ran into the day before. As the Scrum Master or Agile project manager, what should you do?

A. Extend the meeting and encourage your team to find a solution before going back to work.

B. Invite other experts to the meeting to help create a solution.

C. Make sure you help them resolve the issues after the meeting but not during.

D. Do nothing—a Scrum Master only listens during the stand-up meeting.

9. You are the product owner and have just started working on a new Agile team. One of the team members wants to know what your job entails. What do you tell them?

A. "My job is to make sure the team has daily stand-up meetings and continues to embrace Agile methodologies."

B. "My job is to coach management on the different aspects of Agile project management."

C. "My job is to own the product backlog and make sure customer value is realized."

D. "My job is to debate requirements with key stakeholders to make sure we are building the product correctly."

10. As an Agile project manager, you want your team to be which of the following?

A. Totally dependent on your project plans

B. Totally dependent on the product backlog

C. Self-organizing and self-managed

D. Self-organizing and servant leaders

11. You are a practicing Agile project manager, and you are explaining to your new team the value of retrospectives. What will the team understand about retrospectives once you have explained it to them?

A. Retrospectives are a planned review and reflection point.

B. Retrospectives are a necessary function of all Agile methodologies.

C. Retrospectives are when the customer tests the increment.

D. Retrospectives are for helping to groom the backlog.

12. As an Agile project manager, you explain to your team that, as their coach, you are there to provide for the team's needs and remove any roadblocks to their progress. This is also described as which of the following?

    A. Project management

    B. Agile leadership

    C. Management and leadership

    D. Servant leadership

13. Which of the following items does your team need to produce a working, viable product or service?

    A. A definition of done

    B. Approval from the product owner to create user stories

    C. A well-planned strategy to accomplish project goals

    D. A wireframe with a breakdown of the product needs

14. Your customer is asking you to describe what you mean by self-organizing and self-managing teams. How would you describe them?

    A. Your team is colocated, which helps with self-organization and self-management.

    B. Your team is a group of experts who don't need a manager.

    C. Your team can make all project-related decisions.

    D. Your team can make local decisions about how to produce the result of each iteration based on a shared knowledge of the definition of done.

15. The basics of a stand-up meeting are to achieve which of the following?

    A. Identify problems and describe what has been accomplished since the last meeting.

    B. Describe accomplishment for motivation.

    C. Coordinate discussions on problems and work on solutions.

    D. Identify opportunities for improvement.

16. Who is responsible for the product backlog?

    A. The Scrum Master

    B. The product owner

    C. Everyone

    D. The sponsor

17. Your new Scrum team is looking forward to practicing the time box methodologies of Scrum and Agile. When asked how long the stand-up meetings will be time-boxed for, what will you say?

    A. Stand-up meetings are weekly for one hour.

    B. Stand-up meetings are for Waterfall projects.

    C. Stand-up meetings will require15 minutes every day.

    D. Stand-up meetings will require 15 minutes every week.

18. You and the team are working with a visible master list of work to be done and are constantly reviewing and updating it with requirements that will be reorganized and reprioritized repeatedly. This is an example of which of the following?

   A. You are the development team planning the next iteration.

   B. Working with the team to groom the backlog

   C. You are the Scrum Master working with the customer on priority.

   D. You are the customer working with the product owner to keep your priorities up to date on the Kanban board.

19. Julie has just joined your organization as a new team member. She has heard of Agile as a concept and has a bit of Scrum experience, but she is confused about the sprint backlog and where it came from. What is an effective way to explain to Julie what the sprint backlog is?

   A. It's a separate list of things that the development team wants to accomplish on the sprint.

   B. It's basically the product backlog with the items chosen by the development team based on what they can accomplish during the sprint rather than a totally separate list or artifact.

   C. It's the list of value to be created as well as the risk-adjusted backlog items.

   D. It's the development team's "punch list," and it includes the theme of the sprint.

20. Daily stand-up meetings or daily Scrums are designed to work through three questions. What did we do yesterday? What will we do today? Which of the following is the third question?

   A. What impediments are in our way?

   B. What solutions have we created?

   C. What risk events have occurred?

   D. What backlog items need to be accomplished?

Chapter

3

Key Aspects of Additional Agile Methodologies

THE FOLLOWING PMI-ACP® EXAM TOPICS ARE COVERED IN THIS CHAPTER:

✓ **Domain I: Agile Principles and Mindset**

- Task 1: Advocate for Agile principles by modeling those principles and discussing Agile values in order to develop a shared mindset across the team as well as between the customer and the team.

- Task 2: Help ensure that everyone has a common understanding of the values and principles of Agile and a common knowledge around the Agile practices and terminology being used in order to work effectively.

- Task 3: Support change at the system or organization level by educating the organization and influencing processes, behaviors, and people in order to make the organization more effective and efficient.

- Task 4: Practice visualization by maintaining highly visible information radiators showing real progress and real team performance in order to enhance transparency and trust.

- Task 5: Contribute to a safe and trustful team environment by allowing everyone to experiment and make mistakes so that each can learn and continuously improve the way he or she works.

- Task 6: Enhance creativity by experimenting with new techniques and process ideas in order to discover more efficient and effective ways of working.

- Task 7: Encourage team members to share knowledge by collaborating and working together in order to lower risks around knowledge silos and reduce bottlenecks.

- Task 8: Encourage emergent leadership within the team by establishing a safe and respectful environment in which new approaches can be tried in order to make improvements and foster self-organization and empowerment.

- Task 9: Practice servant leadership by supporting and encouraging others in their endeavors so that they can perform at their highest level and continue to improve.

In this chapter, you will continue going through the first domain of the exam content outline about the mindset of Agile. Understanding different best practices and applying them (regardless of your choice of method) is a large part of absorbing Agile.

In Chapter 1, you covered the beginnings of Agile and the reasons it was necessary to find better ways to manage technology projects. In Chapter 2: Scrum and eXtreme Programming (XP), you covered Scrum and XP. In this chapter, you will finish moving through the final frameworks and mindsets that complete all nine tasks found on the exam content outline under the first domain.

Dynamic Systems Development Method

Dynamic Systems Development Method (DSDM) is considered to be a framework, much like Scrum, rather than an Agile methodology. DSDM is based on best practices and lessons learned with a major focus of being on time and on budget, keeping a competitive advantage, and adhering to philosophies about getting to market first. DSDM is flexible enough to be implemented as a hybrid with Scrum, and it is compared with the *Crystal family* of methodologies of Agile development that you will cover later in this chapter.

The DSDM Consortium is a not-for-profit organization that was formed in the United Kingdom in 1994. One interesting fact is that it is based on the Pareto principle, or the *80/20 rule*, and has roots in Waterfall and *rapid application development (RAD)*. Further flexibility allows it to be utilized with ITIL and PRINCE2, which will be discussed shortly. Even though this framework was created earlier than the Agile Manifesto, you'll see that it is tightly integrated with it based on its major principles.

DSDM Principles

While you won't be tested on the following concepts, it is relevant to review them to understand DSDM and other project management frameworks fully.

The Pareto Principle

The 80/20 Pareto principle was created by Vilfredo Pareto in 1906 after studying the distribution of wealth in Italy. The principle was adapted for business by Joseph Juran, a management consultant who is best known in the quality management arena. In the business arena, this rule basically states that 80 percent of the effects come from 20 percent of the causes. This was used to determine defects in products.

Rapid Application Development

Rapid application development (RAD) was created and utilized to overcome the challenges of Waterfall methods for software projects. The term rapid applies to less time on upfront planning and more time on the process. Prototyping was then easier to manage and changes and adaptability were expected rather than the philosophy of up-front planning found in Waterfall types of projects.

Information Technology Infrastructure Library

Information Technology Infrastructure Library (ITIL) focuses more on IT services rather than on software design. This is why it can be used with DSDM. First you create the software and then you focus on the support of the results by using ITIL principles. ITIL was created to align support with business and customer needs. There are many certifications, from foundational to more in-depth best practices, in the ITIL certification track.

Projects IN Controlled Environments

Projects IN Controlled Environments (PRINCE2) is a structured project management framework that can be adapted to any type of project, not just IT. PRINCE2 was developed for the UK government to help with systems projects, and it is utilized at the government level as well as at the United Nations. The principles and themes of PRINCE2 closely mirror many Agile frameworks, but it is often confused with a Waterfall type of methodology. There is a certification as well for PRINCE2 for those interested in working globally.

Another comparison of DSDM with other frameworks like Scrum and XP reveals that the features are flexible, but the schedule is not.

The Eight Principles of DSDM

There are eight principles of DSDM, and you'll find that they are very much like Scrum and XP. The eight principles also reflect aspects of the Agile Manifesto. These eight principles of DSDM are represented graphically in Figure 3.1.

Focus on the Business Need: You're probably starting to see a pattern between frameworks and methodologies like Scrum, XP, and now DSDM, because many are about focusing on the business needs and understanding the priorities necessary to meet requirements. For many projects, a valid business case must come before any official kickoff or planning of the project/iteration can begin.

Part of maintaining that business need is to ensure that there is continuous business sponsorship and commitment. Another aspect of this is guaranteeing delivery of a minimal usable subset or aspect of the whole that can be used and tested. Basically, like XP and Scrum, DSDM is a piece/part that is usable but not the finished product. To do that, the team must determine the most notable features and make sure that they are in the ultimate solution no matter what.

FIGURE 3.1   The eight principles of DSDM

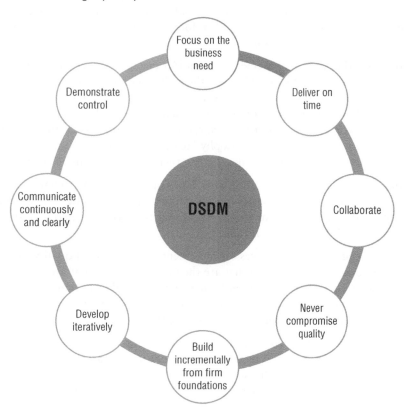

One of the ways that the most important features make it into the ultimate solution is to determine exactly what those features are using a brainstorming approach called *MoSCoW*. This is an acronym that you will see on your exam, and it is important to know that this prioritization method can be used with any Agile methodology or framework.

The MoSCoW Approach to Focusing on the Business Need

- *MUST* have this requirement to meet the business needs

- *SHOULD* have this requirement if possible, but the project success does not rely on it

- *COULD* have this requirement if it does not affect the business needs of the project

- *WON'T* have this requirement, and the stakeholders have agreed that it will not be implemented in a release but may be considered for the future

Deliver on Time: Timeboxing the work is a theme in Agile projects as is focusing on business priorities, always working to hit your deadlines, and building confidence through predictable delivery of usable increments. Therefore, all iterations in all methodologies are timeboxed in some way, shape, or form.

Collaborate: Another universal theme is stakeholder engagement, collaborative environments, and involving the right stakeholders at the right time throughout the project life cycle. The collaboration efforts are proactive across the board, and business representatives are not protected from the potential of being included in those collaborations. All teams are empowered to make decisions in order to best represent customer needs and to maintain a "one team" culture. This cultural philosophy creates buy-in. If everyone is on the same team, from business representatives to developers, then everyone owns the result.

Never Compromise Quality: No matter what types of project management methodologies you subscribe to, quality management is always important. Many notice a distinct overlap between Scope and Quality, and I'm often asked about the difference *Scope is building the right thing, and Quality is building it right.*

Never compromising on quality focuses on agreements on the level of quality that is necessary before any development begins. What are the tolerance levels that are acceptable if quality results fluctuate? How can you build quality into the plan so that you build quality into the increment? The focus here is to ensure that quality is not a variable that can come and go but rather that everyone agrees never to compromise on quality.

Quality is a pay me now or pay me later situation. If you pay now to build quality into the design, it costs less than fixing defects after the fact, not to mention an organization's reputation can be damaged exponentially, which in most cases isn't a quantifiable loss but one that is felt the most. Quality can be managed effectively by testing early, often, and appropriately with frequent reviews.

We haven't talked much about Agile documentation yet, and even though the Agile Manifesto suggests that too much documentation is a waste of time and effort, it is worth noting that designing appropriately and documenting effectively at the last responsible moment is a theme across all Agile types of projects.

Build Incrementally from Firm Foundations: Much as you wouldn't want your home built on a foundation that wasn't solid, the DSDM framework is about building incrementally from firm foundations. What this really means is making sure that appropriate analysis is done and there's "enough design up front," or EDUF, to create as strong a foundation as possible. We do know that priorities change, and with that foundations change as well. Thus, you will need to reassess priorities formally and determine whether the project is still viable after the delivery of each increment.

Develop Iteratively: What makes Agile methodologies so different from Waterfall is the understanding that iterative developments and change are a fact of life in the Agile world.

Not to say that Waterfall projects don't experience progressive elaboration, changes, and even the dreaded scope creep! However, because Waterfall is more focused on a front-loaded plan with formal change control, making substantial change decisions on a regular basis is less likely to occur.

Waterfall methodologies plan first rather than going headfirst into a project knowing that most details will emerge later rather than sooner. Agile projects, on the other hand, focus on finding the right solution and proceed with the knowledge that the solution will not occur without embracing adaptability and change.

Part of iterative development is making room for business feedback and building it into each iteration while at the same time encouraging creativity, experimentation, learning, and even mistakes. Part of making mistakes is learning from them to help create the right solution.

> Anyone who has never made a mistake has never tried anything new.
>
> *Albert Einstein*

Communicate Continuously and Clearly: Communication is very important in all project methodologies and frameworks. Most project managers (Agile or not) spend about 90 percent of their time communicating. But what about the rest of the team?

If 90 percent sounds high to you, it is because it is a *best* practice. But like all best practices, the correct communication percentage is relative to your organization and your team. Most project managers say that they spend between 65 percent and 85 percent communicating about their projects daily.

One of the coolest things about Agile methodologies is that there's total encouragement of informal face-to-face communication at all levels on a regular basis. There is also encouragement for many different forms of timeboxed communication, including daily stand-up meetings, facilitated workshops, modeling, and prototyping, all designed to help manage the expectations of stakeholders at all levels throughout the project.

Part of the importance of communicating continuously and clearly is that everyone understands the evolving solution, and it is demonstrated early and often enough to maintain that understanding. Notice that I didn't say heavy documentation and massive amounts of status reports, because in this case, documentation is expected to be lean and timely. Face-to-face communication is the preferred method. The overarching philosophy of continuous and clear communication is making sure that we always aim to be honest and transparent in all communication.

Demonstrate Control: You can demonstrate control effectively by using DSDM by utilizing low-tech, high-touch information radiators that are visible to all. All Agile frameworks promote visual information radiators.

In later chapters, we will look at all the types of information radiators and low-tech, high-touch tools that will allow progress and plans to be transparently communicated. You will see that is isn't totally necessary to use software to design and communicate about software!

Demonstrating control is also a philosophy of proactive management and continuous reassessment and evaluation of the project viability based on the current objectives of the business. Finally, control is demonstrated by understanding what level and format is considered appropriate for formal tracking and reporting.

The following are an overview of great guiding principles to get you into the mindset of DSDM :

- Everyone is actively involved, including the end user.

- Teams are empowered.

- There are frequent deliveries of products.

- There is a big focus on quality.

- There is both iterative and incremental development.

- All changes are reversible.

- Requirements are baselined at a high level.

- There is integrated testing of the increment.

- It's a no-blame culture.

Kanban

In the late 1940s, Toyota started studying US supermarkets after noticing that they were not storing a lot in warehouses or in the back rooms of their stores. They also noticed that customers generally retrieved what they needed at the time—no more, no less—because they knew they could always come back the next day and get what they needed again.

If you have ever been in a supermarket while they're stocking the shelves, you might have noticed that they stock only what they expect to sell within a certain time frame and replace what they have already sold. Granted that much of that has to do with spoilage and expiration dates, but these observations by Toyota sparked a new way of perceiving inventory. Now, with the use of computer systems and inventory software, it is easier for a system to be lean and *just in time (JIT)*. Toyota took the observation to its factory floors and created the *Kanban* system as a way to utilize it as an inventory control system.

Kanban (看板) means signboard or billboard in Japanese; "Queue Limitation" in English.

Because Kanban means signboard or billboard in Japanese, the manufacturing system created the use of a card displaying the sequence of the process or events and instructions so everyone knew how to manage the process and what the instructions were to manage the just in time (JIT) model. It was sent all the way through the production line to communicate better through visual management and stay with the concept of using only what is needed.

 Real World Scenario

An Observation of Manufacturing

I've spent some time in China and Thailand as a project management subject-matter expert, and I observed the assembly line in an organization that provides technology that you use every day. I saw the use of Kanban cards at the beginning of the production flow all the way to the end. I also saw a color-coded board that was updated and other visual items designed to help the system along.

In that moment, I wasn't totally sure what I was witnessing, since I was heavily involved in Waterfall project management at the time. When I asked about it, the answer was "To make sure that we are meeting requirements, we use a Kanban (pull) system. We always know what is next because the card signals us to move materials within the production facility or even from a supplier as needed."

The color-coded board I saw was explained as a visual wall schedule to maintain production capacity. I can tell you from that experience that I really started to think about Kanban and other Agile methods. Honestly, the use of Kanban cards and boards is something I can no longer do without.

As a devotee of Microsoft Project for many years, using it to manage my workflow, working with its Gantt charts and work breakdown structures, and suffering as it fought back against any changes, it was so refreshing to find a better way. When I learned how to use Kanban boards, it changed my paradigm of how I viewed workflow. Switching to Kanban changed the way I looked at scheduling forever. No going back now!

The Kanban method emphasizes a focus on the customer and the work that services their needs rather than on the activities of individuals. Moreover, the principles of Kanban are quite simple, starting with change management and service delivery principles. The change management principle is all about understanding current processes and respecting roles, responsibilities, and job titles. There is a constant focus on pursuing improvements and evolving through change and encouraging every level to practice leadership no matter what their role is in the organization. Like the philosophy of cross-functional teams in many other Agile principles, Kanban mirrors adaptive leadership.

On the service delivery side, one key aspect is really understanding and focusing on what the customer needs and expects. One way to do this is to consistently evolve your policies organizationally to improve outcomes for both the customer and the business. The way this is done is quite simply to manage the work and let your team self-organize around it. Thus you have self-organized, self-managed, and cross-functional teams.

There are two aspects of Kanban that are a great introduction of the low-tech, high-touch tools that are used in Agile methodologies—the *Kanban card* and the *Kanban board*. The Kanban cards signal the need to move materials within the production facility or to get the materials from an external seller or supplier into the production facility. The primary technique, however, which is used most of all in many Agile methodologies, is the Kanban board.

Most Kanban boards are front-and-center whiteboards with swim lanes that represent the work as it travels from backlog to work in progress (WIP) to the work that is done or deployed. The uncomplicated process utilizes Post-it notes to represent the individual work items or the Kanban cards. It isn't always possible to have colocated teams and onsite customers, so there are many software programs out there that can mimic a Kanban board virtually. Jira, Smartsheet, and many others can provide your remote team with the option to use one of the most popular information radiators out there.

Kanban Board

The Kanban board is not only a visual representation of work that needs to be done, is being done, and *is* done, but it is one of the most popular ways to radiate information to multiple stakeholders at one time. The Kanban board is considered to be low-tech and high-touch, meaning no technology is used and everyone has a hands-on way of moving work through the process flow Figure 3.2 shows an example of a Kanban board.

FIGURE 3.2   Kanban boards

Backlog	Work in progress (WIP)	Done	Accepted	Deployed

What is so cool about the visual process that Kanban uses is that it represents a *pull system*. Work is pulled into the iteration when other work is completed. You know that a backlog is dynamic and ever changing. You also know that value changes based on the needs and wants of the customer. By using a pull system, the product owner can determine what backlog items should be done next. The team will select the work that they can accomplish in the sprint or iteration. Once the work is accomplished, it moves to acceptance and other work is pulled into progress. Once the work is considered done, it can be deployed. Many people who use this process use large white boards and Post-it notes to display backlog items, selected work, *work in progress (WIP)*, and what's been done and deployed.

It's relevant to discuss Scrum boards at this point because they're very similar in nature to a Kanban board, but there are some distinct differences between the two. A Scrum board uses the same pull system, but rather than new work being continuously pulled in, no additional items can be added during a sprint other than what the team has chosen to work on during that sprint.

A Scrum board is an excellent visual representation of workflow moving from left to right through the sprint, and it keeps everybody on top of the work. At the same time, it is used as an information radiator that is not only easy to read but easy to use. Once all of the work has been done and one sprint is over, the Scrum board will be reset when new work is chosen to be done during the next sprint. The other difference between the two is that Scrum boards use epics, user stories, and tasks with story points to represent the amount of work that can be accomplished in a sprint.

We'll discuss user stories and story points in a later chapter focused on *Domain V: Adaptive Planning*. At a high level, story points represent the size of the work. Much like Kanban boards, the Scrum boards provide visual aids and tangible items that are updated on a regular basis.

The Six Principles of Kanban

The six principles of Kanban are as follows:

1. Visualize the workflow
2. Limit work in progress (WIP)
3. Manage flow
4. Make policies explicit
5. Implement feedback loops
6. Improve collaboratively, evolve experimentally

The Six Principles of Kanban Simplified

The six principles of Kanban review the cycle of understanding the workflow intellectually and allowing for consistent feedback and improvement as work progresses.

1. *Visualize the Workflow:* See the work and the policies that determine how the workflow is currently and will be executed. This does several things: It improves the overall process iteratively, helps to embrace necessary changes, and allows for learning from ineffective changes. This is why the Kanban boards are so useful, because they keep the workflow front and center, and they show a map of where you begin and where you end. Once workflow is understood then change for the better and optimized workflow can occur.

   The Kanban board is always within eyesight, leaving very little question as to the work that needs to be done or what work has been completed or deployed. This low-tech, high-touch way of radiating information is more effective than status reports because it is so visual. The brain processes visual images 60,000 times faster than it processes text, and therefore Kanban/Scrum boards are highly valuable in a fast-paced Agile environment.

2. *Limit Work in Progress (WIP):* Limiting work-in-progress is the crux of Kanban. Nobody takes on too much or too little work. If WIP is limited via the pull system and implemented on parts or all of the workflow, then each step in the workflow is limited. New work is only "pulled" into the next step when there is available capacity. Limiting WIP is a large part of many Agile methodologies and frameworks. You'll review WIP in the chapters based on adaptive planning and continuous improvement.

3. *Manage Flow:* Even though change is necessary to improve process or products, sometimes too much change can wreak havoc on process flow. A key aspect of managing the flow effectively is to only create changes in the process once the change is understood. This can be done by assessing all impacts on other areas of the project that could be a result of the change.

   If you have ever attempted to make a change in one area of a project and then witnessed the domino effect after the change was implemented, you know why this is so important. For example, let's say that you change the scope of work without consideration for time and money and now you are over budget and behind schedule. This is all due to not assessing the impact of the change and how it was implemented. Managing the flow and only implementing changes that are really necessary keep the things moving efficiently and remove waste from the process.

 Real World Scenario

How Golf Balls Led to Continuous Improvement

During my training for Scrum certification, the instructor broke us up into groups of six. He then proceeded to hand us a bucket of 60 golf balls and gave us two minutes to determine how we were going to meet the requirements. The goal was to get as many golf balls back in the bucket as possible in two minutes. Sounds simple, right? I thought so too until I heard the rules. Each person must touch each golf ball. The first person to touch it was also the last person to touch it before it went back into the bucket, and if the golf ball hits the floor it doesn't count. Finally, you could not hand it to the person next to you on either side.

Needless to say, during the first few rounds, people were chucking golf balls at each other, dropping them, and in general it was (best case) an epic fail! We regrouped after each round and discussed ways to improve the process. For sure, we learned by doing and then discussing what was and what was not working. It took us five iterations of execute, regroup, reset, and execute again before we discovered how to manage the flow.

Once we understood the changes we were making to the process, the wasteful extra steps that we were taking, and how poorly we worked together as a team, we could then work continuously to improve the process flow. We went from 10 balls in the bucket to 50 in five iterations. Still not perfect, because project management isn't an exact science. Nevertheless, I learned a valuable lesson that day about continuous improvement and only changing parts of a process if they absolutely do not work. If the processes work but are executed poorly, you have to self-adjust around the work and the processes. That involves honestly defining your failure without finger pointing, being transparent around it, and working together to improve.

Who knew golf balls in a bucket would change my way of thinking about everything? Being agile is more than crossing the finish line—it's about how you run the race that matters the most.

4. *Make Policies Explicit:* Having rules and policies that are well known by everyone takes the guesswork out of the equation. Having a rule that all policies are explicit seems odd, but if everyone understands the policy and procedures, or the definition of done, there is a better chance that rational changes in process when and if needed will be better implemented and more effective.

5. *Implement Feedback Loops:* Better understanding through feedback improves the process and the result. In a continuing trend of effective communication and colocated teams, it's easy to see that everything under the Agile umbrella follows a similar theme. Visual workflow and self-directed and self-managed teams that are colocated are all considered important aspects of effective feedback loops.

 Osmotic communication is a term that you will also see on the exam. It relates to having colocated teams who can overhear conversations and tap into things they want to know or need to know, as if through osmosis. Osmotic communication is testable as an effective way of knowledge transfer. You will cover communication in more depth in Chapter 7, "Effective Team Performance on Agile Projects."

6. *Improve Collaboratively, Evolve Experimentally:* For sure, this is easier said than done, and there are a variety of methods, both scientific and not, that can be used to evolve as an organization.

You may see the word *Kaizen*, which is a combination of the two Japanese words *Kai* and *Zen*, meaning continuous improvement. It isn't a distinct process but more of a way of being. If your organization is going through a Kaizen, it is unique to your organization rather than a specific set of rules to follow.

Many of the Agile and quality management methodologies came from collaborations between Japan and the United States as organizations moved from the industrial age and entered the technical age. The knowledge transfer of Kanban still applies whether you are mass producing bicycles or creating cutting-edge software. Kanban is a deep concept with very simple ideals. Improve your process, use only what you need at the time until you pull more work in, organize around the work, and utilize visual workflow.

The following are great guiding principles to know to get you into the mindset of Kanban:

- Kanban is a way to manage work easily and keep work in progress (WIP) limited.

- Derived from Japan, Kanban is a visual sign that is used to trigger an action.

- Kanban work in progress (WIP) is often represented on a Kanban board to reflect processes of workflow.

- A Kanban card will move through various stages of WIP through acceptance.

- Kanban is often referred to as a pull system.

- Kanban is a model for incremental improvements rather than a set framework.

- Kanban can be incorporated into many Agile methodologies like Scrum and XP.

What Is Lean Product/Software Development?

Many philosophies integrated into Agile methodologies come from the Japanese and more specifically from Toyota. It's not unusual in both Waterfall projects and in Agile projects to see the term *Lean*. Many of you have probably heard of *Lean Six Sigma*, which is a quality approach that incorporates philosophies of Lean. Lean Six Sigma projects utilize the Lean philosophy of elimination of waste in the system, and Six Sigma focuses on reducing defects that can affect the overall quality of the result.

When you think of the word *lean*, you probably think thin, skinny, or without extra weight. That's an excellent way to think about Lean product/software development as well. The history of Lean software development began as a translation of Lean manufacturing and IT principles and practices seen in the Toyota production system but were later translated and adapted to outline best practices in software projects.

 Lean Software Development: An Agile Toolkit by Mary and Tom Poppendieck (Addison-Wesley Professional, 2003) incorporates the original Lean principles and compares tools and techniques to other Agile methods. Lean is easily adapted and used in any framework or best practices of most Agile methods, if not all.

The Seven Principles of Lean

The seven principles of Lean are as follows:

1. *Eliminate Waste:* Maximize value.
2. *Amplify Learning:* Via Frequent Communication and Feedback
3. *Decide as Late as Possible:* Early Planning, Late Decision Making
4. *Deliver as Fast as Possible:* Maximize ROI.
5. *Empower Team:* Self-Managed and Trusted
6. *Build Quality In:* Quality Assurance Rather than Quality Control
7. *See the Whole:* See the system not the parts of a system.

 Verbiage may vary on the seven principles, but the meaning or outcomes are the same.

How Lean Complements Agile

Lean complements Agile in four very distinctive ways, and it works to optimize flow efficiency across the entire value stream. The four ways are easily understood and necessary to keep the process flowing in the right direction.

- *Build the right thing:* Understand and deliver real value to real customers.
- *Build it fast:* Dramatically reduce the lead time from customer need to delivered solution.
- *Build the thing right:* Guarantee quality and speed with automated testing, integration, and deployment.
- *Learn through feedback:* Evolve the product design based on early and frequent end-to-end feedback.

Implementing Lean Software Development: From Concept to Cash (Poppendieck, 2006)

Lean has influenced many Agile methods, especially those that strive to keep the framework light and flexible. However, I've seen Lean be influential in Waterfall projects as well. I wouldn't necessarily call Lean an Agile principle, as it is more of an influencer of improved process. Some of the terms and specific principles of Lean have influenced every methodology in Agile today, including some you have already read about and some you will cover in Chapter 9, "Detecting Problems and Working Through Changes." Lean is much more of a variation of the Kanban methodology and pull system rather than a specific Agile methodology.

The Seven Wastes of Lean Manufacturing

The goal in manufacturing is to keep things Lean, which is impossible if you're producing the opposite of value. In any Lean project, waste is the opposite of value. The term *waste* started in the late 1940s at Toyota when they were looking to reduce manufacturing costs to keep the budget, you guessed it, lean. Because Toyota was mass-producing vehicles, the concepts of Lean manufacturing came well before Lean in Agile software development. While there is overlap in some concepts, there was a need to adapt it specifically to software development.

First, it's important to understand where and how the original Lean framework began before jumping directly to software.

The original seven wastes of Lean manufacturing were identified in *A Study of the Toyota Production System* by Shigeo Shingo (Productivity Press, 1989):

1. Overproduction
2. Extra processing
3. Transportation
4. Waiting
5. Motion
6. Defects
7. Inventory

The Seven Wastes of Lean Manufacturing Simplified

To remove waste from the manufacturing process, it was important to identify what the causes were. After the wastes were identified effectively the organization could determine how to remove them from their value stream.

1. *Overproduction: Producing more than the demand requires* Overproduction costs organizations every single year, not just in money but in labor, parts, and leftover inventory, which potentially will not be sold due to lowered demands. It's a gamble for organizations who mass produce to forecast how many/how much they should produce in a market that is typically fickle. Better forecasting methods are necessary not to overproduce, and this is typically why a Kanban pull system approach works well in this environment.

2. *Extra processing: Additional steps in the process that aren't really needed* Extra processing is like the continuous integration practice in XP's software development. If things get complicated or you are spending too much time on the process steps, it is necessary to implement process improvement and simplify the value stream.

> The term *value stream* refers to the process from conception to delivery. It is the stream by which we produce value to the customer. If there are unnecessary steps in the process or other waste in the system, the value stream will not flow correctly. Value stream mapping is a lean way of looking at the current system and then designing a future system that is more effective. We will cover value stream mapping in more depth in Chapter 10, "Tailoring, Quality Management, and Improving Project Processes," which relates to the PMI-ACP exam content outline and *Domain VII: Continuous Improvement.*

3. *Transportation: Shipping the increment from one place to the other* Many manufacturing organizations produce one part or piece of an increment and then transport it to another location that makes a different part or piece. This slows the progress from concept to delivery. Even though this can't be helped in many cases, it is better to have many locations that are all set up to produce one full increment themselves to reduce handoffs.

4. *Waiting: Lag between process steps* If you have ever had to wait for someone else to finish their work before beginning yours, and then you find yourself with limited time to do your piece, you know what this feels like. I would imagine that you would be engaged in much arm crossing, foot tapping, and passive-aggressive sighing. Waiting is time wasted.

5. *Motion: Moving around within the process* What is the shortest distance between two points? A straight line, of course. Too much motion or extra steps produce defects and wastes time.

> I see motion in the process all the time in heavier frameworks like Waterfall. There are too many practices and too much documentation. Those are all great best practices on long-term, set-scope projects, but in Agile projects it is too much motion in the process to be effective.

6. *Defects: Flaws in the deliverables that impact their features/functionality* Defect repair is very expensive, and a lot of quality management methodologies incorporate a pay-me-now or pay-me-later situation. Organizations spend money upfront to make sure that the process produces quality deliverables through quality assurance and quality control procedures. I'm sure that you have heard on the news recently of many companies that have to do recalls on defective parts, equipment, and products. It's expensive and bad for the organization and its reputation.

7. *Inventory: Unfinished goods* Keeping items in inventory that will not be sold, used, or finished takes up precious square footage that could be used for other things. It's what I refer to as *organizational hoarding.*

You might be surprised to know that the concept of Lean didn't just begin with Toyota and certainly was created well before Agile was used as a description of project management best practices. Reputable names of those who influenced Lean and removal of waste include Benjamin Franklin, who in several writings describes his thoughts on how saving money organizationally is much better and more effective than raising the prices of products. This influenced Henry Ford, whose use of just in time (JIT) practices revolutionized manufacturing and assembly lines. Many other contributors influenced Lean throughout the years and Kanban as well, including Sakichi Toyoda, who invented the first automatic loom. The creation included a device that stopped the machine when a thread broke. This was revolutionary at the time and again changed automation for the better as well as saving time, materials, and money and preventing waste in general. Toyoda's son is the founder of what we know of today as Toyota.

After the nephew of Sakichi Toyoda visited Detroit and viewed firsthand the manufacturing of automobiles and how a supply chain worked in US grocery stores, other methods were created at Toyota to improve processes. This then influenced Taiichi Ohno, who created the Toyota Production System (TPS) or "Lean Manufacturing," and the visual control method of a Kanban approach. Ohno worked closely with Shigeo Shingo, who is known as the world's leading expert on manufacturing and specifically on the TPS. The concept of Kaizen—a combination of two Japanese words, *Kai* (continuous) and *Zen* (improvement)—was utilized to help keep things lean and minimize waste.

The Seven Wastes of Lean Software Development

The goal of Lean software development is to apply a framework around reducing the day-to-day items that create noise in the process. The goal is to determine relatively quickly what that noise is and continuously answer the questions of where are the time wasters, the extra steps, or the general problems in our process and our product. Figure 3.3 illustrates the seven wastes of Lean software development.

FIGURE 3.3   The seven wastes of Lean software development

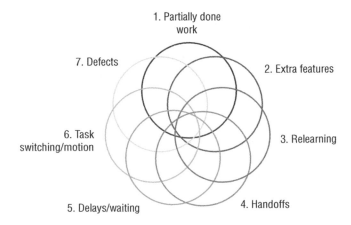

The seven wastes of Lean software development were adapted from *Lean Software Development: An Agile Toolkit* by Mary and Tom Poppendieck (Addison-Wesley Professional, 2003).

The Seven Wastes of Lean Software Development Simplified

Since Lean software best practices were derived from Lean manufacturing, the framework involves a similar thought process. Remove waste from the system of software development and focus on continuous improvement.

1. *Partially Done Work:* Remember when your parents told you to eat all of your vegetables? Of course, you would take a small bite and hide the rest under your mashed potatoes or feed it to the family dog. Afterward, you would triumphantly announce that you were done and hope that nobody noticed. When your parents did notice, they reminded you that you only partially ate your vegetables and were in fact *not* done. Even worse, you were wasting food.

   The same thing applies to partially done work. It does not meet the definition of done, it can't be released or used in a demo, and the code is nowhere near deployable. What may have caused this is that you didn't realize how complex the technology needed to be prior to the plan and have now wasted time and resources. Believe me when I say that it's a similar feeling to getting busted by your parents when hiding your vegetables. Except in this case, it is your customer instead of your parents.

2. *Extra Features:* Goldplating in any project is considered a big no-no! *Goldplating* is, in its simplest form, giving the customer extra features or added functionality that they did not request. This shows that you did not understand the vision or understand the target end user and/or have incorrectly prioritized the value and produced to an incorrect spec. In a lot of organizations, this will result in mediocre quality and scope creep, which will in turn be a waste of time or money.

Example

Let's say that you are creating a bicycle for your customer. They have asked for a 10-speed, cherry red bicycle with a leather seat and highway tires. Instead, you present them with a 12-speed, cherry red bicycle with leather seats, and you have added functionality on the braking system that they didn't request and delivered it with off-road tires.

In this case, one of two things will occur:

1. The customer will say "This is AWESOME! Look at how many extras I got for free! I'm going to tell everyone to come here and get extra features for free!"

The other response is somehow worse:

2. "What did you DO TO MY BIKE? I wanted a 10-speed, not a 12-speed, with highway tires, not off-road ones, and when I hit the brakes they work so well that I nearly flipped myself over the handlebars. Change it back!"

There is no winning in the goldplating game, so it is better to avoid it all together. Many times, goldplating is compared to scope creep, which consists of unauthorized changes to the scope of work. Goldplating, on the other hand, is adapting the quality requirements to improve functionality or giving "extras." Scope is building the right thing, and quality is building it right. Both are necessary for the result to be accepted and deployed.

3. *Relearning:* You might be thinking, "What is wrong with learning?" Learning provides value, and it's important to learn as much as possible. You are correct, but relearning something you already knew at some point is wasted time.

    Think about a time when someone on your team asked you to do something again that you hadn't done in years. You have a vague recollection of how to do it, but you still need to Google it on the sly. Yep, that's relearning. Lack of documentation, poor coding practices, and consistent task switching between team members all create chaos as each one attempts to relearn something they moved on from in the past.

 Real World Scenario

Relearning Project Management

I see relearning situations a lot when organizations decide that their project management practices aren't up to snuff. They begin by bringing in a consultant to implement new best practices and customize something just for their organization. Everyone gets pulled away to train and go through the new way of doing things. Several months pass, and one of two things happens:

1. Some employees go back to the old way of doing things because it's hard to break habits.

2. The rest buy into the new system until the organization decides it isn't working and the original way was better.

In a worst-case scenario, a still newer/better/best way has been identified and is about to be implemented, and so everyone has to reset and relearn, wasting more time and money.

4. *Handoffs:* In many organizations, there is a hierarchical set of processes in place and many hands and eyes will be involved in projects. This is the equivalent of "too many cooks in the kitchen." If you have too many dispersed team members, and the

information is not well communicated or visible, then handoffs will create chaos. Every cook adds salt to the soup, and before you know it the soup is ruined.

This can be managed effectively by using cross-functional teams, which is a major theme in all Agile projects. This means that one team contains all of the knowledge it needs to be effective across all functionalities.

 You may see questions on the exam that relate to *dispersed teams*. It is important to note that if you have dispersed team members across multiple locations, it is a best practice to have a complete team of cross-functional employees in each individual location in order to minimize handoffs.

5. *Delays:* Delays in any form are always a nightmare. Think about sitting in an airport; you're ready to leave on vacation, and then you hear that dreadful announcement that your flight is delayed (or worse still, canceled)! You're vacation has gotten off to a poor start, indeed.

    In this scenario, you are a customer and the delay is keeping you from doing what you want to do. This form of waste is usually due to not having enough people to do the work, or overestimators and overachievers who select too much work than can be accomplished in an iteration. Oftentimes, delays can't be helped because external dependencies get in the way, or there is a significant lack of estimation experience or simply generic estimating, which can result in major delays as well. Delays are the opposite of Lean.

6. *Task Switching:* How many of you are currently working on more than one project at a time? I'm sure that many of you virtually raised your hand or just nodded your head and sighed. This is certainly not uncommon in the project management industry, and in most cases we have more work than we can handle. If that is the case, then you are jumping from one thing to another and going in 800 different directions at the same time.

    The myth of multitasking is the perception that you are being super productive when in fact it is quite difficult. Task switching really muddies the waters and makes it impossible to have a shared vision when you're expected to have visions about multiple projects. Task switching creates waste, and it does so because there are too many projects going on, which leads to poor estimation, poor analysis, and a lack of a shared vision. Having a cross-functional team will prevent many of the handoffs that create waste in the system due to switching tasks on a regular basis.

7. *Defects:* Nothing creates more waste than defects in the increment. Even in Waterfall projects, there are specific quality assurance and quality control processes of audits and inspections to make sure that the process flow is working and that defects are minimized. Is it possible to be 100 percent perfect all of the time? Not at all, but there are steps that you can take to narrow the gap. By *refactoring* on a regular basis, having a shared vision and true understanding of what the customer is looking for can help exponentially. By following a comprehensive quality assurance process, you can continually audit whether the process is working, and you are continuously improving by reducing defects iteration to iteration. This is the key to removing the waste of defects.

Refactoring is changing the code without changing the way the code functions. This has a lot to do with continuous integration and making sure that the code is as simple as possible. This makes it easier to review, test, and change. You will review refactoring more in Chapter 9. Until then, continuous improvement is an ongoing theme in both the work results and the processes you use to produce the work.

Continuous Improvement

Several methods of continuous improvement can be found in Kanban, Lean, or other Agile environments. The main goal is to figure out (using the entire organization dynamic to do so) what is causing the waste or lack of improvement in the process and the results. Many times, as you saw in Lean, waste can happen in the process, the inventory, the team, and the product. To avoid that, you can look to philosophies that guide us in the right direction.

There are three very common philosophies that resonate with Agile frameworks.

1. *The Theory of Constraints (TOC):* The TOC study of bottlenecks in the process flow happens by identifying constraints and focusing on how to alleviate them by restructuring around them. Otherwise, organizations will be affected by a significant lack of meeting or achieving their goals. One bad apple can spoil the bunch, and because of that it is important to focus your efforts on ongoing process improvement to exploit the constraint(s) and remove them.

The *Theory of Constraints (TOC)* is something that you will cover in Chapter 9. The theory describes how you can discover bottlenecks in your process flow, which create waste and impede the implementation of the process itself. Once you know what the constraints are, you can work to improve your process flow and remove wasteful or unnecessary steps as well as produce better-quality increments.

2. The *System of Profound Knowledge:* This is the title of a study by W. Edwards Deming of variation and how it affects processes. Deming's significant contributions to organizations in Japan and the United States are well-modeled theories found in many project management methodologies and quality philosophies. Deming utilized the adaptation of the Shewhart cycle of *Plan-Do-Check-Act* for continuous improvement of best practices in quality management. The cycle can also be translated to follow a Waterfall approach of planning, execution, monitoring, and controlling. The System of Profound Knowledge uses four specific ways (or "lenses") to view the world all at once:

    a. *Appreciate a system* by understanding the processes used.

    b. *Understand variation*, why defects occur, and why there is a range of variation. Statistical sampling in mass production allows for the review of one result that will represent a part of the population. Inspect that and see if there is a range that meets tolerance levels. If not, then the process is out of control.

   c. *Understand psychology* and theories of the mind and human behavior. This allows for a better understanding of the people doing the work.

   d. *Understand the Theory of Knowledge* (Epistemology), a philosophical approach to knowledge and justifiable belief systems.

3. *Lean Economic Model*: This model is based on the concepts of "waste." It was first implemented by Toyota in order to improve its production systems by eliminating the three major constraints to effective production, which are interconnected and work together to wreak havoc in a production system and in process flow:

   a. *Muda, or Waste:* The seven wastes of Lean, which Kanban helps to solve.

   b. *Muri, or Overburden:* Overworked employees or poorly functioning machines will create overburden. It is necessary to remove overburdening from the process flow.

   c. *Mura, or Unevenness:* Variations in the process can create waste (*muda*) and over-burdened employees (*muri*). Mura contributes to a vicious cycle if not managed appropriately.

Much of what you just read is easier said than done, as are most philosophical approaches to project management. I call it "perfect world project management." As organizations recognize the waste in their process flow, identify too many defects in their products, and recognize a faulty process system in general, the more necessary it is to attempt to attain a semblance of order. Lean and Kanban philosophies apply to both industrial and knowledge work, and they have been proven to work time and again in multiple industries and are flexible enough to converge with other frameworks. The theory of Kaizen, or continuous improvement, may be a moving target, but it is a target that all organizations should aim for. Being Agile is the goal.

The following are great guiding principles to know to get you into the mindset of Lean software development:

- Limit work to remove delays and lower interruptions.

- Use time to market ("concept to cash").

- Identify the most valuable work to be done.

- Avoid building what's not needed.

- Have the workflow be in the correct order.

- Remove waste from the system.

Feature-Driven Development

Feature-Driven Development (FDD) isn't the most widely known Agile methodology, but there are several best practices that can be gleaned from each methodology that you review. FDD has important aspects and influences that can be helpful on your Agile projects. FDD was created by Jeff De Luca to help larger teams implement Agile and improve their processes. Larger teams come with more communication channels and more challenges than smaller teams. Remember what Scrum recommends about nine team members. What if you have 30?

The Five Processes of FDD

There are five processes attributed to FDD, of which the first three could be identified as part of Iteration Zero, or in FDD, initial project-wide activities. When you have a much larger team, it is important to get your ducks in a row and figure out how you are going to produce the expected result. Much like Initiation in a Waterfall project, *Iteration Zero*, or initial project-wide activities, helps to create a plan in advance and develop ways to prove the direction in which the project is headed. It also helps answer the question: Will the direction we want to head in work well *before* we actually begin heading in that direction?

1. *Develop an Overall Model:* The first step of Iteration Zero is to develop a model for the tasks and determine how quality checks will occur in execution as well as the problems that will need to be solved.

2. *Build a Features Lists:* A *feature* is a small, client-valued function that needs to be developed and is usually written out and broken down by three aspects: *<action> <result> <object>*. This allows the team to zero focus in on what exactly they are attempting to build and gain consensus on the main features that provide value.

3. *Plan by Feature:* This is the last step in planning, or of Iteration Zero. Initial schedules and assignments are created. The planning team will initially sequence the features based on current business value and determine how to achieve them.

4. *Design by feature:* In this step, a design is created for each feature. A chief programmer selects a small group of features that are to be developed within two weeks but leaves some time and room for inspection to occur.

5. *Build by Feature:* Any activity designed to produce a completed client-valued function (feature) is planned with the idea that it will be built during the iteration. In this case, work is executed in order to produce the feature selected for development.

Because tailoring is becoming so popular in project management, it might be relevant for your team to have an Iteration Zero on a large project, with multiple team members working on something totally unique and new. It's a chance to plot your strategy and map out your way through the project before too much time and money is spent doing the wrong things.

Even though FDD isn't highly testable, Iteration Zero may be the correct answer to a situationally based question when a large team is attempting to develop an overall model for features or trying to prove their strategy or process will work.

Best Practices of FDD

The best practices of FDD are as follows:

1. Domain object modeling
2. Developing by feature
3. Individual class (Code) ownership
4. Feature teams
5. Inspections
6. Configuration management
7. Regular builds
8. Visibility of progress and results

Best Practices of FDD Simplified

Even though FDD isn't the most talked about or popular Agile framework, I find it resonates with many of the Waterfall projects I have worked on in the IT sector. Knowing and
determining what the features were in advance was commonplace, and then working to
determine how to achieve those features involved owning the processes and achieving the
goal. To me, FDD is really a simplified way of running a Waterfall project in an Agile or
software development environment that you can't expect to be successful with the use a
heavier framework.

1. *Domain Object Modeling:* Exploring and explaining the domain of the problems
   to be solved can provide an overall framework and approach. This is very much
   like the Initiation best practices found in the *PMBOK® Guide* and *Project Management Institute, A Guide to the Project Management Body of Knowledge, (PMBOK®
   Guide)*—Sixth Edition, Project Management Institute, Inc., 2017 other Waterfall
   types of methodologies.

2. *Developing by Feature:* Any function that is too complex to be implemented within
   two weeks is further decomposed into smaller functions. This is a lot like taking a
   bigger deliverable to the task level or decomposing a work breakdown structure (WBS)
   used in Waterfall projects to the activity level.

3. *Individual Class (Code) Ownership:* The programmer/developer is responsible for the
   consistency, performance, and conceptual integrity of the code, as opposed to collective code ownership found in other methodologies.

4. *Feature Teams:* These are small, dynamically formed teams that develop a small activity and work on a feature while the rest of the team does the same. They allow pockets
   of cross-functional team members to work together on the same outcome rather than
   one large team working in a swarm.

5. *Inspections:* These are carried out to ensure excellent quality, design, and code, primarily by detection of defects if any.

6. *Configuration Management:* This is the process of identifying features completed to date and maintaining a history of changes. Configuration management is a type of formal change control system that is specific to product changes not seen in many Agile types of projects.

7. *Regular Builds:* Up-to-date systems can be demonstrated to the client and help highlight integration errors early. The more regular the build, the more feedback that can be obtained.

8. *Visibility of Progress and Results:* Frequent progress reports help managers focus a project correctly. Visual progress or transparent placement of progress and results keeps everyone on track and focused on the goal.

The following are great guiding principles to know to get you into the mindset of FDD:

- FDD incorporates high-level planning leading to incremental delivery.

- Each increment has a design and implementation phase.

- The scope of each increment is a single feature.

- FDD defines the overall scope in the beginning but doesn't define the details.

- FDD may incorporate an Iteration Zero to create and approve the process before executing the feature development iteration.

Crystal Methods

Crystal methods are a family of methodologies (the Crystal family) developed by Alistair Cockburn in the mid-1990s. The methods come from years of study and interviews of teams by Cockburn. The Crystal family is Cockburn's way of cataloguing what they did that made the projects successful. Crystal methods are considered and described as "lightweight methodologies."

There aren't any questions on the exam that are specific to Crystal methods *per se*, but you may see questions that do mirror the methodology's focus on adapting a heavier weight process for weightier projects, meaning that the larger the project and the larger the team, the greater the level of criticality increases. Crystal methods shift in criticality depending on the needs of the project. This is also the source of the osmotic communication philosophy, which is highly testable.

Crystal Family Color Codes

Crystal methods are a family of methodologies color-coded and customized by team size and the criticality of the project. Once that is determined, the project is placed based on the scale, and a method is chosen from a range of scalable models. The family of color codes is a lot like when you see a high terrorism alert from the government. They say it is code red, and everyone is on high alert.

In Crystal, it is a similar thought process. If I have a very heavy project with a lot of critical needs, then I need to scale my model to a weight that can work effectively for the outcome. The heavier the project, the heavier the need to scale up in process. The less critical the project, the greater the need to scale down. Crystal is a flexible model, and deciding which to use is based on the criticality of the project and what scale is needed to complete the work appropriately. The family of Crystal begins with Crystal Clear and ends with Crystal Sapphire:

1. Crystal Clear: Smaller projects
2. Crystal Yellow
3. Crystal Orange
4. Crystal Orange Web
5. Crystal Red
6. Crystal Maroon
7. Crystal Diamond
8. Crystal Sapphire: Mission Critical

If I am building a small, noncritical software program for my customer for their own personal use in developing a website, then I would utilize Crystal Clear. On the other hand, if I were building a space rover to run around and take pictures in a galaxy far, far away, then it is a more critical project needing a mission-critical framework like Crystal Sapphire.

The Crystal Family

The Crystal family uses "criticality" to determine what project goes in what color, from low to high, by using a point system based on categories like life, essential/discretionary money, and comfort. Based on the score, a determination can be made of how critical the project is. Then the selected family and their best practices will be utilized. A scalable model like Crystal is something of a one-stop shop for best practices in Agile. It is the most lightweight and adaptable Agile methodology.

The big focus outside of determining the color code are the core tenants of *teamwork*, *communication*, and *simplicity*. Reflection is used frequently to adjust and improve the process. Crystal also promotes early, frequent delivery of working software, high user involvement, adaptability, and the removal of bureaucracy or distractions.

This sounds like many of the frameworks and best practices you have read about already. The resounding themes across multiple Agile methods and frameworks are the focus on communication, delivery early and often, and adapting to changes as needed but keeping things as simple as possible.

The following are great guiding principles to know to get you into the mindset of Crystal methods:

- Crystal is the most lightweight and adaptable Agile methodology.

- Crystal comprises a family of Agile methodologies.

- The Crystal family methodology depends on unique characteristics.

- Choices are driven by several factors, such as team size, system criticality, and project priorities.

- Key tenets of Crystal include teamwork, communication, and simplicity.

- Reflection is used frequently to adjust and improve the process.

- Crystal promotes early, frequent delivery of working software; high user involvement; adaptability; and the removal of bureaucracy or distractions.

- Osmotic communication is highly represented in Crystal, especially with higher criticality or larger teams.

Adaptive Software Development (ASD)

As you have seen throughout, it makes sense that you would need to be flexible and adapt in the ever-changing waters of software development. In the book *Adaptive Software Development: A Collaborative Approach to Managing Complex Systems* by Jim Highsmith (Dorset House Publishing, 2000), Highsmith uses the analogy of mountain climbing to illustrate his points about needing effective teamwork, planning, and the ability to adapt to rapidly changing conditions. Adaptive software development replaces the traditional Waterfall cycle with a repeating series of *speculate*, *collaborate*, and *learn* cycles rather than the Deming/Shewhart cycle of Plan-Do-Check-Act. The planning, execution, monitoring and controlling, and closing process groups found in the *PMBOK® Guide* also reflect the need for continuous improvement and adaptation.

The characteristics of an ASD life cycle are *mission-focused*, *feature-based*, *iterative*, *timeboxed*, *risk-driven*, and *change-tolerant*.

> Rules can be barriers to hide behind or guidelines for the wise to consider and break when the circumstances justify it.
>
> *Jim Highsmith*

Adaptive Software Development Cycle

Rapidly changing conditions mandate the need to be adaptive and flexible. The *adaptive software development (ASD)* cycle very simply represents the continuous sequence of adaptation in software development. Figure 3.4 is a graphic depiction of the adaptive software development cycle.

FIGURE 3.4   The ASD cycle

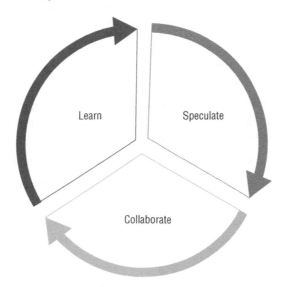

Adaptive Software Development (ASD) Cycle Simplified

The name *adaptive software development cycle* really describes its focus. Develop software, but be prepared to adapt by speculating, collaborating, and learning as you go. Even though the cycle sounds a bit vague, it is a good reminder to all of us working in Agile environments to be constantly checking ourselves, collaborating, communicating, and finally, learning from both our success and mistakes, using what we have learned in an effective and adaptive way.

1. *Speculate:* The project is launched and adaptive cycle planning is conducted using what was learned from project initiation information. For example, the customer creates a mission statement depicting what they want from the results. Typical project constraints like time, cost, scope, and quality are reviewed. The basic requirements are documented to define the set of release cycles or software increments that will be required for the project.

    As the title suggests, this is all speculation at this point because nothing specific has been proven, and you know that customers *always* change their minds. Today's mission statement could be tomorrow's trash, but the act of speculation allows for a direction to be chosen and the ability to move forward while knowing that changes will occur and embracing them.

2. *Collaborate:* Collaboration is crucial to any Agile type of project, as is adapting to uncertainty. Open dialogue is necessary to combat the wrench throwers of technology, requirements, scope changes, risks, stakeholders, and vendors/suppliers.

3. *Learn:* What you will see in a lot of these methodologies is the ability to make mistakes and learn from them. How do you learn? You challenge the status quo and even stakeholders if necessary. You will also run in short iterations of design, build, and test. During these iterations, knowledge is gathered by making small mistakes based on false assumptions and correcting those mistakes as you go. This practice leads to a better experience, better assessment, and eventual mastery in the area where the problem lies.

The following are great guiding principles to know to get you into the mindset of ASD:

- ASD grew out of the rapid application development (RAD) work by Jim Highsmith and Sam Bayer as a way to adapt a typical Waterfall method to software design.

- ASD has less focus on planning and more focus on process.

- Continuous adaptation of the process and the work is the norm in ASD.

- ASD replaces the traditional Waterfall cycle with a repeating series of speculate, collaborate, and learn cycles.

Creating a Successful Mindset

> The servant leader is servant first. It begins with the natural feeling that one wants to serve, to serve first.
>
> *Robert K. Greenleaf*

It seems relevant to end the chapter with everything that it takes to run any methodology successfully and to help you study for and answer questions on the PMI-ACP exam. It is also a good point to review the differences between management and leadership.

Management is focused on big picture items like best practices and whether they have been implemented correctly. It involves being efficient and task-oriented as well as maintaining a position of authority and formal power.

Leadership is much more focused on the human elements of communication, understanding people and your team of individuals, building and maintaining effective teams, and following a core set of principles. Most leadership on Agile projects promotes and encourages the team to be self-directed (and managed), and it stresses the ability to motivate and empower the team on the individual level as well as the collective "we."

Having a good balance of both management and leadership are important and necessary skills for anyone running a team of people. Whether that is a team of salespeople or software developers, good leadership is necessary for effective team development. What you will see throughout most of the methodologies and the exam is the concept of servant leadership. Notice that the word *management* is missing.

 NOTE I've mentioned numerous times that to pass the PMI-ACP exam and improve your mastery of all things Agile, it is important not just to understand content but to get into a successful mindset as well. This is the key to success no matter what type of Agile methodology you implement and no matter what type of questions you get on the exam.

Three Main Aspects of Leading an Agile Project Effectively

The main aspects of leading an effective Agile team are to practice leadership and continuously aspire to learn innovative ways of leading. Servant leadership is a key mindset for Agile, and practicing the tasks of servant leadership is the icing on the cake of a highly effective Agile project manager.

Three Main Aspects of Leading an Agile Project Effectively Simplified

The three aspects, or trifecta, of Agile Project success, is to be an Agile project manager who practices the three principles illustrated in Figure 3.5: leadership, servant leadership, and leadership tasks.

FIGURE 3.5   Leading Agile projects

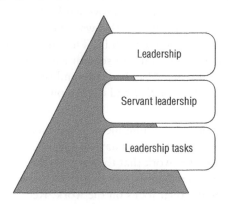

1. *Leadership:* This is the practice of emotional intelligence and being able to adapt and adjust to the needs of your team. A certain amount of extroversion is also a good practice, because without engaging with your team members, you won't know what is going on with them day-to-day. Active listening, being open to new points of view, diversity of thought, and consistent learning are all active traits of good leaders.

I used to call project managers that stayed in their office all day, hovering over spread-sheets, "pod squatters," because they just wouldn't leave their offices to hang out with their team. I thought then (and still do) that they aren't leaders at all—they are simply managers.

2. *Servant Leadership:* The servant leader is servant first and leader second. This may seem counterproductive, or as if their authority is somehow rapidly disappearing. I wouldn't be surprised if this type of Agile project manager is foreign to a lot of managers today—maybe even your own manager!

    Servant leadership is for sure, the key to effective Agile project management. To get into the mindset of a servant leader, you first should know what that entails. The servant leader should provide what the team needs. It's as simple as that. Easier said than done you say? You would be correct! The only way to know what your team needs is to ask them. This requires the emotional intelligence to identify and understand an undercurrent not expressed yet; you'll need to apply your active listening skills to truly understand *what you are hearing without thinking about what you are going to say next.*

    Active listening is probably the biggest aspect of communication. My mother always said, "You have two ears and one mouth, use them accordingly." I wasn't listening at the time. It was only until I ran my first team that I understood what she meant. It's not about me, it's about them. Listening is the best way to know what the team needs and wants. If you are distracted by your own thoughts or words, you'll never understand where the team is coming from.

    It is also your job to remove any roadblocks the team is facing, including pesky stake-holders who are interrupting their work and meetings. Perhaps the biggest aspect of this that makes project managers everywhere scratch their heads in disbelief is help-ing maximize productivity by taking on administrative work if the team starts fall-ing behind schedule. Me take on administrative work? Yep, you read correctly. I hear collective groans everywhere! Think of it this way: The more you help your team to be successful, the more successful they will be. This isn't just fortune cookie rhetoric; it is part of carrying the food and water of servant leadership. Jump in there and get your hands dirty with your team. Also, keep in mind that excessive documentation is considered wasteful, so it won't be *that* bad to take on administrative work in an Agile environment.

3. *Leadership Tasks:* The ability to communicate the project vision as many times as needed for success is a large part of your day-to-day job. Doing so keeps the team focused on the *why* behind the work that they are performing. Keeping the team from being distracted by interruptions, whether from an outside source or by their own creation, helps promote their focus on the work. Remember, you are working in short iterations, so focus is necessary for successful completion. Remove roadblocks preventing the team's success. Motivate, compensate, and encourage. ("Carry the food and water.")

- Here are some tips to keep in mind about the principles of servant leadership as a mindset. Remember that perfect practice makes perfect!

  - Work toward helping your team transform for the better by providing support and coaching as needed.

  - Encourage the personal growth of each team member.

  - Create and help maintain environments that enable your team to be successful.

  - Provide service or servant leadership, rather than managing, is a fundamental reason to be an Agile project manager.

  - Help support and create trusting relationships on your team. You are all in it together.

  - Building commitment is about maintaining the vison and communicating it as often as needed.

  - Create an environment of community and unity by nurturing your team and providing what they need to maintain a sustainable pace and remain motivated in what they are doing every single day.

You will get questions on the exam about doing administrative work for your team to free them up for work on the project as well as questions about active listening. Be aware that active listening doesn't mean that you are thinking about your reaction or even about yourself at all. You will be thinking more about whether the team members look upset, happy, or angry, and if they need your help. It's not "Oh boy, they look angry, so I'm going to have to figure out a way to fix it." Instead it's "My team member looks upset and needs my help." Then you must really listen to what they are saying. It takes practice to do so, and it is an aspirational skill upon which many project managers need to improve.

Summary

This chapter began with an overview of DSDM and the best practices associated with its framework, including the MoSCoW approach to brainstorming value.

Next I went over several other frameworks, including Lean, Kanban, and Feature-Driven Development (FDD), which all contribute to a full understanding of the principles to develop a shared mindset across the team. Much of the Lean and Kanban approaches are complementary to all Agile frameworks and help to trim the waste from your processes and products by embracing a visual pull system to manage your process flow with the use of Kanban/Scrum Boards.

Finally, I went over the essentials of embracing an Agile mindset by practicing servant leadership and some of the important things to keep in mind as you lead Agile projects as well as when you study for your exams.

Everything that we have covered in the first three chapters are incorporated into the tasks found in *Domain I: Agile Principles and Mindset.* Now you have a great foundation to move on to other domains and see how some of the best practices that we covered at the surface level can be implemented and utilized on your next project and on your exams.

Exam Essentials

Be able to understand DSDM and why the MoSCoW approach to determining value is important.   Even though DSDM isn't necessarily testable as a methodology or framework, it does contain the best practice of MoSCoW prioritization. Must, Should, Could, and Won't aspects of MoSCoW help prioritize value.

Understand the Lean and Kanban methods.   It is key that you understand why the Lean and Kanban methods influence Agile frameworks. You must especially appreciate the use of Kanban boards as a way to radiate information of what is in the backlog, what is in progress, and what has been deployed.

Understand the meaning of criticality and heavier weight methods.   Even though Crystal methods aren't mentioned too often on the PMI-ACP exam, the methods lend themselves to the understanding that higher-criticality projects need a heavier method. This is something you may see as a concept on the exam.

Be able to identify waste in a system.   Even though this isn't something that falls under Domain I on the exam specifically, eliminating waste from the value stream is a concept that you will see in *Domain VII: Continuous Improvement (product, process and people).* Understand that removing waste(s) from your Agile process is a continuing theme throughout, and the more waste removed from the system, the better the system works.

Be able to get into the mindset of servant leadership.   The key to passing the PMI-ACP exam is to put yourself into servant leadership mode. Be able to understand the differences between leadership and management. Almost every question deals with the ability to understand this concept and apply it.

Be able to understand all Agile methodologies and frameworks.   You have completed all of Domain I at this point, and you have reviewed at a high level all of the frameworks under the Agile umbrella. This is the foundation to understanding every other domain that we will cover in the rest of this guide. It's always a good thing to review the first three chapters again before you take your exam so that you are really in the Agile mindset and understand the source of the concepts and best practices.

Review Questions

You can find the answers to the review questions in Appendix B.

1. Why is using the MoSCoW Approach in DSDM so important?
    A. To make sure that the least important features are finished last
    B. It incorporates the Pareto principle.
    C. It allows for timeboxing the approach.
    D. To make sure that the most important features are in the ultimate solution no matter what

2. The Pareto principle is seen in many project management and quality methodologies. Why is the principle so important to use when determining cause and effect?
    A. Eighty percent of all effort produces 20 percent of the result.
    B. Improving to 80 percent productivity will produce better results.
    C. Roughly 80 percent of the effects come from 20 percent of the causes.
    D. Twenty percent of the defects are created by 80 percent of the effort.

3. Which of the following is a correct statement?
    A. Lean is the opposite of value.
    B. Haste makes waste.
    C. There are ten forms of waste.
    D. Waste is the opposite of value.

4. Other than defects, which of the following is included in the seven wastes of Lean software development?
    A. Handoffs
    B. Poorly designed backlog
    C. Too many meetings
    D. Lack of pair programming

5. Using Kanban methodology, which of the following is the best way to show performance and WIP to the team and to the customer?
    A. Scrum board
    B. Kanban board
    C. Work radiators
    D. Status reports

6. Why is a pull system so important in the practice of Kanban?
    A. To limit work in progress
    B. To protect the quality
    C. To use the team wisely
    D. To update progressively

7. Why was Feature-Driven Development created?

  A. To accommodate larger teams

  B. To create features that are developed

  C. To incorporate many stakeholders in the process

  D. To complement Scrum

8. Which of the following is the best way to complete the sentence: In Crystal methods, _____ increases with team size.

  A. The number of stakeholders

  B. The framework

  C. Criticality

  D. Output

9. Mission focused, feature based, iterative, timeboxed, risk-driven, and _____ are all characteristics of an ASD life cycle.

  A. Plan-driven

  B. Adaptive

  C. Rule-oriented

  D. Change-tolerant

10. Your team is currently a bit behind schedule, and it is worried that it won't complete the work before the iteration ends. If you are practicing good servant leadership, what should you do first?

  A. Hold stand-up meetings.

  B. Communicate with stakeholders.

  C. Coach them on Agile principles.

  D. Take on administrative work as needed.

11. One of your team members comes to you with a problem about something that they are experiencing with key stakeholders on the project. They seem upset and are looking for you to provide some feedback. If you are actively listening to your team member, what thoughts should be running through your mind?

  A. "I need to handle this very carefully."

  B. "I'll have to make sure to handle it in the appropriate manner because the team member clearly needs me to help them through this problem."

  C. "My team member is upset about something and needs to express him- or herself and gain support."

  D. "I should tell the team member to bring this issue up at the next stand-up meeting as a description of the impediments that stand in their way."

12. If you are leading an Agile team and spend most your time focusing on inspiring and collaborating with your team, what kind of leadership are you practicing?

   A. Effective leadership

   B. Leadership by management

   C. Agile leadership

   D. Adaptive leadership

13. The team space is key in Agile projects. What is the one thing that is recommended above all others for Agile teams?

   A. Scrum boards

   B. Colocation

   C. Caves and common rooms

   D. Information radiators

14. On a colocated team, what is one of the major benefits of everyone sitting together in the same work space?

   A. The Scrum Master can find everyone.

   B. Daily stand-up meetings are easier to organize.

   C. Osmotic communication is enhanced.

   D. It builds relationships and trust.

15. Leadership tasks are designed to help your team be most successful and to remove roadblocks preventing the team's success. Which of the following best describes this mindset?

   A. Motivate, compensate, and encourage

   B. Colocation and osmotic communication

   C. Information radiators

   D. Daily stand-up meetings

16. What percentage of time should an Agile project manager spend communicating daily?

   A. 85 percent

   B. 95 percent

   C. 90 percent

   D. 65 percent

17. Lean was originally designed for which of the following?

   A. Manufacturing

   B. Software development

   C. Waterfall project management

   D. Visual project management

18. Adaptive software development replaces _____ with a repeating series of *speculate*, *collaborate*, and *learn* cycles:

A. Lean

B. FDD

C. Waterfall

D. Kanban

19. One of your key stakeholders comes to you after a meeting and says, "I don't see you doing a lot of normal paperwork associated with project management. Instead, I see you talking to your team a lot. Why aren't you doing your management duties?" How would you respond to this statement?

A. "In Agile project management, paperwork is a waste of time. My team needs me around in case they have questions."

B. "In Agile project management, I do paperwork at the last responsible moment. Until then, I do management activities like hold stand-up meetings."

C. "In Agile project management, we practice servant leadership. I don't do any amount of management tasks, but I serve my team as they need me to."

D. "In Agile project management, my role is that of a servant leader. I do an appropriate amount of documentation, but I serve mostly as a coach and leader for my self-directed team."

20. A key stakeholder has asked for information on the team's progress through the iteration. What would be the best way to present information about team progress?

A. Earned value report

B. Kanban board

C. Detailed notes on stand-up meetings

D. A Gantt chart

21. What would be the reasoning behind having an Iteration Zero?

A. To prove the process will work

B. To determine a process that works

C. To prove that the product should be built

D. To prove that the product will be built correctly

Chapter 4

Agile Initiation and Stakeholder Engagement

THE FOLLOWING PMI-ACP® EXAM TOPICS ARE COVERED IN THIS CHAPTER:

✓ **Domain III: Stakeholder Engagement**

Understand Stakeholder Needs:

- Task 1: Identify and engage effective and empowered business stakeholder(s) through periodic reviews in order to ensure that the team is knowledgeable about stakeholders' interests, needs, and expectations.

- Task 2: Identify and engage all stakeholders (current and future) by promoting knowledge sharing early and throughout the project to ensure the unimpeded flow of information and value throughout the lifespan of the project.

Ensure Stakeholder Involvement:

- Task 3: Establish stakeholder relationships by forming a working agreement among key stakeholders in order to promote participation and effective collaboration.

- Task 4: Maintain proper stakeholder involvement by continually assessing changes in the project and organization in order to ensure that new stakeholders are appropriately engaged.

- Task 5: Establish collaborative behaviors among the members of the organization by fostering group decision making and conflict resolution in order to improve decision quality and reduce the time required to make decisions.

Manage Stakeholder Expectations:

- Task 6: Establish a shared vision of the various project increments (products, deliverables, releases, iterations) by developing a high-level vision and supporting objectives in order to align stakeholders' expectations and build trust.

- Task 7: Establish and maintain a shared understanding of success criteria, deliverables, and acceptable trade-offs by facilitating awareness among stakeholders in order to align expectations and build trust.

- Task 8: Provide transparency regarding work status by communicating team progress, work quality, impediments, and risks in order to help the primary stakeholders make informed decisions.

- Task 9: Provide forecasts at a level of detail that balances the need for certainty and the benefits of adaptability in order to allow stakeholders to plan effectively.

In this chapter, you will begin working on the tasks found in of the exam content outline, *Domain III: Stakeholder Engagement*. Because the tasks in this domain directly relate to the initiation or beginning of an Agile project, it is important to understand how to obtain stakeholder buy-in before actual team execution of iterations, as seen in *Domain II: Value-Driven Delivery* and *Domain IV: Team Performance*. Understanding different best practices, applying them to pre-project engagement, and working with stakeholders on their vision of the increment is the first step to gaining their buy-in and planning around it. This chapter and the next chapter will cover all of the tasks in Domain III and give you a well-grounded idea of how an Agile project kicks off and how knowledge sharing and communication best practices apply.

Charters and Agile Projects

All projects, both Agile and Waterfall, have a formal way of kicking off and methods for defining initial requirements. Some projects will begin with a *Statement of Work (SOW)*, other projects will begin with a contract agreement, and still others will begin with a *project charter*. Typically, how this process unfolds depends on your organizational best practices, and those can fluctuate based on the needs of the project and/or the customer. Many times, an SOW or a contract will kick off charter creation, but it isn't unusual to have just one or the other. There aren't any set ways in any type of Agile framework of how a project's kick-off absolutely has to go, but the recommendation is always to have something formally written.

In typical Waterfall projects, a project charter is necessary to give formal authorization to begin project work. The charter will contain information based on a business case to determine the fiscal health of the decision to charter a specific project, a high-level overview of what success looks like, and actual *deliverables*, *milestones*, *budgetary constraints*, and *initial risks* that have been identified. Finally, and most important, in the Waterfall environment, the project charter gives authorization to begin project work by assigning the project manager formally. In fact, in many scenarios, a Waterfall project cannot begin without a charter, or it is risky to do so.

Chartering will take place in the Waterfall *initiation phase* of the project, and the project manager may be considered a key expert with good judgment about the scope of work and a key contributor to the charter itself. Once the project manager has their what I call "ticket to ride the roller coaster of project management," they can begin a *cost-benefit analysis* to make sure that it is a feasible request both financially and based on the currently defined scope of work. Once that is determined, the *project sponsor* (check writer) will sign off, and work begins by identifying stakeholders and planning project efforts.

You might notice that there is a lot of initial information in the Waterfall charter that covers the big constraints like scope requirements, cost, and scheduling as well as risks. This doesn't mean that things won't change, but at this point the result is pretty much set in stone. Whether you are building a bridge, a skyscraper, a railroad, or a massive datacenter, even though the scope may be too large to determine cost accurately and time definitively, at least you know what the result should be.

After the collection of requirements, the project manager will put together a *scope statement* with specifics and will get sign-off. This is the point in the Waterfall project where you hand the scope statement to the customer and sponsor and say, "Is this what you meant? Does this look right to you?" This is a key step because that scope statement evolves from the charter, and it will drive the budget, schedule, resources, and procurement, and it is the crux of the result. In essence, *"Here is what we will do, and here is what we won't do."*

> We will build you a 12-speed bicycle that is cherry red with leather seat and road tires. We will not add a bell.

This is a crucial step because it helps prevent assumptions and lowers the possibility of scope creep later. Yet again, you can see a vast difference between Waterfall and Agile projects. Waterfall scope is well known, and in Agile projects it simply is not. How then can you use a project charter in Agile? The answer is to keep it simple, keep it flexible, and update it as needed. Chartering sets the stage for what is to come, and it allows everyone to get on the same page for now or at least until the scope changes—as it always does.

Simply put, traditional charters won't work on Agile projects because they aren't flexible enough to accommodate the changes that will occur. Does this mean that you shouldn't use a charter on your Agile projects? Not at all; the best practice is there for a reason. Switching from a Waterfall framework to an Agile one takes some adaptation of best practices and a flip of the script to facilitate a flexible response to changing needs and technologies. It would be impossible to put together a totally static document that describes what success looks like when you don't even know yourself. I can pretty much guarantee that the customer isn't exactly sure either at this point.

What Waterfall and Agile charters *do* have in common is project selection techniques to determine the fiscal output and input of the organization sponsoring the project. It is necessary to engage your stakeholders early and often to determine the jumping-off point of the project and decide to charter. Therefore, some organizations will consider the conversations with the customer and any currently known requirements as well as any additional information they have and determine the fiscal health of chartering that specific project as part of initial project-wide activities. This means that they will get their ducks in a row before they start pulling out the corporate wallet or asking the customer for theirs.

The top three tasks of the exam content outline for stakeholder engagement at the beginning of the project and throughout are as follows:

1. Identifying and engaging effective and empowered business stakeholder(s) through *periodic reviews* to ensure that the team is knowledgeable about stakeholders' interests, needs, and expectations.

2. Promoting *knowledge sharing early and throughout* the project with current or future stakeholders to ensure the unimpeded flow of information and value throughout the life span of the project.

3. Establishing stakeholder relationships by *forming a working agreement* among key stakeholders in order to promote participation and effective collaboration.

Even though the top three tasks are expected to continue throughout the project, it is important to note that the development of a project charter is setting the stage for a general understanding and agreement.

Waterfall and Agile projects alike have a kick-off point designed to engage current and key stakeholders and form a working agreement of at least the financial aspects and a general understanding and agreement on *who, what, where, when, why,* and *how.* Without this type of interaction, the flow of communication is impeded and a working agreement won't occur. The theme of collaborative communication will continue throughout the iterations of the project because everyone knows the scope will change. By starting out the project on a collaborative footing, it can pave the way for open and transparent communication and consensus building very early in the project. The momentum can then continue throughout.

Traditional vs. Agile Project Charters

It's a good idea to know the difference between a traditional project charter for Waterfall and a generic Agile project charter. As you move forward throughout this chapter, you will see all of the pre-project initiation steps to build out the Agile charter, but knowing what the result of charter creation will be is helpful for the exam and for your real-world projects, whether they consist of best practices in Waterfall, Agile, or a hybrid of both. I have seen plenty of Agile project charters that look more like Waterfall charters and vice versa. Remember, you decide what works for your projects and organizations.

Traditional Project Charter Headers

Project Name   XYZ Project

Executive Summary   Business case overview and a statement summarizing what will be done. Usually this is written last after key stakeholders review the information in the charter. They will then summarize and justify why the project is necessary.

Project Overview   A general description of what success looks like is documented in an overview. For example, "Our organization is partnering with ABC Company to build a new housing development of 25 homes to improve living conditions in that area."

Project Scope Requirements   This is usually the end result or planned scope of work. This can also include aspects of the actual project scope, such as, "We will need 25 engineers who will meet the scope baseline estimates within +/- 15 days."

Goals and Objectives   This can be anything from profits to what the inevitable product/service/result will be or what it will be used for.

Organizational Impacts   This can be inclusive of things like being first to market, meeting contractual obligations, or updating corporate policies to meet a regulation. Typically, this is generic as well.

Project Deliverables   This can be the scope results or actual documentation or deliverables needed during the project. Deliverables can also include cost, scope, and schedule baselines or documented or current procurement relationships.

Estimated Costs and Durations   Costs will come from the business case development and project selection techniques, while durations usually come from the customer or mandatory milestones. Both estimates tend to be optimistic.

Assumptions and Constraints   Assumptions are documented to help identify risks and also to make it known what the sponsor/organization/customer assumes will occur during the project. Constraints are anything that limits the project, such as not enough resources or absolute dates to finish project work.

Project Risks   Such risks are occasionally documented (if you are lucky) and are typically presented in categories such as, for example, technical risks, weather risks, or project management risks. Risks also have the potential for an opportunity instead of just threats. These could be being first to market and/or landing a new customer.

Project Approach   This may be a very lightweight generic statement about phases or processes needed. It could also include formal change control approaches.

Project Manager and Level of Authority   This gives the PM formal authorization to begin project work.

Signatures   The sponsor and other key stakeholders will sign off on the charter.

It's important to note that the project manager and other key stakeholders are typically contributors in Waterfall charter creation because they are all considered expert judges.

Agile Project Charter Headers

Who   This section will document who is known now, such as key stakeholders, the team, and the customer.

What   It is key to document a high-level description of what success looks like today. The goals and vision for the project should be documented with full knowledge that they will change. As an example, "Our customer needs a new document storage solution that will accommodate 15,000 employees."

Where   Knowing where most work will be done is important to note due to the fact that many teams are remote or virtual. Even though it is best to colocate the team, it may not always be realistic to do so in the real world.

Why   Knowing why a project is being chartered helps to set the stage for buy-in by stakeholders, and it begins to perpetuate the vision that will be carried throughout the project.

> **How**   Since so much of today's project management is tailored to be appropriate for the result, it may be relevant to document how the project will run. If your organization strictly follows Scrum, XP, or another framework, it is still an innovative idea to document so that the customer/key stakeholders understand the "how" behind your work flow.
>
> **Signatures and the Date**   Formal authorization to begin is still needed to launch an Agile project.

I'm sure that you noticed that there is a smaller focus on specifics in the Agile project charter and a greater focus on brief explanations of what we know today. There is less scope, and it is more flexible and less informative. That is not to say that Agile charters are a waste of time. As you'll come to see, there are many pre-project engagement techniques designed to get everyone on the same page, even if that page is brief and changeable.

Since Agile project management focuses on *transparent* and *interactive* communication, the goal is to promote knowledge early and often when it is known. The team will answer whatever questions they can in the beginning and ask their own questions for clarification. The result may just be "I need a software program that can manage my team schedule and vacation time." That is enough information to begin to ask probing questions and to start the process of getting them answered. The end goal is the same, but what goes into the final release may change exponentially throughout the course of the complete set of iterations.

Determining Return on Investment

Let's face it, organizations are in the business of making money. Yes, they are also about providing goods and services to their customers, but rarely will an organization invest in a project without knowing what the benefits are versus the costs. To charter a project effectively, it is necessary for organizations to trim down from "We should do this!" to "Let's see what it costs first." Once costs are identified, it becomes about the benefits. How much will this cost, and what will the organization get in return. What is the *return on investment (ROI)*? To determine ROI, a business case is usually created.

Much of what you are tested on in the PMI-ACP exam is about providing value to the customer and understanding what they need from the increment you are designing and building. The reason for this is that proving value iteratively is a large part of why Agile project management is more effective than Waterfall types of frameworks in this context. Value is malleable and changeable as the project progresses. Value isn't set in stone, and it always will change and adapt.

On the money side of things, no organization wants to see funding rise and then drop off or, worse yet, make nothing from the venture at all. The project needs to be flexible to accommodate customer changes, but not too risky on the cost side of things. It makes organizations a bit nervous not to be able to pin down some information on cost versus benefits.

There are many techniques to determine whether an organization will gain their return on investment by determining the cost versus the value of chartering one project over another. Some techniques will determine how fast the money is going out the door, while others will calculate how fast the expenditures will be recouped and what the profit will be.

The best way to begin a project is to determine the cost versus the benefits, and there are many ways to do this. Usually, this determination is one of the roles of a business analyst working with the sponsor or key stakeholders. They do this by having one eye on the prize and one eye on the market.

Development of a *business case* incorporates a lot of market knowledge, reading of a crystal ball, and forecasting the future. I'm sure that the business analyst in your organization wouldn't be happy to read that I just called them a crystal ball reader, but the market fluctuates and changes daily. Inflation, varying exchange rates, and market shares should be considered and built into the process. It is a bit of a psychic forecast because anything can change, and change rapidly.

Many of the best practices of project selection involve big scary formulas that you don't need to know, unless you are a business analyst. For our purposes, let's focus on an overview of the techniques and why they are important.

The first thing to note is the concept of ROI, or return on investment. ROI is often used as a corporate buzzword; however, ROI is a very serious concept without a whole lot of structure in its definition. My organization's ROI may be very different from yours. It all depends on what is considered valuable. In that context, ROI is subjective, so other financial analysis must be done to determine prospective ROI. Typically, project selection techniques begin with a payback period and end with net present value, which we will discuss shortly.

Payback Period

Payback period is pretty much what is sounds like—it answers the question of how fast the organization will get back the money spent on the project and begin generating a profit. Certainly, the faster the payback period, the better off the organization will be.

Think about it this way, if you lent your best friend money, would you rather they pay you back sooner or later? If you say later, you are a very good friend! Most of us would want that transaction to go as quickly as possible before things get awkward. Organizations are no different, and there is a reason for that. First, profit is generated faster if the payback period is shorter and, second, because today's money will more than likely not be worth the same tomorrow. The longer it takes to recoup initial investments, the less the return on the investment.

Payback period is always represented in time, and if you have a choice, you would charter a project that pays you back the fastest. Unfortunately, that isn't the only variable to consider. Organizations still have that pesky problem of determining the allocation of funds across your project and others in the organization, plus spending money means it isn't being invested in expansion, new equipment, and other projects. Here is where the crystal ball comes into play. You can forecast out when you will be paid back, but it is also necessary to look at the market and see what it is going on at this point in time in order to determine an accurate and effective forecast. That is where things like internal rate of return (IRR) and net present value (NPV) come into play.

Internal Rate of Return

If you were given a choice of whether to invest your money with an annual return percentage of 3.5 percent versus a 10.5 percent, which one would you choose? Those of you who play the market might say things like "it depends on the market, I could lose more with risky investments," or "I like to play the long game and invest wisely." That makes sense. What if the market or any other external factors weren't there? Would that change your answer? Probably! You would most likely choose the highest percentage of return and get the biggest bang for your invested buck. That's a very simple example of the concept of *internal rate of return (IRR): internal* (meaning no external influences), *rate* (what percentage), and *return* (ROI).

If I'm an organization, I'm going to compare my proposed investment in a project to my projected rate of return and determine if it is the right way to go. Just as you would choose the highest return if no external risk were present, an organization will choose the highest return as well—especially if they are trying to decide between chartering similar projects. The highest return wins.

There is a lot more that goes into all of this, of course (remember big scary formulas and business analysts with crystal balls), but the bottom line is that the higher the IRR the better, and this will be a contributing factor in financial decisions. Once the payback period and the IRR are determined, it's time to take a look at the *time value of money*.

Net Present Value

What is today's money worth tomorrow? My grandmother used to be very specific in her disgust at rising prices for things like movies and travel. In fact, I'm pretty sure that I heard this on a regular basis: "When I was your age, movies cost a nickel and we took a train rather than hurtling through the sky in a tin can to the tune of a year's salary." The point is that yesterday's money isn't worth the same today. There is inflation and an ever-present market that is constantly unpredictable.

What are big organizations to do? They run big scary formulas that let them know as of right now—today—the present value of net return. Therefore, payback period and internal rate of return are important inputs because they will help drive the resulting *net present value (NPV)*.

All organizations have incoming cash flow and outgoing cash flow, and both hold their own values. Outgoing cash flow is a negative value, and incoming is a positive value. If the organization compares the value of an outgoing cash flow to a project (including what they spent initially) and the incoming cash flow over the payback period, they can start to see the benefits versus the costs. If you spend a million dollars one month and only receive $500,000 back over the course of the next six months and have to wait another six months for the other $500,000, it won't be worth as much. Your million-dollar investment is now worth less.

Granted that financial worth rarely fluctuates that quickly with those numbers, but you catch my drift. As an organization, I would want the highest NPV possible to drive my decision to charter a project. If a company is forecasting that they will break even on the venture, they may determine that it isn't fiscally healthy to charter that project. Although, I've seen organizations charter a break-even project based on an opportunity that may provide more ROI somewhere down the road, or one that has a chance of landing a big customer, or even one for future growth. Some organizations and industries are considered risk takers, and in technology a lot of projects are cutting edge and risky. Sometimes, however, the opportunity is worth the risk.

Most of you would probably agree that if you knew in advance that you were going to lose money on something, you probably wouldn't do it. Organizations and the market are sometimes favorable in the odds, and so, like playing craps in a casino, an organization will roll the dice and cross their fingers. You see this a lot in the movies, which now cost an arm and a leg to make and frankly to take your family to these days. This is due to the massive amounts of expense invested in the project and the need to make it back quickly. Think of those huge budget movies with high-paid talent and crazy special effects that tank in the theaters. A studio may have taken a quarter of a billion-dollar gamble and only made $30 million back. Ouch! Why would an organization take on a loser project like that? Because they don't expect to lose.

Most organizations wouldn't ever consider taking on a loser project if they knew in advance that it would provide zero profit and run way over budget. The problem is that projections can be optimistic, and sometimes the crystal ball is cloudy and not reliable.

There are only a few reasons an organization would take on a financial loser. First, because they flat out have to. Regulation or compliance demands it, and money that will never be seen again must be spent to be compliant. Nonetheless, because they spent the money, the organization continues on its merry way as compliant. Second, organizations may do this because they hope the market will reset or adapt before they lose money in profits. Usually, you see a lot of this before elections. It's still a gamble, though and any financial advisor with whom you speak will tell you the same: It's a risk. So how much are you willing to risk? This is where you leave it to the business analysts to determine that amount.

As Agile project managers, you will wait until you get the green light to begin, and then you will go forward with the stakeholder interactions and determine aspects of the project scope. That is where you begin to determine who, what, where, why, and how.

It's unlikely that you will see many (if any) questions on project selection techniques and financial decisions on the exam. If you do see any questions asking you to choose the best project based on certain forecasts, here's a very easy way to remember the variables:

Payback Period   Always choose the fastest payback if that is the only variable that you are looking at in the question.

Internal Rate of Return (IRR)   Always choose the highest IRR percentage if that is the only variable in the question.

Net Present Value (NPV)   Always choose the highest NPV dollar amount, regardless of other information in the question. NPV is the only factor since, to calculate it, you would use the payback period, present value of money, and IRR as inputs to the formula. Those would-be values help to calculate the results.

Otherwise, these concepts are more of a way to answer the question, "Where did you come up with that number?" Business analysts love that question... well, not really. It's worth asking it anyway, especially if they hand you a budget to work with and it's not aligning with your own projections of what things should cost. It never hurts to question the number, and in fact many times it is your responsibility to do your own cost-benefit analysis and provide expert judgment on the numbers. Therefore, it is a good idea to have a basic knowledge, at the very minimum, of how those numbers are calculated.

Techniques of Pre-Project Engagement

Getting everyone on the same page at the beginning of a project can be difficult. There is not a lot of information to go on, and it is known that throughout the project the scope will undoubtedly change. How can an Agile team get on the same page with the customer and other stakeholders? Talk to them! It's important to make sure that the team knows at a high level what the reason is behind the chartering of the project and to generate an understanding of what the customer finds valuable today. There are few ways to do this with limited information, except by what is currently found in the project charter.

The two ways to get the ball rolling on what success looks like today are as follows:

- Elevator Statements
- Tweeting

Elevator Statements

If you were riding on an elevator with someone, could you in a short ride explain what it is that your customer wants from a finished product? This sounds easier said than done. The process of compartmentalizing and being concise is a profound way to express the needs of the project and describe what a successful result would look like.

Elevator statements provide a tangible vision of what the work will produce and what the ultimate goal is as the result. I find it is best to articulate a *vision statement* or elevator statement in the present tense instead of some far-off increment to be developed in the future. Many times, the terms *vision statement* and *elevator statement* are used interchangeably, but the product owner is the one who needs to make sure that the ROI is met. Thus, the product owner will often ask for the vision and/or elevator statement to determine the end goal(s). Provided the product owner and the team understand the direction in which they are headed, how they get to that point is less stringently enforced in many frameworks. Whatever term or process is used, the goal is to keep the team focused on the here and now. This allows for conversations and better direction toward the jumping-off point prior to the iteration beginning.

One thing that you'll notice about Agile frameworks like Scrum, XP, DSDM, FDD, and others is the concept of *transparent communication*. In a Waterfall mentality, the team is very dependent on the project manager in the very beginning to set the requirements and describe what the project will entail. In Agile projects, the *team* and *product owner* are working with the customer to determine the potential results while trying to fully understand them as they are discussed. Even though the product owner/customer will determine what is valuable to them as the iterations progress, it is the team who needs to describe and understand the vision in the beginning. This will be done with input from stakeholders and customers and from discussions, of course, but ultimately if someone asked you to describe your current project in an elevator, you would have to understand it first yourself.

🌐 Real World Scenario

Group Brainstorming an Elevator Statement

I like having a group brainstorming session with a set list of questions that will help the group develop the elevator statement. It is important to me to have all of the options and opinions heard and all expert judgment explored so that consensus can be reached. Many believe that you should be able to describe everything in 30 seconds or your project isn't ready to be launched due to lack of understanding. I disagree; I think in some cases that the projects are more in depth and intricate, so getting to that 30-second mark isn't my big focus. After all, some elevators have more floors than others.

Elevator Statement Template

A good template to follow for an elevator statement can be a combination of introductory statements to get the brainstorming going. These include the following:

For   Can we explain the customer and have a good understanding of what their end goals are as well as their needs for the product that we will produce? This can also be represented as who or for whom.

The   What are we calling THE end result or deliverable? What does success look like today?

Is A   Can we put the deliverable into a category or box? If so, what kind of category would it be?

That   What benefits to the customer will this deliverable provide? If it were totally complete today, what would "that" provide to them?

Unlike   Who is the competition? Can we identify what they do or don't do, and can we determine how they would undertake something like this project? Most of us know who our competitors are in our industries. If you don't, this is a good time to check them out and let it motivate your team to improve continuously.

We   This is where we pat ourselves on the back and compare ourselves to the competition. Why are we the best choice? What do we do better than our competition?

Elevator Statement Example

This project is *FOR* the XYZ company who reached out to us to build them a better software program to manage their sales leads. *THE* program will allow for easier entry of prospective customer information and keep track of the amount of times that they have been contacted with services. This *IS A* necessary sales software program that can be duplicated and adapted for other customers in need of a similar result. A software program *THAT* is providing ease of use and easy implementation and support is much needed to replace the customer's antiquated web-based system that regularly crashes and loses information. This program is *UNLIKE* the competition's because it isn't an out-of-the-box solution or one-size-fits-all programming—it is adapted to the customer needs and uses. This is why *WE* were chosen to produce this for the customer, because we understand what their needs are and WE will create it with those needs in mind. WE will also change features as necessary to provide the best result (because we are awesome!).

I think it's safe to say that everyone starting the elevator statement with the customer and ending with the team is a good sandwich approach. It allows us to focus on both sides of the project equation and provides the team with the ability to buy in to their role in the result. This gives the team a good idea of who they are dealing with and why they are the best people to take it on. This builds the beginnings of motivation, better team dynamics, and the ability to reach consensus right out of the gate, or right out of the elevator as it were. The format for the elevator statement is graphically represented in Figure 4.1.

FIGURE 4.1 Elevator statement format

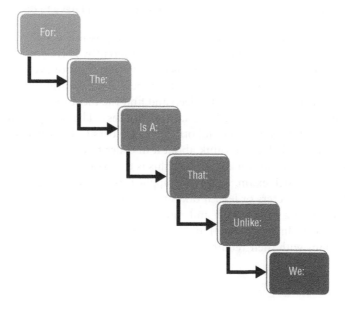

Tweeting

#tweetinghelpspromoteunderstanding

Tweeting takes the elevator statement and trims it *way* down to about 140 characters or less. This is a very difficult thing to do, and if you hang out on Twitter you know sometimes it takes a few tweets to get your point across. The good thing about Twitter or other social media is that people are used to tweeting now and, therefore, it isn't outside of the realm of possibility to tweet an overview of your product.

I find it is very helpful when the customer does this for the team. It causes the customer to really think about what the most important aspects of the result are and really narrow it down to its most concise description.

Remember, I use the term *customer* loosely and as a blanket statement for both internal and external customers. This may represent an internal customer in XP or a product owner in Scrum or an actual *customer*. To keep things generic across best practices, it's important to separate from specific frameworks and methodologies.

> #sales_software: Need sales software to keep track of our client info and contacts. Must be able to install easily and be easy to use.
>
> That's it! That's all of the characters that you will have to describe something.

I know what you are thinking—I mean how could you possibly collect requirements this way? I totally understand! Let me put it to you a bit differently. Have you ever had a laundry list of requirements thrown at you by a customer who seems not even to be sure what it is that they want? If you have, you know that it can be a bit frustrating.

This exercise is for the *customer* to dig deep and find the most important things and describe the result they are seeking in 140 characters or less. The best part about this exercise is that it forces both the customer and other stakeholders to be very concise in their descriptions, and they really have to think about it in order to do this effectively.

One thing to consider while you are reading this is that you will eventually fill out your application for the PMI-ACP exam. Part of the application piece is describing your project work in about 1,000 characters or less. It takes time to put it all together in a concise manner, but you are describing your project and Agile experience in a very long tweet so that the Project Management Institute (PMI) understands your experience and can validate that your experience aligns with their requirements.

 Real World Scenario

The Case of the Confused Client

In this case, I was the confused client! I consider myself a patient person. I'm very willing to help anybody, at any time, in any way. This gets me in trouble sometimes because it leads to hand-holding and walking people through a process that they probably should do themselves. This case was "one of those"!

My husband and I went out to dinner and used a popular driving service to get home. Our driver was about 25, and he had big aspirations for the app that he and his friends were developing. I asked him what his app did. Simple question—or not. The conversation went something like this:

Driver: "We are creating an app that can be used by social media to pay bills, like if you have a contractor and you want to pay them immediately, right? So, you can use this app to pay them."

I said: "You mean like a PayPal app?"

Driver: "No, it's more that you can have access to all of your customers' accounts and help them pay for everything that they are doing. We are hoping Twitter will buy us."

I said: "So, it's like Salesforce?"

What followed was the equivalent of tech speak jargon that in my mind didn't make any sense at all. I won't bore you with all of the details, mostly because my eyes glazed over and I don't remember the main points. Probably because there were so many and they were so scattered. Let's just say that not a single word of what he said made any logical sense and in fact confused me even more.

I said: "If you had to explain this app in a tweet or were riding in an elevator with the person who could buy your app for millions of dollars and you had one shot at it, what would you say?"

Driver: ".......". (The silence was equivalent to crickets when you tell a bad joke and nobody laughs.)

He was stumped and then repeated what he had already said in ten thousand words or more. I was stumped, and I do this for a living!

I said: "I'm not trying to give you a tough time, and I appreciate your passion about the project, but if I do this for a living and can't understand it, chances are that any big company that would think about acquiring it won't understand it either. That severely limits your ability to sell it. Think about how you would describe Snapchat, and think about the fact that they turned down a three-billion-dollar purchase offer from Facebook in 2013. Snapchat is so easy to explain that it's almost complicated in its simplicity. Create simple explanations that show the benefits to the customer."

I also reminded him that most contractors don't bill. They expect payment at the time of service. I'm certain that he was totally exasperated with me at this point, but I was really trying to help him understand that knowing how to explain your product quickly and concisely is one of the most important things that you can do: First so you know your own end goal, and second so that you can provide it to your clients. Third, understand that most people have very short attention spans these days, so it's important to hook them quickly and answer their questions once they are interested.

I recommended that he and his team get together and start thinking of ways to explain what it is that they do as if they were explaining it to Twitter users in a tweet.

In a world where almost anyone can create an app or a web page, it's important to be able to stand out in a crowd, and if the explanation of your product or service is simple, then you've got a better shot at someone saying, "Tell me more" instead of "Next!."

I'm hopeful that the message sunk in, and someday we will see him ringing the bell for his Initial Public Offering (IPO). More than likely, it will be someone else because they helped everyone "get it' quickly.

There are a variety of ways to collect requirements, and occasionally I like to revert to my Waterfall experience to design best practices that will work in an Agile environment. This is called *project tailoring*, and that ability is on deck to be the next important thing in project management best practices, especially with the updates to *A Guide to the Project Management Body of Knowledge (PMBOK® Guide), Sixth Edition*, which focus on tailoring best practices for the benefit of your project, not for your process framework.

I see the value in a lot of best practices in both arenas, one of which is a Waterfall practice of surveys and checklists. I like to use surveys with customers as well as specific interview questions and checklists when explaining process or framework implementation. These are excellent ways to keep me organized personally and not digress into a rabbit hole topic (as you may have noticed I tend to do). At the same time, it keeps the focus on the matter at hand by collecting the right information in real time.

Surveys are helpful when trying to get to the bottom of what the result could be and what the customer sees as a successful completion. These questions can reflect anything from what they see as a successful completion to what the end user is looking for in the increment that you are building. I don't have a set list of survey questions because each project is unique, but I do have some go-to questions I always ask. I use them as a way to keep the focus on the same issues and information and to reduce my tangent potential.

Prototyping is also an effective way to determine what success looks like. Prototyping usually brings up thoughts of creating an entire result, showing it, and then mass-producing it—like in the old days of automobile mass production. A prototype of a new model of a car would be created, shown, and then mass-produced.

This is simply not fiscally responsible anymore. Not to say that organizations don't create prototypes—they certainly do, and for some engineering organizations it is worth it to build something correctly once before mass-producing it. In technology, however, we are more focused on finding out what the build should be rather than telling the customer here it is—just what you want! Now that is prototyping type casting! These days, due to 3D printers and computer-developed models, as well as low-tech ways to work through to the solution, it's easier in an Iteration Zero or through pre-project engagement to collect the right requirements, or at least to begin to do so. Obviously, whether you prototype or not is dependent on the types of products or services that you create.

The Definition of Done

Perhaps one of the biggest and most well-known phrases in an Agile environment is the *definition of done*. And by done, I mean finished. Think about what a tough question that is in the very beginning when you know that the scope will change and that the customer is mostly focused on the final result as it stands today.

Your team needs to know what *done* looks like, not just for the finished product or result (we will call the finished product done-done), but at the end of each iteration. Keep in mind that iterations are designed to produce a usable increment at the end of each sprint or iteration, so the definition of done will change and adapt. It's a moving target. If you and your team don't know the stakeholders' definition of done, then it is totally impossible to know when the project is finished or the increment is done-done.

For now, let's focus on engaging stakeholders in defining what done actually means. This allows your team to focus on the specific and main items needed to produce a working, viable product/service that is considered done-done at a certain point.

There are many ways to engage your stakeholders and get to the bottom of the question of "What does done look like to you?" Wireframes are a good way to begin.

Wireframes

Wireframes are a super easy and cool way to work with stakeholders to define their needs and to help create a mock-up of what will be built before you get into the business of building. I use movies and television shows when I explain wireframes to my customers. I give them an idea of how each scene in the movie is plotted out in advance on paper and, in many cases, is hand-drawn. It is a visual representation of the scene before it is shot. I'm sure that when you look at big blockbuster movie budgets, you can imagine how important it is to plot out the scene in advance. Having a script is great, but that is mostly for the actors to see their lines and when they enter and leave a scene. The storyboards are there for the director so that they can *see* what they will create on film and use that to plot out the visuals and stunts and to correlate with the actor's lines. If you consider yourselves the director of the project, then it's important to see what it is that you are about to create.

A lot of tools used in Agile are surprisingly low tech, and wireframes are considered *low-fidelity prototypes* or mock-ups of the scene. This allows for a better definition of done because it's visual, it doesn't cost anything except for time, and you can work with stakeholders to show what it might look like when it's finished. Just as in the movies, scenes may be cut or re-created until they are just right.

In Figure 4.2, you'll see a very basic wireframe. The question you have to ask yourselves is do you understand it? Do you get the gist of how you would mock up the app? At this point, you wouldn't have all of the information, and the wireframe can be used as a tool to see what the customer wants. If there is open real estate, you can ask what the customer wants in that space and begin building out the vision.

FIGURE 4.2   Basic wireframe for phone app

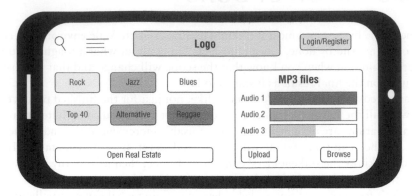

I find that not being able to draw very well, by making it a bit messy I allow the customer to feel more empowered to grab a pen and show me what they want. Or, they think I draw like a two-year-old. Either way, it gets the conversation flowing. There are several wireframe apps out there now to help, and you can always revert to PowerPoint as needed as a quick and easy way to draw or mock up a wireframe. It's also much less formal than a kick-off meeting. Wireframes are a way to show what you are thinking visually you are going to build. If not, then certainly crumple it up and throw it away. I call it the Pictionary of Agile.

The description *is* the tweet, and the wireframe *is* the picture of the tweet. Now we are getting somewhere!

User Stories

User stories were originally created in the XP framework as a way to determine the definition of done and are now used in just about every single Agile framework.

Not only are user stories an effective way to determine what done looks like, but they are also used to determine how much work could be accomplished in any given sprint or iteration. You'll see in *Domain V : Adaptive Planning* how you can estimate amounts of work by utilizing user stories. In this chapter, you'll see them as a way to engage stakeholders, and as task 6 on the exam content outline for this domain clearly states, "*You will need to establish a shared vision of the various project increments (products, deliverables, releases, iterations) by developing a high-level vision and supporting objectives in order to align stakeholders' expectations and build trust.*" User stories help you accomplish that.

Most user stories follow a similar format of: As _____ I need/want _____ so that I can _____.

This keeps things very simple, and as the title suggests, allows the key stakeholders and customer to work through the *why* as well as gives the team a better idea of *who* they are and *where* they are coming from.

It's a powerful thing for a customer to say any one of the following:

"As a customer and key stakeholder, I need to be able to log in from anywhere in the world so that I get better at client relations and service."

"As an end user, I need an app to keep track of my teenager so that I get updates on her whereabouts and can keep her safe."

"As a decision maker in my organization, I need an app that can access my sales-people's daily results, regardless of where they are in the world, so that I get the sales updates in a timely manner."

Even though the above examples could be viewed as vague and nonspecific, they can be better vetted as the user story creation progresses. Remember right now that you are trying to engage your stakeholders—you are attempting to understand their needs and why they want the product, service, or result.

The goal of any user story is to make sure that you can break it down to a specific, individual amount of work (about 1 to 3 days of work) and test it for completion. It's okay in my book to allow them to start big and work their way down to more specifics. It's our job as a development team, product owners, and Agile project managers to get the customer to the point where we understand their vision enough to define the specifics to the point where we can execute them.

User stories give us some insight and a way to see stakeholders and end users as people needing something from us rather than some random customer. This will create buy-in on the team side of things, and the client will feel heard and understood.

 NOTE Always remember during the exam and throughout your projects that stakeholder engagement, transparent communication, buy-in, and reaching consensus is ever present. If you are in the role of an Agile project manager, Scrum Master, coach, and so on, it's important always to provide your team with the vision. Reiterate it as often as possible, and make sure that as the vision changes, so too does your message to reflect those changes.

Ron Jefferies is one of the founders of eXtreme Programming as well as one of the 17 contributors who created the Agile Manifesto. Jeffries also contributed to the idea of a user story by providing Agile with the Three C's:

Card

Conversation

Confirmation

Jeffries felt that all user stories should be written on a card. This makes a user story tangible and singular, and it also limits the amount of space you have to write it. There can be many user stories in one iteration/project, and each can be as important as the other. It's up to the product owner to determine which of the cards or user stories are most valuable today. Just like the Kanban card approach or Scrum boards that use Post-it notes to describe user stories or tasks, the first *C* is used in the same way. The story is written on a *card*.

The second C is *conversation*, and it is perhaps the most important. I could write user stories all day long about what I *think* my customer wants, but unless I have a conversation with them, I'll never know for sure. I also have a self-directed and self-managed cross-functional team who frankly knows more than I do—people who do the work, know the work, and therefore, are the best people to be creating user stories with the customer and other stakeholders. The communication, engagement, and conversation aspect is the crux of Agile. Without it, you would never build the right thing or build the thing right.

The third C is *confirmation*. Have we done it correctly? Have we built the right thing? Is it fit for use? Have we tested it to make sure? Can we test it to make sure?

Confirmation is a bit like the validate scope process in Waterfall project management, meaning that the customer needs to sign off on the result and validate its correct completion. You'll have to have some kind of formal thumbs-up to call it done, and much of that comes from testing early and often to make sure everything is working correctly and meeting the needs of the customer's definition of valuable.

Reviews with the customer will also provide the opportunity to demo the increment at the end of a sprint or iteration. This allows the customer to confirm that it's correct or not by utilizing *acceptance testing*.

User Story Workshops

User story workshops are an excellent way to get everyone working together and communicating. Some of the best explanations I've ever gotten from my clients resulted from asking them to tell me a story. The workshops are a collaborative way of gaining valuable insight into what the end user needs and what the requirements are, and it also engages stakeholders by including them in the design process. Much like wireframes, it's a way to get everyone on the same page. I like the workshop aspect of user story creation because I believe that to truly reach consensus and design a vision, everyone needs to have input and it's worth spending the time to get it.

You can certainly timebox these workshops from one to two hours as needed, and you can provide facilitation or structure to the event as well. Otherwise, you have a free-for-all that's free for all. I like to keep it to just one free-for-all and facilitate the rest.

The key to most planning in Agile environments, other than engagement and communication, is determining your workflow and improving it as you go. By collaborating on the needs of the end user *with* the end user and the team, everyone can begin to see a path to the workflow necessary to achieve it.

Epic and Personas

I think it is important to give day-to-day guidance on how to run a user story workshop. It's easy for someone who has done it to say, "Oh this is super important, and you should do it." Just as you are about to say, "Yeah, but how?" they have moved on to a new topic. User stories and workshops designed to create them are important, so I want to give you some tips and tricks on the how, not just the why!

There are a couple things that can help you in a user story workshop and throughout the project, and those are *epics* and *personas*. Let's start with epics.

Epics

When I think of the word *epic*, I think of something that is massive, with many pieces of a whole put together. Sometimes it's impossible to jump to a small user story about a couple of days' worth of work just like that. The customer also may have a challenging time narrowing down what they want in a short sentence. In this respect, epics are a good jumping-off point, and then you can begin decomposing down to the user story and finally to the task level. Remember, all of this could adapt and change, but you have to start somewhere and the better that you understand the big picture as the customer sees it, the better you are able to break it down into an actual workflow.

I know that in Waterfall project management, the decomposition of scope is a big deal. If a sponsor says that you are going to be assigned to a year-long technology project to introduce broadband (yes, I'm aging myself) to other areas of the world, that's a BIG ask! It's too much information to process in its vastness. I could never in that moment answer the question of how much it will cost, how long it will take, and how many or what resources it would require. It's too, for lack of a better word, epic. So, we begin to focus on big deliverables and break those down to a level that we can most accurately estimate. We could still be wrong, but it's easier to zero focus than to determine specifics from a 50-thousand-foot overview.

You'll find that your customers also start 50 thousand feet up, and they will describe something much larger and with too many moving parts to it. Guess what? That's okay. I encourage it! The reason I do encourage those thoughts and discussions is that you have to start somewhere and, once everyone has a direction, it's easier to map it out.

A good epic metaphor or story is useful to help explain the importance of this technique.

An Epic Metaphor

I'll revert to my normal pop culture references to explain epics, and how user stories help me understand the needs of the customer or end users.

If someone asked me to explain the entire Harry Potter series to them in a short sentence, could I actually do it? Sure, but would they totally get all of the nuances of it or understand the intricacies of the story lines? No way—it's too big. I would explain that there are seven books in the original series. I'd explain that it is an epic story filled with magic, good against evil, friendship, and loss. Now that everyone is interested in the epic, we break it down into multiple user stories and explain the first book, then the second, and so on. Each book is part of the same whole but with specifics all its own. Obviously, one whole book or movie isn't going to fit on an index card, so we may have to utilize more time in a workshop focusing on the important aspects and reduce the noise.

Eventually, user stories will be broken down to tasks and used to estimate work effort, so we have to make sure that we keep our eye on the prize. That is what is great about creative collaboration—it allows us to start big and work our way down from there, together.

Another way to explain an epic is by using a jigsaw puzzle as an example. When you go to the store and buy a jigsaw puzzle, you buy it because the picture on the box resonates with you (Oh Paris!!!), and it tells you exactly what success looks like—nothing more and nothing less.

When you get home and open the box, all you see is a mess of pieces, colors, and shapes. You can't right then in that moment start to put the pieces together and voilà, the Paris puzzle is done-done. You will have to work at it a bit to get it organized. Corner pieces in a pile, gray pieces in another pile, and so on until you have smaller chunks of work. Then you can refer to the picture on the puzzle box and begin to put it all together—like with like. Epics are the puzzle box, and user stories are the piles of pieces. Make sense?

Personas

Personas are a great way for the team to understand the end users or customers in a way that keeps the focus on their needs while bringing a personal aspect to the users. The key to personas is to make them realistic and goal oriented. The advice from experts is to use someone who isn't real but who can be related to in a real way. I agree with that if it is in the very beginning of the project and the team doesn't really know the customer well yet. After that, I believe in the getting-to-know-you process of customer collaboration and communication. I like to make the personas become more realistic and more specific to the customer. It makes everything more real in our world, and it allows me to empathize or even sympathize with their needs.

Whatever way you use personas, it's best to keep them front and center on visible cards or flip charts so that everyone can see them and use them in correlation with user stories. Keep things goal oriented but personal to the real or fictitious customer and be creative. The better everyone understands the persona, the closer you will get to creating the thing right.

Knowing your audience is a big part of Agile project management, and therefore personas are useful in a workshop environment and in sprint planning meetings. Even if the customer isn't part of the discussion, or the team has run a couple of them and is getting better at identifying who is the customer, personas can help you walk in the customer's shoes for a bit.

 **Real World Scenario**

Bill's Story

Bill is a manager of a health insurance company, and he has 35 employees. Bill is getting more and more frustrated every single day because the computer program that he uses to check on processed claims crashes if he looks at more than 50 claims in one sitting. As you can imagine, Bill is ready to throw his computer out the window, and who could blame him? If only Bill had a software program that would allow him to view as many claims as he wanted to per day, track his team's performance, run reports, and keep track of the paid claims all on the same dashboard in his program. Bill would be totally thrilled! Our team is going to build that for Bill based on his requirements and how they unfold during the project.

A persona is a description of a person and what they want from the end result. Because scope of work changes, it is very vague in the beginning. This is a way for our team to feel Bill's pain and ask the right questions to collect those requirements.

You can probably tell that epics, personas, and user stories are a large part of collecting requirements to determine the definition of done. The more times that you produce a workable increment at the end of an iteration, the deeper you can get into what the customer wants and needs. That in and of itself is pretty epic.

Figure 4.3 shows the very simple steps to consider when holding a user story workshop. Whether you incorporate all or just the ones that are relevant to your current project is up to you. One of the major trends in Agile is to keep things simple. The process can be as well.

FIGURE 4.3 User story workshop process

Agile Knowledge Sharing and Communication

Project managers in any framework spend about 90 percent of their time communicating in some way. In an Agile environment, this applies to the team as well. Whether it's face-to-face communication, osmotic communication, body language, Kanban boards, other types of information radiators, or written communications, the team is in constant communication with each other, the customer/product owner, and the Agile project manager/Scrum Master/coach.

As part of the domain that incorporates stakeholder engagement, the focus in this chapter is on understanding the needs of the customer and determining how the team will go about producing the increment. When we review *Domain 4 (IV): Team Performance* tasks in a later chapter, you'll see the trend of open and honest feedback and communication continue specifically to the team environment.

In this chapter, the focus is on engaging the stakeholders to determine what they need. With user stories being such an important aspect of that determination, your focus will be on the communication used to engage stakeholders in the development of user stories.

Part of the *how to* of user story workshops is to utilize your time wisely, have effective communication, collaborate, and develop the epics and stories effectively. You may have noticed earlier in the chapter that it seemed to be a very simple user story format of "as _____ I need/want _____ so that I can..." That format doesn't provide a whole lot of distinct information, but it's important to note that whatever format works for you and your team is the format that you should use.

If the product sounds like it could be or is certainly a highly complex result, there may be a variety of options on who is the actual user. If there are many users, how do you account for their needs without reaching a state of analysis-paralysis? An effective way is to focus on what information is needed to lead communication and collaboration to other questions and clarification.

As a customer, I may only know that I need a website that allows me to upload my speaking voice, and people can hire and pay me for voice-overs through the site. Questions, collaboration, and communication can help to drill down to the main points.

- What kind of uploads are possible and in what format?
- Can you use any mic or recording device?
- How will the buyer search for your specific talent?
- How will they pay you?
- If by credit card, which ones are accepted?
- What about PayPal?

You are a user, but so are the people who would want to hire you. The credit card companies are on the periphery as well as any advertisers. How about investors in the web business? How do they check their stats? How do you determine end user needs if you aren't really sure who the end user is and there are layers upon layers of things to consider? Working with a set system to approach this is very helpful, and I tend to revert to the INVEST process flow to achieve what it is needed.

INVEST for User Stories

Remember back in Chapter 2, "Scum and eXtreme Programming (XP)," you were introduced to the acronym INVEST created by Bill Wake. The INVEST acronym applies to having superior quality in the product backlog, which essentially means that you have effective user stories that can be estimated and produced to spec. INVEST is an effective way to check ourselves and not produce defects or waste in the process flow. Part of our ability to provide that quality is to communicate the needs of the business and the customer effectively.

The INVEST acronym is an excellent way to develop user stories during a workshop to communicate those needs, and even though you were introduced to it before, this is where it really matters—the creation of effective user stories.

It's also important to balance both what the customer wants and what the organization needs. NPV is present here, and ROI needs to be met. This balancing act is the main reason a workshop or collaboration involves everyone—customer, development team, Agile PM, and other key stakeholders.

The INVEST Acronym

The INVEST acronym stands for the following attributes:

- Independent
- Negotiable
- Valuable
- Estimable
- Small
- Testable

Let's look at user stories in the context of the INVEST acronym to gain effective insights into what the customer wants and that this is understood by the team.

Independent

When writing user stories, you will want to keep them independent from each other. This literally means that each user story isn't created in order of occurrence—do this, then that, and then that. Remember the puzzle pieces? A gray piece and a black corner piece may fit together when all is said and done, but you aren't there yet. In my voice-over website example, if you want different upload speeds or sound quality encoding and features for MP3 or other audio file types, then each one of those features gets its own independent story.

 Real World Scenario

Voice-Over Format Options

Each user story needs to be independent because the technology or how requirements would be built out may be different. Keeping each feature separate allows you to zero focus on one user story at a time.

"As a voice-over talent, I need to be able to upload my audio in an MP3 format so that I can provide the best quality in my voice-over material and minimize background sounds."

"As a voice-over talent, I need to be able to upload my audio in a WAV format so that my customers who use that format can hear the sound quality in a format they use."

"As a voice-over talent I need to be able to upload my audio in an AAC format so that I can provide the best quality in my voice-over material."

Negotiable

Just because there is a user story on a card that is three-dimensional, it doesn't mean that it's absolutely going to be done. What is considered valuable is likely to change, and some of the features that are requested now may never make it into the final result.

You may negotiate that the AAC format is unnecessary, and not many people even know what it is unless they are real audiophiles. It may ultimately become a useless feature for which the customer pays. The same goes for the WAV format. That is negotiable because it's proprietary and only able to be used on a Windows-based computer. Everyone knows what an MP3 is, however, and it plays on all devices. Thus that may be the ultimate solution. Unless there is a contract in place, the user stories are all negotiable.

Valuable

User stories may be valuable to the user but not to the customer and vice versa. The goal is to provide enough details in the story to the person who will find it valuable and be able to describe the feature and the benefits that are relevant and valuable to the customer and/or users or both, depending on the outcome.

Remember, you are probably dealing mostly with the customer. Clearly the person who wants the voice-over website to be built isn't going to be the only one on the site. They may charge a subscription fee for other users of the site. The developers of the site may see value in the technical specifics, and the end users may see value in how easily they can pay their subscription fee, upload their audio, and even promote their content.

The backlog is never complete, and it is ever changing in value. You don't have to have it all figured out in one workshop, and this isn't the only workshop that you will have throughout the project. This is an important one, though, because you are just beginning to collaborate with the customer and gather requirements so that you can perform backlog grooming with the product owner and estimate how much of the work will be completed in the iteration.

Value-driven delivery is a direct result of knowing what is valuable first. The user stories should be developed to show the value and the benefits as effectively as possible with the information that you have today.

Estimable

Just as you wouldn't be able to say how long something would take or how much it would cost if the project concept was too large, you occasionally will find an epic or user story that is too bulky or complex to get an effective read on it. The inability to define complexity may be influenced by the lack of current knowledge that the developers have about the technology they are being asked to create, or the customer may not know what they want in the finished product at this point. That leaves a very epic story that can't yet be estimated. More information is needed to truly understand the scope and make effective estimates.

Keep in mind that the team will determine how much work they can accomplish based on user stories, and user stories represent the work that needs to be done. Both should align in order to estimate correctly. Typically, I like to get user stories down to a few days' worth of work, and that is easier said than done. You'll see this especially if the complexity of the story is hiding vital information or assumptions.

Questioning assumptions is a large part of risk management in any project, and it is an iterative process as well. I see more complex or assumption-riddled types of user stories on teams that are newer to Agile project management. Typically, they haven't ever planned this way before. Many are used to a Waterfall type of framework where dependencies exist between activities, and assumptions lead to scope creep. Newer Agile teams have a harder time being concise, and they may be harvesting unknowns in their user stories right out of the gate.

If you are experiencing the quandary of how to deal with something that you can't effectively estimate, it may be necessary to perform an *architectural spike* to determine how to solve a problem or use a *proof-of-concept* or prototype during a sprint or iteration.

Spikes can occur throughout the project, but most especially at the beginning if not enough information is available. The spike may be necessary if it is difficult to determine the tech approach, durations, or workflow from the information you currently have. All assumptions amp up the risk factor on the project. Unknowns are difficult to deal with when they become known on a project because they are almost always a costly surprise.

Spikes

An architectural spike (or just a spike) can be in the XP framework to solve a technical problem brought about by a user story that can't be effectively estimated or that doesn't explain the technical side of the story well enough. The spike can be performed like a mini-sprint or iteration to develop something that can provide the solution without trying to perform the work without a solution that isn't present currently or hasn't yet revealed itself. You want to make sure you are on the right track, but if you have no idea exactly what that track is, a spike may be necessary to prove that something will or will not work.

A spike may not necessarily involve the entire team, and it has to be approved as relevant time spent. Overall, though, a spike may be necessary even on seasoned development teams due to rapid changes in technology. Spikes are used in risk management as well: they are used to help mitigate risks and to adjust the backlog to accommodate the mitigation efforts. We will cover spikes in greater detail in the chapter related to *Domain VI: Problem Detection and Resolution* which are found in Chapter 9 of this guide relating to detecting problems and risk.

Proof of concept (PoC) isn't just native to Agile frameworks, as it is seen in many organizations that work with prototypes or feasibility studies. For example, the pharmaceutical industry has to prove that a drug works with trials before the FDA will approve it for mass production and public consumption. Cybersecurity firms must prove that they can protect an organization from security breaches by creating or showing a demo that they have used in the past as proof that their service works. It wouldn't be unusual for an epic or user story to lead to a proof of concept first before moving forward, although this is rare due to the changing nature of scope and unclear requirements in the beginning of a project. It may be that the proof that the concept can work for the current customer comes from something similar that was created previously for another customer.

Small

All user stories need to be small enough to reflect about three to five days of work at most. It's important to keep the user stories small enough that all questions about the story can be easily answered and what needs to accomplished is understood.

If too many questions are asked and can't be answered without further clarity, it may be because the story is too large or encompasses several different related features. At that point, it would be necessary to collaborate as a team on what the story should represent without any additional noise or misunderstandings. That way the team can determine the size of the work, what the definition of done is, and be able to produce a minimally viable increment during the iteration. Keeping stories small and simple helps maintain focus on the goal and allows the team to execute the work appropriately.

Testable

How will you know that a user story has been accomplished? Test it and test it again! Think about it this way: To graduate high school or college, you had to take tests that proved that you knew the information well enough to pass. When you take your PMI-ACP exam, you will be tested on your knowledge of Agile environments. Testing is the proof that something is correct and that it works and meets requirements.

Much of the testing piece in Agile environments is currently or eventually will be automated. In fact, many tests are written in advance knowing that the increment will fail right out of the gate. It is expected.

When the test is passed, it meets requirements. To create the right tests to prove that something is working or completed, it is important to understand what it is that you are trying to develop. Therefore, user story workshops are an integral part of Agile frameworks. What you produce in the workshop will go into the backlog, be groomed by value, and be used by the development team to estimate what they can accomplish in each sprint or iteration.

If you rolled all selected and developed user stories together across iterations, all stories combined should align with the definition of done and the definition of done-done or deployed.

The INVEST acronym is an important one to remember. Not just for your PMI-ACP exam but when you are holding your user story workshops. Figure 4.4 is a simplified version that you can keep close by the next time you host a user story workshop if you are not already familiar with it and/or using it currently.

The concept of communication and knowledge sharing in a user story workshop environment, as well as other communication opportunities, provides many keys to a successful result. Stories allow us to put ourselves into the shoes of the user or the customer, and it allows the development team to practice *empirical process control* by utilizing observation, conversation, and experimentation as ways to make decisions.

Originally rooted in the Scrum framework, but applicable in many frameworks, empirical process control keeps things transparent in the communication, allows for ways to inspect or test the increments being developed, and can be adapted as needed. Regardless of how you run your workshops and how you go about getting to the point where you can build out the increment, user stories are one of the key aspects of communication and knowledge sharing.

FIGURE 4.4   INVEST

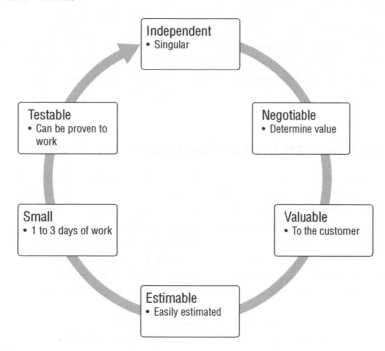

Most of the time your team and organization will be working directly with a customer who may want you to develop a website, get it up and running, and then fix any bugs with updates later. That's realistic because you want to produce something workable and usable, or what's called a *minimal marketable feature (MMF)*. It's not unusual to have tech debt from past projects to work on throughout your current iterations as well.

Tech debt involves doing bug fixes or updating software from past projects, websites, or apps that you are still supporting as an organization. Many times, you will add time into the iteration duration for tech debt.

Much like any financial debt, the longer the debt sits unpaid, the more expensive it becomes. It gathers interest. Therefore, tech debt and planning accordingly to address it is part of many iterations.

A good example of tech debt is waiting for your computer or mobile phone operating system to go through an update. These consist mainly of bug fixes. If you read the disclaimer to agree to the update, you'll see exactly what the updates are designed to fix.

Perhaps your mobile phone has been out on the market for a year, but updates are still to come. This is because the mobile phone manufacturer produced something that was minimally marketable with the knowledge that they would have tech debt. They were aware that they would need to push out those fixes to the market even while they were engineering the next version of the phone.

You know going into a project that some tech debt may occur in the future, but you can't depend on a future update to get it right. So you focus on the here and now using communication, collaboration, and knowledge transfer to keep everything above board. You work with the customer to understand exactly who the users are and how to build the thing right and how to build the right thing. Finally, you produce a usable increment that has a minimal (the smallest amount of what is needed and valuable) marketable (you can push it out to the market as is and fix the bugs later) feature (one feature of many until done-done).

Communication and Knowledge Sharing Basics

The concept of communication is a large one to tackle because there are so many ways that humans communicate with others. We have so many ways to communicate these days, and the options aren't fading—rather they are increasing. We have social media and colocated versus remote/virtual people that need to communicate differently as well as texts, mobile phones, and the Internet. Soon holograms and virtual reality will be a part of organizational day-to-day communication. In Agile, though, a lot of communication is low-tech, high-touch as well including visual communication via information radiators. Body language can influence the final message, and it is a large part of overall communication in a colocated environment.

Albert Mehrabian, professor of psychology at UCLA, performed a study in the 1970s on communication. This study suggests that body language makes up 55 percent overall of a face-to-face message, even if we aren't fully aware of it. Tone of voice makes up 38 percent of the message, and only 7 percent comprises the words spoken. That's a pretty powerful reminder that our brains are receiving more visual communication than the words themselves. The brain is said to process visual images 60,000 times faster than spoken words. That is a good part of the reason Agile teams use so many types of information radiators. They are front and center and easy to understand because they are so visual.

What happens when the communication isn't face-to-face? Tone takes over. If you have ever read and reread your emails before sending them out to someone, that is why you are doing it. What is the message and, more importantly, what is the tone? Perception is 100 percent reality to the person decoding the message. If you don't really like someone, and you get a message that you perceive to be a bit salty or cranky, you'll take more offense to it. If your best friend wrote the same exact message, you'd think that they were just having a difficult day and didn't mean to come off that way.

Communication is considered an aspirational skill, meaning that we all aspire to be better communicators. Some people pursue this more than others. In an Agile environment, the entire framework you use (regardless of method) is dependent on effective, transparent communication. The act of knowledge sharing on an Agile project can be specifically targeted communication with your team or your customer, or it can be very passive like osmotic communication. Because humans use a variety of methods to communicate, and each method is affected by many things, it seems better to address some of the influences on and challenges of effective communication and knowledge sharing one by one.

Osmotic Communication

Osmotic communication is important for many questions on your PMI-ACP exam because it describes one's ability to pick up information whether you are directly involved in the conversation or not. This is a direct result of *team space tooling*, or how your team is colocated and seated near each other. You will pick up information just by overhearing it. At that point, you can decide if it is information that you need to retain or let it go because it isn't applicable to your current situation.

Once the information is retained, this becomes *tacit knowledge*, which is very different from explicit knowledge that can be looked up in a book or written down. Tacit knowledge is something that is understood but may be difficult to explain to others. I sometimes refer to this as *tribal knowledge*. It's something that everyone on the team understands but that would be very difficult to explain accurately to others.

> We know more than we can tell.
>
> *Michael Polanyi*, The Tacit Dimension, *University of Chicago Press, 1966.*

Communication Channels

There are many different channels of communication in a normal feedback loop. You send a message in some kind of format: verbal, email, and so on. That message must travel through channels and battle either physical noise or the noise of perception from the receiver, who decodes it according to their own perception and response.

If you ever played the game of whisper down the lane or telephone as a child, you know that the more channels there are, the more the message is diluted based on perceptions and how much noise the message travels through. The first kid in line says, "I like your hat, pass it on." The last kind in line hears, "She doesn't like your cat."

It's important as Agile project managers and team members to practice clear and effective communication. The more channels you have, the greater the chance that your message can go horribly, horribly wrong. This is probably why in most frameworks, the team is kept to a smaller size, therefore reducing the number of communication channels.

Perception

Perception is an individual thing. It's based on our upbringing, how we see the world, and how we think the world sees us. No matter what, it's 100 percent correct to the individual until proven differently.

There are so many perception problems permeating the world right now, especially on social media. Everybody's opinion is right and justified to the individual, and every individual's way of thinking is right in their own minds as well. Everyone else has a problem, and it's the job of the commenter to prove them wrong.

There have been times on projects when I've identified that there is a perception problem. If a customer is expressing something one way and my team is hearing something else from their perception, we will inevitably produce the wrong thing. I think it's totally realistic to say, "I think we have a perception problem. Please explain from your point of view what you are looking for, then we will express ours and see if we can't meet in the middle." It isn't always going to work, but sometimes the perception elephant in the room needs to be addressed before you can get down to the work at hand.

Visual

If the brain processes visual images 60,000 times faster than language, then it is important to be as visual as possible. I know that I'm a visual learner—I need to see it and then do it.

So many best practices in an Agile environment are visual. User story cards, wireframes, Kanban boards, process-flow diagrams, and others that you will review as you move forward through this book. The bottom line is that *visual communication works better than words.* The more visual you are in your processes, the better your team and customer will understand you.

Body Language

Our brain processes micro expressions and picks up signals based on our perception. You can tell when someone is mad, sad, or glad just by looking at them in many cases.

Some people are harder to read than others, and some are more effusive. This is originally why emoticons were created in written communication so that you can see when someone is just kidding or is actually not very happy.

As an Agile project manager, it is important to know your team well enough to be able to gauge how they are feeling above and beyond what they are saying. There are common signals and gestures that relate to certain thoughts and feelings, but even those can be misread based on your perception or knowledge of the individual.

One common type of body language is crossing of the arms. It is a signal that the person is closing themselves off from the other person, or isn't at all happy. If foot tapping and sighing is also occurring, then you know for sure that they are not happy. But what if the person is just cold? Reading body language isn't an exact science, and it is actually more of an art form. The better you know your team, the better you'll be able to read them.

Jargon

The use of *jargon* is prevalent today. It could be industry-specific jargon, some of which you are learning in this study guide, or it can be geographical or cultural.

It's important to keep jargon to a minimum when working with new customers. They may not understand a lot of the technical jargon without explanation. They may not even understand an Agile approach or what a sprint is. I usually start by reviewing the project charter and explaining our framework: how we meet, how we communicate, and our timeboxes for planning meetings and reviews or tests. It's basically a crash course in Agile without overwhelming the customer.

When you are communicating with people who don't understand programming or precisely what the process is, it's important to give examples or metaphors that can help explain it. You may have noticed that a lot of what we do involves communicating and interacting with customers. You can tell by the confused looks on their faces whether your jargon is understood or not. Then you can go on to explain in words they can understand. Be especially diligent in email communication to avoid too much unexplained jargon. Otherwise, it may take many feedback loops to address the confusion.

Mirroring

The practice of *mirroring* is an important aspect of effective communication. When someone communicates in a similar manner as you do, it's easy to get along and understand the message. This can occur in a variety of ways. For example, how someone signs off in their email is how I sign off in my response. If they say, "Best Regards," "Sincerely," or "Kind Regards," I do so as well. The only two that I don't use are "Cheers," because I am so not cool enough to pull it off (even though I wish I were!) and "Thanks." I bet a lot of you are thinking what is wrong with "Thanks?" It's dismissive. Believe me, many people read that as responding with "Whatever" or "Because I said so."

> Dear so and so:
>
> Have that report on my desk by 5 PM EST.
>
> Thanks...

In fact, in a lot of countries in Europe, it's seen as dismissive and rude to use "Thanks" as a signature. If I get a "Thanks," I'll reply with "Thank You" or even "Thanks!" Those are the only two exceptions.

I also attempt to mirror how emails are sent. If they write in bullet points, I'll answer in bullet points. If they write in paragraphs, I'll respond in paragraphs. Now obviously this can't be applicable to every single email. I may need a paragraph before the bullets, but people send emails in the way they want to receive them. I attempt to match that whenever possible.

In a face-to-face dynamic, it's a bit more difficult because of personalities, body language, position in the organization, and so forth. Nonetheless, there are some phrases that show you are listening and attempting to understand:

> If I'm hearing correctly, you are saying XYZ.
>
> Help me understand.

It's yet another thing that we don't really think about when we communicate, but every little bit helps.

It's like passing a stranger who has on your favorite sports team's logo or the university you attended. You feel an instant connection with them, and you may even give them a nod and a smile. They are mirroring your favorite team, and that creates instant recognition and an instant bond no matter how briefly. The same can be said for mirroring communication.

Emotional Intelligence

Having the ability to understand and sympathize or emphasize with another human being and to understand what they need from you in the moment is a big sign of having *emotional intelligence*.

If you are aware of your emotions and of someone else's, and you can determine how they are feeling regarding your interaction with them, you display emotional intelligence. That does not mean being everyone's best friend or allowing things to slip by that are incorrect because you understand why someone did what they did. It means that you understand why they did what they did, but you can still guide them in a direction to do what needs to be done instead.

As a servant leader, it's important to practice this skill as much as possible. You can emphasize if you have experienced something similar, and you can sympathize if you intellectually understand something and feel from it. This will help in how you communicate, not just with your team members, but also with significant others, family, and friends.

Trust me when I say those who display emotional intelligence and an understanding of human behavior are far better leaders than those who don't. More and more organizations these days are looking for those traits in their project managers, more so than their technical skills. It is a large part of understanding and engaging in servant leadership, which is the crux of all project managers running Agile types of projects.

Feedback

Giving effective feedback isn't always the easiest thing to do. Many of you may prefer the nonspecific "You did a great job today" type of feedback over the specific "Here's what you need to work on" conversation.

Providing effective feedback is a communication skill that needs to be practiced. The cool thing about Agile is that so much revolves around open and transparent communication, as well as the team taking the onus upon themselves for successes and challenges because they are self-directed.

When you delve a bit deeper into other domains, you'll see the value of retrospectives and team collaboration games as windows into feedback and transparent communication. In this domain, the focus is on stakeholder engagement, and some stakeholders or even team members new to Agile frameworks may require some warming up to get to a place where they are comfortable with true feedback. In this case, it is important to explain how things work right from the beginning, and with user story workshops, tweeting, and elevator statements, you are gently guiding them through a highly engaging communication best practice and providing help in the development of the features and needs of the result.

Active Listening

Of course, there isn't any communication that is effective without active listening. Part of being a good servant leader is not just to hear the words, but rather to understand them.

The hardest part about active listening is not to be thinking of your next response or anything else for that matter. Yes, our brains shift and these days most adults have the attention span of a one-year-old, so it takes practice and work to become proficient in this skill.

On the PMI-ACP exam, you will see questions about you as a servant-leader, listening to one of your team members and expressing a problem with something or someone. The questions will test your ability to choose the best answer that represents the thought process of someone who is actively listening versus someone who is thinking about solutions or the next thing they need to do. You'll see some examples in the review questions for this chapter. See how you do, and as you are studying for your exam, try practicing your emotional intelligence, mirroring, reading body language, and active listening.

No matter how good anyone is at communicating, there is always room for improvement, and in an Agile environment, communication is among the top three most important skills you should have to be the best and most effective servant leader or team member.

Summary

This chapter started with pre-project engagement and the creation of an Agile project charter. You saw a comparison of and the differences between a more formal Waterfall project charter and a flexible Agile project charter. No matter what type of framework you use to manage your projects, a charter is a good stepping-off point to begin pre-project engagement.

Next we went through the various techniques or project selection methods of pre-project engagement, including payback period, internal rate of return, and net present value. All of the methods are typically used to determine the fiscal health of a chartering decision as well as determining ROI for the organization. Keep in mind that even though you may not see any questions specific to these methods on the exam, it's often important in your day-to-day work life to understand the derivation of these numbers.

In the next section, we went through two very specific techniques for pre-project engagement, which are elevator statements and tweeting. Both allow you and the stakeholders to get a better idea of the scope of work for the project and to create concise ways to explain the results. This then leads to understanding the definition of done and developing better user stories utilizing user story workshops. You reviewed epics and personas as well in order to understand better what the customer's needs are for the increments as well as knowing yourself when it is "done."

Finally, we went through an overview of knowledge and information sharing for better communication. You'll notice that this topic will continue throughout the rest of this book.

Exam Essentials

Be able to describe an Agile project charter. Understand why it is important to kick off a project with a good understanding of the who, what, where, when, how, and why. Determining some of the key information during the pre-project engagement process is an excellent best practice.

Understand how to determine ROI. Even though you may not play the role of a business analyst or need to truly understand the ins and outs of project selection techniques, it is important to absorb what happens in the background to determine fiscal health in project chartering decisions.

Be able to explain the importance of elevator statements and tweeting. Having the ability to explain the increment of a project concisely in a short tweet or having the ability to explain what it is you are going to produce to someone in an elevator is a key skill when determining what success should look like. It also allows for better stakeholder engagement and communication as you work together to get to the point where you can build the right thing.

Understand what is the definition of done.   Utilizing epics, user stories, and personas allows you and your team to engage with stakeholders effectively and have a true understanding of what it is you are attempting to create. If the concept is too big, or if it can't be tested, then it's important to break it down further to the user story level. Personas help you understand the needs of the customer, whether the person represented is fictitious or not.

Be aware of effective communication techniques.   Effective communication is a common theme in all aspects of Agile. In this chapter, you reviewed stakeholder engagement tasks to determine the needs of the customer and how to get to the point where your team could start working on the priority user stories and produce a usable, done increment. A lot of those strategies include wireframes, elevator statements, and user story workshops. Also, be aware of things like emotional intelligence, active listening, providing feedback, and mirroring communication. Practicing those aspects of communication will help you be more Agile in your communication as well as make you a better and more effective servant leader.

Review Questions

You can find the answers to the review questions in Appendix B.

1. You have colocated your team, and during the day the team discusses the things they have learned, what they are working on, and various solutions to issues they confront. Even though not everyone contributes to every conversation, they are picking up the information. This information can be internalized or thrown away depending on the individual's need for that information. This is known as which one of the following?

   A. Tribal knowledge

   B. Osmotic communication

   C. Tacit knowledge

   D. Team knowledge

2. Which of the following items can your team use to help visually show what a viable product or service might look like in a type of low-fidelity prototype?

   A. A definition of done

   B. Approval from the product owner to create user stories

   C. A well-planned strategy to accomplish project goals

   D. A wireframe with a breakdown of the product needs

3. Your organization is working to determine a project to charter officially, and it is looking at various financial information for project selection. Which technique contains the most information necessary to make a final decision?

   A. Project charter

   B. Internal rate of return (IRR)

   C. Net present value (NPV)

   D. Payback period

4. During a user story workshop, your customer says, "As a customer, I want a web page so that I can do business." Is this considered an effective user story?

   A. No, because it isn't specific and therefore not testable.

   B. No, because it doesn't follow the structure of a user story.

   C. Yes, because it follows the structure of a user story.

   D. Yes, because you will work through the details later.

5. During a user story workshop, you ask your customer to explain to you the result they are looking for in 140 characters or less. Which of the following are you requesting?

   A. Wireframe

   B. User story

   C. Elevator statement

   D. Tweet

6. Kelly and Jim are working together on an architectural spike to help determine what process they will use. They have come to you as their Agile manager and expressed some frustration with the process. If you are practicing active listening, what would you be thinking as they expressed themselves?

   A. "Kelly and Jim are upset. I need to help them find a solution."

   B. "I'll need to jump in and see if I can help them fix this."

   C. "Kelly and Jim are upset, and they need my help."

   D. "Kelly and Jim are really upset. I'd better get other team members involved to get all of the information."

7. How can you tell when you have a user story that isn't going to be effective?

   A. It can be tested.

   B. It is large enough to explain the work.

   C. You can negotiate items in it.

   D. It stands alone as an independent item.

8. You are a business analyst working to put together a business case utilizing project selection techniques. Project A has a net present value of $555,926 and Project B has a net present value of $787,454. Based on this information alone, which would you choose as the project to charter?

   A. Project A because the NPV is less than Project B.

   B. No decision can be made accurately until ROI is determined.

   C. Project B because the NPV is higher than project A.

   D. No decision can be made until the payback period and internal rate of return are determined.

9. You are working with your customer and sketching out what their website will be like. This is an example of which one of the following?

   A. Wireframe

   B. User story

   C. Persona

   D. Tweet

10. You are working with a customer who is used to Waterfall frameworks and formal project charters. They ask you to explain the difference between a Waterfall project charter and an Agile project charter. How do you explain it to them?

    A. "Waterfall project charters are mandatory, and Agile charters are not."

    B. "Agile project charters are more flexible and describe who and what."

    C. "Waterfall project charters don't get to the definition of done like Agile charters."

    D. "Agile project charters aren't formal, and Waterfall project charters are formal."

11. You are working with your team to develop a persona, and one of your team members says that they were in the same position as your customer once and can understand where they are coming from. Your team member is expressing which of the following?

    A. Emotional intelligence

    B. Empathy

    C. Active listening

    D. Effective user story development

12. An effective user story follows which of the following formats?

    A. As a(n) _____ I want _____ because _____.

    B. As a(n) _____ I need _____ in order to _____.

    C. As _____ I need _____ so that I can _____.

    D. As a user _____ I need _____ so that I have _____.

13. A user story workshop is important because of which one of the following?

    A. It allows for collaboration and determination of scope while engaging your stakeholders.

    B. It is important since it is a large part of Agile frameworks.

    C. It allows all of the user stories for the project to be created.

    D. It isn't important, as it is up to the team to decide whether or not they use them.

14. Payback period is a less effective way to determine ROI on a project because of which of the following reasons?

    A. Payback period only shows the period of time to recoup the money spent, not the net present value.

    B. Payback period isn't an effective way to determine ROI if it is used with internal rate of return only.

    C. Payback period is only ineffective when combined with net present value.

    D. ROI isn't determined using payback period.

15. Your team is working to engage with your stakeholders, who are very interested in what your team thinks the eventual result will be. Your team works with the customer and draws out the web interface they are thinking of developing based on what the customer is describing. Which of the following wouldn't be involved in this process?

    A. Wireframe

    B. User story workshop

    C. Elevator statements

    D. Project charter creation

16. You are responding to a key stakeholder via email, and you decide that you will follow their lead and write with bullet points and sign your email in the same way as they do. This is an example of which kind of communication best practice?

  A. Effective email writing

  B. Emotional intelligence

  C. Mirroring

  D. Feedback

17. If you received a project charter and it fully described the scope of work, milestones, risks, and key stakeholders, as well as budgetary estimates, would that be a good reflection of an Agile project charter?

  A. No. This is closer to that of a Waterfall project charter where the scope of work is well known.

  B. Yes, because the more information you have in the beginning, the better off the project will be in the end.

  C. No, because an Agile project charter isn't necessary.

  D. Yes, because it helps with the user story workshop.

18. You are in a meeting with a new customer to agree on requirements and basic starting points of the project. Your customer is going on and on about a long list of things that they want done, but they aren't really giving you a clear explanation of the project's end result. How can you encourage your customer to provide a clear, high-level explanation of the project's result?

  A. Have a kick-off meeting.

  B. Build a project charter.

  C. Have them create a tweet.

  D. Have a detailed planning meeting.

19. Which of the following items does your team need in order to produce a working, viable product or service?

  A. A definition of done

  B. Approval from the product owner to create user stories

  C. A well-planned strategy to accomplish project goals

  D. A wireframe with a breakdown of the product needs

20. A persona is based on which one of the following?

  A. Someone who had similar goals on another project

  B. The organization and its culture

  C. A real person or a descriptive placeholder for the customer

  D. A fake placeholder of a future user and what they may or may not want

Chapter 5

The Human Side of Agile Project Management

THE FOLLOWING PMI-ACP® EXAM TOPICS ARE COVERED IN THIS CHAPTER:

✓ **Domain III: Stakeholder Engagement**

Understand Stakeholder Needs:

- Task 1: Identify and engage effective and empowered business stakeholder(s) through periodic reviews in order to ensure that the team is knowledgeable about stakeholders' interests, needs, and expectations.

- Task 2: Identify and engage all stakeholders (current and future) by promoting knowledge sharing early and throughout the project to ensure the unimpeded flow of information and value throughout the lifespan of the project.

Ensure Stakeholder Involvement:

- Task 3: Establish stakeholder relationships by forming a working agreement among key stakeholders in order to promote participation and effective collaboration.

- Task 4: Maintain proper stakeholder involvement by continually assessing changes in the project and organization in order to ensure that new stakeholders are appropriately engaged.

- Task 5: Establish collaborative behaviors among the members of the organization by fostering group decision making and conflict resolution in order to improve decision quality and reduce the time required to make decisions.

Manage Stakeholder Expectations:

- Task 6: Establish a shared vision of the various project increments (products, deliverables, releases, iterations) by developing a high-level vision and supporting objectives in order
  to align stakeholders' expectations and build trust.

- Task 7: Establish and maintain a shared understanding of
  success criteria, deliverables, and acceptable trade-offs by
  facilitating awareness among stakeholders in order to align
  expectations and build trust.

- Task 8: Provide transparency regarding work status by communicating team progress, work quality, impediments,
  and risks in order to help the primary stakeholders make
  informed decisions.

- Task 9: Provide forecasts at a level of detail that balances the
  need for certainty and the benefits of adaptability in order to
  allow stakeholders to plan effectively.

In this chapter, you will finish the tasks found in *Domain III: Stakeholder Engagement* in the exam content outline. The tasks in this domain directly relate to the initiation or beginning of an Agile project as well as to the interaction with stakeholders utilizing interpersonal skills. It is important to understand how to obtain stakeholder buy-in, resolve conflict, and practice adaptive leadership before actual team execution of iterations, as seen in *Domain II: Value-Driven Delivery* and *Domain IV: Team Performance*. Understanding the different best practices for the human side of Agile project management while working with stakeholders on their vision of the increment is the best way to gain buy-in. This chapter will cover the rest of the tasks in Domain III and give you a well-rounded idea of how to apply interpersonal skills to knowledge sharing, adaptive leadership, and communication, which will carry over to all of the domains.

Interpersonal Skills

Interpersonal skills, while hard to quantify, make up a large part of an Agile project manager's role on a project. A major part of what you will be doing is leading, communicating, motivating, and perpetuating the vision.

Many interpersonal skills come naturally to some personalities, while others may have to work a bit harder to sharpen their skill sets. Some personalities may find that they need to step outside of their comfort zones to immerse themselves in an Agile culture, while others will jump right in without any culture shock at all. Those who have a tougher time adapting to a new way of doing things could be external customers and stakeholders who may be more used to a more rigid set of processes for project management. This is especially true if the organization or the customer is used to or has worked in a Waterfall environment for the majority of their careers.

It would be difficult to say exactly what you should or could do in any given situation because neither the Project Management Institute nor I know your team on a personal level or your organizational culture like you do. Therefore, much of what you will read in this chapter will appear as generic information. I would ask that you think about your stakeholders and your team and how you interact with them. You can use this chapter as an opportunity to reflect and adapt your daily interactions with your team and stakeholders. This could result in giving yourselves a pat on the back for doing a fantastic job with your team as well as identifying areas that need improvement.

NOTE   Even though I'm giving generic examples in this chapter, the PMI-ACP exam will test your ability to put yourselves into an interpersonal situation with your team or stakeholders and be able to adapt to the scenario as presented to answer questions correctly.

Many questions on your exam will be on interpersonal skills, engaging stakeholders, servant leadership, and shared collaboration. In the last chapter, you spent a lot of time reviewing things like pre-project communications and stakeholder engagement. Most of the questions may not be specific to the project charter, but instead they test on things like engagement with metaphors, elevator statements, and tweets as well as good interpersonal skills and adaptive leadership throughout the project. Engaging stakeholders doesn't end with a charter or one definition of done—it continues from planning through deployment.

As you go through the main categories of interpersonal skills, ask yourself if any of the areas represent aspirational skills that you would like to work on. If there are skills that you already possess, then ask yourself if there is any improvement you need in those areas.

Communication

How people perceive you is how they will receive you.

Ashley Hunt

Obviously, *communication* is a big deal on any team, but in Agile it has a greater focus due to the importance of face-to-face communication, colocation of the teams, and visual information radiators like Kanban boards and other charts. If the communication in your organization is largely too many emails and too many meetings about meetings to discuss meetings, then a shift is necessary to work appropriately with an Agile team and properly engage your stakeholders. If you are an Agile novice (or your organization is new to Agile), then a bit of a culture shock will occur when things change over to a more interactive, communicative environment.

The key thing to remember about Agile teams is that the Agile Project manager is the *coach*. Your job is going to be to make sure that good, collaborative communication is occurring during facilitated workshops and even provide individual and group coaching as needed.

The stakeholders and your team are the *who*, and the product owner provides the *what*. The Agile project manager is the balance point on which it all hinges.

The goal in any Agile environment is to determine how best to communicate on many levels and truly understand where the stakeholders are in their thought processes while determining the definition of done. Otherwise, the team could unfortunately experience a very real situation called the gulf of misunderstanding.

The *gulf of misunderstanding* is when the customer is thinking and explaining something one way and the team understands it in a different way. All of a sudden, everyone believes that they are on the same page, until the review comes where the customer is wondering what the team has built and you are wondering why the customer isn't accepting it.

The gulf of misunderstanding can be a very real thing on Agile projects. Therefore, effective communication is very important, especially if your customer isn't very technologically savvy, or if they don't understand the jargon you are using to describe something. They may give up and say, "Do whatever you think is best," and then end up getting something that is very far from what they thought they were getting, or the conversation comes to a standstill until communication improves.

Figure 5.1 is a good visual of the confusion of not understanding which direction to go in, even though there are signs that are supposed to guide you.

FIGURE 5.1   The gulf of misunderstanding

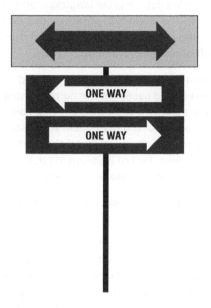

 Real World Scenario

Avoiding the Gulf of Misunderstanding

When I first started down the Agile road, I knew that I was entering unfamiliar territory because I was so used to a Waterfall way of doing things. All things were documented, all things were regimented, and everything needed signatures. Even though I am totally convinced that my customers did not read every single item of documentation I presented to them, I knew they got the gist of it since they signed off on it. They knew the scope of the work. They might not have known the ins and outs of how we would execute it, but they knew what they were getting themselves into because everything was preplanned. That was a big deal for the team and me, since we knew it would be tough for stakeholders to argue with their own signature.

In an Agile environment, many of our communications were conversations, much of the scope of work or documentation was done at the last responsible moment, and the definition of done-done was foggy at best. We did use personas, user stories, and INVEST, of course, because those are best practices and an important aspect of collaboration and communication. Nonetheless, I was concerned our communication wasn't completely effective.

One thing I did bring from my Waterfall project experience was a *glossary of uncommon terms*. The company I worked for at the time had massive lists of TLAs or, three-letter acronyms. Everything was in coded license plate language, and I knew my customers didn't speak that language at all. The worst thing that you can do is to start throwing jargon and acronyms at people who may not want to admit that they don't understand. That in and of itself creates the gulf of misunderstanding.

The glossary of uncommon terms was very simply laid out and easy to read. The terms were grouped by logic and assembled based on our current knowledge of what the key stakeholders wanted. I also felt that there should be a group called "Agile terms." Did my customers know what a user story was? Did they understand story points and other ways to estimate? Did they understand Agile frameworks? If they did, no harm, no foul. If they didn't, that could be a major problem. Part of a Scrum Master or Agile project manager's job is to teach the how and why of Agile to those who need to understand it.

The glossary was distributed during pre-project engagement, and terms were added to it as necessary throughout the project.

A gulf of misunderstanding can occur on two different, yet important, levels. First, it can occur between the customer and the team on what the definition of done is and understanding the scope of the work, and second, between the team and the customer due to a misunderstanding of our terms and best practices. The important thing about the glossary is that it is constantly growing, and it can serve as an excellent template for any projects for which it is needed in the future.

If you break down the exam content outline for stakeholder engagement, much of it describes behaviors and communication needs throughout the project. In Chapter 4, "Agile Initiation and Stakeholder Engagement," you spent time on the best practices for determining the definition of done and the aspects of pre-project engagement. Throughout the chapters of this study guide, there will be reference points to effective communication between the team and the product owner, the team and the Agile project manager, and everyone and the customer, as well as team communication on a team level.

The exam content outline points to some very specific needs from a stakeholder point of view, and it is important to delve a bit deeper into those to truly understand what the outline is describing and why it is so important—not just to pass an exam, but to truly get into the mindset of Agile. To be Agile.

> To effectively communicate, we must realize that we are all different in the way we perceive the world and use this understanding as a guide to our communication with others.
>
> *Tony Robbins*

Task 2 in the exam content outline for stakeholder engagement clearly points to identifying and engaging all stakeholders (current and future) by promoting knowledge sharing early and throughout the project to ensure the unimpeded flow of information and value throughout the life span of the project. I think that it is also realistic to find out their preferred method of communication, provided that it doesn't eat up too much time that could otherwise be used to produce what it is they are requesting. I'm speaking of too many meetings or too many phone calls, just because that is what the stakeholders are used to.

It is going to be up to the Agile Project Manager to coach stakeholders, current and future, in the ways of Agile and protect the team from too many interruptions. However, with that caveat in place, it is still a good idea to ask someone their preferred method of communication. It's unrealistic to assume that every single team member is colocated and every single stakeholder is wandering around the building ready for a conversation at any given moment. With that thought in mind, asking your customers and stakeholders what is most effective for them in the realm of communication isn't outside the boundaries of any Agile method or framework. This is especially true if the stakeholders already understand that they are key contributors in timeboxed events like reviews and sprint planning.

How do you like to communicate or what is your preferred method? This would be above and beyond other communication types necessary on the project and a quite useful question to ask. Think about it; has anyone ever asked you how you prefer to communicate? If left to our own devices, some may say "face-to-face," others may say "just send me an email," while still others may say "formal events or ceremonies work best to focus the message." It's up to you how you engage your own stakeholders based on your own styles of communication and your organization's culture. Remember, there would be no way that I could say this is best or that, unless I came to your organization. We can then, and only then, rely on best practices of effective communication.

 Real World Scenario

Miscommunication and the Emails They Rode In On

One of my clients asked me to visit their organization and do a workshop on communication skills. They were concerned because too many emails were going unanswered by the development teams, and the teams felt that there were just too many. An impasse had been reached, and neither side was willing to budge in their preferred methods of communication. So there they sat—all in one conference room around a large table. The operations side of the house sat on one side of the table and the development team sat on the other. It took a while to get any useful information out of them, but the major issue was this from each perspective:

> *Operations*: "We send emails out attempting to get information from the development teams on staffing needs and approvals of certain things, and we get back one word answers or none at all, plus they seem to be a cranky bunch."

I asked to see one of the emails operations had sent to the development team, and it went something like this in 12 paragraphs or more.

> *Operations email*: "Hi! Hope you are all having a wonderful day!!! We are looking to get some information on question 1, question 2, question 3, question 4, and question 5, comment 8. Also, don't forget it's Brenda's birthday and there will be cake in the break room from noon to 1:00. Let us know as soon as you can possibly get the answers to the questions, and I hope you all have a fantastic day!!"

> *Development team response:* "Yes, thanks."

> *Operations responded with:* "Hi again everyone!!! Hope you are all having a great day!! I'm not really sure which questions you were responding to, could you clarify for us? Whenever you have a chance that would be great! By the way, you missed Brenda's party but there is leftover cake in the breakroom fridge. THANKS!!"

> *Development team response:* "Yes, No, Maybe, No, Yes... Thanks."

You can see where I'm going with this. The complaint from the operations side was the development team gave short, one-word answers, and they rarely if ever respond to the entire email. They also came across as rude and not very helpful. The development team's complaint was that the operations emails were filled with useless noise, emoticons, and paragraphs, and they didn't have time to read a novel when they were working.

There was an ah-ha moment in the room. Lightbulbs were going off everywhere. Operations asked how the development team wanted their emails to be written to gain the best responses. The development team said to use bullet points, keep it simple, and, if possible, submit one question at a time in the emails submitted to the team. It's easier to respond quickly to one question, and a one-word answer should be good enough. If more was needed, they would expand on it. The development team also agreed that they could be a little nicer in their responses and maybe throw in a "Have a great day!" for good measure.

I followed up about a month later and was told that the email back and forth had been cut down exponentially, and everyone was communicating on a better level with better efficiency.

The moral of the story is that once you know the preferred, or even expected, methods of communication, you are better able to mirror that and provide information in a way that is realistic, appreciated, and well understood.

I could literally fill a book with communication best practices, but I'll conclude the communication piece with this: The better you know someone, the better you will be able to communicate. Communication is two way and action based, but perception is 100 percent reality. How people perceive you is how they will receive you. It's your job to determine what that looks like and adapt your communication strategies accordingly.

Self-Directed Teams

What exactly is a self-directed team, and why is it so important for an effective Agile environment? Think about this scenario: Your boss hands you a list of things for you to do for a customer and then says, "I don't care what order you do them in or how you split up your time." Your boss then asks you how long will it take you to do all this?" How would you react? You would give them a realistic estimate on duration, and get as much done as you could in an order that seemed realistic. You probably wouldn't drag your feet, but you would work diligently in a realistic time frame. You would likely get most of it done, and you would have a good reason for what you didn't get done. That is a self-directed team.

Give the team the valuable items, let the team decide how much they can accomplish in an iteration and in what order they will do it, and then step away and let them fly. Provide coaching as needed and when requested, but otherwise be hands-off.

This is a very different dynamic from a project team that has directives and daily activities that are structured in a set order because the Gantt chart says so and the baselines demand it. This is a new way of thinking and working on a team level, and some who are newer to Agile frameworks may be a bit befuddled by it all in the beginning because they have been conditioned to work a certain way. This is, again, the job of the Agile project manager—to coach in the ways of self-directed teams, providing guidance and reassurance. Let them know that it is okay to do things this way and to block out any disturbances from pesky stakeholders who haven't yet been schooled in Agile. Remember, Agile is easy to talk and think about, but it is very difficult to do. You are the Yoda of Agile project management, and it is up to you to teach others the ways of Agile.

> Always pass on what you learn.
> *Yoda*

Negotiation

When you think of the word *negotiation*, what do you think about? Do you automatically think about winning something, or do you see it more as a healthy give-and-take, a win-win situation, or a collaboration? How you view negotiation can significantly influence your ability for the good or not so good in an Agile environment.

> Every time we interact with another person at work, we have a choice to make: do we try to claim as much value as we can, or contribute value without worrying about what we receive in return?
>
> *Adam Grant, author of Give and Take: A Revolutionary Approach to Success*
> *Adam M. Grant*
> *Weidenfeld & Nicolson, 2013 - Altruism - 305 page*

Negotiation in an Agile environment is akin to both sides winning. You can probably tell with the amount of collaboration, communication, and teamwork that sharklike negotiation behaviors don't have a comfortable spot on an Agile team.

Think about what you would need to negotiate on an Agile project. If you are a product owner, much of what you negotiate is based on what is valuable today and on what the customer wants. Sometimes, you would have to tell them no; otherwise, there would never be a defined "done" point. Keeping it simple and creating something minimally marketable every iteration isn't about cramming as many features as you can into something during a one-month iteration. It's give-and-take.

If you are part of the development team, you may be negotiating with your team members on work assignments and with the product owner on what can and can't be accomplished. Regardless of the type of negotiations you do, it won't be about you winning and the other party losing. It's about *compromise, collaboration,* and *win-win environments*.

There are several philosophies of effective negotiation. Some suggest that you should understand your own negotiation style first. Do you play your cards close to the vest, or do you throw them all down on the table to create and maintain a good relationship? Other philosophies recommend that you mirror the style of the other party by doing research and knowing your audience. Other methods still suggest that you always show your cards first to set the bar and then work around that through give-and-take. This particular method never worked with my teenage daughter, but it's been successful in my professional career. Come to think of it, not a single negotiation method or strategy prepared me for a teenage daughter! She's considering law school—go figure?

Honestly, my feeling is that if it is unnatural to you to act one way over another during a negotiation, then that method probably won't stick, much less allow you to work toward a good solution.

No matter what method you subscribe to, it is always good to be prepared in some way for the negotiation. If you are asking for a raise, then know what you want. If you are negotiating a feature that you feel is a "must-have," then do the research to back it up.

A very basic, generic plan would be to establish your requirements and determine the value of the item being negotiated. Is it something you can live without, or are you negotiating for something that you must have to be successful? The answer to this question can determine how much preparation you need to do and how much of the outcome affects you.

I always find it is best to have two options: what you really want and what you can live with. I always start with what I really want first, because you can always come down to a different level but you can never go up.

Even though negotiation can sometimes have a negative connotation, it can involve a very healthy give-and-take to reach a conclusion on which everyone agrees. The first step to a good negotiation is to be aware that the other party has ideas that may differ from yours. If both sides are allowed to express those ideas and collaborate on them, something new can be achieved that both parties may never have considered. To truly be Agile, negotiation can only be done one way, and that is that both parties walk away feeling as though they were heard and can agree on the direction in which they are headed. In that respect, it is a win-win endeavor.

Aspirational Skills

There are many other core aspects of interpersonal skills that are hard to quantify as well, or even put into the context of your personal day-to-day thoughts and feelings. Many of these skills are learned behaviors, and many of you came into the world doing them intuitively as part of your personality or nature.

The Project Management Institute's Code of Ethics and Professional Conduct places items into two categories: aspirational skills and mandatory skills. *Aspirational skills* are things we *aspire* to be better at, such as always working on being better communicators, negotiators, and servant leaders.

Mandatory skills are things like don't break the law, don't discriminate, don't have any conflicts of interest. Things that would be illegal or unprofessional in any industry fall under this category. The Code of Ethics and Professional Conduct is designed to highlight the importance of always aspiring to learn new skills and master them while at the same time being a good, ethical person. You will have to accept the Code of Ethics and Professional Conduct before you take your exam, and you will be held to it. I highly recommend that you read it prior to accepting it.

The aspirational skills that all servant leaders strive to obtain and perfect include the following, among others:

- Empathy
- Respect
- Integrity
- Fairness
- Patience
- Responsibility
- Flexibility
- Self-discipline

I also highly recommend an excellent sense of humor as well as good communication and negotiation skills.

Just as all things in Agile, these are easy to say and much harder to do; what we can do is make it easier to function in an Agile environment and sharpen our aspirational skill sets. Colocation of the team as much as possible, even if only for an iteration or so, will improve communication. Making effective decisions in a collaborative environment, using good negotiation and communication skills, and voting are all needed to reach a conclusion or direction.

The practice of active listening is especially important. By listening actively, you are making sure that you are not thinking of the next thing to say or passing judgment on what you are hearing. Hearing and listening are two different things. The more we listen, the more we hear, and the more we hear, the better our understanding of the information that is being communicated and our chance of retaining it. Active listening can also help you respond effectively to conflict while practicing empathy and understanding to manage it correctly. You will cover conflict resolution a bit later in this chapter.

Motivation

If I were to ask you what motivates you, what would your answer be? Would you say that you're motivated by money? Would you say that you're motivated by the work you do? Would you say that you're motivated because you like the people with whom you work? What motivates each individual is a very personal thing, but there are some common motivators that are identified and can be utilized when practicing servant leadership.

  It's unlikely that you will be tested specifically on motivation or any motivational theories that you will review in this chapter. To be the best servant leader you can be, however, it is very important to know how to motivate and develop your team of individuals.

If we look to the past at some of the theorists and experts on psychology and human motivation, it's easy to see why these philosophies have stood the test of time—from the 1940s until today.

One such theorist is Abraham Maslow. Maslow's hierarchy of needs was first proposed in an article in 1943, and again in his book *Motivation and Personality*, Third Edition (Longman 1987). Maslow concluded that all humans have several levels of needs and motivations and that all people must have very basic needs met before they can move up the hierarchy. Figure 5.2 shows Maslow's hierarchy of needs, which is typically represented in a triangle.

FIGURE 5.2   Maslow's hierarchy of needs

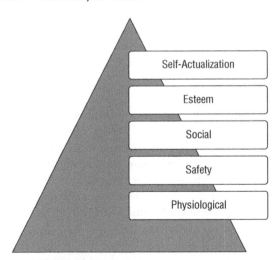

Maslow concluded that all humans must first meet their physiological needs of air, food, and water and then safety and freedom from harm followed by love and friendships. Those are the three core needs that all humans need to attain. Once they have met the core needs, they can work on building their esteem and finally reach self-actualization.

Maslow was not convinced that everyone reached self-actualization because that is the level that defines doing things for the greater good and not being self-absorbed. It is also the level where people learn new things about others just because they want to do so. Maslow felt that our society is so caught up in self-esteem and relationships with other people that many humans rarely, if ever, reach self-actualization and stay there. Mostly, we humans are sliding up and down the hierarchy as life throws wrenches at us and forces us to adapt and overcome.

The only reason I bring up Maslow is because his description of self-actualization is very close to what makes a great servant leader. We won't ever be perfect at it, but we can attempt to put others first and work for the greater good. It's just something to keep in mind.

A lot of what a good servant leader will do is to practice a bit of intuitive mind reading until they know their team well enough to motivate them accordingly. Something else to keep in mind is that many people are uncomfortable or embarrassed by public displays of recognition of individuals only. In an Agile environment, it is very much a Three Musketeers mentality—all for one and one for all!

Keep a good focus on motivating the *team of individuals*, get to know them as individuals, and coach and support the team so that they can reach their goals, whether those goals are to make more money, to advance their careers, to work with people they like, or to love the job they do. It takes emotional intelligence, active listening, and transparent communication to build up a team. Your job as an Agile project manager is much more focused on these aspects than pretty much anything else you do.

Conflict Resolution

Conflict isn't about if—it is about when. If you are like me and give conflict the big dislike, you aren't alone. Most humans do not like conflict in general—much less in a professional environment. I know there are people who love drama and gossip, and I wouldn't be surprised if someone's name just popped into your heads, you know...THAT person! However, most of, if not many, of us would rather not deal with it.

Obviously, there is *dysfunctional conflict*, typically between individuals, which is tough to manage. The conflict that you'll be reviewing is professional conflict, or what could be called *functional conflict*. Perhaps you disagree with the way things are being managed on your projects, or you disagree with a solution that someone is proposing to a problem the team is addressing. Maybe lack of clear expectations or effective communication is causing unnecessary conflict and risk. If you find yourself nodding along, you know what I mean.

What would you say is the number one cause of conflict on your current team?

- Differences in objectives, values, and perceptions?
- Disagreements about roles or responsibilities?
- Technological issues?
- Management styles?
- Scheduling issues?

- Personality issues?
- Lack of communication?
- Lack of support from stakeholders or senior management?
- Unclear expectations?
- Unexpected risk events?
- All of the above?

Most folks would probably say unclear expectations, lack of communication, and personality issues. One of the nice things about Agile is that communication and interactions are such regular occurrences that lack of communication is the last thing to worry about. Effective communication? Well, that is a different story.

As a servant leader, it is your job to make sure that communication is occurring on a regular basis, that you support the team, and that you help the team learn how to deal with conflict in a healthy way. In Chapter 7, "Effective Team Performance on Agile Projects," you will delve a bit deeper into team development and mastery of skills. However, one of the key aspects of developing a brand-new team is getting them from the forming stage to the performing stage. In Figure 5.3, you'll see a visual of Tuckman's Ladder. Bruce Tuckman presented his theory on group or team development in 1965 and expanded upon it in 1977.

FIGURE 5.3   Tuckman's Ladder

The expansion of the theory included another step called *adjourning*. This is the step where people leave the team or the team disperses to other projects. The concept is that if one person leaves the team and another person joins the team, everyone will have to reset and repeat the stages, though much more quickly this time.

In an Agile environment, the best practice is to have a core self-directed team that doesn't adjourn but that works together all of the time. In Tuckman's Ladder, which is shown in Figure 5.3, the second phase of team development is storming. The team isn't able to manage conflict totally on their own and may look to the Agile project manager to step in and help guide the resolution. This is due to the team not being completely comfortable with each other, and they may be prone to disagreement on the direction the project should take. You are more likely to see conflict as part of a team storming and moving from storming to constructive disagreement in performing. Teams diverge with conflict and converge with negotiation.

Just as it would be difficult to give you a one-size-fits-all motivation or communication strategy, it's also difficult to give you a specific way to manage conflict on your team. I can only present ideas and categories of risk responses. Table 5.1 shows the distinct categories of conflict resolution and whether they are considered a good direction or not.

TABLE 5.1   Conflict resolution categories

Conflict Resolution Strategy	Description
Collaborate or Problem Solve	Identifying the underlying problem and working out solutions in a way that allows all parties to work through their disagreements. Recommended as a *Win-Win* and the longest lasting. Very Agile oriented.
Compromise or Reconcile	Finding a middle ground that satisfies all parties to some degree. Considered *Lose-lose* because both sides have to give up something, but it can be useful.
Smoothing or Accommodating	De-emphasizes differences between points of view and focuses on commonalities. Recommended as a *Win-win*, but short term. Best if used with problem solving and compromise.
Forcing or Directing	Requires others to yield to the point of view of one side or another. Not recommended unless necessary. Becomes necessary when a decision must be made quickly or to force regulatory compliance. *Win/Lose.*
Withdrawal/ Avoid	Avoiding or retreating from the conflict or potential conflict and allowing the involved parties to work out the conflict on their own. Not recommended unless it is a very heated or dangerous situation, or it is a strategic withdrawal. Considered *Lose-lose.*

I realize that in a conflict situation, you won't be sitting around saying to yourself, "I'm accommodating." Many times, conflict is a slow burn that builds over time, or a total and complete surprise. On an Agile team, it is important to encourage the team to discuss things that are causing conflict or problems.

For the most part, you will be coaching your team and helping them to manage functional conflict and reach a consensus. This is especially true when a team is in storming. A performing team is more likely to manage their own conflict without input from the Agile project manager unless absolutely necessary.

> In the middle of difficulty lies opportunity.
>
> *Albert Einstein*

Adaptive Leadership

This chapter wraps up with adaptive leadership. Even though this chapter and the last one have a much larger focus on stakeholder engagement, we have discussed the team as well. As an adaptive leader and Agile project manager, you must be able to pivot, roll with the punches, and adapt to your environment to lead effectively. This allows you and the development team to focus on value-adds and to reduce waste and thus meet stakeholder expectations.

I read somewhere once that "nobody actually does Agile—they ARE Agile!" This resonated with me because being a servant leader who can adapt is the definition of true agility. The meaning of it is more to the point that Agile is a way of being, not a set process of doing. Even with all of the methodologies and frameworks you have covered, the constant theme throughout all of it is effective and adaptive leadership. It's a way of being, not of doing.

> I'm going to give you a little advice. There's a force in the universe that makes things happen. And all you have to do is get in touch with it, stop thinking, let things happen, and *be the ball.*

Ty Webb
Caddyshack
Warner Bros., 1980

Inspire, communicate, and collaborate. Easier said than done, right? Nobody expects you to be perfect all of the time. Remember, in Agile there is a no blame culture, so mistakes are expected and embraced. Mistakes are how you learn and how you grow as a leader. You adapt and become a lifelong learner. You manage change effectively, and you practice servant leadership. You resolve issues, provide coaching when needed, and accept coaching when you need it yourself.

Adapting to your team and environment is the crux of being Agile, because no position on an Agile team controls the other. They all have a role to play. Your job is to model best practices and behaviors by practicing them yourself and leading by example.

Almost the entire PMI-ACP exam involves adaptive leadership and situational questions of "What do you do next?" or "What do you do?" The exam questions drop you right into the shoes of an Agile project manager, product owner, and team member, and based on the Agile Manifesto and your servant leadership abilities, it will be up to you to choose the best response to the scenario.

> At any organizational level, people are leaders not because of what they do, but because of who they are.
>
> *Jim Highsmith*

As you wrap up this chapter on the human side of Agile that corresponds with stakeholder engagement and team development, it's always a good thing to reflect back and ask yourself, "How can I help my stakeholders, my team, and myself to be more successful today?" You can achieve this by walking the talk and being a lifelong learner. Be the ball!

Summary

This chapter began with an overview of interpersonal skills and the best practices associated with them, including communication and your role as a coach to help avoid a gulf of misunderstanding with your stakeholders.

Then I went over the self-directed team dynamic, and why is it important to be a good coach and block the team from unnecessary disturbances from stakeholders to achieve an effective Agile environment.

Next I reviewed negotiation and other aspirational skills, including motivation and Maslow's hierarchy of needs. It's important to have a way to identify where your team is in the hierarchy and to help motivate on the level of the team member.

After that, I covered conflict resolution strategies and categories that can be used depending on the situation. Some are considered win-win, while others may only be used in very specific situations.

Finally, I went over the essentials of embracing the mindset of adaptive leadership and being able to inspire, communicate, and collaborate while practicing servant leadership, as well as some of the important things to keep in mind as you lead Agile projects and study for your exams.

Everything that you have covered in this chapter is incorporated into the remaining tasks found in *Domain III: Stakeholder Engagement*. Now you have a great foundation to move on to other domains and see how some of the best practices that we covered at a surface level can be implemented and utilized on your next project and during your exam.

Exam Essentials

Be able to absorb different interpersonal skills.   Understand why it is important to practice good communication to avoid the gulf of misunderstanding with your stakeholders and be able to use emotional intelligence to ask the right questions while actively listening for the answers.

Understand the concept of adaptive leadership.   Having the ability to adapt your leadership style based on what stage of development your team is in and to truly understand what your team, product owners, customers, and other stakeholders need from you is the crux of being truly Agile.

Be able to understand the differences between aspirational skills and mandatory skills. Much of the exam will focus on aspirational skills like communication, negotiation, and conflict resolution. It's also important to read through the Project Management Institute's Professional Code of Ethics and Professional Conduct because you will be asked to agree and abide by it as an Agile professional.

Understand categories of conflict resolution.   Knowing when to problem solve, versus smoothing or compromise, is the sign of an effective leader. Also, knowing when to stay out of a conflict and let your team work through it is equally as important. The majority of conflict on an Agile project team may be due to a misunderstanding of requirements or disagreement on the direction to take with the work. Because communication is constant, conflict is typically less impactful on an Agile team versus a Waterfall team.

Be aware of effective communication techniques.   Effective communication is a common theme in all aspects of Agile. In this chapter, you continued reviewing stakeholder engagement tasks to determine the needs of the customer and how to get to the point where your team could start working on priority user stories and produce a usable, done increment. Practicing aspects of communication and adaptive leadership will help you BE more Agile in your communication, as well as to make you a better and more effective servant leader.

Review Questions

You can find the answers to the review questions in Appendix B.

1. Your team disagrees on the direction a requirement should take, and it is convinced that the customer hasn't explained it correctly. As a servant leader, what can you identify as the reason for the misunderstanding?

    A. Not enough information was gathered from the customer.

    B. The gulf of misunderstanding has occurred, and more information is needed to determine the correct direction.

    C. You should practice good conflict resolution skills.

    D. Team knowledge is limited because they are in the storming stage.

2. Bill and Ally are having a disagreement in the break room about something they saw on the news the night before. You are walking by, and you overhear the disagreement. As a servant leader, what is the best conflict resolution technique to utilize in this situation?

    A. Help them reach a compromise.

    B. Tell them to stop the disagreement, as it is inappropriate at work.

    C. Try to get them to compromise.

    D. Avoid getting involved as it isn't relevant to project work.

3. Your team has been working together for several iterations now, and they seem to be working well together. They are making decisions as a team and determining what work they should do and when. This is an example of which of the following?

    A. A storming team

    B. An Agile team

    C. A self-directed team

    D. An adjourning team

4. As an Agile team member, you are working with the product owner and the customer on several of the user stories and requirements the customer is requesting. You witness the product owner suggesting that the customer choose one requirement over another because it will function better with their result, and the customer agrees that it is win-win for everyone. What did the product owner do effectively?

    A. Negotiation

    B. Requirement gathering

    C. User story development

    D. Servant leadership

5. Task 5 of the exam content outline for stakeholder engagement states that you will need to establish collaborative behaviors among the members of the organization by fostering group decision making and conflict resolution in order to improve decision quality and reduce the time required to make decisions. If there is a conflict and you have an option, which of the following is the best conflict resolution strategy?

    A. Compromise

    B. Smoothing

    C. Collaboration

    D. Avoiding

6. Your team has reached the performing phase. What types of management and leadership do they need?

    A. A lot of feedback and interactions

    B. Feedback, coaching, and help only when they ask for it

    C. Help with conflict resolution and expectation settings

    D. Helping getting to know each other and building trust

7. The team space is key in Agile projects. What is the one thing that is recommended above all others for Agile teams?

    A. Scrum boards

    B. Colocation

    C. Caves and common rooms

    D. Information radiators

8. On a colocated team, what is one of the major benefits of everyone sitting together in the same work space?

    A. The Scrum Master can find everyone.

    B. Daily stand-up meetings are easier to organize.

    C. It enables improved communication.

    D. It builds relationships and trust.

9. Your newly formed team is experiencing some conflict in the way they estimate time. Several team members have withdrawn from the conversations, while others are still arguing about the best ways to do things. This is an example of what team stage?

    A. Forming

    B. Norming

    C. Storming

    D. Adjourning

10. As an Agile project manager, you explain to your team that, as their coach, you are there to provide for the team's needs and remove any roadblocks to their progress. This is also described as which one of the following?

    A. Project management

    B. Agile leadership

    C. Management and leadership

    D. Adaptive leadership

11. Misunderstandings of value, product, and customer needs can best be described as which one of the following?

    A. The gulf of evaluation

    B. The gulf of Agile

    C. The gulf of misunderstanding

    D. The gulf value stream

12. For an Agile project manager, active listening is an important aspect to practicing adaptive leadership. If a stakeholder is talking to you about an issue, what should be your primary focus?

    A. Solving their problem

    B. Assessing their facial features

    C. Thinking of what you will say next

    D. Listening to what the person is saying and assessing the information

13. Your stakeholders are engaged in a conversation about what direction to go in with an aspect of the software that is being built. The team is divided on how to proceed. The conflict is more of a collective disagreement than an outright conflict. What should you do as the Agile project manager?

    A. Engage in the conversation, and help the team solve the issue.

    B. Call a meeting to have a formal discussion about the issue.

    C. Discuss conflict resolution techniques at the next retrospective.

    D. Do nothing.

14. One of your stakeholders is asking about your PMI-ACP certification and wonders what code of ethics you need to abide by as a certified professional. You explain that there are two categories of conduct you abide by. Which of the following describes these categories?

    A. Legal and aspirational

    B. Motivational and legal

    C. Mandatory and motivational

    D. Mandatory and aspirational

15. During a heated exchange over what the definition of done is to the stakeholders, you have determined that there isn't any way anyone is going to be able to collaborate on solutions. Which of the following conflict resolution strategies would work best in this situation?

    A. Compromise

    B. Forcing

    C. Withdrawal

    D. Smoothing

16. In Maslow's hierarchy of needs, what term expresses a person who has everything and determines that they will give back for the greater good?

    A. Social

    B. Physiological

    C. Safety

    D. Self-actualization

17. You and your development team are working with the product owner on user stories in the backlog. Your team is asking questions about what stories will be done next and what they think that they can accomplish. The product owner asks the team to consider adding two more stories to the sprint for the customer, and the team explains that they are unable to do any additional stories. The product owner explains why it is important, and the team agrees to take on one more story but not two. What does this exchange represent?

    A. A poorly run negotiation

    B. A balanced win-win negotiation

    C. The product owner overstepping their position

    D. Good communication

18. Engaging with stakeholders involves having the emotional intelligence to understand their concerns and to work to determine what they value. In order to be effective in this role, which of the following skills are necessary?

    A. Interpersonal skills

    B. Adaptive leadership

    C. Creating an elevator statement

    D. Having a detailed planning meeting

19. One of your stakeholders is new to Agile and is asking that the team take on more user stories per iteration to get things done faster. As an adaptive servant leader, what is the best thing to do?

    A. Listen to what they are saying, and then explain to them that they should go talk to the product owner.

    B. Tell them no.

    C. Listen to their concerns, but explain the concept of a self-directed team.

    D. Negotiate with them to protect the team from interruptions.

20. You are a product owner, and you are working to sort various user stories by value during the current sprint. A key stakeholder comes to you in the middle of the current sprint and asks you to add a feature that was deemed unnecessary by the customer. What is the best thing to do?

   A. Call a team meeting and explain that you are adding another feature to the increment in the middle of the sprint.

   B. Tell the Agile project manager, and let them deliver the message to the team.

   C. Explain to the stakeholder that the feature will be put at the back of the backlog for a potential future revisit, but right now the customer doesn't see it as valuable.

   D. Tell the key stakeholder that the best thing to do is bring it up at the next sprint planning meeting and discuss it then.

Chapter 6

Agile Estimation and Planning

THE FOLLOWING PMI-ACP® EXAM TOPICS ARE COVERED IN THIS CHAPTER:

✓ **Domain II: Value-Driven Delivery**

Define Positive Value:

- Task 1: Define deliverables by identifying units that can be produced incrementally in order to maximize their value to stakeholders while minimizing non-value- added work.

- Task 2: Refine requirements by gaining consensus on the acceptance criteria for features on a just-in-time basis in order to deliver value.

- Task 3: Select and tailor the team's process based on project and organizational characteristics as well as team experience in order to optimize value delivery.

Avoid Potential Downsides:

- Task 4: Plan for small releasable increments by organizing requirements into minimally marketable features/minimally viable products in order to allow for the early recognition and delivery of value.

- Task 5: Limit increment size and increase review frequency with appropriate stakeholders in order to identify and respond to risks early on and at minimal cost.

- Task 6: Solicit customer and user feedback by reviewing increments often in order to confirm and enhance business value.

Prioritization:

- Task 7: Prioritize the units of work through collaboration with stakeholders in order to optimize the value of the deliverables.

- Task 8: Perform frequent review and maintenance of the work results by prioritizing and maintaining internal quality in order to reduce the overall cost of incremental development.

- Task 9: Continuously identify and prioritize the environmental, operational, and infrastructure factors in order to improve the quality and value of the deliverables.

Incremental Development:

- Task 10: Conduct operational reviews and/or periodic checkpoints with stakeholders in order to obtain feedback and corrections to the work in progress and planned work.

- Task 11: Balance development of deliverable units and risk reduction efforts by incorporating both value producing and risk reducing work into the backlog in order to maximize the total value proposition over time.

- Task 12: Re-prioritize requirements periodically in order to reflect changes in the environment and stakeholder needs or preferences in order to maximize the value.

- Task 13: Elicit and prioritize relevant non-functional requirements (such as operations and security) by considering the environment in which the solution will be used in order to minimize the probability of failure.

- Task 14: Conduct frequent reviews of work products by performing inspections, reviews, and/or testing in order to identify and incorporate improvements into the overall process and product/service.

In this chapter, you will cover all of the tasks found in *Domain II: Value-Driven Delivery* of the exam content outline. The tasks may overlap in some respect with *Domain V: Adaptive Planning* as well, since Agile best practices are iterative in nature. Both of these domains directly relate to planning around what is valuable in an adaptive way. You will cover specific aspects of *Domain V: Adaptive Planning* in Chapter 8, "Agile Execution and Tracking of Iterations," when you cover key performance indicators that would adjust or adapt the planning of value-based work. This in no way means that it is the end of these best practices; in fact, they carry through from iteration to iteration. It is important to address them together, at least initially. Both domains work through the analysis of work based on business value, the concepts of timeboxing, epics, features and user stories, story mapping, relative sizing, planning poker, sprint calculations, iterations, spikes, and initial velocity planning. While these concepts repeat during every iteration, with the exclusion of a potential Iteration Zero or lack of need for a spike, it is important to understand how to determine value and plan accordingly. This chapter will cover the tasks in Domain II and give you a well-rounded idea of how to apply good planning best practices for efficient and valuable execution that will carry over to all of the domains.

Iteration Zero

There are different schools of thought when it comes to *Iteration Zero*, or *sprint zero*. The entire concept of Iteration Zero is to not create a usable increment during the iteration but instead to use the upfront time to create goals, usable processes, and a game plan. Most of the time that type of planning is done in the chartering step of Agile and not in its own separate iteration.

One side of the discussion is that to have an iteration without producing value and doing planning to create artifacts that will change is a colossal waste of time. I agree that to totally preplan is wasteful because plans will change, and you are supposed to wait until the last responsible moment to plan. "Working software over comprehensive documentation" is one of the key tenets of the Agile Manifesto.

Iteration Zero, in some cases, may also be used or viewed as an excuse to keep stakeholders at bay when the first iteration doesn't go so well, wasting time and effort.

The other side of the conversation sees value in teams that are very new to Agile taking some ramp-up time to set their goals, help the product owner build up a backlog, write user stories, get differing views of how the process should go, and inevitably have a game plan that is, at least initially, workable.

Iteration Zero could be a week in length rather than a month, and that time can be used to understand the goals, help Waterfall teams transition to Agile, and get comfortable with an entirely new and diverse set of processes. Waterfall to Agile is a big project management culture shift, and conducting a dry run may work out in the long run. An Iteration Zero also allows for converting a typical Waterfall project plan into a backlog, and it allows for setting up the environment needed to be successful in future iterations.

Some of the benefits of an Iteration Zero are as follows:

- It can be used to groom the backlog.

- It allows time to write user stories.

- The team can understand the definition of done.

- You can generate an understanding of technical processes that will be used.

- It may not be an entire iteration in length.

- It can act as a buffer or bridge between Waterfall and Agile.

I think of Iteration Zero as similar to the *initiation process* of Waterfall project management, which involves collecting stakeholder information, plotting a course via the project charter, and having formal authorization to begin project work in general.

Iteration Zero is like a diet soda. It has all of the taste of an iteration without all of the calories or the guilt. Whichever side of the conversation you fall on, the more comfortable teams become in their Agile environment, the less likely you will have a need for an Iteration Zero.

Keep in mind that some highly technical projects could come about in the future and be totally new and unique. Even the best Agile teams may see the need for Iteration Zero at some point in their projects.

Be quick, but don't hurry.

Jim Highsmith

Analyzing Based on Business Value

Different stakeholders find different things valuable based on their position in the organization or project. It can be difficult to determine value completely without understanding the roles on the project and what drives return on investment (ROI).

In Chapter 4, "Agile Initiation and Stakeholder Engagement," you read about project charters and stakeholder engagement to kick off a project and to determine what the increment could, would, or will be. Once you have that information, it becomes necessary to get it to the level where you can create it.

Domain II: Value Driven Delivery contains the information about how to execute the work that provides value to maintain stakeholder engagement iteratively. The stakeholders and what they value include the sponsor (check writer), the product owner (backlog owner), developers (increment creators), and testers (those who prove that things work).

- The sponsor values ROI and workable, sellable products, which can be pushed out to the end users or consumers as quickly as possible.

- The product owner places at the front of the backlog on a regular basis items that are valuable to the users and promote the vision of what the result will become.

- The developers value completing a done increment that is accepted during reviews.

- The testers value increments that work and pass their tests.

So how does an Agile team analyze what is valuable?

Some of the ROI and value is determined during the business case creation, at least from the sponsor/customer side. The net present value (NPV), internal rate of return (IRR), and payback period are all estimated and determined by business analysts so that the money side is covered initially. Most organizations will review all corporate ROI on a yearly, quarterly, or monthly basis and even at the iteration level above and beyond the business case.

The majority of what determines business value is vetting the features that can best create market value, reduce risk, and create better value streams. There is also a focus on improving the capability of the team to produce better value faster.

As you move forward through this chapter you will see a lot of information on epics, user stories, backlog grooming, and other ways that value is determined. The goal is to work with the product owner, sponsor, developers, and testers to push the most valuable items to the front of the line and determine the features to be produced that make everyone happy. It's easier said than done for sure, and that is why this chapter is broken down into the many ways that value is determined and how to prioritize from iteration to iteration. It is easiest to explain when you know what each role plays in the determination of value and then to look at the techniques to see how the team works together to produce value in the form of a usable increment.

The Product Owner

The *product owner*'s job is to create user stories that can be turned into workable increments. Think of user stories as descriptions of about two to four days' worth of work for now; you'll delve much more deeply into the creation of user stories later in the chapter. The product owners have a good idea of what they are trying to accomplish or what the end result *could* be, but they may not have a lot of the details yet.

The product owner knows *why* the team is building the product and what the end result should be because they are in charge of the backlog and collecting all potential requirements. Product owners communicate frequently with stakeholders and the development team to promote the vision, gather information, and work to create the user stories needed to solve a problem and produce value.

The product owner also ultimately knows *who* will be the recipient of the result and why the result will be created. The stakeholders may have a lot of ideas of things that they want in the increment, and the product owner will need to turn those requests into user stories. The product owner will then prioritize the stories based on value and be able to describe the results that will allow the team to complete them.

The stakeholders may have even more ideas as things progress, and it is the product owner's job to manage the ideas and requests and help them determine what is valuable right now. The product owners also need to say no when the ideas and wish lists become too long or go in a direction that doesn't support the total vison.

It's a lot like when it was your birthday as a child. You probably had a long list of what you wanted, but your family knew that it was either too expensive to get them all or they simply didn't want to spoil you. Your parents also knew which items were at the top of your wish list (because you never stopped talking about it!) and that is what they got you.

Your parents were in charge of providing the most valuable items to you based on your list. That is the product owner's job; that is, to take a wish list and organize it with the most important and valuable items first, perhaps allowing a secondary wish list as a maybe and saying no to the rest. This sorting of value can change frequently, which is why the product owner is continuously looking at the backlog and grooming the backlog to adapt and adjust to the latest needs and wants.

Three months before I was to turn 12, I thought I really wanted a tree house, a Barbie, a bicycle, Asteroids on Atari (Yep...I just dated myself), and the list went on and on. Closer to my birthday, my parents asked me again what I wanted and I decided that what I wanted most was a bicycle and that is what I got. My brother got the Atari console and Asteroids. To this day, I'm still a bit salty about it, but I got what I wanted most at the time—the freedom to roam. The product owner is the one that takes a very long list of items and sorts them in order of importance.

Somebody actually has to build the important items, though, and that is where the development team comes into the picture.

Development Team

In a perfect world, the *development team* is typically made up of about nine people. Those nine people will work on the increments that the product owner designates. If you are thinking that you have 20 people on your team, that's okay too, as long as it works for your projects. The smaller the team, the fewer the chances are that there will be misunderstandings and lack of communication. There may be many small teams working on different aspects of a large project, but typically the best practice is to keep teams to nine or fewer people. Too many people, and the complexity of communication on the project increases, give or take, depending on your own organizational influences. In a perfect world, the team would be colocated, even if it is only for the first couple of iterations, or even better yet, colocated for the entire project.

The development team will determine how may user stories it can accomplish in each iteration. This is totally up to the team, based on what they think they can accomplish and what they determine is their capacity. Notice it is the team who determines this and not the Agile project manager, product owner, or other stakeholders. We will cover how the team determines capacity a bit later in the chapter, but for now assume that the team has chosen their work for an iteration.

That doesn't mean that the customer isn't asking for more items to be accomplished, and it doesn't mean that the product owner doesn't have more stories on deck. What it *does* mean is that the team has chosen the amount of work that they can accomplish in that iteration only.

If, in fact, the team took on more work than they could handle, it would create a bottleneck in the process flow and demonstrate that they took more on than is feasible. It's like shoving too many clothes into the washer than it can handle, and the result is that nothing gets totally clean. Over time, it would reduce performance and may even break down. It's the same thing for a development team. The goal is maintaining a sustainable pace and creating a result that can be considered finished or deployable at the end of the iteration.

Making an overly confident estimate does happen occasionally, especially in the beginning of a project that is totally unique to the team or with a newer team that isn't used to estimating in an Agile way. In general, the team decides together how much and how many, and they get better at estimating as the iterations progress.

Fluctuating estimates are all taken into consideration when the team determines how many stories or what work they can accomplish in an iteration. The team also wants to limit work in progress (WIP) or set WIP limits so that too much work isn't pulled in at one time, which could create an overflow of work into the next iteration. That isn't very Agile.

In Scrum, the limits are set, and no new work can be pulled into a sprint until the next sprint is planned and it begins. In Kanban, when an item is completed and tested, more work can be pulled into the iteration in a continuous flow, but WIP limits are still present. No matter what framework or method is used, the goal is that the team will not be working on more than they can handle at any given time.

To keep the flow working, and allow time for testing the results at the same time, the team may develop tests in advance of the creation of the increment. The team knows that the increment or story result will fail initially, but once it passes the test, the increment is ready for review. This allows for a minimally marketable feature to be produced in each iteration. It's complete and it works. Once the increment passes a review of the stakeholder, customer, and end users, the process of selecting work begins again based on the product owner's updated backlog.

Keep in mind that stakeholders want lots of things, but the team decides how many things they can work on at once. The product owner transparently communicates the backlog to the development team so that they understand the vision and can select priority work accordingly.

It's easy to see that with many stakeholder requests coming into the queue or backlog at any given time, and the team selecting only the work that they can accomplish in any given iteration, the potential of a backlogged backlog is possible. If the backlog isn't managed effectively by the product owner, the team is probably delivering on value that is several months old, may have changed, or is no longer relevant.

To prevent that from happening, the product owner is working with the stakeholders and the team to reset and sort the backlog on a regular basis, as well as saying the all-important "no" when some items are requested that aren't relevant or truly important to the result. It's a balanced and Agile approach involving a lot of transparent communication.

Value and what makes it to the front of the backlog isn't determined based on the size of the story or work effort. This is a case of bigger not always meaning better. Some stories are large and cost a lot, and some stories are small and don't cost very much at all. Value isn't determined by size and cost; it's determined based on choosing work that creates a workable feature in each iteration and how it applies to the overall increment that is being produced. Remember, value is viewed differently from all positions on the project.

Think about something that you use every single day that has a cool feature that you never use. That feature probably cost a lot of time and money to make, but it isn't valuable in the day-to-day life of the end user—you.

I know that I have tons of features on my smartphone that I have used once or not at all. The compass is a good example of that, and I only know this because I read an article about cool features that you never use. The next time I get lost in the woods maybe I'll use it, provided I don't have a signal to call the ranger, then the compass feature is rendered mute once again. I walk around life directionally challenged just fine, thank you, and never even think about a compass. I pretty much can't live without my fantasy football app, on the other hand, from August to January.

Tons of features are produced that don't provide value to end users. There may very well be one of you reading this who is thinking, "I use the compass on my phone all the time, and I could care less about fantasy football." Value is different to different people. The product owner's job is a difficult one because they have to figure out what stories come first as a must-have, and the team's job is to select from that list what they can accomplish in any given iteration or sprint. Then they must create it, test it, and demo it for acceptance.

Agile Project Manager

The Agile project manager's job in all of this is to help the product owner (as needed) sort the key features and functions that go to the top of the list, help the team determine what work they can accomplish, and perpetuate the vision. You help facilitate events that contribute to effective results as well as providing transparent communication to stakeholders about the processes being used. You are the support mechanism for the entire show.

I was watching a documentary on a famous band and how they created one of the biggest speaker setups that any band had ever had at the time. The system was also very technologically advanced for the early '70s. They called it the Wall of Sound! The person who created it dealt with very specific technical problems, like how to prevent reverb by using two microphones stacked together and how to set it up so that anyone could hear live music a mile away. He and his group were the development team. They had to determine how to put together something very technologically difficult, work around issues, and deliver what it was that the band wanted. They also had to do a lot of testing to get it right, and when it was done it was like nothing anyone had ever seen or heard before.

The band was the product owner. They explained what they most wanted from the system and how they wanted it to look and sound. They provided the list of what they needed by importance, and the development team created it.

The band manager who oversaw the setup in each location, brought water to the band, and helped with sound checks was the Agile project manager. You keep it all together and help where needed while at the same time maintaining the vision for your team. That is how the music happens.

> I don't feel that one instrument has more weight than others. Any sound
> that you can produce adds to your vocabulary of possibilities.
>
> *Jerry Garcia*

Timeboxing

In Chapter 2, "Scrum and eXtreme Programming (XP)," you learned about different timeboxed events, which are standard in the Scrum and XP frameworks. For example, in Scrum a sprint is timeboxed anywhere from a month or less, and in XP the iterations are usually timeboxed for two weeks. Sprint planning meetings can be timeboxed for eight hours for long sprints or less for shorter ones. That eight hours may be split up as an hour a week, or four hours upfront depending on your team and your process. Typically, you plan for two hours multiplied by the number of weeks of you sprint. Two weeks would be four hours and so on.

The great thing about timeboxes is that they allow the team to know for sure how long things will take and that helps with planning. Timeboxing is important at this point because you will begin sprint/iteration planning, and much of what the team does during the timebox of four hours is to determine what work needs to be done and what work will be done.

Other important timeboxes include daily stand-up meetings for 15 minutes and timeboxing reviews of the increment to no more than four hours per one-month sprint or iteration. The retrospective is timeboxed to no more than four hours for a one-month sprint or less for shorter sprints.

It will be up to the Agile project manager to keep things inside the timebox and to focus everyone on the reasons the events are occurring. Newer teams may find it difficult to get into the groove of planning and reviewing this way, especially in the beginning. If they are anything like my team, they will get it sooner instead of later and prefer it to too many meetings, unknown expectations, and work being dictated rather than discussed.

Timeboxed events are very different from scheduled durations of activities in a Waterfall environment. In Waterfall, scope of work is fixed and the time and money adapt around it. In Agile, time and money are typically fixed and you work the scope around those constraints.

In Figure 6.1, you can see how keeping the timeboxes static and the work flexible allows the team to organize around the work they select to accomplish. It may sound like a lot of time is dedicated to planning, reviewing and reflecting, but if you think about how many hours you sit in meetings every week and nothing gets accomplished, you can see that dedicating a specific amount of time for very specific reasons lets everyone know it's time to get down to business.

FIGURE 6.1   The generic timeboxes of an Agile life cycle

Sunday	Monday	Tuesday	Wednesday	Thursday	Friday	Saturday
	Iteration Planning 8 Hours	Stand-up 15 mins	Stand-up 15 mins	Stand-up 15 mins	Stand-up 15 mins	
	Stand-up 15 mins	Stand-up 15 mins	Stand-up 15 mins	Stand-up 15 mins	Stand-up 15 mins	
	Stand-up 15 mins	Stand-up 15 mins	Stand-up 15 mins	Stand-up 15 mins	Stand-up 15 mins	
	Stand-up 15 mins	Stand-up 15 mins	Stand-up 15 mins	Stand-up 15 mins	Stand-up 15 mins	
					Review 4 Hours	
					Retrospective 3 Hours	

Themes, Epics, and User Stories

No matter what types of projects you work on, they always start with a projected deliverable and some idea of what the result will be. Even in Agile, when the team is aware that the backlog can and will be adjusted and that the result you thought you would create could inevitably change, there is still planning that must be done. In Waterfall project management, you always start with big deliverables and decompose them down to a level where you can most accurately begin to estimate time, money, and resources to build the scope of work. In Agile, it is a similar concept, except instead of a *work breakdown structure (WBS)*, the use of themes, epics, and user stories are applied to help determine the what and how of the iteration's work.

There is a common misnomer that Agile teams don't plan, and that is simply not the case. Agile teams plan at the *last responsible moment* and *elaborate progressively* when new work is prioritized in the backlog. The product owner communicates with the team to explain the work and also to review upcoming work. This helps the team better understand the work for improved estimation. It also allows for communication with stakeholders/customers to review and add new requirements to the backlog.

While the team and other stakeholders can contribute to the backlog information, the product owner is in charge and responsible for making sure the backlog is organized and understood by the team and other stakeholders.

Themes

> I can't make a movie unless I believe in the themes behind it. I mean, the first question I ask myself, always, is, "What is this movie about?"
>
> *Jake Gyllenhaal*

In any Waterfall project I have ever worked on, a theme has always been present—I just didn't always realize it at the time. It was sometimes difficult to see the forest through the trees until we were knee deep in it.

In Agile project management, you seek the connections and the theme as much as possible because it helps to drive the vision and provide a shared understanding of the overarching goal. This doesn't always mean that it's present or identifiable right away, but seeking patterns in the deliverables and grouping them together provides the big picture.

It's similar to reading movie reviews. They don't give away all of the spoilers, but you get the gist of what the movie is about and then you can decide if you want to see it or not.

A *theme* in Agile is basically just a collection of user stories or requirements with shared attributes that will allow for grouping of like with like but can't be produced in one single iteration. Those themes are too large to produce specific features in one sprint or iteration.

It reminds me a lot of a WBS where you break deliverables down to the work package level. Remember the jigsaw puzzle box and sorting all of the pieces by color or corner? That is what themes represent. Getting organized.

Theme Example

An example of a theme could be the grouping of "requirements" that may have the same function with different elements. If the customer says that they want to develop a website that would enable the user to upload their music by category, that upload becomes the theme.

Music Page: As a music lover, I want to be able to upload all of my music and sort rock music into a Rock category.

Music Page: As a music lover, I want to be able to upload all of my music and sort alternative music into an Alternative category.

The theme is presented with a similar context: uploading music. The theme is that each music upload can be sorted by category. Without the categories and the breaking out of each upload type, there is too much information to effectively understand what the requirements are.

Think about it this way: If you were to go through all of your CDs (if you still have any!) and organize them by artist or by music type, you are developing a theme in your collection. It is easy to see the big picture. Here are all the blues CDs, here are all the rock CDs, and so on.

If someone asked me to explain all of blues music in a short overview, I would have to stick to a theme to answer that question and then break it down from there. It's a vast topic with many stories included. Grouping each one of the genres by theme allows you to see the 50-thousand-foot overview to which each story or artist contributes.

Another aspect of themes is that you don't necessarily need to work on each one in order. I could start with one blues artist and randomly select others. I don't need to listen to them in chronological order unless I want to, or if there is a good reason to do so.

Epics, on the other hand, are a way of taking a potentially vague or large user story and getting to the point where you can clarify much more specifically.

Epics

The easiest way to describe an *epic* would be a large, vague user story that includes information that needs to be clarified. This is typical in the beginning of a project where you have several large epics that need more clarification and usually can't be completed in one iteration.

Epics need to be broken down into several stories before being worked on. It will take effort on the team's part to uncover the various user stories and truly see what the work will be.

You might be thinking that themes and epics seem very similar and you would be correct. Epics differ from themes because most of the stories in an epic are related to specific business value, and they should be broken down and done in the order necessary to produce that value. Stories that are part of a theme can be done in any order and produce value independently. It may take many iterations to complete the stories in the epic, but until all of the stories are completed, business value cannot be achieved.

It's also important for the team to be able to estimate effectively, and an epic is too large to estimate. Because there are so many stories in one epic, it makes for a slow moving Post-it note across the task/Scrum/Kanban board. The epic will just sit there until all the stories are completed. The goal is to *be* Agile and move work though process flow. Using a static task board, it's difficult for the team to truly see the user stories without some kind of decomposition of the scope of work to the story level. Furthermore, in many cases it is a demotivator, since nothing is moving through the swim lanes with any kind of regularity.

Epic Example

As a lover of music, I want a website that allows me to access all of my music, upload multiple formats, and open it up to the public as a paid service so that they can upload and access their purchased music on the cloud wherever they are in the world.

The epic example may seem pretty innocuous and make perfect sense to you right now. All of us are constantly accessing music sites, storing our music on the cloud or a variety of websites. What's the big issue with an epic?

Imagine if someone asked you to build the site and you had never done it before. I guess you would need more information and clarification on the ins and outs of such a project. The epic itself may represent final business value, but until you can achieve the epic's result, that value will not be realized.

Requirements versus Epics

Many times, students in my classes will ask me about the differences between requirements and epics. Because the project management arena in general revolves around the *must do* features, it seems a logical time to bring up the differences.

Requirement   Create marketing materials for a web campaign.

Epic   As a marketing manager, I need to develop an interactive web campaign to drive sales so that customers know of new products.

Both represent something that you would need to break down further in order to accomplish. Both have numerous tasks that need to be done to provide the result, and both may be something about which the customer has no flexibility. The difference is that you can understand why the result is necessary because of the epic.

 Real World Scenario

What Do They Want? What Are They Interested In? What Do They Need?

When I was running sales teams (in another lifetime), one of the major tenets of our philosophy was that when selling, always do your best to determine their wants, interests, and needs; that is, the customer's "WIN." I always remember this when I'm in a planning meeting and attempting to determine what success actually looks like in any given iteration. Even though it is obvious that an epic is too large to manage in its current state, it helps to determine the end user's list of must-haves, should-haves, and won't-haves. As an Agile project manager, it's our job to perpetuate the vision, and epics allow us to do that. Epics also give us a springboard into the actual user stories that we would accomplish.

The original definition of epic began as a descriptor of long poems that were narrated as a way to show achievement and heroic feats of success. It makes sense, then, that in Agile we would take a large epic story that describes success and break it down into smaller stories that allow us to attain the success described.

User Stories

> Fast is fine but accuracy is everything.
>
> *Wyatt Earp*

User stories are the result of a well-refined backlog, transparent communication, and the understanding of what it is the team is going to create. Epics and themes are too large to accomplish or truly understand at their core, so the team will have to work together and be realistic and goal-oriented as they generate the user stories.

The team, coach, and product owner work together to clarify requirements and understand the user stories. User stories were designed in the eXtreme Programming (XP) process and are used by multiple Agile methodologies to determine when a team has accomplished a usable increment.

User stories describe the end users and what they want. The team will use the stories to determine how much they can accomplish in an iteration. Some stories are larger than others, but if the team understands them enough to produce something that can be reviewed, tested, and deployed after every iteration, then the user story was effective.

You covered a high-level overview of two best practices for user stories. In "Chapter 2: Scrum and eXtreme Programming (XP)," the INVEST acronym that helps make sure user stories is independent, negotiable, valuable, estimable, small, and testable. Ron Jeffries's three Cs method of developing user stories with a card, conversation, and confirmation were mentioned in "Chapter 4: Agile Initiation and Stakeholder Engagement." Both concepts are utilized as best practices in the development of comprehensive user stories.

There are many ways to create effective user stories, and in many cases, it is more of an art form than a science. If you have designed into your best practices a creative and interactive way of optimizing work flow and are regularly engaging your stakeholders in the design process, how you develop your user stories may fluctuate until you have a good system in place that works for your team.

 You will be tested on your ability to identify good user stories based on best practices on the PMI-ACP® exam. Typically, they will be in the following format:

As _____ I need/want _____ so that I can _____.

User stories are a collaborative way of communicating and gaining valuable insights into the requirements and needs of the end users and breaking them down to a level of the best understanding of priority. Once that occurs, then user stories are reviewed based on current priority, and once the priority is determined, the team will decide what they can accomplish in the iteration.

High Priority

- Will be worked on first
- Could be main functions or features to be built

Medium Priority

- Worked on later depending on the dynamics of the backlog and changes
- Will move up in priority

Lowest Priority

- May not ever be built
- Will always be replaced with higher-priority items as they are determined by the product owner

The creation of user stories from themes or epics involves a lot of communication. The team will make decisions based on the information they have *today* and make those decisions often.

User Story Workshops

The goal of a user story workshop is to brainstorm collaboratively as a team and to allow for effective decision making. User stories don't just suddenly occur either: Remember, you are working with epics and themes, and you want to get to the point where you have a story or stories that you can not only estimate but actually produce during the iteration.

It takes some work and creativity to elaborate on the work progressively and write as many stories as possible. Remember, the product owner is usually in charge of writing stories, but the development team produces the increment. Thus, user story workshops are a collaborative effort to gain information and have a plan for execution. In this respect, the entire team attends the workshops and may also invite other stakeholders to get clarification and discuss the work.

Typically, user story workshops occur more in the beginning of a project when many are unclear on the true scope of work outside of a charter description. However, I've seen workshops held during backlog refinement/grooming or during iteration planning meetings.

To be truly Agile, it's important for the team to know what it is they are trying to create, and without that clarification they may not produce the right thing or the thing right. It's up to you and your team what works best. Many teams new to Agile frameworks may find this type of collaborative communication to be highly effective for estimation efforts and acceptance of the increment.

The workshop may not initially involve prioritization or order, but order and priority can be discussed. Epics will be broken down to the user story level, and then the bigger picture becomes more focused on the work that needs to be done.

In Figure 6.2, it's easy to see that one epic can generate many questions that need answers. Once those answers are discussed and determined, then an effective user story can be created. Details are needed and questions will be answered so that the team has enough information to know when they have achieved what they set out to do and what types of testing will be done to prove that the increment functions correctly. Details are then added to the user stories to help determine the tests needed for completion.

FIGURE 6.2   From epics to user stories

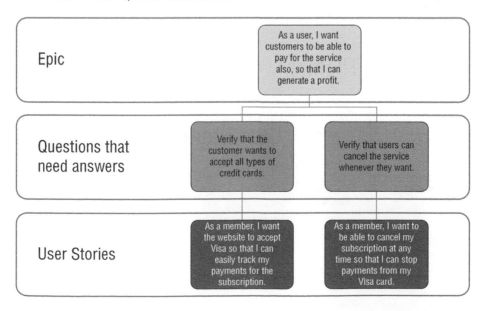

User Stories versus Requirements

Why are user stories so effective? Because if I tell you a story, you are more likely to remember it than if I give you a list of the main points. Stories are easier to understand than a list of requirements. User stories encourage communication and clarify questions to be asked and answered. User stories also make estimating easier for the team because it helps to determine how much work it will take to accomplish the user story based on the definition of done.

I know that there have been many Waterfall projects where I was given a long list of requirements in no particular order and found myself faced with a gigantic puzzle that I needed to sequence correctly. I often tell my classes that requirement sequencing in software is my nemesis. It is my least favorite and the most stressful aspect of my job. Some people love it and some people don't. I'm in the "don't" category! Why? It's difficult to understand the reason why certain requirements come first or second, and if sequenced incorrectly, you have wasted time, money, and resources.

With user stories, the puzzle is already put together in the form of epics or themes, and the user stories are the chapters that are needed to finish the book. Lists of requirements may not provide enough information or may cause confusion; therefore, user stories are a better way to communicate and determine what is necessary to assure the successful conclusion of an iteration.

In Figure 6.3, it's easy to see the progression from a large epic broken down to the user story level. This is why it is important to have open and transparent communication. Even though the product owner owns the backlog, they also work with the team to define the backlog to the point where the team can select which stories they will work on in the iteration and understand them enough to produce the increment.

FIGURE 6.3   Epics, themes, and user stories

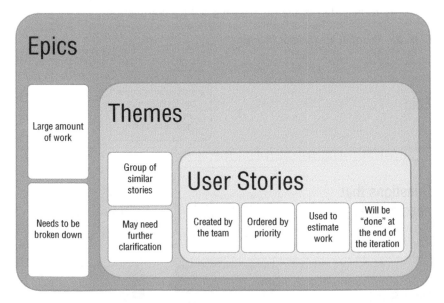

Personas

Personas help the team understand the end users or customers in a way that keeps the focus on the customer needs while bringing a personal aspect to the user.

The team will work to create a persona for their end users/customers and build it around a real person or create a descriptive placeholder or character for the customer.

 Real World Scenario

Carol's Persona

Carol is a very busy marketing professional who works on a lot of projects to promote her business. Lately, there has been a slump in the marketing campaigns to promote new products, and customers are not responding to it well.

Carol needs to create a web-based interactive media blitz. Carol wants something slick with video and audio capabilities and with easy navigation for new customers. She also wants to use it as a template for future campaigns.

Carol has come to you to develop her page since she has seen examples of web-based development that you created for other customers.

Carol has an idea as to how she wants the page to look, and she will be a part of initial brainstorming and wireframe creation.

It is amazing how much the team can better understand why we are building what we are building when using personas. It allows for immediate, personalized understanding. Even if you aren't in marketing, you can see Carol's point of view through the eyes of the user and not just the creator. I like to keep personas posted somewhere front and center so that my team doesn't lose track of the people behind the reason for the product.

Wireframes

You might have noticed that this entire chapter is dedicated to understanding what you are building, why you are building it, and for whom. It's always great when a team knows exactly what they are doing and a customer understands the ins and outs of your process. What happens, though, when the end user has no idea what goes into building a website or software program, or even mass-producing a car that they want to drive? Then it will become necessary to show them what they are getting. Much as stories are easier to remember than a list of requirements, visuals of the result are easier to explain and understand as well.

Wireframes are an excellent way to produce a low-fidelity prototype in a short amount of time. In Chapter 4, you went through the basics of wireframes, but now is a good time to address how wireframes may be relevant to your planning process. The end user/customer may see the wireframe plotted out and decide that a web page button should go elsewhere, or even point out a feature that is no longer considered valuable. Most of the time, your product owner will promptly get a new list of wants, needs, and interests after the end user/customer views a wireframe.

A wireframe allows a better focus on the definition of "done," even when the entire project involves a moving target.

Backlog Refinement

Backlog refinement, or what is sometimes called *backlog grooming*, is the process of addressing all of the different requirements that are currently known and then prioritizing them so that everything at the front of the line and top of the backlog are prioritized stories ready to be pulled into an iteration by the team once they decide on the amount of work they can handle. The result can then be ready for delivery at the end of the iteration.

The product owner is inevitably responsible for the refinement of the backlog, and the rest of the team and the organization respect their decision on prioritization.

Refining the backlog isn't a one-time occurrence—it is an ongoing process. Depending on your organization or chosen framework, there may be timeboxed activities designed to help the product owner refine the backlog items, or the product owner may just make time daily or weekly to keep on top of the backlog items.

A lot of refining/grooming is exactly what it sounds like. Out with the old, and in with the new! User stories that are no longer relevant or necessary will be removed from the backlog, and new stories will be created when new requests are made.

It's also part of refinement when user stories that are high priority but too large to fit in one iteration are split into smaller stories. This is usually referred to as taking something that is course-grained and making it fine-grained. It's a lot like using a salt grinder. Large kernels of salt would be too big to enjoy on your food, so you grind them down to finer-grained salt and it works for your meal. Many fine-grained particles of salt make up one big kernel. The same thing goes for user stories.

Refining the backlog takes review, prioritization, and decomposition from large down to small. A large part of having a refined or groomed backlog is that the development team will use the backlog to estimate user story sizes and determine how many they can do in each iteration. It also is relevant to mention that sometimes the initial estimates are off and need to be reestimated once new information is present.

The backlog is a living, breathing thing. It will always include a variety of user stories that are of assorted sizes or scope, and the product owner will prioritize the most important user stories. The team will determine how much and what work they will do in the iteration. We will cover how the team selects the work a bit later in this chapter, but as an overview, the work is sized and the team determines how many user stories they can produce based on the size of work.

The levels of value provided during each iteration will bring the result closer to being able to predict when certain items will be completed. It is difficult, however, to predict a schedule end date when you don't completely know what you are creating in the beginning. Moreover, it is impossible to predict a schedule since change is expected, plus users review each increment and always want extra things added to the backlog. This is why the definition of done is so important. It helps the product owner prioritize, the team select work to accomplish value, and everyone to understand what being finished or done looks like.

Most of the time, you will hear Agile teams say that the backlog is never complete. That is a true statement. This doesn't mean that you won't finish your project; it means that the backlog evolves as the product evolves. As long as the product is still in existence, then so too is the backlog—mostly because when a product is released, the organization gains feedback from customers, end users, and the market. This could drive updates or bug fixes to get pushed out, or even new features to be created.

 Real World Scenario

A Living Backlog

A good way to imagine a living, breathing backlog is to think of Office 365, which is the cloud-based version of Microsoft Office. Every other month or so, a new feature is added to Word, Excel, Outlook, PowerPoint, and the rest of the Office system of products. You don't have to wait until a whole new version comes out anymore; it simply updates when your computer updates, or when Microsoft pushes out the new features.

The backlog for Office 365 is never complete, not as long as new features can be pushed out and bugs can be fixed. That backlog won't be completed until they retire Microsoft Office totally and replace it with something else.

When Microsoft Office went from the 2003 to the 2007 version, the world stopped turning a bit when nobody could find the drop-down menus and were now staring at something called a "ribbon"! Office 2003's backlog is now extinct and Office 2007's was going full force at that point.

Definition of Done

Without knowing the stakeholder's definition of done, it would be impossible to determine when the project is finished. Having a comprehensive definition of done allows the team to focus on the main items needed to produce a working, viable product or service that is considered done-done at a certain point.

The *definition of done* can be seen in a lot of Agile projects in acronym form as *DoD*. No matter how it is represented the definition of done is the team's responsibility. Just as the product owner owns the backlog, the development team determines the definition of done. Not to say that the team won't accept feedback that the software is slow or buggy, or that it needs tweaking somehow. They will accept this feedback, and it may create a shift in direction. Either way, the product owner owns value and the development team owns quality, meaning that they produce it, test it, and present it for acceptance. The development team needs to know what the result will be and when they can call something done-done.

The definition of done is created by the team based on several variables, and one thing that they consider is the overuse of the word *done*. Think of it this way: When is an epic done? When is a user story done? The team has to determine what done actually looks like. For the sake of simplicity, done usually means that the product has passed acceptance tests, has been approved during an iteration review, and/or is deployable.

The team may put together a checklist for themselves that describes when done means finished, from creation of the increment all the way through its testing. The goal is to remove confusion and to know what the end game is.

Think about the last time you were lost in the car without GPS and how confusing it was not to reach your destination in a timely manner. You know that feeling. You are lost somewhere strange. Maybe you stop to ask directions along the way, and the person you ask says things like go east. East? You mean left? That would probably be another good time to bring out the little-used compass app that I mentioned before. It's confusing being lost, and it is also confusing not knowing where you are going.

Having a distinct definition of done, a comprehensive checklist that says go this way and then that way and run this test to make sure that it is correct is the best compass for a development team. It's also helpful to have a map as well as a compass, and story mapping is something that provides a visual plotting out of all of the roads to take to done.

Story Mapping

Why does anyone use a map? They use it to determine the best path to follow to reach a destination. On some road trips, there are priority stopping-off points, like major monuments or scenic overlooks, and then lower-priority stop-offs, like the largest ball of twine, the Hollywood sign, or South of the Border. All make up your trip, but without mapping it out you don't know how to get there and you don't know which is most important and in what order you will see them.

Think about software features that you use every single day and find valuable. Hello spell check! Imagine if the spell check button were there taunting you but it didn't actually work. That could happen because spell check was considered a high value or high priority item but the inner workings of the code to launch it might have been overlooked or put lower in value. Mapping allows you to place items in a map or order them by priority and then look to see if anything got missed. *Story maps* are also sometimes called a *walking skeleton*, which is also an apt description of what we are doing.

You can see in Figure 6.4 that themes are placed at the top, epics come under the theme that they belong to, beneath that are features, and then user stories come under features.

FIGURE 6.4 Story mapping

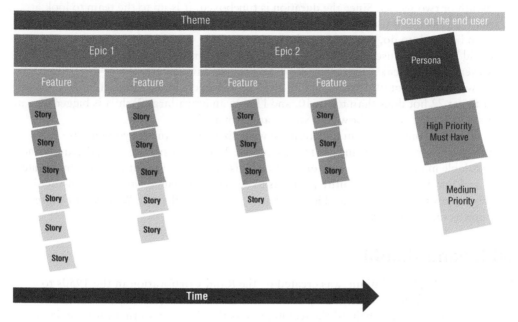

Typically, higher-value user stories will be represented in a distinct color code from the others, but that is totally up to your team. I also like to put the persona on the map as well, in order to help us focus on the end user and remember why it is we are doing this project in the first place. This allows the team to plot their course based on the definition of done, the priority of user stories, and the ability to produce an epic over time.

As with most best practices in Agile, the way that you do a story map isn't necessarily the most important thing—doing the story map is. For example, some maps use headers like Goals ➤ Activities ➤ Tasks ➤ Stories as the decomposition of the map. How you determine your headers and your format can be unique to your organizational influences and culture, but as with everything in Agile, the simpler the better. The goal is agility, not a ton of documentation for the sake of having it.

Relative Sizing

I just read an article today about the Nathan's annual hot dog eating contest in Coney Island, New York, and the winner ate 72 hot dogs in 10 minutes! That's not only totally insane, but it got me thinking about how to explain relative sizing.

If I asked you, "How long would it take you to eat 72 hot dogs?" you might not be able to answer that question because only one person in the world has done it in 10 minutes. But what would your answer be if instead I said, "Which would take longer to eat, 72 hot dogs or 10 hot dogs?" You would most definitely say that it would take longer to eat 72 than 10. Welcome to relative sizing!

Planning iterations involves determining how much work can be done in a timebox of one month or two weeks. Since the duration is timeboxed, it is up to the team to look at a variety of prioritized user stories and determine how many can be done in one iteration. That can be tough to do, especially in the beginning.

I could look at one user story and say that it will for sure take longer than another, and I may even have to break a user story down to a couple days' worth of work to truly get an idea of what it may entail. I know that an elephant is bigger than a kitten, I know it takes longer to eat 72 hot dogs than to eat 10, and I know an extra-large T-shirt is bigger than an extra-small T-shirt. That is how user stories are estimated.

It's up to you and your team to determine what sizing mechanisms you will use to describe your user stories. Some use fruit, some use T-shirts, some use animals, and some use a scalable model of points from one to five. This all makes estimating much more interesting and fun. However, the entire team has to determine what constitutes extra-small and what constitutes extra-large. That is where something called the *Wideband Delphi* technique comes into play.

Wideband Delphi

The original Delphi technique was created by the Rand Corporation in the 1950s to 1960s. This technique was originally created as a way to do organizational facilitated forecasting. The thought behind the technique was that it assumes that group judgments are more valid than individual ones. The Delphi technique was used as a way to promote group consensus without groupthink.

Groupthink is what happens when the stronger personalities within a group lead the charge and the rest of the group just goes along with it.

The Wideband Delphi technique took things to a wider thought process and embraced collaboration to reach consensus rather than individuals giving their opinions and having a facilitator collate the results. Many Agile teams use a variety of Wideband Delphi techniques to determine story sizes or story points. The most popular among them is *planning poker*, which we will cover a bit later in the chapter.

The Fibonacci Sequence

I'm kind of a nerd when it comes to history, and so I always think it is relevant to tell a story about the background of a concept that you may very well use for every iteration. I also know that when you tell a story, people remember better than when you give them a bulleted list of points. With that thought in mind, here is a story about the *Fibonacci sequence* as we know it today. The Fibonacci sequence is credited for being brought to light in 1202, but prior to that the first inkling of what the Fibonacci sequence would become emerged in India in 200 BC, relating to Sanskrit and what was called *prosody*. In the simplest of terms, prosody is discerning patterns of sound and rhythms in poetry.

The Fibonacci sequence represents patterns in nature, and nature is exactly how an Italian mathematician Leonardo of Pisa, known as Fibonacci, applied the theory. *Fibonacci* is loosely translated to mean son of the Bonacci, and he is sometimes referred to as Leonardo Bonacci or Leonardo of Pisa. Fibonacci's father was a wealthy merchant in Italy who frequently brought Fibonacci with him on his travels. It was in the country of what is now known as Algeria that Fibonacci learned about the Hindu/Arabic numbering system, as he spent much of his time on those trips meeting with merchants and learning about mathematics. In 1202, Fibonacci introduced the numbering system in his book *Liber Abaci* after studying the overpopulation of rabbits. (Yes rabbits!)

Today, the Fibonacci sequence is known as the numbering system in nature, and without it being known at the time, the Fibonacci sequence is relatable to the golden ratio, or Phi. I can't confirm or deny whether the plants are aware of the sequence or golden ratio, or if it is just that they grow according to the most efficient way to do so. Either way, it's fascinating and efficient.

The Fibonacci sequence itself is 0, 1, 1, 2, 3, 5, 8, 13, 21, 34, 55, and so on until infinity. Each number is the sum of the preceding two numbers.

For the mathematically challenged (like myself) 0+1=1, 1+1=2, 2+3=5, and so on.

You might be asking yourself, what in the heck does this all have to do with Agile (and why would I need help with such basic math)? Good questions! Story point estimates using a type of Wideband Delphi technique, like planning poker, use the Fibonacci sequence to apply story points to user stories.

Planning Poker

You've got to know when to hold 'em Know when to fold 'em

Know when to walk away, know when to run.

You never count your money when you're sittin' at the table

There'll be time enough for countin' when the dealin's done.

The Gambler by Kenny Rogers

 Real World Scenario

Planning Poker

Planning Poker® was originally created by James Grenning in 2002, and it was brought into mainstream Agile best practices by Mike Cohn, who contributed to the development of the Scrum framework and is one of the founders of the *Scrum Alliance*. Cohn, whose company, Mountain Goat Software, trademarked the term *Planning Poker*, has many great references for you if this is something that you have never done before and are looking for ways to implement it on your next project.

If you play poker, you know that you hold your cards very close to your chest and you don't give the other players the satisfaction of seeing your facial features, which can *tell* them what you have in your hands. I've never seen professional poker players sit around and discuss why they decided to call, fold, or choose certain cards. This is where the line between actual poker and *Planning Poker* diverge. The entire goal is to get an idea of what people think and then discuss it until a consensus or majority is reached.

You got a bit of a history lesson on the Fibonacci sequence, and now you can use that sequence to assess story points. I know 55 is larger than 3, and I know that 1 is smaller than 13.

Now the team will get together and start assessing the user stories and applying a bit of a game and relative sizing using the Fibonacci sequence as its guide.

In Figure 6.5, you will see the cards represented with the Fibonacci sequence on them, and each player will have a full deck as pictured. Now the team can start looking at the work and determining how to assess it. There are several ways in which the cards can be numbered. I prefer the infinity symbol representing an inability to estimate, or something that is too large to adequately estimate and may have to be broken down further before estimation can occur. Some teams prefer to go higher than 55 on their decks. It's up to you and your team to determine what works best.

FIGURE 6.5   Planning poker cards

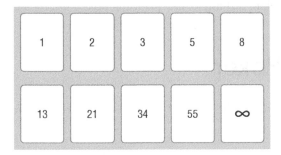

Planning Poker Best Practices

The goal of planning poker is to determine the relative sizes of development work in the form of user stories and use that information to plan for the amount of work that can be done in a given iteration.

There are several schools of thought on how and when planning poker is played. Some teams will spend time on the front end working with the product owner after a user story workshop. Everything is fresh in everyone's minds, and it allows for discussion and clarification as well as contributing to the product owner's job of prioritizing the backlog.

Other best practices or suggestions are also to play planning poker once an iteration/ sprint and plan out everything all at the same time. Typically, you would play during or directly after a backlog refinement/grooming meeting (since the entire team attended those meetings) but before the iteration/sprint planning meeting. Again, you and your team will have to find your groove. Keep in mind that the goal isn't to spend as much time as possible planning—that isn't very Agile.

There is going to be a fine balance between playing too early and playing too late. Too early won't work because things are bound to change in priority or value, and all the work you did would be nearly a waste of time. Depending on the situation, it may not be a total waste of time because some things won't change, or it saves you time later if a priority is pushed back a bit. In the grand scheme of things, however, those unusable hours will add up. If it is done too late in the process, like during an iteration/sprint planning meeting, it's almost too late for the product owner to shift priorities for the upcoming work.

Some teams prefer to do four big workshops a year and knock out as many backlog items as they can in that meeting and then run one workshop each iteration. It depends on what type of framework you are using. If you have a tailored or a hybrid method, it will be up to the best practices you choose to implement.

The beauty of a Wideband Delphi approach like Planning Poker is that it is zero focused on the work—it forces collaboration and communication in a fun way, and it allows the team to get their heads wrapped around upcoming work. As with any game, though, there are some rules and best practices to help make it the most effective that it can be.

1. **Have a moderator:** The moderator can be the Agile project manager, and typically that is the best choice since you want the entire team playing and discussing the work. The moderator can also be the product owner so that they can explain the stories and provide clarification to the team. It depends on the team's need for additional information whether the product owner attends. In general, if the team doesn't understand the work or needs technical questions answered or clarification, it is the product owner who needs to provide that to the team. Whoever you decide should moderate, their job is to facilitate the discussions to make sure that everyone is involved in the process, reads the stories, and keeps groupthink from occurring, but the moderator should not contribute to the estimations. The moderator is there for facilitation only.

2. **Have a timer:** Typically, a two-minute timer is used to allow for discussion before the cards are laid out with each person's choice of story points. It can always be restarted after a vote if more discussion is needed. The main goal is to avoid analysis-paralysis and spending too much time in discussion on one single item.

3. **Have a full deck of cards:** Each team member will have a full deck of cards. Each player will hear the story from the moderator, ask questions for clarification, and then each will make their estimate. It's important that all of the cards selected are placed face down and then flipped over at the same time and that nothing is said out loud. If I said I think this is a five out loud, I might inadvertently convince someone that I'm correct. This is called *anchoring*, and it works great in negotiations but this process doesn't benefit from convincing—it benefits from discussion.

4. **Have the big reveal:** Once everyone has flipped their cards over, you may see a variation of results. It's statistically unlikely that everyone will select the same number, especially in the beginning. The person with the highest and lowest estimates will explain the thought process behind their choice. Sometimes one person recognizes technical complexity that the others didn't see or know about before, so that would

be explained. The low score may very well be too optimistic for the rest of the team to accept comfortably. Once the moderated, timed discussion is completed, the team votes again until consensus is reached. If the team can't agree and you've reached that analysis-paralysis point in the conversation, it's best to go with the pessimistic vote. Don't worry, you'll get better at estimating as you go. It's not unusual to be more pessimistic in the beginning.

5. **Repeat:** It's important for the moderator to make sure that people aren't just estimating their own effort for the work but are seeing the well-rounded bigger picture as well as building other variables into the estimate. For example, it may be a score of five to do the work but no testing was built into the estimate. This is where more heads are better than one.

Even though time and calendars are front and center in our day-to-day work, it is easier to assess work based on relative sizing and honestly a lot more accurate than applying a duration to something. Trust me when I say that I've gone into projects sideways because customer estimates were too optimistic. The customer was estimating in what we call ideal time, meaning that in a perfect world without any distractions whatsoever, the work could be completed in that time frame. Uh. No. Not possible! This is a way of sizing the work, understanding the work, reaching consensus on the amount of work, and agreeing to be as realistic as possible.

Initial Velocity

When I think of the word *velocity*, other concepts come to mind, like speed, acceleration, and hurtling through space in a time machine. These concepts, however, are very different from one another. Without getting too much into the physics of velocity and scalar quantities, or addressing the time/space continuum, *velocity* is very simply defined as having a constant speed in a constant direction. Speed is how fast something is moving, and acceleration is gaining speed in a short time frame. So, what is the deal with velocity in Agile? It's important to note here that having a very good definition of velocity and how it applies to your projects is an important conversation. For most of us, velocity is basically how much work can we accomplish in a specific time period. How the amount of work is determined is by planning for a certain amount of story points to be calculated in any given iteration and then looking back when the iteration is over and figuring out what really got done.

Many people look at initial velocity as goal setting, and in a way, it is. It is closer to realistic goal setting for the future using past velocity as a guide. Velocity predictions aren't deadlines or milestones; these are ways to see progression and forecast future work. Initial velocity is the jumping-off point, and you can expect your team's velocity to fluctuate for several iterations and then plateau as your team gets better at estimates and is seeing the results of iteration work.

Velocity Example

As an example, let's say that your team went through several rounds of planning poker and determined the story points for several user stories. Then, in an iteration/sprint planning meeting, you determined that your team could accomplish 30 story points in the first one-month iteration. When that iteration is over, the team will look back and see what has been accomplished and how many points of work they actually completed.

In Agile, it is typically an all-or-nothing situation, meaning that you calculated 30 points and have a story that is incomplete and worth 10 story points. You don't get partial credit for that story. Looking back, the team would surmise that they got 20 story points completed and therefore the velocity is 20. During the next iteration, your team uses the last iteration's velocity and selects the stories. Maybe this time there was room for another 10 points that didn't get accomplished, and on it goes until things stabilize and your team has a better idea of what they can and will accomplish. This doesn't mean that it's a perfect science, but like anything else, the more you do it, the better you get.

Iteration/Sprint Calculations

Let's go with the assumption that your team selected five user stories worth 20 story points for your second iteration. This is based on your initial velocity from iteration one. The total number also incorporates testing, bug fixes, refactoring of code, and *tech debt*. While this offers no value to the current increment being delivered, it does provide value in the long run and keeps things from eventually adding up.

Tech Debt and Bug Fixes

In the simplest of terms for those of you who don't code software for a living, *tech debt* is what happens when a team creates software code that is the bare minimum needed to get things to work so that they can deploy it. Then, in later iterations, it is quantified and updated. Tech debt is created by choice to meet a deployment need. You will repay tech debt by refactoring code along the way; otherwise, the cost of rework would be too high, just as if you borrowed money from a bank. You would have the immediate gratification of spending the money, but the longer it takes you to pay off the loan, the more expensive it becomes due to increasing interest payments.

Bug fixes are not planned for, and they are needed to resolve glitches in the code that cause things to not work properly. Most of us would agree that if you see a bug in software that you're developing, you squash it immediately and absorb it as a part of developing testable, deployable code. If you don't spot it in the current iteration, you'll have to make time to fix it in a later iteration.

Both tech debt and bug fixes may have to be accounted for in story point estimates to keep the ship running straight. In both cases, value is provided but not immediately evident in a release at the end of an iteration/sprint.

As your team gets better at estimating the amount of points that they can achieve, they will have a better idea of how to answer the question of "How long will this project take?" In Figure 6.6, you will see how iteration forecasts work based on current velocity and a prediction of how many story points are left in the prioritized backlog.

FIGURE 6.6   How many iterations?

Backlog	Points	Backlog	Points	
Priority A	3 points	Priority A	3 points	Iteration 1 = 9 points
Priority B	6 points	Priority B	6 points	
Priority C	4 points	Priority C	4 points	Iteration 2 = 7 points + tech debt
Priority D	10 points	Priority E	3 points	
Priority E	3 points	Priority D	10 points	Iteration 3 = 10 points

Team Velocity = 10 points
Iterations = 3

You can see that prioritization plays a large role in when work is accomplished, and also in how the team is the one that says how much they can do. Many times, when a customer is asking for a certain amount of work to be done at a specified date, the team can look at the amount of work left and determine how much they *can* accomplish by that date rather than cramming more story points into an iteration to please a customer and in the end not getting everything done. It's better to say that you can get X amount of work completed by Y date. Then it will be up to the customer/product owner either to trim the tail and cut the scope of work when dealing with a set deadline or to ask if scope is more important than time and give a prediction of how long the current scope of work would take based on current velocity.

One more thing to consider with velocity calculations: If your team has accomplished four iterations and in the first iteration your team completed 10 story points, in the second iteration 12 story points, in the third 15 story points, and in the fourth 14 story points, how do you calculate future velocity effectively? You go with an average!

$$10 + 12 + 15 + 14 = 51 \text{ points}$$

$$51/4 = 12.75 \text{ points as an average}$$

In this case, your team can decide to bump that up to 13 points or bump it down to 12 points, since there isn't partial credit or partial points. That can be decided on a case-by-case basis, depending on the situation. If there is a lot of tech debt, it may be better to round down to 12 points because there is still the work involved to produce the increment. If there isn't a lot of tech debt, round up in order to knock it out more quickly. Again, it depends on the specific situation and how that decision is made. Either way, it gives you and your customers a good idea as to how long the project will take and how much prioritized work will be completed and reviewed at the end of the iteration/sprint.

You may see questions on your exams regarding the calculation of how many iterations it will take or in which order your team will perform the stories based on priority and velocity. Priority is always first and velocity second. If a priority story has 3 points and the next story has 10 and the third has 5 and your velocity is 10, then you perform the first and third story in iteration one and the second story in iteration two. The amount of points will allow you to calculate the amount of iterations.

Also remember that incomplete stories don't count. If you have one outlier activity that is 2 story points, and you have maxed out your points in the other iterations, then the last story will be 2 points' worth of work and buffered out with tech debt, bug fixes, refactoring, and so on.

Typically, velocity is represented in big visual charts or information radiators so that everyone knows at any time what it is. You will cover velocity tracking in greater depth in Chapter 7, "Effective Team Performance on Agile Projects," when the team is executing the work and tracking begins. At this point, the velocity chart is an overview of what it will become once work begins.

In Figure 6.7, it's very easy to see the progression across iterations. You will notice in your own charts the eventual plateau that happens about three to six iterations into a longer-term project. This will allow for more accuracy in your projections and forecasts as well help to determine the amount of story points your team can actually accomplish.

FIGURE 6.7   Velocity chart

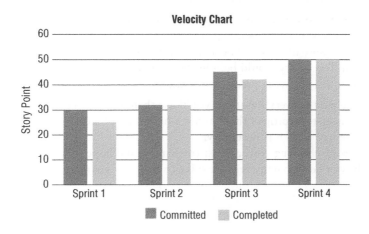

Story Point Estimates and Spikes

> We keep moving forward, opening new doors, and doing new things,
> because we're curious and curiosity keeps leading us down new paths.
> *Walt Disney*

On occasion, there are going to be stories that carry risk or some kind of technical problem that can't be solved in the moment, and it may be necessary to perform an *architectural spike.*

A spike was created within the eXtreme Programming (XP) framework as a way to solve a technical problem, reduce risk to the story, or help clarify a story that isn't able to be estimated or broken down further due to a lack of knowledge. The contributors to the XP concept of spikes explained a spike in terms of rock climbing and the necessity of hammering in spikes. Those spikes are used to move you higher and higher up the rock face while removing the risk of falling. The spike itself isn't actually climbing, but it is necessary to get to the top.

A spike may be requested by some of the members on the development team, and it would need to be approved, prioritized, and scheduled by the product owner just like any other story. The difference is that nothing will be produced from a spike other than attempting to solve the problem or walk away with a proof of concept or prototype of some kind. Taking the time to lower the risk and investigate the problem works better in the long run than producing something that doesn't work.

These are some best practices to keep in mind during a spike:

- The development team proposes the spike, and one or two developers will work on it. It is unnecessary to involve the entire team because they are working on other stories during the iteration/sprint.

- The product owner and the development team will work together to reach an agreement on the objectives of the spike and how much time should be dedicated to it.

- Typically, the spike is a timeboxed event lasting anywhere from four to eight hours at the extreme. If you still don't have a workable solution, you at least walk away with more information than you had before and can use it to reestimate the story.

- Spikes are not necessarily given story point estimates because the spike itself doesn't contribute to producing a workable product in this iteration but may contribute to one later. A spike is more like research time, but I've seen spikes included in an iteration's velocity much like a story would be. On the framework side of things, XP is less stringent than Scrum is in having precise estimations.

Spikes won't be part of every iteration; you'll use them maybe once or twice as you move forward with a longer-term project that carries a high level of technical intricacy or risk. It's worth the time to do it if it is necessary.

Sometimes in rock climbing you can just freehand it and hope that you don't fall; occasionally, though, you need to hammer in a spike to help you get the rest of the way up.

Summary

This chapter started with an overview of Iteration Zero and how some teams newer to Agile frameworks may find value in having a trial run. Iteration Zero may only last for a week, or it may take up an entire iteration. However, many view Iteration Zero as a type of initiation in a large, technically complex project. While an Iteration Zero is not necessary for every single project, it is a good thing to consider when and if your team decides to move forward with a specific Agile framework, or if your team is heavily steeped in Waterfall project management and needs a bit of a springboard or trial run at Agile best practices.

Next, we went through how business value is analyzed on the organizational level and how each team member views value. Value isn't always money, and it can mean very different things to very different people. How value is determined is based on a good understanding of the product backlog and what can be created in each iteration or sprint.

In the next section, we went through the concept of timeboxing as well as analyzing epics, features, and user stories to help determine value and to be able to map out the story of what it is you are going to create on the project. Walking skeletons, or story maps, help to focus the team on the result they are attempting to accomplish.

Next, we went through all of the ways that a team can determine the sizing of the work in the prioritized backlog. Relative sizing, planning poker, and effective iteration/sprint calculations allow for initial selection of stories that the team thinks they can accomplish, which will allow tracking of velocity and forecasting the future.

Finally, we wrapped up the chapter with some information on the need for a spike if the team finds that they have a high-risk story or one that is technically vague. A spike can be used to do research or create a workable solution to the problem that is occurring. Even if the solution is elusive, the team at least has more information than it did before the spike and can use it to move forward.

Exam Essentials

Be able to understand the concept of value.   Understand why it is important to see the different viewpoints of what is considered valuable and apply that to your planning. Value is more than just ROI, and it is important to understand that value drives the prioritization of the backlog, which will then drive the team's selection of work to accomplish.

Understand the concepts of epics, themes, and user stories.   Epics are large amounts of work that need to be broken down to a level where the team can work to create user stories that will be sorted based on priority in the backlog. Themes are groups of related stories that may still need further clarification. User stories are the result of working together to create the stories, ordering them by priority, and selecting the work to be achieved in an iteration/sprint.

Be able to understand the concepts of planning poker and relative sizing.   Having a good understanding of the processes a team might use to size work is not only important for the exam, it is also very important in your day-to-day work. Whether you use T-shirt sizes, fruit, or the Fibonacci sequence, the goal is still the same. Understand the user story, apply a sizing solution to it, and reach consensus. Practicing a Wideband Delphi technique is an excellent way to involve the team, transparently communicate, and have your self-directed team see the work that needs to be done and organize around it by selecting what can be accomplished (we think!) in each iteration/sprint.

Understand velocity estimates.   It makes sense that first estimates of any kind can and will be initially flawed until your team gets to the point where their velocity plateaus and the team has a better idea of how many user stories they can accomplish. The team will also need to accommodate tech debt, refactoring, and bug fixes after the first iteration begins, or to accommodate products that came before. Either way, be aware for the exam that you may be asked about calculating how many iterations/sprints it will take based on the current backlog and assumed velocity and that partial stories don't count as completed. You may be asked to sort stories based on priority and points to determine the order in which the team will perform the work.

Be aware that a spike may be necessary.   Spikes are designed to provide more information or a proof-of-concept approach. Many times, a spike is run by a couple of the development team members and those team members would need to gain approval by the product owner in advance of the team members performing the spike. There are spikes that are used specifically for risk mitigation efforts and others that are used to work through a technical conundrum. You will cover risk spikes in more depth in Chapter 9, "Detecting Problems and Working Through Changes."

Review Questions

You can find the answers to the review questions in Appendix B.

1. Which of the following best describes a team's velocity from the first iteration on?
   A. Velocity is based on the decomposition of activities and their sequence.
   B. Velocity varies in the first iterations, increases, and eventually plateaus.
   C. Velocity is determined by the product owner.
   D. Velocity is based on approved deliverables, milestones, scope, and resource management plans.

2. Your team has determined that there are 500 points of functionality left in the backlog to complete. The first four iterations' velocity has been tracked at

   22 points

   30 points

   39 points

   45 points

   Approximately, how many more iterations will it take to complete the project based on velocity?
   A. 15.1
   B. 25.7
   C. 14.7
   D. 13.6

3. Utilizing decision delays in an Agile environment allows teams to do all of the following, except _____.
   A. Mitigate risks
   B. Adapt to changes
   C. Implement based on the most up-to-date information
   D. Have "fine-grained requirements" until they can become "course-grained"

4. The concept of ideal time is _____.
   A. How long something will take with distractions
   B. What you put on your schedule for approval
   C. How long something will take without any distractions
   D. The total duration plus risk events

5. Which of the following represents a user story?

    A. As an end user, I want to be able to shop online.

    B. As a team member, I want to be able to see my progress.

    C. As an end user, I want to be able to review status reports daily so that I can track project performance.

    D. As a customer, I need to be able to use the software you create.

6. As a product owner, it is important to determine the priority of user stories that will be performed next. This is an example of which one of the following?

    A. Backlog sorting

    B. Retrospective

    C. Sprint review

    D. Backlog grooming

7. Decomposition of requirements could best be described by which of the following?

    A. Epic, task, user story

    B. Epic, feature, user story, sequenced activities

    C. Theme, epic, feature, user story

    D. User story, feature, tasks

8. It is important for the Agile team to be able to see the "Big Picture" in a visual way. Which of the following would be the best tool for prioritization?

    A. Epic

    B. User story

    C. Wireframe

    D. Story map

9. Which of the following items does your team need in order to produce a working, viable product or service?

    A. A definition of done

    B. Approval from the product owner to create user stories

    C. A well-planned strategy to accomplish project goals

    D. A wireframe with a breakdown of the product needs

10. A persona is based on which one of the following?

    A. Someone who had similar goals on another project

    B. The organization and its culture

    C. A real person or as a descriptive placeholder for the customer

    D. A fake placeholder of a future user and what they may or may not want

11. As an Agile project manager, you are tracking the team's work capacity and getting a sense of how much work is going to be done in the current iteration. What are you tracking?

    A. Features completed

    B. Scope of work completed

    C. Velocity

    D. User stories completed

12. Your team has been averaging 50 points' worth of work per iteration and has determined that there are 201 points left to complete. In how many iterations will the team complete the work?

    A. Four

    B. Two

    C. Six

    D. Five

13. Your team has stabilized their velocity throughout five iterations and commits to 15 story points in the current iteration. Due to a risk event during the iteration, the team only completed 14 story points. What happens to the leftover point?

    A. The team will work overtime to complete the work to which they have committed.

    B. The team will adjust their sprint plan from 15 to 14.

    C. The team will do 14 story points and put the remaining work or 1 point into the backlog for another iteration.

    D. The team will do nothing; points are only estimates.

14. Agile teams work with timeboxes. A customer asks, "What is the point of timeboxes in an iteration?" What do you say as an Agile project manager?

    A. It's a fixed time period applied to activities.

    B. It's a rough estimate of velocity.

    C. It's something we use instead of Gantt charts.

    D. It's a way of tracking performance.

15. Your team is working with the customer on a brand-new project. The customer has established the primary scope of the work, but your team doesn't quite have a process intact. You suggest to the team that they run an iteration that allows for process discovery but doesn't yet deliver releasable value to the customer. This is otherwise known as which one of the following?

    A. Iteration one

    B. Initiation

    C. Iteration Zero

    D. Iteration discovery

16. Your team is estimating that it will take two weeks for the next sprint if there aren't any interruptions to their work flow. Which of the following describes this estimate?

    A. Likely time estimate

    B. Ideal time estimate

    C. Bottom up estimate

    D. Expert judgment estimate

17. Whose position is it to determine the priority of user stories that will be performed next based on value?

    A. Scrum Master

    B. Development team

    C. Project sponsor

    D. Product owner

18. You are working with a visible master list of work, and you are constantly reviewing and updating it with requirements that will be reorganized and reprioritized repeatedly. This is an example of which of the following?

    A. You are the development team planning the next iteration.

    B. You are a product owner and are working on grooming the backlog.

    C. You are the Scrum Master working with the customer on priority.

    D. You are the customer working with the product owner to keep your priorities up-to-date on the Kanban board.

19. You and your teammates are debating how long something should take to accomplish. Which of the following ways is the best way to estimate project work?

    A. Story point estimates for user stories based on lessons learned

    B. Using scheduling software approved by management

    C. Parametric estimates

    D. Using storyboards and pull systems

20. Your team is estimating work using planning poker. All team members agree that the work size is a 5, except for Bob. Bob thinks it should be a 10 in size. What could the reason be for this discrepancy?

    A. It could be due to product uncertainty or technical uncertainty.

    B. Bob is being difficult so that he can add padding to his work.

    C. The team should have used T-shirt sizing to get a better result.

    D. The team should talk to the Scrum Master for leadership in the matter.

21. How many sprints will it take to complete the work providing the team's current velocity is 10 points a sprint?

Stories	Points
Priority A	3 points
Priority B	6 points
Priority C	4 points
Priority D	10 points
Priority E	3 points

A. Five

B. Four

C. Three

D. Six

Chapter 7

Effective Team Performance on Agile Projects

THE FOLLOWING PMI-ACP® EXAM TOPICS ARE COVERED IN THIS CHAPTER:

✓ **Domain IV: Team Performance**

Team Formation:

- Task 1: Cooperate with the other team members to devise ground rules and internal processes in order to foster team coherence and strengthen team members' commitment to shared outcomes.

- Task 2: Help create a team that has the interpersonal and technical skills needed to achieve all known project objectives in order to create business value with minimal delay.

Team Empowerment:

- Task 3: Encourage team members to become generalizing specialists in order to reduce team size and bottlenecks, and to create a high-performing cross-functional team.

- Task 4: Contribute to self-organizing the work by empowering others and encouraging emerging leadership in order to produce effective solutions and manage complexity.

- Task 5: Continuously discover team and personal motivators anddemotivatorsin order to ensure that team morale is high and team members are motivated and productive throughout the project.

Team Collaboration and Commitment:

- Task 6: Facilitate close communication within the team and with appropriate external stakeholders through colocation or the use of collaboration tools in order to reduce miscommunication and rework.

- Task 7: Reduce distractions in order to establish a predictable outcome and optimize the value delivered.

- Task 8: Participate in aligning project and team goals by sharing project vision in order to ensure the team understands how their objectives fit into the overall goals of the project.

- Task 9: Encourage the team to measure its velocity by tracking and measuring actual performance in previous iterations or releases in order for members to gain a better understanding of their capacity and create more accurate forecasts.

In this chapter, you will finish the tasks found in *Domain IV: Team Performance*. These tasks in directly relate to the Agile development team and how to help drive skill mastery and determine how the team is performing. The tasks in the content outline include building a collaborative working environment, encouraging transparent communication, and tracking velocity as well as creating visual charts. This is all designed to give you a well-rounded idea of how to review your team's performance and to help guide the team to Agile mastery. It includes elements of knowledge sharing, adaptive leadership, and communication techniques that will carry over to all aspects of your Agile projects.

Tuckman's Ladder

In Chapter 5, "The Human Side of Agile Project Management," you reviewed a lot of information on interpersonal skills and adaptive leadership, including Tuckman's Ladder, which is the theory by which one can identify the team's progression from a newly formed team to one that is considered performing. It is relevant to mention it again at the beginning of this chapter on team performance because the goal is to have a team that is high performing, self-directed, and self-managed.

No team ever begins as a performing team, especially those that have never worked together before. I would imagine that any organization that is trying to implement Agile approaches at any level has team members who may have worked together on other projects or have chatted in the break room. It may seem like a best bet to place those people together and call it a development team and have lofty expectations of exceptional performance right out of the gate. That simply isn't the case.

In 1965, Dr. Bruce Tuckman published the forming, storming, norming, and performing model, which describes the stages of team development. In line with his research and thought processes, Tuckman believed his model demonstrated that all of these phases are necessary and inevitable regardless of the type of team, type of work, or type of industry.

In 1977, Tuckman revised the original sequence with then doctoral student and now psychologist Mary Ann Jensen. Their work together added adjourning (or what some refer to as mourning) as the final stage. This additional stage expresses the feelings of loss at the end of a team dynamic or the loss of a team member from the group.

In order to develop a high-performing team, it is important for the manager to understand the stages and be cognizant of their role in getting a team from forming to performing. It's also important to mention that this sequence happens regardless of skill set. You could have high-performing individuals who, when put onto a new team, will still go through the process of forming and then eventually reach the performing stage.

Agile project managers practice servant leadership rather than management, and in the case of a newly formed team, it would be your job to maintain the vision, lead by example, and realize that your team may be a bit more dependent on you in the forming stage. During storming, you will guide your team through conflict resolution and promote collaboration and transparent communication. During norming, it is appropriate to function in a supportive role or that of a coach, unless the team or an individual asks for help. When the team is performing, they have reached the ability to be self-directed and self-managed, and that is the goal.

Shu Ha Ri and Skill Mastery

In the late 1920s and early 1930s, the martial arts were given a new or more modern way to practice. Rather than simply beating your opponent, you would now also attempt to use your movements to protect your opponent from harm. The Aikido practice of martial arts was developed in Japan based on several years of martial art studies. Added to this was a mix of philosophy and religious beliefs of the Aikido creator Morehei Ueshiba. The entire premise was to have the skill set both to defend and to protect: Defend oneself and protect the attacker from harm.

As with any type of martial art or mastery of a given craft, it takes many years to reach the pinnacle of what could be considered expert or master. What does that have to do with Agile, you may be thinking? Agile is easy to talk about but very hard to do. A practitioner of Agile will have to work and learn to master their craft.

Martial arts also influenced Agile in the sense that anyone learning something new would be a follower of the rules as they learn them, and then, over time, they would become more comfortable with their skill sets and branch out a bit or break some rules for the good of the outcome. It is assumed that within that consistent practice and learning, eventually the individual would reach mastery. Therefore, *Shu Ha Ri* and skill mastery became a part of Agile.

As a contributor to the *Manifesto for Agile Software Development* and the *Declaration of Interdependence* and the creator of the Crystal Method approach to Agile projects, Alistair Cockburn also incorporated the concept of Shu Ha Ri into Agile environments.

Loosely translated. *Shu* is to protect or obey, *Ha* is to detach or digress, and *Ri* is to leave or separate. When the same philosophy is applied to adopting Agile frameworks, there is a learning curve that follows the same patterns when applied to learning new skills.

At its highest level, Shu Ha Ri describes the progression of learning both in martial arts and in Agile frameworks. At the Shu level, when learning something new, the student follows the master and their practices precisely to learn the skills needed to perform the tasks. In our case, the Agile project manager would be guiding the development team in the ways of the chosen Agile framework.

No such thing as bad student, only bad teacher. Teacher say, student do.

Mr. Miyagi from The Karate Kid

At the Ha level, the student uses their new skills and applies their own innovation or way of doing things—still not breaking rules, but detaching from the way they were strictly taught to reach mastery.

Ri is about allowing yourself to become as creative as seems appropriate to you personally but still not breaking the rules or laws. It allows us first to follow the rules but work toward gaining mastery that resonates with our way of doing things and without losing the framework with which we started.

In a lot of ways, this explains Agile project management in its entirety. The frameworks are more flexible than traditional project management, and there is room to grow and be creative in our execution of work. Knowledge work is not tangible, and it is a lot more of an art form than a best practice. Therefore, as teams new to Agile work to implement best practices, they look to frameworks like Scrum to provide the timeboxes and solid foundation so that they can learn.

Once we have learned, we can begin to work with our teams to branch out a bit and find a groove that works for us while still following the framework and rules. This can include a variety of tailored approaches to Agile project management. Once the team has reached the performing stage, it has also reached mastery, or the Ri Level. It is suggested that an Agile team reach mastery before trying to adapt the frameworks. However, I disagree. I think part of learning is attempting to gain mastery while still knowing and understanding your own organizational dynamics. What works for one may not work for another. In Chapter 10, "Tailoring Quality Management and Improving Project Processes," I'll go through some tailoring approaches and other frameworks that have been adapted as their creators addressed their Ri and their organization.

Dreyfus Model: Five Stages of Skill Acquisition

Throughout the last 40 years or so, there have been many studies of human behavior and skill acquisition. While those studies have been done for a variety of reasons and recipients over the years, it is easy to see a trend of how humans learn and the stages necessary to achieve skill mastery.

In 1980, Stuart and Hubert Dreyfus published a report about skill acquisition based on their research at the University of California, Berkeley. The Dreyfus Model was designed to show how people learn necessary skills through formal instruction and by regularly practicing what they have learned. While the model is self-explanatory, it is an excellent overview of what teams new to Agile frameworks will experience and to what level an Agile project manager needs to get involved.

The goal on any Agile team is to have a self-directed and self-managed team, but that takes time and coaching. In Figure 7.1, the Dreyfus Model is represented by some ideas for how to guide your team to self-direction and become an expert-level practitioner of Agile frameworks.

FIGURE 7.1   The Dreyfus Model

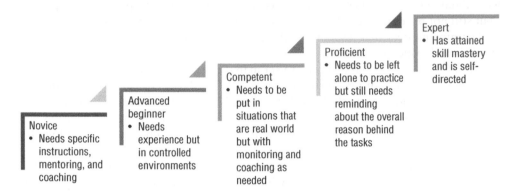

Many of these models are a lot like Agile, easy to talk about but hard to implement. It's always a good idea to ask yourself where you fall on the model with regard to Agile practices as well as where your team of individuals fall on the scale. That identification can help you with coaching your team through a challenge or new learning environment either now or in the future.

🌐 Real World Scenario

To Train or Not to Train? That Is the Question

Nearly my entire career over the past 10 years has been in the training industry. The goal I set for myself before any new class is how to present information that is "perfect world project management," and then tie it into the real world in which we all live. That is challenging these days, because there are so many different global industries, and each could be considered technical in some way. Everyone has an IT department, everyone has cybersecurity risks, and everyone needs project management.

The goal is always to help people master skills in a creative and fun way and to obtain the certifications they want and/or need. The biggest issue that I see is that many people don't feel like they have time for training, or they are so used to their way of doing things that mastery never gets reached.

Mastery is a lofty goal in any case, and simply having too many projects or too busy a life becomes the reason for not improving skill sets. I challenge that reality every day.

Mastery isn't given, it is gained, and perfect practice makes perfect. We don't live in a perfect project management world, so the best we can do is to prepare ourselves, practice our craft, and strive for mastery. Training and learning provides that, and coaching, mentoring, and support maintains it.

If the goal is mastery, then simply following the rules without expanding into your own best way of managing your projects won't work in the long term. The fact that you are reading this guide now demonstrates your desire for expansion of knowledge and working toward goal attainment. I think that is fantastic! Congratulations and enjoy the journey to mastery!

Collaborative Working Environments

Speaking of perfect world project management, a collaborative working environment for Agile teams is recommended as the best way to manage your projects. Since Agile frameworks are best in an environment of colocated team members, the way the team space is created, or "tooled," allows for the best interactivity and collaboration.

For the best setup of your colocated space, it is key to remember that Agile teams tend to be smaller in size. In fact, the optimal team size is about 12 people. If you have more or fewer people on your team, that's okay, because many of the tailored approaches you'll review in Chapter 10, "Tailoring Quality Management and Improving Project Processes," address how to work with best practices on a large or enterprise-sized project. For exam purposes, though, we'll stick to the thought process that everyone could practice perfectly if you have no more than 12 people working on a project.

Above and beyond the size of the team, the rest of the team space is designed for a high amount of collaboration for several specific reasons, as described here:

Shared Vision   When the team sits together, it allows for free-flowing osmotic communication and a shared environment. Because of this, all of the team members are more likely to hear the same message from the Agile project manager, whose job it is to continue to perpetuate the vision for the project and the increment. Even though the scope of work will change the result, the focus of the team will remain on point.

Realistic Goal Setting   Because the team is self-directed and self-managed, it is the team who will determine their goals for the iteration. The team selects the work, which will determine velocity. Limiting work in progress (WIP) allows for realistic goal setting. Having retrospectives at the end of the iteration for continuous improvement and a refocus on the goal of the next iteration also allows for goal setting to remain in the realm of realism.

Self-Organized   The team's ability to select prioritized work and then organize around it is a key tenet in all Agile frameworks. Unless you are using a tailored approach that is closer to a Waterfall methodology or framework, it is highly likely that the team will chart their own course through the iterations. The team will also self-adjust if the primary direction didn't work effectively.

Empowered   Much as with self-organization, the team is empowered to make decisions and to determine their work in progress (WIP) as well as to be creative and make mistakes. Mistakes are how the team learns, and with that information the team is empowered to adjust, reset, and reach consensus. The product owner is in charge of the backlog, but the team is empowered to determine what will be accomplished from iteration to iteration.

Consensus Driven   The Agile project team doesn't have a hierarchy as you might see in some more projectized organizations with a bigger focus on protocol and traditional project management best practices. The team works together with the same focus on the vision, and therefore they must agree together how to move forward. Reaching consensus may be a bit time consuming, especially in the beginning with a newly formed team. Over time, the team will reach the performing stage and make better decisions together. Much of this type of decision making falls on selecting the work that they will achieve and a collective understanding of the definition of done.

Manage Conflict Effectively   Resolving functional conflict is a challenge, even for the best, most functional performing teams. As the team learns to self-manage, conflict resolution will become more effective. The ability to collaborate in a colocated environment helps this process, as does open and honest communication and collective decision making.

Safe Environment   Having a safe environment applies more toward the emotional side of the human aspect of projects. If you have ever been afraid to bring up changes that should be made or to share your ideas, then your team space isn't necessarily "safe." To have a safe environment in which to work is less about removing hostile work environment influencers (of which I hope none of you work in) and more about a cultural shift in which the team feels comfortable and is able to work and learn while promoting the no-blame culture. If someone makes a mistake, the team owns it, and because of that philosophy the finger-pointing diminishes and the team rallies to support each other.

Generalized Specialists   Having specialists on the team usually isn't viewed as a terrible thing in most organizations. The more specialists, the better, right? It's tough to disagree with that thought process. However, what if you have 10 to 12 specialists on your team who could also do a myriad of other things and who have a wide range of skill sets that reduce the need for larger teams? That would be a better situation for sure. The goal of smaller, more effective teams isn't always achievable. In some organizations, the specialists do their thing and that is what is necessary to be successful.

Being a generalized specialist means that you are good at your job but that you can also do other things. Many expanding skill sets fall under good mentoring or training programs to expand skills outside of the specific things that you do daily. Expanding your knowledge and abilities is promoted in an Agile environment, and knowing how to roll with the punches, adapt, and adjust is key for effective Agile team members.

Task/Scrum or Kanban Boards/Whiteboards   Big visible charts and graphs that are front and center go a long way toward open and transparent communication. The team contributes to the updates and isn't dependent on a project manager to inform them weekly on their own progress. Anyone who walks into the team space will see what the team is doing, what they are working on, and what has been completed. This leaves very little question as to the efficiency of the team and the work that is being accomplished. If the brain processes visual images 60-thousand times faster than text, it is easy to see why these tools are so effective.

Round Tables   Having round tables increases the ability to have free-flowing conversations and increases eye contact and the ability to read body language. It also signifies equality of everyone at the table. There is a reason King Arthur had the knights at a round table. Aside from chivalry, it's a great practice to have round tables for, at the very least, conversations, brainstorming, and planning poker games if your organizational dynamic has a different setup.

No Barriers   Like round tables, the removal of barriers helps increase osmotic communication as well as removing the need to pop your head over someone's partitioned wall space, thus surprising them in the middle of an email. Many organizations have partitioned desk spaces and that's okay. The best dynamics I have seen keep the partitions low enough to maintain eye contact and keep the flow of communication going but high enough that someone's "hang in there" cat poster doesn't end up next to your coffee cup.

Face-to-Face Communication   Seeing a trend here? Round tables, no barriers, and face-to-face communication? It's all dependent on the next item, colocation.

Common Team Area of Colocation   Best practice suggests having your entire team occupy the same space within 33 feet of each other without barriers. The thought is that having a common area will supply multiple tools for team use as well as face-to-face communication. Having the ability to share information easily allows for tacit knowledge to be shared, and it saves substantial amounts of time that could be spent in meetings trying to obtain the same information. I don't know anyone who can't get behind that thought process. You might be thinking to yourself, "What happens if I need to make a private call?" or "All of that chatter and sharing can be distracting—I like quiet when I work." You would not be alone in that thought process, so a best practice is to have a secluded area dedicated to the team. These are fondly known as "caves" or "common rooms." These areas can be used to protect privacy as needed while working on the same iteration/sprint.

There are many questions relating to work environments on the PMI-ACP exam because of how team space tooling is vastly different from a more traditional or Waterfall approach to project management. Even with an open-door policy by the project manager, the team may be scattered or even distributed in different departmental areas of the organization. Colocation is the key to Agile team development.

The team space is designed in such a way that all team members are playing on a level playing field. Everyone knows where everyone else is located and what everyone is working on. Colocation is always suggested on any project team for a lot of the reasons that you just reviewed. It isn't always possible in the real world, so consideration must also be made for distributed or virtual teams.

Now let's take a quick look at the roles or players on the team, whether they are virtual or not. In Figure 7.2, you'll see a table of roles on an Agile project team and what titles you may see on the exam.

FIGURE 7.2 Team role designations

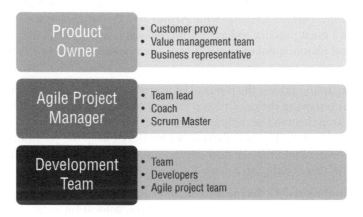

Product Owner
• Customer proxy
• Value management team
• Business representative

Agile Project Manager
• Team lead
• Coach
• Scrum Master

Development Team
• Team
• Developers
• Agile project team

You may see a variety of questions that utilize different titles to represent job functions or roles, such as, for example, designating you as a product owner or a customer. Both titles define the same role. Understanding the overlap of titles or roles on an Agile project team and how they relate to other titles or job roles in a generic way is important for the exam. You may be asked to answer questions based on your role. That role may tie back to a specific methodology like Scrum, but it's typically a very generic term. You may see multiple job roles represented in multiple ways. It's a good idea to know them for your exam.

Even though having everyone colocated isn't always possible, it is recommended that your team is colocated for the planning phase, at the very least, and for one iteration if not two.

If your organization has distributed teams across multiple locations, it is recommended that you colocate one entire team's worth of positions so that each location has a fully functioning, cross-functional team working with the other teams on the same project. You may find in your own world that this can be very difficult to pull off and that your virtual or distributed team members may very well be working on an island by themselves. If that is the case, it is important to understand some of the challenges found on virtual teams.

Distributed Teams

If you have ever worked on or managed virtual teams, then I'm sure a lot of what you will read about in this section will resonate. Don't get me wrong: There are a lot of benefits to having virtual team members, including, but not limited to, the ability to have people from all over the world as candidates for your open positions. I had a friend who used to say, "Brilliance isn't always found in one place," and she was correct.

Organizations can have team members who are in multiple time zones, who speak a multitude of languages, and who understand global markets. Or, people can work from home and cut down on their environmental footprint by not commuting every day. Yes, there are many benefits to having virtual teams, but there are also some challenges that, if not addressed, can wreak havoc on an Agile project team.

One of the items of which you should be aware is the *PMI Code of Ethics and Professional Conduct*. You will be asked to review, accept, and abide by the code as a practitioner of project management for any certifications that you obtain through PMI. It's especially relevant to give you a glimpse into the code as it pertains to people who are colo-cated or virtual.

Section 3.1 of the PMI Code of Ethics and Professional Conduct reminds us that respect in all forms is our duty. The sidebar "Code of Ethics and Professional Conduct" provides a snippet of the code as it pertains to the human side of project management.

Code of Ethics and Professional Conduct

3.1 Description of Respect

Respect is our duty to show a high regard for ourselves, others, and the resources entrusted to us. Resources entrusted to us may include people, money, reputation, the safety of others, and natural or environmental resources.

An environment of respect engenders trust, confidence, and performance excellence by fostering mutual cooperation—an environment where diverse perspectives and views are encouraged and valued.

3.2 Respect: Aspirational Standards as Practitioners in the Global Project Management Community

3.2.1   We inform ourselves about the norms and customs of others and avoid engaging in behaviors they might consider disrespectful.

3.2.2   We listen to others' points of view, seeking to understand them.

3.2.3   We approach directly those persons with whom we have a conflict or disagreement.

3.2.4   We conduct ourselves in a professional manner, even when it is not reciprocated.

3.3 Respect: Mandatory Standards as Practitioners in the Global Project Management Community

We require the following of ourselves and our fellow practitioners:

3.3.1   We negotiate in good faith.

3.3.2   We do not exercise the power of our expertise or position to influence the decisions or actions of others in order to benefit personally at their expense.

3.3.3   We do not act in an abusive manner toward others.

3.3.4   We respect the property rights of others.

SOURCE: www.pmi.org/about/ethics/code

I chose to add snippets of the PMI Code of Ethics and Professional Conduct to this section of this study guide for the following reasons:

- First and foremost, you'll have to agree to abide by the code as an Agile practitioner.

- Because in the world of global, virtual environments connected by a web of technology, it is easy to forget our manners sometimes.

There are some things to keep in mind and avoid if you are part of or working with virtual team members from a different country or even a different part of your own country. All of this applies to colocated team members as well, but since virtual team members don't have the ability to be face-to-face all day and build relationships as quickly, much of this is experienced at the virtual level. It's important to avoid these at all costs whenever possible, or at the very least be aware that they exist. Be diligent in your own world and the virtual world of your team members to identify and communicate anything that may waver outside the respect bubble.

The following list of challenges are not meant to be in any particular ranked order, but I feel that it is an important reminder to review the big challenges, if only to establish a list of things to consider while working with virtual employees.

While I put away my soapbox, ponder the main offenders:

Stereotypes   I've heard people say that stereotypes are there for a reason. One such stereotype I heard recently is that all Philadelphia sports fans are obnoxious. I take umbrage with that and would counter by saying that is only the case when we are playing a football game against a team from a large city in Texas. Otherwise, we are very well mannered, thank you very much. Okay, okay, except that one time when people were whipping snowballs at Santa. It happened the year I was born, so I can't be held accountable for that piece of our history. All joking aside, even if you *do* think that all Philly fans are obnoxious, it doesn't mean that you should say it out loud, express your thoughts at the next stand-up meeting, let it interfere with your professional interactions with said football fans, or spread those terrible rumors in general. Your thoughts are your thoughts, and you think what you want, but in a professional environment all stereotypes should be kept out of the workplace and not influence your day-to-day work by making offensive jokes or treating people differently because of how you happen to view them.

Generalizations   See above! Also, it is *always never* a bad idea to avoid words like... *always* and *never.* Nothing will demotivate a colocated or virtual team member more than being told that they *always* do (insert business task here) or that they *never* do (and here) correctly. This is especially helpful information to use on the home front as well. Generalizations can be hurtful, and frankly they are not accurate statements at all. I *always* try very hard *never* to generalize.

Ethnocentrism   *Ethnocentrism* is the thought or feeling that one's country or culture is better than anyone else's. It's shocking to me that this mindset continues, but I feel it is safe to say that any person who feels or professes that their culture is better than any others hasn't traveled or actually met people from another culture. You can and should love your country, but you should respect another's at the same time. The global environment we find ourselves working and living in should always include respect—no matter what. As an Agile project manager or team member, it is up to you to perpetuate best practices and lead by example. Ethnocentrism may be something you tolerate on your daily Facebook feed, but it should never be tolerated in a work environment. A big no-no!

Culture Shock   Believe it or not, culture shock doesn't just occur when you step off an airplane into another country and attempt to get your bearings while suffering from jet lag. Culture shock can happen when you join a new team with new management and a different vibe from your old team. If you have ever experienced anxiety when starting a new job, you can chalk that up to culture shock. It doesn't mean that the new thing is necessarily bad or good; it just is different from the organizational culture that you are used to. Culture shock can often be experienced when a new team is in the forming stage and everyone is a bit uneasy and on their best behavior. There are several ways that you can practice adaptive leadership and servant leadership when you have a newly formed Agile team.

Culture shock can occur or be created by the following:
- Work habits
- Communication styles
- Time differences
- Lack of understanding of context
- Misreading body language
- Ethnocentrism

Best practices for avoiding culture shock are the following:
- Avoid ethnocentrism.
- Base team building events on each person's country or culture.
- Educate each other about other cultures.
- Recognize different work styles, habits, writing styles, and language differences.

- Create ground rules as a team for meetings, emails, and other communications and set deadlines with very specific terms.
- Create mission statements, goals, and ground rules.
- Identify stakeholders and their expectations.
- Build relationships and generate trust.
- Recognize conflict even if it isn't stated, and manage it according to organizational or team culture as much as possible.
- Have a casual meeting or gathering to help orient the team.
- Keep the team colocated for at least two iterations if possible.
- Make sure the team has a good understanding of the purpose of the project and what success looks like.
- Understand the definition of done.
- If distributed, make sure Agile teams are complete groups in each location with matching skill sets to the other locations if possible.

Context and Culture

If you were wondering what I meant by the lack of understanding of context as a cause for culture shock, I was referring to different countries and cultures and how communication is different. There are high-context and low-context cultures, and if you have ever struggled to communicate effectively via email or on a conference call with someone from another country, you have probably experienced a difference in context.

We know that much of face-to-face communication and the general understanding of one's message evolves through the reading of body language, shortly followed by tone of voice and then the actual words that are spoken. If you take face-to-face communication out of the mix on a virtual team, guess what takes over? Tone. If you have ever read and reread your emails before you send them, you are reading for the tone of the message and reviewing the words for clarity. Emoticons were created to help replace body language and help the correct tone come through. Mostly, emoticons are frowned upon as a "thing" during the daily professional deluge of emails flying around. That leaves us with tone and words. If the context of the message isn't read correctly, it can shift the tone.

For example, in a country that typically expresses things in a low-context way in business interactions, including the United States, Canada, the United Kingdom, and others, there is a heavy reliance on the written word and direct, clear short messages. In other countries, where a high- context approach to communication occurs, such as China, Japan, and Russia, for example, the message may not be as clearly understood by those who communicate in a low-context way. This may be due to unwritten rules and not understanding what those rules are. Neither is right or wrong, or good or bad. It may never happen at all since it's now a small world after all. I don't mean to generalize after I just gave you a lecture on not generalizing, but the low- and high-context communication breakdown is a real thing. It's legit. It's worth doing your research.

I'm just happy that I'm getting better at asking the Google and the Google is getting better at reading the question while ignoring massive amounts of typos. Anytime you have global team members, it will be up to you to perpetuate the right vision and the right behaviors and to get to know your team of individuals. Any research you undertake is time well spent.

 Real World Scenario

Kiss, Bow, or Shake Hands?

I had the pleasure of reading Terri Morrison and Wayne Conway's book the first time I flew to Asia for business. I was embarking on a whirlwind work tour that included two cities in China and a stop in Bangkok, Thailand. I was also visiting countries in Europe on that trip, but this was the very first time I had ever gone to Asia. I was nervous because I knew very little about the Asian culture except what I knew from my adopted brothers and sister from China (my mother is a saint), and even that was limited as they were much older than I at the time they lived with us.

I knew that in order to redirect my ignorance ship in the right direction, I had to do my research. I had a good 20 hours of travel ahead of me, so I bought the book. It is filled with proper protocol for international business and useful tips of things about which I needed to be aware. I learned so much about what I should and shouldn't do. There have been numerous books published since then, so pick one that resonates with you or search around the Internet for information.

I still tell my classes about that trip, and now I'm giving you some of that information as well. I'm sure that I didn't do everything correctly, but I do know that I didn't inadvertently insult or shame myself or anyone else due to not knowing something about the culture and how business is conducted.

I loved Asia and have returned another time to China for work and extended the trip to include Singapore, where I had clients at the time. I admittedly have the adventure gene, and I love to travel and immerse myself in other cultures, and as we know, knowledge is power. Understanding another's culture and working to learn more about it is the key to unlocking good relationships with people from all around the world. I highly recommend doing your research whether traveling for fun or for work, or if you are simply trying to connect with an international virtual team member. You won't regret it.

Kiss, Bow, or Shake Hands by Terri Morrison and Wayne A. Conway (Adams Media, 2008)

Frankly, anytime you are dealing with the written word, no matter where you come from, there is a real opportunity to miss the message completely. We are getting better, however, with text-oriented communication. With all the tweeting, texting, and Facebooking the world does these days, it's no wonder there are some improvements.

There is also a significant uptick in ethnocentrism, disrespect, and false bravery behind a keyboard. Be careful what you post, tweet, and say. Many people are being fired or let go these days because of bad behavior online; plus it also diminishes your ability to call yourself a servant leader.

Communication in any sense is a skill that we all aspire to improve upon, and being aware of your team, their communication styles, and how your message is being received is of the utmost importance in a servant leadership role.

Aside from all of this, anytime you have virtual employees, there is the potential for a lack of effective communication, a lack of relationship building or team cohesion. That doesn't mean it can't work. I'm a virtual employee. I work from home and have for almost seven years. Do I feel separate from the rest of my team in Arizona? Totally. Do I make the most out of every single visit to HQ? You bet I do! Colocation for any length of time is great for the virtual employees and the team in general.

Technology is getting better and better, and before we know it, a virtual employee will be popping into the breakroom in hologram form. Until the beaming up occurs, it's always a promising idea to avoid the out-of-sight, out-of-mind dilemma experienced by virtual teams.

Osmotic Communication

You have already learned about and have probably experienced osmotic communication. The recommended best practice is colocation, which promotes a specific setup for your team space and encourages open, honest, and free-flowing conversations. The goal of any communication is for the message to be received and understood by the intended recipient. In a situation involving osmotic communication, even more people will receive the message and choose either to use the information or toss it away.

Have you ever sat in a crowded place, heard the buzz of conversations, and mostly ignored it as background noise until someone says something with which you are familiar or something that is interesting to you, so you zero in on the information and you begin to listen to the conversation more intently? That is osmotic communication. With an open environment of sharing and communication, the Agile team is set up a bit differently from other types of project teams in the sense that a prescribed and highly suggested best practice is to be colocated and to engage in communication on many subjects, including reaching consensus, learning new things, and being privy to transparent communication across all team members.

> Information flows into the background hearing of members of the team, so that they pick up relevant information as though by osmosis.
>
> This is normally accomplished by seating them in the same room. Then, when one person asks a question, others in the room can either tune in or tune out, contributing to the discussion or continuing with their work.
>
> *Alistair Cockburn*

Team and Individual Coaching

A team that has access to coaching will be a team with high performance. It's as simple as that.

A bit later in the chapter, you'll be reviewing velocity tracking as well as how to use burn up or burn down charts to track team performance. Nonetheless, even a great high-performing team may need some coaching at some point.

Lyssa Adkins, president of the Agile Coaching Institute, suggests some guidelines for one-on-one coaching:

- Stay a half step ahead.
- Guarantee safety.
- Partner with managers.
- Create positive regard.

Much of the advice is designed around creating an environment that is comfortable for the person receiving the coaching. The goal is to help the person feel like they are in a safe environment in which they can learn, grow, and totally make mistakes. Mastery isn't earned; it is gained, and we could all use some coaching some of the time.

The part about partnering with managers would only be necessary if your team or part of your team belonged to another Agile project manager, or even a functional manager. That can happen in the real world. I borrowed generalized specialists from other functional departments as needed, and I always felt that it was a best practice to document all of the things that they learned and did on the project. My reasoning was twofold:

1. A lot of managers or bosses only remember the last two weeks of your life, and particularly the one stupid thing you did all year, so having documented proof that their people are awesome helps overcome some of that.

2. Documenting successes and learned skill sets helps to perpetuate growth in the team member because they have the support of their manager.

Hopefully it helps the manager understand the team member's role on the project a bit better, and it also helps them develop the team member further since they are already on a growth trajectory from being coached on the project.

Agile best practices would suggest that part of being a servant leader of a self-directed team is knowing when to step in and help. That time is when someone asks you for help. If an individual comes to you and asks for guidance, or for you to drop some knowledge on them, then by all means hook them up! When it comes to the team, though, it can be a bit trickier to know when to facilitate, when to lead, and when to coach. My best advice is to coach the team as needed at specific points in the project. Typically, do so between iterations or specific planning points if the team is having trouble and needs more than a facilitator.

For me, coaching is best received on the team level during the retrospectives. This is the point when the team is looking back at the last iteration and asking themselves what they could do differently going forward and what they did well. This is especially true with teams newer to Agile frameworks. The coaching is mission critical then because there is a tendency to slip back into the "we always did it this way" habits of yore, especially when best practices are still freshly out of the chaos zone.

To wrap up the first part of this chapter about the team, here are some PMI-ACP exam tips to keep in mind:

- Colocation for kick-off and first iteration is key for virtual teams.

- Osmotic communication is highly effective with colocated teams, and it is necessary for the growth of the Agile team members individually and of the team as a unit.

- Be aware of how and when to coach, and know the process outlined by Lyssa Adkins.

- Be aware of some of the struggles of virtual teams and how colocation is a way to avoid a lot of the feelings of not being a part of the team or missing out on crucial information, which could only be received through osmotic communication.

- Situational leadership is a large part of being an effective Agile project manager. Understand the situation and react accordingly. You'll see a lot of questions on the PMI-ACP exam related to understanding your environment and choosing the best course of action.

Velocity Tracking

I'll be the first person to admit that creating charts and graphs from scratch is not my strong suit, and many times I'll be scouring the Internet for free templates that I can use to knock out a status report. I tell you this for two reasons:

- There are actually free templates online that you can use to knock out a status report (yay!).

- You will be using charts and graphs for a lot of your transparent reporting. Those charts will be front and center and hanging on the team space wall, hence the frantic search for something functional and a bit easier on the eyes as well.

Smartsheet has a ton of templates out there, and they are awesome, free, and easy to use and they work with Excel. And, if you are looking for software, Smartsheet is a good one! (I'm not a paid representative for Smartsheet, but I'm all for spreading the joy when it comes to free, usable stuff and giving props where they are due.) What you are about to see in chart form is 95 percent Smartsheet and 5 percent me.

I'll now show you the charts and graphs that you can use to track team performance during the iterations measured in the units that the team determines best suits the project. For our purposes, we'll look at a velocity tracking chart as well as tracking the scope of work in burn up charts and burn down charts. These are probably the big three, most-used charts or visible items other than a Kanban/task/Scrum board.

Remember, the team's velocity varies in the first iterations, increases, and eventually plateaus. Whether your team is still experiencing fluctuations in their velocity or things have stabilized, it is important to track velocity and for the team to know where they stand from iteration to iteration. Eventually, it becomes easier to predict when the increment will be done-done, once velocity stabilizes. *Velocity tracking* is all based on what has been done in the past to predict the future and to determine the time frame for completion.

In Figure 7.3, you can see the velocity from each iteration climb and eventually plateau as the team tracks how many story points they were able to complete in each iteration.

FIGURE 7.3   Velocity tracking

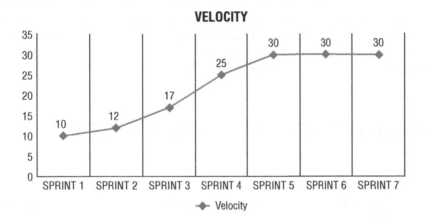

Because velocity fluctuates and plateaus, it is not always easy to answer the question, How long will this project take? It is better to give an estimate based on the average velocity of the first several iterations. That will give you and the team the ability to estimate more accurately going forward, before the team has determined the velocity plateau value.

Iterations

You may be asked to calculate how many iterations are left to complete based on your assessed velocity on your exams, and the best way to predict this is based on what has been done to date and the number of stories currently in the backlog.

An example of the question you might get is where your team has determined that there are 500 points of functionality left in the backlog to complete. The first four iterations' velocity has been tracked as follows. How many more iterations will it take to complete the project based on velocity?

22 points

30 points

39 points

45 points

Step One

What is the average amount of points completed to date?

$$(22 \text{ points} + 30 \text{ points} + 39 \text{ points} + 45 \text{ points}) / 4 = 34$$

Step Two

$$500 \text{ points left} / \text{average points } 34 = \text{approximately } 14.7 \text{ iterations until completion}$$

If this were an exam question, I would look for a whole number answer since iterations aren't partially finished. If all of the work can't be completed, the remaining work would go back into the backlog to be added to the next iteration as needed. I would always round up and say 15 iterations, in this case, just to be safe.

Burn Down and Burn Up Charts

Charts and graphs in an Agile environment are supposed to be simple, easy-to-read dashboards of how the project and the team are progressing. No more Gantt charts, network diagrams, and critical path determinations. I'll wait until you complete your happy dance and then we'll begin.

The goal of any chart is to show visually the result of a lot of data manipulation and make it easy to understand. For both burn down and burn up charts, the simpler the better. As an overview, *burn down charts* show the progression of work completed, and *burn up charts* track completed work and document comprehensive scope changes along the way. Both charts are designed to help the team stay focused on the goal and work toward improvement and will significantly shorten the confusing status report conversations that tend to utilize conference rooms for much longer than necessary.

Burn Down Charts

Let's start with burn down charts. A *burn down chart*, in the simplest of terms, tracks work completed in each iteration and allows for predictions to be made about how many iterations are left based on the amount of work completed and the amount of work remaining. How fast the team is burning through or completing user stories is a great way to show work in progress and work completed visually as well as to provide some insight into how the project is going.

The chart is rather basic in nature, with a projection line moving down as work is completed. Since nothing is ever perfect, don't expect to see your burn down charts with a perfectly formed downward trajectory throughout the project. Real life shows that there are always fluctuations due to changes, tech debt, bug fixes, and perhaps a scramble to complete the project toward the end. Either way, the information is front and center. Everyone knows what is going on during the project, and they are very well aware when work isn't being burned through at a high or even pace.

One thing always to consider in Agile project management is that when the team selects the work and someone asks the big question, "How long will this project take?" the team can make a prediction when that date will be, based on current work and velocity.

Another thing to consider is how differently this question is answered for an Agile project compared to a Waterfall or traditional project.

In a traditional project, which is fully scope-driven, since the scope of work is fairly static and set in stone, it is common for the time and money-related aspects to work around what is happening with the scope of work. That doesn't mean that a customer or sponsor isn't setting deadlines, because they certainly are. Those deadlines tend to be optimistic in nature, and that is precisely why many Waterfall projects come in over budget and behind schedule. But the end goal is always the scope of work. If you want it completed, you'll have to provide contingency money and buffer time to get what you want.

In an Agile environment, the iteration length is static, and typically the budget is rendered due to the iteration length and the work predicted to be accomplished in that iteration. Scope of work isn't fixed, but time and money may be. If a customer asks when the project will be done-done, the team will use a burn down chart to predict that based on what is currently in the backlog and what the definition of done is right now. The answer may be six months. The customer may want it in four months. Now it will be up to the customer to decide what is more important, time or scope. The team will explain how much they can get accomplished by the deadline, and the customer will have to decide whether to trim the tail off the scope of work or allow the team to take the time they need to produce to spec. It's as if everything is flipped. I'm pretty sure that if I told my Waterfall sponsor that if they wanted something specific, they would have to wait X amount of time longer than they not-so-gently requested, I'd be creating an RPE for myself; that is, a resume-producing event.

In Figure 7.4, you'll see a typical burn down chart and be able to understand just how easy it is not only to read but to create (with free templates!). This burn down chart shows the effort and iterations across time more realistically to the real world. Everything will fluctuate based on how the team is performing the work. The fluctuations will continue even if a plateau has been reached because it doesn't necessarily mean that we are static and perfect going forward.

FIGURE 7.4   Burn down chart

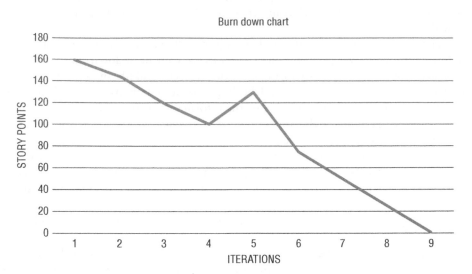

It looks simple, right? In this case, the burn down is showing that the team originally predicted that they would be finished in a certain amount of iterations based on the amount of points they needed to complete the work. My invisible team appears to be on track. In some cases, work gets added and begins to show a burn up on the chart, or the team adapted some of their estimates to accommodate something else on the project. After the burn up, the team returned to the original or close to the original projected velocity and pace.

I realize that the chart looks simple, and in reality, it is supposed to be. Will your charts be *as* simple? Probably not. In the case of a real project, there may be a lot of fluctuation in the beginning, and as velocity shifts and changes, more or fewer story points will be accomplished depending on how the project is going. The goal of any visual in Agile is to keep it as simple as possible, easy to read, and easy to explain. A burn down chart shows the team's progress as they chip away at story points and practice continuous improvement on each iteration.

Burn Up Charts

The purpose of a *burn up chart* is to track completed work as with a burn down chart, but also to show very clearly the changes to scope and what is considered an ideal burn through the project. In this case, the burn line is moving up and scope can be added and removed as the team works through the chosen user stories. Both burn down and burn up charts show very clearly the visible result of knowledge work.

In Figure 7.5, you can see the three main variables plotted out on the chart. The first variable is the number of stories planned to be accomplished. This means that the team selected the number of stories they felt they could accomplish in a day, or week, or month.

You can design your charts to match the iteration length on which your project is running. The second variable is the actual work accomplished, and the third variable is a visual of the ideal burn up; meaning that, if everything goes perfectly, this is what it will look like.

FIGURE 7.5 Burn up chart

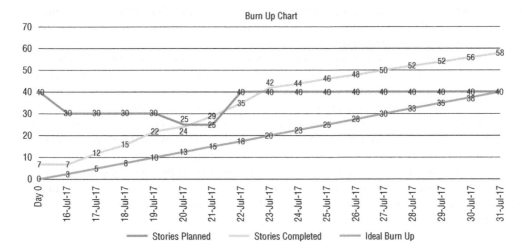

A Kanban board, velocity tracking, and burn up or burn down charts are all designed to be as easy to read as they are to create. Granted that there are many templates out there for you to use as well, and all you have to do is search for them and then adapt them as you go. If you are the guru in the office where Excel is concerned, then this will be a snap for you, or they can be hand drawn on a whiteboard or on flip charts. Either way, everything is supposed to be front and center in the team space and transparent in its communication of team performance.

- Understand the differences between burn up and burn down charts.
- Know that information radiators are the *best* way to show performance.
- Velocity starts out with an estimate, fluctuates, and then plateaus once the team has reached their effective velocity.
- The product owner sets the value/priority; the team sets velocity.

Summary

In this chapter, we covered some additional items relating to the human side of Agile project management and reviewed some of the items of team performance that you saw in previous chapters. Because team performance builds on many of the best practices that you have already seen in different frameworks, plus ways to engage other stakeholders, this may seem redundant, but it is, in fact, the keystone to the rest of the Agile best practices working effectively.

We reviewed some skill mastery theories like Tuckman's Ladder, Shu Ha Ri, and the Dreyfus model of the five stages of skill acquisition. Even though there are numerous theories out there about how people learn, communicate, and behave, these are the most prevalent on the PMI-ACP exam. Along with that, we went through some information on coaching your team and the best practices to do so.

Next we covered the best practices for collaborative team space tooling and some of the ideal configurations for an Agile team. Even though you may not be able to follow all of them, there are some great ideas on how to set up your space for maximum interaction, including but not limited to, the ability to experience osmotic communication.

We also covered some aspects of the PMI Code of Ethics and Professional Conduct that point to a need for all of us to practice respect and to avoid behaviors that can damage relationships and how that ties into a virtual or distributed team dynamic.

Finally, we covered some ways to see how well your team is performing with visual charts. We discussed burn up and burn down charts and graphs representing the team's velocity, how much work is being accomplished, and the influence of scope changes mid-iteration.

Exam Essentials

Be able to understand different levels of skill mastery.   Understand why it is important to know the level at which your individual team members are in their skill mastery and some ways to work with the team to reach the Ri stage and become a self-directed generalized specialist.

Understand the concept of collaborative work environments.   Setting up your colocated team space to maximize your interactions will increase the ability to communicate and place everyone on an even playing field. This setup involves much more than moving desks around. The team space tooling is designed to encourage the team all to sit together and work as a unit while gathering information through osmotic communication.

Be able to understand the differences between working with a colocated team and a virtual team.   Much of the exam will focus on colocation as the best practice, and many questions will place you in situations that involve a team space designed for colocated teams. It's important to remember that currently there are more virtual Agile teams in the world than colocated. If you're lucky enough to be in a perfect world, then certainly colocate as much as possible, but also be aware that your virtual team members need a slightly different kind of servant leadership.

Understand team and individual coaching.   If you have a high-performing Agile team, then your role is that of a servant leader. This doesn't mean that your team won't occasionally benefit from coaching. Best practice states that you coach an individual when they ask for it and the team during planned meeting times, such as, for example, in a retrospective environment.

Be aware of different ways to show work effort visually. Velocity charts, burn down charts, and burn up charts are just a few of the visuals used to illustrate team performance metrics quickly and easily. It's important to know what each chart does and what information is reflected in order to answer questions on the exam about how they differ.

Review Questions

You can find the answers in Appendix B.

1. Which of the following describes a generalized specialist?
   A. They are specialists in their field, but they have additional skill sets that can be used on a project.
   B. They have limited experience in Agile and may need coaching to be more successful.
   C. They have general knowledge about Waterfall projects but not Agile.
   D. They have reached skill mastery.

2. Your team has reached the performing phase. What types of management and leadership do they need?
   A. A lot of feedback and interactions
   B. Feedback, coaching, or help only when they ask for it
   C. Help with conflict resolution and expectation settings
   D. Helping the team get to know each other and build trust

3. The concept of Shu Ha Ri is one of _____.
   A. Obey, detach, mastery
   B. Learning, communicating, mastery
   C. Novice and then proficient
   D. Follows plans and process

4. The team space is key in Agile projects. What is the one thing that is recommended above all others for Agile teams?
   A. Scrum boards
   B. Colocation
   C. Caves and common rooms
   D. Information radiators

5. On a colocated team, what is one of the major benefits of everyone sitting together in the same work space?
   A. The Scrum Master can find everyone.
   B. Daily stand-up meetings are easier to organize.
   C. Osmotic communication can be achieved.
   D. Colocation helps with understanding of velocity charts.

6. Your team has reached the performing phase. What types of management and leadership do they need?

   A. A lot of feedback and training

   B. Coaching as needed during retrospectives

   C. Help with improving velocity

   D. They don't need any help.

7. The team space is key in Agile projects. What can be provided to the team in case they need privacy and quiet to work?

   A. Time off

   B. The ability to work from home

   C. Caves and common rooms

   D. Nothing. The team should always be colocated.

8. All the following are guidelines for one-on-one coaching except _____.

   A. Stay a half step ahead

   B. Guarantee support

   C. Partner with managers

   D. Create positive regard

9. Which of the following best describes a team's velocity from the first iteration on?

   A. It's based on the decomposition of activities and their sequence.

   B. Velocity varies in the first iterations, increases, and eventually plateaus.

   C. Velocity is determined by the product owner.

   D. Velocity is based on approved deliverables, milestones, scope, and resource management plans.

10. What is the main difference between a burn down and burn up chart?

    A. A burn down chart tracks the time and effort left, and a burn up chart tracks completed work and changes.

    B. A burn up chart tracks the time and effort left, and a burn down chart tracks completed work and changes.

    C. A burn down chart tracks risk averted, and a burn up chart tracks risks left to manage.

    D. A burn down chart tracks the burn rate of project costs, and a burn up chart tracks scope of work left to complete.

11. Your team has determined that there are 500 points of functionality left in the backlog to complete. The first 4 iteration's velocity has been tracked as follows:

20 points
35 points
55 points
50 points

Approximately how many more iterations will it take to complete the project based on velocity?

A. 12.5

B. 10

C. 14.7

D. 16

12. A key stakeholder has asked for information on the team's progression through the iteration. What would be the best way to present information about the team's progress?

A. Earned value report

B. Burn down chart

C. Detailed notes on stand-up meetings

D. A Gantt chart

13. Your key stakeholder is asking for comprehensive Gantt charts to determine how the project is progressing. What will you tell them?

A. "Sure, I'll put one together for you."

B. "In Agile projects, we don't use Gantt charts."

C. "I'll ask the team to put it together."

D. "Agile projects use low-tech, high-touch tools to radiate performance rather than Gantt charts."

14. Your team is colocated and has a common room to work and communicate. Bill is getting distracted while working on a specific line of code, and he has to have a private call with his doctor in a half hour. Bill gets up to go into another room to work privately and take the call with his doctor. Is this an acceptable practice for Agile teams?

A. Yes. Bill went to a "cave," and even though teams are colocated, it doesn't mean that they can't work privately as needed for a short period of time or to take private phone calls.

B. No. Bill needs to be coached in osmotic communication since his team could have found his code solution valuable.

C. Yes. Bill is perfectly within his rights to work separately from his team whenever he wants.

D. No. Bill is antisocial and may not be the best fit for your Agile team.

15. You are working on a large project, and many of your team members are going to be virtually distributed. What is the best way to help your virtual team be successful for your upcoming project?

A. Distributed teams are not recommended on Agile projects.

B. Set up ground rules.

C. Set up a live stream of video feeds to keep everyone virtually colocated.

D. Colocate the team for the planning meetings and two iterations if possible.

16. Of the following, what is the best way that you can help your team stay connected when they are virtual?

A. Daily stand-ups

B. Mission statements, goals, and ground rules

C. Kickoff meetings

D. Video calls

17. What is the following statement defining?

Information flows into the background so that the team members will pick up relevant information that they can choose to learn more about or dismiss.

A. Nonverbal communication

B. Active listening

C. Osmotic communication

D. Stand-up meetings

18. Your newly formed Agile team makes a mistake during the first iteration that results in 500 lines of code needing to be redone. As their coach, what do you think is important for the team to know?

A. Nothing. Teams are self-motivated and don't need a manager.

B. That Agile teams are most effective at problem solving when they feel that they have permission to make mistakes.

C. You need to create a clear action plan for the team so that same mistake never happens again.

D. You need to determine whether or not your new team understands your chosen Agile framework, or if your team would be better suited using a specific project plan.

19. A key stakeholder is asking what is the estimated time for the entire project to be completed. Which of the following will you show them to help answer that question?

A. Kanban board

B. Gantt chart

C. Burn down chart

D. Process flow diagram

20. An Agile team shows its progress visually and has created a specific chart/graph to show work that has been completed as well as make scope changes visible across iterations. What are they creating?

   A. WIP

   B. Cumulative flow diagrams

   C. Kanban board

   D. Burn up charts

Chapter 8

Agile Execution and Tracking of Iterations

THE FOLLOWING PMI-ACP® EXAM TOPICS ARE COVERED IN THIS CHAPTER:

✓ **Domain V: Adaptive Plannning**

Adaptive Planning—Levels of Planning:

- Task 1: Plan at multiple levels (strategic, release, iteration, daily) creating appropriate detail by using rolling wave planning and progressive elaboration to balance predictability of outcomes with ability to exploit opportunities.

- Task 2: Make planning activities visible and transparent by encouraging participation of key stakeholders and publishing planning results in order to increase commitment level and reduce uncertainty.

- Task 3: As the project unfolds, set and manage stakeholder expectations by making increasingly specific levels of commitments in order to ensure common understanding of the expected deliverables.

✓ **Adaptive Planning—Adaptation:**

- Task 4: Adapt the cadence and the planning process based on results of periodic retrospectives about characteristics and/or the size/complexity/criticality of the project deliverables in order to maximize the value.

- Task 5: Inspect and adapt the project plan to reflect changes in requirements, schedule, budget, and shifting priorities based on team learning, delivery experience, stakeholder feedback, and defects in order to maximize business value delivered.

✓ **Adaptive Planning—Agile Sizing and Estimation:**

- Task 6: Size items by using progressive elaboration techniques in order to determine likely project size independent of team velocity and external variables.

- Task 7: Adjust capacity by incorporating maintenance and operations demands and other factors in order to create or update the range estimate.

- Task 8: Create initial scope, schedule, and cost range estimates that reflect current high level understanding of the effort necessary to deliver the project in order to develop a starting point for managing the project.

- Task 9: Refine scope, schedule, and cost range estimates that reflect the latest understanding of the effort necessary to deliver the project in order to manage the project.

- Task 10: Continuously use data from changes in resource capacity, project size, and velocity metrics in order to evaluate the estimate to complete.

In this chapter, you will work through the tasks found in *Domain V: Adaptive Planning.* The tasks directly relate to the team's ability to plan in an uncertain environment and adapt to the changing scope of work while maintaining focus on providing value.

The tasks in the content outline include creating and refining initial plans in a progressive manner and managing stakeholder expectations. This is all designed to give you a well-rounded idea of how to plan, adjust, and manage changes throughout the project. This includes elements of identifying key performance indicators and avoiding the misunderstandings that can occur in an Agile project while at the same time tracking performance across the project.

Much of project initiation and determining return on investment was covered in Chapter 4, "Agile Initiation and Stakeholder Engagement," in the form of business case development and focusing on measuring benefits compared to costs. This chapter will address the planning that comes after initiation while keeping an eye on original value determinations.

Return on Investment and Benefit Measurement Methods

In Chapter 4, you reviewed all of the influencing factors that help to create a business case. Those included payback period, internal rate of return (IRR), and net present value (NPV). As organizations determine which projects to charter, a lot rides on the organization's ability to obtain some type of *return on investment (ROI)*. Even though ROI differs from organization to organization, the financial bottom line is always a concern. In this chapter, you will be fast-forwarding to the execution of a project and how value is both determined and tracked.

You will review many techniques, which can be executed at a variety of stages in the project. Since each iteration in an Agile project is itself like a mini-project, these best practices may be recycled as many times as necessary to determine budgetary constraints and need for changes as well as checking to make sure that you are building the right thing and building the thing right. All projects follow a type of *progressive elaboration*, or elaborating progressively on current plans as more information becomes available.

You will start with an approach called the *earned value technique*. The technique itself is a way to review current performance and compare it to what you thought the performance would be. In traditional project management, earned value is something that is used frequently to compare the current baselines to actual performance. If there is a variance that is too great, then a formal change may have to be enacted to put the project back on track in terms of scope, time, and costs.

While earned value may never show up on your PMI-ACP exam, earned value analysis will show up on the PMP exam should you ever want to pursue that as well. If you have already obtained your PMP, then you know that this section in class required you to memorize a lot of formulas in order to accurately answer questions on the PMP exam. Time to breathe a sigh of relief, mathematically challenged people, since you won't see this on your PMI-ACP exams, at least not yet anyway. There are always updates and changes to these exams as new best practices are realized and older best practices resurface.

So, you may ask, why the heck are we going through this? Because you may have some old-school customers or stakeholders who want this type of information. You may also be tailoring your projects to contain both Waterfall and Agile best practices and may be called upon to run a report with this information. Therefore, it's a good skill to have in your back pocket just in case.

Earned Value Analysis

The beginnings of earned value occurred in manufacturing, but it was widely embraced in the 1960s by factions of the US government, specifically the Department of Defense (DoD). You can blame the DoD for the next several pages, because I know will! All kidding aside, the technique is designed to look at the three major constraints on a project—scope, time, and cost—and determine if the project is being successfully executed to the original baselines or not. NASA and the US Department of Energy also use earned value analysis to track their budgets and schedule performance based on the scope of work completed.

A fun fact on earned value is that a massive navel military project was cancelled in 1991 by then Secretary of Defense Dick Cheney because of the results found after an earned value analysis—not satisfactory results, as I'm sure you figured out. There was too much deviation from the plan and too much time and money being spent on the scope of work.

The Project Management Institute incorporated earned value into the first edition of *A Guide to the Project Management Body of Knowledge* (*PMBOK Guide®*) in 1987, and there it has remained as a way for organizations to review project performance and make decisions.

To this day, I still have PMP students email me and say that they were asked about the technique in job interviews, and I also get my share of email from students freaking out about the math on the exam. So, now that all the hoopla as to why you should know this has been covered, here is what it is and how it pertains to your Agile and Waterfall projects.

First, we'll start with an overview of schedule control, and then we'll move to cost. I'll review all of the formulas after the introduction to the technique in both areas.

Controlling the Schedule

Earned value can be used in both predictive and Waterfall projects, and with Agile projects, it is important to recognize that there are vast differences between the two where schedules are concerned.

Predictive Projects

Predictive, or traditional, projects set baselines that are approved by the powers that be before the execution of project work. This is done to keep performance on the radar during the entire project and also to know when you have veered off your schedule. The baseline is static (unless a formal change updates the baseline at some point) and the work is fluid and is in the process of being executed.

Tracking schedule performance is iterative in nature and decisions will be made once performance has been tracked. Usually performance reporting is done weekly or even biweekly on longer-term projects. The project manager will check the current status of the schedule and ask for real-time updates from the team in order to acquire the data they need to run the analysis.

Typically, you'll overhear project managers in their current environment saying things like, "So what you are telling me is that it took you four days longer than planned to complete the work?" or my favorite, "Wait, *how long* did it take?" Either way, the project manager is keeping track of performance and progress. Often, formal changes to the scope of work will create a change in the schedule and cost baselines, and the domino effect of those changes is tracked across time and cost.

Reserves, buffer time, contingency time, padding your schedule, or whatever you want to call it, is tracked as well. This is to make sure that there is additional time somewhere in the schedule to accommodate a massive swerve from the baseline. Usually, there isn't additional time *ever*, but contingencies are often added for schedule risk. FYI, padding your schedule is bad; contingency, though, is fine! (They mean the same thing in the real world.)

Once a deviation is reported, it is then up to the project manager to determine if the deviation is outside the tolerance, and if so, then it's time to make some changes to fix the deviation. Keep in mind that predictive projects tend to be longer than Agile projects and have more of a set scope of work. Therefore, it is preplanned, baselined, and tracked.

It's rare that the scope of work would change so much from the original and not result in closing out the current project and starting another project from scratch—charter and everything.

How a Scope Change Can Cancel a Project

If you are working on a project to build 50,000 12-speed bicycles for a customer and in the middle of the project they decide that they want motorcycles instead, that scope change is exponentially different from the original scope of work. The project manager would need to have the customer sign off on the partial completion of the bicycle project and formally close it out. A new charter would then be created, new scope of work, and so forth.

> Unlike Agile projects, Waterfall projects do not support substantial changes in the middle of a project very well. Either way, a scope change can affect the original baselines and estimates and require updates to the current plans in order to track performance effectively. Small additions to the scope of work will need change requests as well. For example, the customer wants a bell on all bicycles. Now you would need to assess the impact of the change on scope, time, cost, and possibly quality. You would then need to come up with a solution to implement the change and then get a formal sign-off on your solution. The customer would also need to approve this as well, since they may not know what a bell costs or how long it might take to implement. Either way, baselines would be updated and then performance tracked against the new information.

Agile Projects

Performance is tracked a bit differently in Agile projects, and much of tracking takes place on information radiators like Kanban boards, velocity tracking, and burn up and burn down charts. However, this doesn't mean that there aren't aspects of schedule control in the form of more distinct status reports, including earned value reporting. The difference is that in Agile projects, there is a bigger focus on checking the current status of work by comparing what has actually been completed and accepted versus the estimates for completion. There is bound to be a variance due to the potential of pull systems like Kanban, where work is pulled into the iteration once other work is completed. This is less likely in a Scrum environment, where work is chosen and not added to in the middle of a sprint.

In all Agile frameworks, reviews and retrospectives are a large part of keeping track of performance and focusing on continuous improvements. Couple that with a consistent reprioritization of the product backlog and a team focus on velocity, and it's easy to see that the analysis of performance factors happens on a regular basis.

Regardless of the project type, or if the project itself is tailored to conform to your organizational dynamics, you will have a schedule, budget, and scope of work to complete, all of which can be managed using the earned value technique as needed. The difference is that Agile works from iteration to iteration to improve on processes and results and a predictive Waterfall environment uses up-front baselines and formal change control to fix problems across multiple constraints.

Controlling the Budget

Every project has budgets, which were originally created based on a business case and the decision to charter the project. How organizations determine their financial return on investment (ROI) is mostly based on the costs compared to the benefits.

The majority of projects are funded to provide a financial return to the organization after the project ends. This is based on the philosophy of having to spend money to make money. If too much is spent and not enough is gained, then the budget is experiencing *sunk costs*, meaning that money that has been sunk into the project will never be returned.

It happens more than you might think, and in general it isn't really a strong, singular, influencing factor when making the decision to pull the plug on a troubled project. It's typically not even up to the project manager to make that decision.

The organization may determine that not throwing good money after bad may be relevant in their industry or with respect to a specific project. Who are we to freak out unless it thinks we should? Throwing good money after bad is not typical or realistic in many cases, and usually once it happens, it is then actually time to freak out.

The goal to keeping an eye on cost performance is effective tracking systems, preventing scope creep, and preventing excessive expenditures for risk events that were unknown/ unknown or otherwise known as a *surprise*! Those unfortunate surprises are typically going to happen while the sponsor is keeping a pirate eye on project costs due to current and excessive project expenditures. Murphy's Law is a very real thing in project management.

One of the unfortunate results of scope creep, surprise risk events, sunk costs, and unapproved changes is that they skew the original baseline data, create a deviation from the plan versus actuals, and create cost overruns in predictive, preplanned, and pre-baselined projects.

Predictive Projects

Think about the meaning of the word *predictive*; that is, the ability to know or predict what will happen. Waterfall projects predict based on the current scope of work, much planning, and budgetary constraints, all based on *how* and *what* we *think* will happen on a project. The prediction is documented fully, and a baseline will be created for the core constraints of scope, time, and cost.

Once work is being executed, the actual performance will be compared to the baselines. Each baseline impacts the other. If the scope of work changes, it will affect the budget, schedule, and on it goes.

So how can costs be predicted and controlled? The main baseline items that control the prediction revolve around controlling changes as well. There is a very static procedure for formal change control, and it often includes *change control boards (CCBs)* whose entire role is to approve or deny changes. I often felt like I was standing in front of the Supreme Court when asking for minor changes and awaiting their response. Typically, that response was no.

To control costs effectively in a predictive or traditional project environment, it is necessary to control those influencing factors that create changes to an authorized (read, "set in stone") baseline. If changes were necessary, then all change requests need to be assessed for impact on other project factors, a solution created for implementation, an approval obtained from the powers that be, an update issued to affected baselines, and finally, the change needs to be implemented and validated to make sure it actually worked!

If a variance from the baseline is identified, then it's your job to find out what caused it, isolate it, and understand how it occurred. It's exhausting really, if I'm being honest. The good thing is that we have software that can keep us updated on variances if we set it up correctly. That software setup will directly reflect your ability to manage scope, time, and cost with an earned value approach.

Agile Projects

Change is a bit more accepted in an Agile environment. Since change is expected and more fluid, then how is it possible to control costs as well? The first thing to realize is that even though change is acceptable without all of the hoopla of formal change control, changes aren't made willy-nilly. Oh no. There is a very busy product owner who is attempting to balance customer value and organizational return on investment (ROI). There is a sponsor whose job it is to keep on top of project expenditures and, frankly, who typically finds it easier to budget per iteration or quarterly in many cases.

Effective budgeting in an Agile environment and how budgeting is done may be based on the framework you choose to use. If you keep things in the one-month iteration time frame, then budgeting can occur based on the team's selection of work, their velocity, their salaries, their burn rate, and, of course, something set aside for risk events as a contingency.

Reviewing the planned iteration or using lessons learned from past iterations allows for more effective budgeting. Plus, as the team learns more about the true definition of done, it will be easier to forecast out future costs.

The downside of this type of budgeting is that it often makes the *powers that be* uncomfortable. Those who aren't used to hearing a month-by-month prediction may ask for one large number for the entire project budget and that can be difficult to do as well as fiscally dangerous, because the numbers could be wrong when you are trying to predict an unpredictable project.

Of course, there are templates and forecasting processes that organizations use based on typical costs for similar projects. In that regard, it may be easier to budget for the unknown a bit more easily. Regardless of how the budgeting happens in your organizations, there is always somebody who wants the answer to the question, How much is the thing going to cost us?

Earned Value Technique

In order to use earned value analysis effectively, one must first have a budget in mind. In predictive environments, a baseline would be approved for both cost and time. Those baselines are created using a bottom-up estimation, which basically means attaching price tags to all instances of scope, resources, and risk and then aggregating all those price tags together into one big number. That big number gets approved as a baseline, and it is called the *budget at completion (BAC)*.

It's almost a misnomer to call it that because it sounds like something you discovered after the fact when the project has ended. Actually, it is the total number that gets approved in planning as the budget for the entire project in a Waterfall environment or for the iteration in an Agile environment. It is simply the number that you think the project or iteration is going to cost based on what you know today.

The thing to realize in this type of analysis is that time is money. We have all heard that statement at one time or another. In my experience, I often heard that statement coming from my mother when I was running late for something. If time is money, then when looking over your schedule, you are looking at what it will cost to accomplish the work that is scheduled, or to put together a *time-phased budget*.

A *time-phased budget* is where you have work that you need to accomplish within a scheduled time frame, and as you attach resources to the work, so too do you attach the costs of those resources (people, equipment, or materials), and an itemized cost estimate for each activity over time is created. This is what is known as *planned value (PV)*. This will help determine how much money you *planned* to spend on an activity over its time to completion—in other words, the budgeted cost of work scheduled.

Roll up all those itemized price tags or planned value numbers and you'll have your budget at completion (BAC). Conversely, if you took an entire budget and parceled it out over work to be accomplished, those would be your planned values (PVs).

As of right now, we are still in the planning phase and have not actually executed any work. We have laid the groundwork for the budget and the schedule, and we'll assume that it has been approved as a baseline or iteration budget.

Once work begins, so too do the questions of how long it actually took and how much did you actually spend. The money actually spent on the work is called the actual cost (AC).

 Real World Scenario

How Earned Value Mirrors Real Life

If you aren't familiar with earned value, let me explain it in a different way. It's kind of like when you go to get your car's oil changed. You go in there thinking, "Hey, I have a coupon for a $39.99 oil change, so I will only spend $39.99, which is my budget for the completion of this task," or your BAC. You also think, "It should only take an hour to complete," which is your PV. Then you find yourself sticking your head under the hood with the mechanic who proceeds to show you that you need a new oil filter, brakes, fluids, and some kind of alternator thingy. Now your $39.99 oil change becomes $3,000 dollars in actual cost, or your AC. It took twice as long as you planned, and you have a brand spanking new alternator thingy that you never intended to buy.

As your team is doing the work, you will be keeping an eye on that work and determining if they are moving as quickly as you thought they would as well as if they are getting as much accomplished as planned. This is where earned value comes into the mix. *Earned value (EV)* is the budgeted cost of work completed, meaning what percent has the team completed on project work and what is that work worth based on the original budget. Essentially, you can calculate earned value by taking the percent complete and multiplying it by the budget at completion:

$$\text{Earned value} = \% \text{ complete} \times \text{BAC}$$

If I were walking around with a checkbook in my hand to pay people for what they have actually accomplished, I would only pay them based on what the work is worth. This doesn't mean that they are on time or on budget; it means that I'm looking at the financial value of the work and what they have earned by accomplishing it.

Let's take a painting project that I had done at my home last year as an example to keep things very simple, mostly because the concept of earned value has a tendency to put the hardiest math whizzes to sleep, and put those who are mathematically challenged in general (raises hand) into a bit of a panic. I'll remind you again that unless your organization demands this or you are taking the PMP exam, you won't have questions related to earned value at this point in time.

If that has changed from the writing of this chapter to when you read this book, that's totally my bad. However, please know that I'm empathetic and sympathetic about it, and I know the difference between the two!

 Real World Scenario

Painting by Numbers

I hired two people to paint my living room last year. I asked them how long they thought it would take and they said four days. I also asked them how much it would cost for their labor and materials. They said $2,000 (apparently the paint in my living room is made of gold or something? Outrageous! I digress.) I approved the budget at completion (BAC) of $2,000 and the schedule of four days, which worked out to be (with all things being equal in distribution) approximately $500 dollars a wall (PV). At the end of day three, I walked in to check their work and noticed that there were two walls that had been completed, which is 50 percent of the work, or one $1,000 worth of work (EV). I then asked for the receipts for the materials, and they equaled $1,500 (AC). So, what did I know about how my project was progressing?

Original budget, or budget at completion (BAC) = $2,000.

Planned value (PV) at this point in the schedule (end of day 3) = $1,500 worth of work *should* have been done at this point.

Earned value (EV) is 50% × $2,000 = $1,000 of *actual* work completed.

Actual cost (AC), or what they spent on materials to date = $1,500.

How do you think I was feeling about my painters without even doing any math at all? I'm not happy at all, and here is why:

They are behind schedule: They should have done $500 more work at this point in the schedule.

They are currently over budget. If I review what they have spent to date, it looks like they did $1,000 worth of work and spent $1,500 on it.

I know what you are thinking: Maybe they bought all of the materials up front, and when all is said and done they won't be over budget, and you would be correct. These things fluctuate daily, weekly, and monthly, but right now in my living room it looks sketchy.

Now, maybe they will work like crazy on the last day and bang it all out within schedule. Again, you would be correct, but right now in my living room they appear to be behind schedule. The entire point of tracking performance is to see red flags and determine whether they need fixing with corrective action or if the work is still bouncing between tolerance levels and may reset itself to what it should be.

If you are wondering, it took them a half a day longer to finish the living room than forecast, but they didn't charge me any additional money. Behind schedule but on budget. Needless to say, my husband and I have done the rest of the painting in the house ourselves. We are typically behind schedule and over budget, but we are also our own sponsor and don't have to answer to anyone else, and that makes all the difference in the world.

The Formulas

There are two variations of performance tracking, and while both use the same data, the result gives you different information. First there are variances, or the difference between what we thought would happen in planning and what is actually occurring. There are also indexes, or ratings of efficiency on the schedule and budget, still based on what you thought would happen and what is actually happening. Let's start with variances.

Variances *Variances* give us information on how far over or under budget or schedule we are compared to the approved baselines. The resulting data is represented by whole or negative numbers. Negative results are bad for the project, positive results are good for the project, and break even means we are right on track.

The formulas for schedule and cost variances include the earned value (EV) compared against planned value (PV) for schedule variance (SV) and earned value (EV) compared against actual cost (AC) for budgetary performance or cost variance (CV).

$$\text{Earned value (EV)} - \text{planned value (PV)} = \text{schedule variance (SV)}$$
$$\text{Earned value (EV)} - \text{actual cost (AC)} = \text{cost variance (CV)}$$

A good rule of thumb at first glance is that if the earned value is less than the planned value, you are behind schedule, and if the earned value is less than the actual cost, you are over budget.

Indexes *Indexes* measure efficiency of cost and schedule. This information allows for replanning or preventative actions to be taken. The formulas for schedule and cost indexes include the earned value (EV) compared against planned value (PV) for schedule performance and earned value (EV) compared against actual cost (AC) for budgetary performance.

The resulting data is represented by percentages or decimal results. Any result below 1.0 is bad for the project, while any result above 1.0 is good for the project. 1.0 means that you are exactly where you are supposed to be. The same rule of thumb applies here. If the earned value (EV) is less than either the planned value (PV) or the actual cost (AC), then the project is not progressing with the efficiency for which you had planned.

Earned value (EV) / planned value (PV) = schedule performance index (SPI)
Earned value (EV) / actual cost (AC) = cost performance index (CPI)

I like to think of 1.0 as 100 percent efficiency in schedule performance. If schedule performance is above 1.0, it means that you are performing above 100 percent efficiency, and if it is below 100 percent, then you are less efficient and therefore behind schedule.

On the cost side of things, I like to think about a 1.0 as one dollar, so if you have a CPI that is less than a 1.0, you are getting less than a dollar's worth of work done and paying a dollar for that work. Over time, you'll end up over budget if you aren't already there. If the CPI is above 1.0, then you are getting more than a dollar's worth of work done and only paying a dollar for it—more work is accomplished, while less money is spent. You'll be under budget if things continue the way they are today. If the result is exactly 1.0 for cost or schedule, you are exactly where you are supposed to be—100 percent efficient on your schedule and paying one dollar for one dollar's worth of work.

When you are running earned value analysis in a software program, you will see that every task or user story has a value, a schedule, and a price tag. When looking at the big picture of the entire project, it would be easy to see just exactly where the project is going sideways and to apply corrective actions where they belong.

The downside is usually that those tasks or stories are attached to other things, and the domino effect of low performance in one area could certainly squeak by and affect other tasks or stories, in essence, guilt by association. That is why we take a lot of the results with however many grains of salt we need, with the realization that performance could change for the better or for the worse. We don't wait until something magical happens that improves our performance one minute before we take the long walk to the sponsor's office for a status meeting (as tempting as that sounds, it's unrealistic unless you are Harry Potter). Instead, we start looking at ways to improve performance and take away lessons learned about our estimating prowess or lack thereof.

Earned value gives you a snapshot in time, comparing planned data with what is actually happening today. That information allows for change, new decisions, and a heads-up of what could follow.

What you do with that information depends on the type of projects on which you work. In a predictive Waterfall environment, you may decide to process a formal change request to adapt the schedule or cost behaviors and wait for approval. Once you have the approval, you implement the change and then validate that it actually worked. You may even choose to do nothing if the tasks don't really impact your bottom line too much.

In an Agile environment, project performance would be discussed during a retrospective, and the team would determine ways to improve performance in the next iteration. Perhaps the estimates were too optimistic or the velocity wasn't what was predicted? Maybe your team is taking extra steps that cost time and money, and they can work to streamline their efforts and remove waste from the process going forward?

Continuous improvement on performance is key in Agile projects, which is why I think earned value is a topic to discuss whether exam testable or not. It's hard to argue with hard data.

Key Performance Indicators

Key performance indicators (KPIs) are ways that most Agile teams track performance. That is not to say there aren't tailored approaches that include earned value, but it's more to the point that earned value results could be a key performance indicator. KPI is a bit like ROI, meaning that it is dependent on what the organization or the team determines is valuable information to improve performance. You have reviewed burn down and burn up charts, velocity tracking, story points, and the like for running an Agile project. All of those results plotted out on charts and graphs could be considered information on performance in key indicators.

How much work is the team accomplishing in an iteration or sprint? What is the difference between what they thought they would get accomplished and what was actually presented to the customer in a review? These are questions that will need answers, and much of performance tracking includes real-time work and real-time results.

What are the key performance indicators that show how performance is being managed and how the work is being executed? That is up to your organization, and it is the key data necessary to drive the implementation of improvements.

We know that velocity fluctuates, and we know that scope will change. If everything is so uncertain, then how can you track performance? Many times, there are two types of data to review. The first is team performance, including but not limited to the amount of story points that they select versus what they accomplish. There is always a big focus on continuous improvements and working to improve the value stream or to output more value in less time. It's part of the culture of Agile teams.

All that focus on team performance is important, but what about the product and its quality? It's one thing to bust out a new software program in the time frame that we said we would, and it's quite another situation if that software is buggy, doesn't work, or doesn't perform to standards. Then the team performance is really a moot point. I'd rather see that they slowed down a bit and did it right the first time.

As you determine how you and your team will perform, it is important to set some goals and, moreover, to make them smart goals. The mnemonic of SMART was originally referred to in 1981 in a magazine article written by George T. Doran as a way to help organizations make goal setting more explicit and to help zero in on the reason goals don't get met.

> There's a S.M.A.R.T. way to write management's goals and objectives.
>
> *George T. Doran, Management Review, AMA FORUM (1981)*

Later, the idea of setting smart goals was attributed to Peter Drucker and the philosophy of management by objective, or MBO. Throughout the years, the mnemonic or acronym adapted and adjusted to different verbiage, but the crux of the thought process remains the same. How do you make smart goals and work to attain them?

In Figure 8.1, you can see how the SMART process of setting goals allows for a focus on each item and a way to determine what a goal should look like to make it more likely to be achieved.

FIGURE 8.1   SMART

S {	• Specific
M {	• Measurable
A {	• Assignable • Achievable
R {	• Realistic
T {	• Time-bound • Time-related

I once read an article that said 92 percent of all New Year's resolutions end up failing by February. That is why the gyms are filled with people on January 2nd and by February they're empty, and you can actually hear crickets.

What are the other 8 percent doing differently? They are setting realistic, smart goals. The key to specificity is removing the vagary from the equation. Instead of "I want to lose weight," which is too vague, it could instead be "I want to lose 10 pounds." That goal is more specific and it is measurable. How about assignable? Oh, I wish I could assign someone else to lose 10 pounds for me! Instead, we'll focus on attainable for our goal. Is it attainable? Sure, people do it all the time. Not me, but you know, "people" do it all the time. How about realistic? That is a personal question, thank you very much, but a question nonetheless. Is losing 10 pounds realistic for the way life is rolling right now? If not, the goal will not be met unless my time frame is such that I can work around my crazy life and make it happen. Time-based goal, hmm: 2030?

In all seriousness, when I make goals now for life or for when I'm working with a team of people who need a bit more help to design their career goals, I use SMART goal setting. It's a very different way of compartmentalizing what you want to achieve. If the stars don't align across all SMART aspects, then that goal most likely will not be met.

If you have ever watched *The Simpsons* on television and seen the episode of Homer singing, "I am so smart, SMRT," then you know if one piece of the equation is missing, it's not so smart, D'oh!

Real World Scenario

Setting SMART goals

When I first started my management career, I was tasked with fixing a team of product specialists who needed a bit of help getting their act together. My sponsor at the time was a huge movie buff, and the way he explained my new role to me was "The first rule of fight club is, don't talk about fight club." (*Fight Club*, 20th Century Fox, 1999). What he meant was, don't bring me your problems, just fix them, and oh by the way, "May the force be with you" (*Star Wars*, 20th Century Fox, 1977). Alrighty then.

My new team consisted of five people who had never worked in the industry before, one person who had a tendency to go off on a break numerous times a day and could not be found anywhere right about the time they had to talk to customers, and another seven people who really appeared to me as people who couldn't care less about the job. In other words, I had a big task at hand.

I worked with the team on goal setting over the course of three months. I had one-on-one meetings with everyone once a week, and they would work to set goals. I found that if I discussed with them where their struggles were and asked them to focus on three things to improve upon, they were very clear on the things they needed to work on but didn't have any idea how to fix them

At about the same time, I took a management class and the concept of SMART was discussed. It was eye opening, not just for myself but for my team as well. Over the next three months, my team focused only on goals that they could attain. These were goals that were created using SMART as a guide. Little by little the team's morale improved, their performance improved, and the motivation to continue to improve was high. At the end of five months, my team was one of the higher-performing teams in the organization, and when asked how I did it I said, "Elementary, my dear Watson" (*The Adventures of Sherlock Holmes*, 20th Century Fox, 1939). We were SMART about it. Ever since then, any goal that I set for myself or encouraged my teams to make follow a very simple process; that is, to make specific goals that are measurable, attainable, realistic, and time-based. We make them SMART.

Key performance indicators tend to be based on both tangible results, like work completed or time and money, and intangible items, like how the team works together, whether they have reached the performing stage, and what the Agile project manager's day-to-day influence looks like. If you are having to remind your team every single day that stand-up meetings literally mean standing up, then you have your work cut out for you. If you are more of a servant leader, motivator, and coach, then the team performance is up to snuff.

Just as setting SMART goals is an important aspect of improving performance, keeping track of other team performance improvements are crucial to the project's success as well. What is seen as a key performance indicator may rest solely on the framework you choose to use. Scrum KPIs may be different from XP KPIs. If you are designing software programs, performance indicators may be very different from a team that is implementing a new process or producing something more tangible.

From a business or customer standpoint, the scope, time, and money performance is crucial. From a team perspective, it may be improving best practices from iteration to iteration in how stories are estimated, what the definition of done is, velocity improvements, or actual stories completed versus planned.

As an Agile project manager and servant leader, coaching your team when needed begins with knowing what types of indicators show a high-performing team versus one that needs additional help and possibly a SMART goal-setting session. It's always best to have the team determine what success factors need tracking and to understand management goals.

Those success indicators and goals need to be explicit so that there isn't any question as to what information will need to be reviewed and reported. The keys to success are performance indicators that are well defined and well reviewed throughout the course of the project.

The Triple Constraints

Most projects have a semblance of balance between competing constraints. The term the *triple constraints* or the *iron triangle* describes what was initially a way to document the big constraints of scope, time, and cost. Quality was later added to the mix because it is so closely tied to the scope of work. Now with risk and resources added to the list, the triangle has gotten a bit busy and is now referred to as the *competing constraints*. Our focus, however, will be on the big constraints of scope, time, and cost.

In a Waterfall project environment, the scope of work is fixed, while time, cost, and quality work around that constraint.

In Figure 8.2 you'll see that in an Agile environment, the triangle is flipped because cost and time are fixed, while scope is flexible and quality is dependent on the scope of work. In some cases, quality is very flexible if the development team knows they will be pushing out bug fixes or software updates in the very near future. The goal is to create a minimally marketable feature that is the simplest thing that works.

FIGURE 8.2 The competing constraints

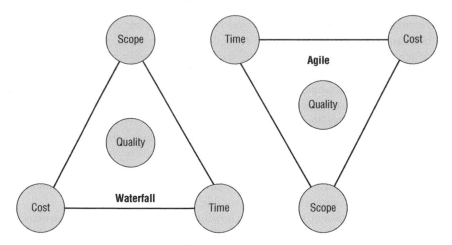

Determining what the scope of work really is will be the key to meeting requirements and providing value to the user. That scope will be driven by a fixed budget and schedule per iteration.

The Gulf of Misunderstanding

The *gulf of misunderstanding* sounds very much like the Bermuda Triangle of Agile and in fact is a fairly good description of what can happen when the customer/end user and the team totally miss each other's point and land in the deep end.

The concept of the gulf of misunderstanding is more often called the *gulf of evaluation* in a software development environment. The gulf of misunderstanding is a catchier and more apt description, though. Both terms mean that somebody missed the point.

When applied to software development, the gulf of evaluation is the difference between what the end user wants and what is created for them. Because of the misunderstanding, the true results won't match up to the needs of the end user and are a waste of time and money.

The hard part in a software design project is that the end user may not know what they want, or they may not understand the jargon. *GUI* sounds like something that sticks to the bottom of your shoe instead of actually meaning graphical user interface. It would be easier if someone just said, "You know those icons on your desktop? Yeah, that helps the computer understand what it is you want it to do without you having to know the language of the computer. So, what icons do you want?"

An end user may not understand the technical jargon and tell the team to "do whatever you want or think is right." Now you may get some software developers working on something they think is cool but is completely out of scope for what the end user wants or needs. The gulf of misunderstanding strikes again.

> Abbott: No. What is on second.
>
> Costello: I'm not asking you who's on second.
>
> Abbott: Who's on first.
>
> Costello: I don't know.
>
> Abbott: He's on third, we're not talking about him.
>
> Costello: Now how did I get on third base?
>
> Abbott: Why you mentioned his name.
>
> Costello: If I mentioned the third baseman's name, who did I say is playing third?
>
> Abbott: No. Who's playing first.
>
> Costello: What's on first?
>
> Abbott: What's on second.
>
> Costello: I don't know.
>
> Abbott: He's on third.
>
> *Bud Abbott and Lou Costello*

A large part of making sure time, effort, and money aren't wasted on producing items that aren't wanted, needed, or understood is the concept of prioritization, so there is a firm understanding of what will be created and in what order.

The product owner will communicate as often as possible to help the customer understand and/or help the team create something of value if the product owner is in fact the customer. The team will then work with the product owner and/or customer to prioritize what is most valuable or necessary now. All activities and transparent discussions are utilized to avoid falling into the gulf.

The rest of this chapter is designed around ways to provide value without misunderstandings. Some of the techniques you have reviewed in other chapters. Others are there to help you help yourselves and your customers/end users get what they want without rework due to misunderstandings. Remember, this all goes back to providing value and the organization getting the return on investment they expected for the time and money they allotted. It's a win/win for everyone.

Dot Voting, or Multi-Voting

If you have a long list of items that need to be sorted in order of importance or in order of occurrence, it can be difficult to get everyone on the same page. However, if everyone has a say and that leads to a cumulative agreement, then it may not be so bad. This is where dot voting, or multi-voting, can help your team make decisions in a facilitated, orderly fashion—plus you get to play with stickers!

The concept of a democracy comes from the Greek word meaning *rule of the people,* or *rule of the majority*, and in this sense the best practice of voting was born. In an Agile environment, a *dotmocracy* may be necessary to reach consensus through voting.

Dot voting is a facilitated event in which the team has a set amount of dot stickers to their name. They are then asked to vote on certain options. The individual uses as many dots as they want for a cross section of options, and in general the options with the most dots are priorities.

In some cases, the team will use red and green dot stickers to represent what they agree or disagree with. There is often a lot of discussion around the decisions, but the goal is not to create an environment of groupthink. Groupthink is the opposite of a facilitated decision-making exercise, meaning that the strongest personalities usually influence the rest of the group. Meanwhile, the rest of the group doesn't want to create conflict or analyze the options thoroughly, so they go along with whatever decision is made or whatever options are presented. The upside to groupthink is that decisions are made quickly and consensus *appears* to happen. The downside is that relevant information may not be discussed and major features may not be built. Now the stronger personalities get to win because they said so. Dot voting allows each person to have an opinion and openly vote on their opinion. They are then asked to explain the reasoning to the rest of the group as needed for the group to make informed decisions. Groupthink is the easy way out, and many risk events and key features have been missed because of it.

If this is a bigger group event that includes senior management or the customer, different color dots can be used to represent senior management's votes versus team votes and even customer votes. That way, who voted for what is much clearer.

There is literally no wrong way to do dot voting, and I've found that, in some cases, it opens up the lines of communication a bit and allows everyone to have an opinion. When the dust settles and the votes are counted, it just "is what it is," and everyone agrees to the decisions that were made. In a perfect world, the number of votes something gets describes a clear winner and that is that. However, since the scope of work changes regularly, voting doesn't happen just once.

Embracing a dotmocracy may occur at every review or during backlog refinement or even in a retrospective when things didn't go so well. Mostly, the process is about prioritization, discussion, and embracing all ideas. Dot voting is a quick, straightforward way to reach consensus.

Much as with everything we vote on, there are some downsides to dot voting. There could be a sense that even though something has been explained as necessary, others don't buy in and views aren't heard. There is also always the possibility that someone isn't fully caffeinated and that they just stick stickers wherever so that they can get to the break room as quickly as possible.

This is a good lesson for Agile project managers whose job as facilitators rests on how the team engages with each other. With that in mind, it is better to set some ground rules about time to make decisions or time for discussions when holding any kind of voting. You know your team, and you will also know if this type of engagement would be effective in your own environment.

The first time I tried this, there were more stickers on the team members' backs than on the board due to rowdy team members who thought they were being funny. A week later, I still found dots stuck everywhere. That onus is on me for not setting ground rules and facilitating appropriately. It's a cautionary tale. Otherwise, have at it! It can be a fun, relaxed way to make decisions as a team and to help get priorities straight.

MoSCoW

This section is just a *reminder* of the prioritization technique of *MoSCoW* that you covered in Chapter 3, "Key Aspects of Additional Agile Methodologies." The entire premise of using the acronym is the process to determine what *must* end up in the result no matter what, what *should* be in the result, what *could* be, and what *won't* be in the result. Obviously, things change, and in some cases what should be included will rise to the top and become a must-have, and what could be in the result can slide down the ladder to the won't pile.

The MoSCoW Approach to Focusing on the Business Need

- *MUST* have this requirement to meet the business needs.
- *SHOULD* have this requirement if possible, but the project success does not rely on it.

- *COULD* have this requirement if it does not affect the business needs of the project.
- *WON'T* have this requirement, and the stakeholders have agreed that it will not be implemented in a release but may be considered for the future.

Prioritization is a moving target, but by simply asking the right questions during backlog refinement or in selecting work to be done, it is easier to use a categorization schema than to go in a million different directions and not get anything accomplished. The minimally viable product or minimally marketable feature would contain mostly must-haves. The goal is to have end users understand what value is and what items need to be in the increment. Reaching an understanding of the classifications can be difficult, though. Allow me a quick tangent.

In risk management, we often use a high, medium, or low classification for probability and impact. This can be difficult to quantify because if I have stakeholders who are risk takers, they may not look at an identified risk as high probability or impact, whereas someone who is a catastrophic thinker may see red flags everywhere. Who is correct?

It's important to get everyone on the same page as to what is high, medium, or low. The same concept applies to must, should, and could. In risk management, you are considering the stakeholders' level of tolerance for certain risk events, and in prioritization methods like MoSCoW, you are seeking an understanding of what is valuable. That can be difficult since what is valuable to one may not be valuable to another. I find it is best to quantify classifications and communicate around them.

Monopoly Money

If I were to hand you a million dollars today, how would you spend it? Would you travel the world? Buy properties? Start a business? Invest it? Buy a very expensive sports car? What is most important to you?

What I might do with a million dollars may be very different from what you would do with the same opportunity. I'm also aware of the curse of the lottery winners who spend all of their money in all the wrong places and end up with nothing in the end. From a business and financial perspective that sounds terrible, and you might think to yourself, I would never do that if I won the lottery; yet it happens all the time.

Organizations spend billions (with a *b*) every single year on projects that aren't successful: good money being thrown after bad money. Such projects include customers who are disappointed with the quality of the work or the result that isn't what they expected, recalls that end up on the news, and projects that are cancelled before they ever get off the ground. It's the cost of doing business.

This is where a cool little exercise called *Monopoly Money* makes all the difference in the world. If you have never played the game of Monopoly, which originally was sold by Parker Brothers and now by Hasbro, then here is a quick overview. The object of the game is to become the wealthiest player by buying and selling property. There are also some pesky interruptions to that process, like not being able to pass Go without a payout and the possibility of landing in jail. The bottom line is that to win the game, you have to gain as much money or assets as possible before someone in your family flips the board over in frustration and announces that they are finished with the game. At least that's how it works in my house anyway.

The interesting thing is that the game was originally created as an educational tool to explain the downsides of the single tax rule or having land concentrations in private monopolies. The game's patent and sales history is quite fascinating if you are looking for ways to waste time at work, and if you find yourself playing trivial pursuit instead, it may come up in a question.

> Rule No.1: Never lose money.
>
> Rule No.2: Never forget rule No.1.
>
> *Warren Buffett*

The question of what you would do with a million dollars and how you would spend it is the premise behind Monopoly Money as a prioritization technique. The sponsor or customer is given Monopoly Money in the equivalent of the current project budget and then asked how they would spend it and where. This eye-opening experience for both the sponsor and the team is an excellent way to see what is deemed a priority over another.

We always stick to features during this process because what the team might find as a valuable day-to-day practice, the sponsor sees as having no value and vice versa. I know I'm not throwing money at an earned value report lest someone ask for one, and the sponsor may not see value in our little dotmocracy. Stick to the features. For some reason, when money, fake or otherwise, is in the mix, the seriousness of decision making becomes more prevalent. Fun with stickers is one thing, but with money, oh now we are *really* getting somewhere!

Just like any other conversationally driven, facilitated event in Agile frameworks, you will walk away with a better understanding of what is valuable to everyone involved. The sponsor will understand how their money may be spent, and the team can now determine of all the valuable items, what stories need to be written and selected to accomplish in the next iteration.

The goal in any project is to provide a quality result in a way that is within budget, within schedule, and within the scope of work. The almighty dollar speaks volumes in this technique, and it quantifies the work for all involved.

100 Points

The 100-point method is like Monopoly Money in the sense that there is an allocation or distribution of something across features and the ability to vote on features. Everyone has 100 points that they can allocate however they want to. Some team members may feel very strongly about one feature and use all of their points to prove a point, but mostly the team will use their points in a way that shows priority. Much of the time my team agrees on the big features and the priority of them, but the features that have less priority to some are higher in priority to others.

Because the team is voting and can use their points, however, like our facilitated voting event, it will often include a rousing discussion by technologically savvy people speaking in code and using sci-fi references to make a point. (I'm usually the one using the sci-fi references.) The rest of the team is discussing the ins and outs of the features and the technology behind the features, and with that stream of consciousness some support items may come to the surface. This happens more times than not due to some supportive features becoming necessary.

If a main feature is a priority but it needs something in a lower priority ranking executed so that it can actually function, then that lower-priority feature has moved up the ranks.

Just as with any other activity to determine priority, priorities change, and, using a technique of 100-points can help the team distribute priority across multiple features in multiple iterations.

Kano Analysis

What defines priority may come down to personal opinions of what is most interesting or exciting about a result. I know that if I have some technology that I love because it does something I really want it to do, I can forgive it crashing a few times or being a bit buggy. That is because something I see as super cool was created: I bought it and I use it. There are some reasons consumers line up around the block for the next big technological thing, even though in most cases it's just an updated version of the thing they are currently using. "Did you hear the headphone jack is at the bottom now? Somebody please take my money!"

What excites us about software and technology are all the things that can help make our lives easier. In order to do that, there is a fine balance that must be met of whether or not the product works well, or whether or not it has exciting features that I want, or whether it contains any deal breakers that would make me go to the competition. Welcome to software development! *Kano analysis* is a model of determining distinct categories of needs or wants and quality of product.

The beginnings of Kano analysis were created by Professor Noriaki Kano in the 1980s as a way to classify the preferences of customers. The theory was based on quality. The various category labels may have changed over the years, but the premise remains the same. There are certain things that cause customers to buy and other things that cause them to walk away. That is the beauty of a capitalistic society; everyone has the option to do either based on their needs at the time.

If that is the case, then as an Agile practitioner it's important to be able to classify features based on very distinct categories.

Delighters or exciters, satisfiers, and dissatisfiers.

Delighters or Exciters   These are the features and functions that the customer finds super cool and is excited to begin using.

Oh my. There is a watch that is like a phone, and I can use it to track my sleeping patterns? I must have one right now.

Satisfiers   My watch answers phone calls and allows me to receive emails and texts even when my actual phone is somewhere else.

Dissatisfiers   My watch keeps telling me to breathe every hour to relax, and frankly I find it annoying and it's stressing me out.

Here's the deal with exciters and satisfiers—they change over time. What I find exciting about technology today will be replaced with something else tomorrow.

> I forget things almost instantly. It runs in my family… well, at least I
> think it does.
>
> *Finding Nemo*

The odds of customers finding new shiny things to be excited about on new or updated products on a regular basis is very high. What once was an exciter is now simply a satisfier. We still like it and want it, but we are not jumping up and down about it anymore.

The importance of continual analysis of what is deemed valuable and necessary today also has to be balanced with what the end users find exciting. The goal is to attempt to balance that and add it to the mix if the feature doesn't take away from the performance of a satisfier.

Kano analysis shows that innovation and exciters become basic needs in the long run. The goal is to make sure that the satisfiers are always included in the product and that they work. If satisfiers don't work effectively, then dissatisfaction occurs. In Figure 8.3 you can see a very simple example of Kano Analysis which can be used as a discussion piece when determining features.

FIGURE 8.3   Kano analysis

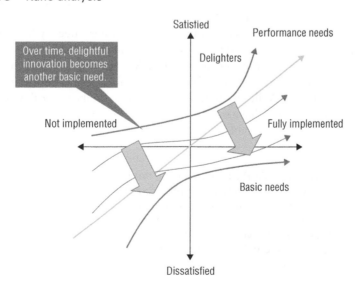

Customized Procurement

Procurement is pretty much always necessary on any type of project. Whether it be Waterfall or Agile related, there will always be a need for goods and services, materials, and equipment from an outside source.

Most organizations that run projects have a procurement department, or at the very least a legal team who helps with terms and conditions and negotiates the agreement. It is rare that an Agile project manager or a Waterfall project manager would be doing the actual negotiations and contractually binding their organization to that of another without an attorney present.

The bottom line is that the project manager will understand the scope of work and may be tasked with creating a *procurement statement of work (PSOW)* that is itemized for the procurement needs. They would then need to understand what constitutes a viable option when bids start coming in. Basically, that involves determining if a bid or proposal goes into the Yes or No pile and understanding the source selection criteria, or in other words, the criteria by which we select our seller.

Many times, in a more traditional Waterfall environment, the project manager would be the one who is responsible for protecting the organization from future costs and litigation (litigation bad; negotiation good!) as well as having the skill sets to weed through a variety of bids, quotes, and proposals to determine which sellers meet the project needs.

Also, traditionally contracts have been very rigid in their terms and conditions. For traditional projects, *fixed-price agreements* were good for the project because the scope of work is well known and the project can budget the costs easily. *Cost-reimbursable contracts*, on the other hand, are more flexible for scope changes but a little too flexible on the cost side, so budgeting is more difficult. No matter what, though, when I think of a contract, I think of something that would be very difficult to change or adapt as needed on an Agile project where change and flexibility are necessary.

You can adapt to different flavors of contract types in either category by adding words like *incentive fee* or *fixed fee* and adding tons of terms and conditions, but a contract is still a contract, and a breach of contract isn't acceptable. What to do? Create a change control procedure that is a bit easier to work with but have an attorney present for all changes? That is a lot to ask for in an Agile environment. Because of the need for flexibility on the scope side of things, and to still have some semblance of planning ahead, much more flexible procurement options are available.

On your PMI-ACP exams, you will not be asked to understand different procurement types in depth. You may get questions on how flexible procurement is more necessary in an Agile environment, but you will only need a surface-level understanding of the contract types; that is, unless you are working with flexible procurement in your organization. In that case, you will find these questions very generic to your day-to-day environment.

As far as the assorted flavors of Agile procurement, there are many more than what you will see here, and some may have different terminology based on your organization. As a high-level overview, here is a list of the types that you could see in your organization or as they pop up in an exam question.

Fixed-Price, Fixed-Scope (and possibly Fixed-Time)   Good when requirements are known or stable and very common in both Waterfall and Agile environments. Very simple terms and conditions, and it just "is what it is" for cost, scope, and time as needed.

The Fix and Switch   Fixed-price, fixed-scope (and possibly fixed-time) but vague enough that the contract can be altered to meet customer needs. The downside is that it isn't the easiest contract to get sellers to agree on due to the vagary of the contract itself and because collaboration is needed with the product owner/customer in order to alter scope.

Time and Materials   This contract is very common in all project types. Basically, it is designed to pay for the work as it gets accomplished, or for materials/equipment as they are needed and used. Good for flexible scope, and typically has a ceiling price or not to exceed number.

Not-to-Exceed with Fixed-Fee (NTE/FF)   This type isn't so flexible but might be relevant if it is used for an iteration or a point in the project where the specific scope of work is known. There is flexibility to a point, but as soon as the ceiling is hit, it's done, and the seller will receive a fixed fee as a profit. It will have a definitive ceiling price.

Fixed Price per Function Point or Story Point   This type allows for reprioritizing scope and calculations based on velocity and embraces the agility of many project types. Keep in mind that velocity tends to fluctuate in the beginning and then plateau, so costs may be a bit wonky until that happens.

Graduated Fixed Price   Finally, this contract type allows for incentives and focuses more on other items in the project that may be more important than money. This agreement may provide for different hourly rates for early, on-time, or late delivery of work in a tiered approach.

Regardless of the types of contracts your organization works with, you may find that the sellers or suppliers are also part of your team or are for sure considered stakeholders. With a lot of the more flexible contract types for Agile projects, both the buyers and the sellers share some of the risk, especially the cost risk. When the scope of work is flexible, it's more difficult to set requirements in stone. With fluctuations in scope come the inevitable fluctuations in cost. This can be concerning for sponsors or customers because typically time and cost are fixed while scope is flexible. Because budgets may be created per iteration, it can lead to some creative contracting.

Many organizations find it better to work with adaptive contracting across the board. A *master service agreement (MSA)* may be more realistic for your organization due to its flexibility regarding future changes. Many times, a master-level service agreement allows for acceptance of terms and conditions that will apply in the future as well, regardless of scope changes. Both parties will agree to those terms and conditions on the front end about how decisions will be made in the future. This keeps all necessary negotiation focused on the scope of work changes rather than continuously updating or negotiating on other terms and conditions.

Master service agreements may also include open-ended fields that can be adapted throughout the project. In most cases, a *Statement of Work (SOW)* is written into the service agreement as well. Along with the scope of work, there are also provisions (as in all contracts) for risk allocation and indemnification.

Risk allocation is setting very specific standards for how risk will be handled during the agreement and who are the responsible parties. Indemnification allows one party legally to exclude the other party from payments or damage in the future. In simpler terms, it would be written in the contract that Party A will not hold Party B accountable for financial losses in the future based on decisions made today regardless of who is at fault—lots of legalese that you don't need to know about unless you are managing procurement in your organization.

Here are some concluding thoughts on procurement. It is typically the project manager's role to protect the organization from future litigation and to manage good, working relationships with the sellers, meaning don't breach contracts, don't allow them to breach contracts, and engage the sellers as you would any other stakeholders on the project regardless of the framework or methodology you practice.

Summary

In this chapter, we covered the execution of work on an Agile project and revisited some of the items that not only can determine return on investment (ROI) by using benefit measurement techniques but can also show whether ROI has been met. We reviewed some of the specific key performance indicators (KPIs) that drive project performance, and I included an overview of the earned value technique (EVT) used on many project types to track scope, time, and cost completions. This data can also be used to predict project performance should the project move forward with the same performance trends.

Next we reviewed some of the many ways that value is determined both by the customer and the team. Some of these were reviewed at a high level in other chapters, like the MoSCoW technique of determining what must, should, could, and won't be included in the deliverable or result.

Then we covered other techniques that allow specific ways to help determine value and gauge if the ROI is being met while avoiding the gulf of misunderstanding between customer and team. Techniques like dot voting, Monopoly Money, and 100 points allow for transparent communication and consensus to be reached before anything is produced.

We also reviewed Kano analysis, which is likewise used to determine value for features and items that can create excitement in the end user while maintaining that the satisfiers are met as well.

Finally, we covered some ways that Agile organizations utilize a more flexible procurement approach. This allows an organization to enter into a contractual relationship with sellers while allowing for changes in scope to be added and removed more easily. Having more flexibility in procurement is key to creating and maintaining good relationships with the sellers and to reduce the risk of breach of contract or other alternative dispute resolutions like arbitration, mediation, and litigation.

Exam Essentials

Be able to understand how return on investment (ROI) is determined.   Understand why it is important to know how your organization views what is considered to be valuable and how benefit measurement methods extend past a simple business case and creation of the project charter.

Understand the concept of earned value technique (EVT).   While you may not be tested on actual formulas and equations, it's important to understand how project execution can be tracked using schedule and cost variance information as well as indexes of efficiency. This can lead the team to adapting and adjusting their strategy to meet organizational goals.

Be able to understand the different ways to determine value.   Having a misunderstanding about what the customer or end users want will lead the team to create an incorrect increment. This causes lost time and money and a significant amount of rework. Avoiding the gulf of misunderstanding is crucial to project success. Dot voting, MoSCoW, Monopoly Money, and 100-point assessments can clarify the requirements and allow for a consensus to be reached.

Understand Kano analysis.   You won't be heavily tested on this concept, but this analysis technique is an excellent way to categorize qualitatively what the end users find exciting in a feature and what is necessary to maintain satisfaction in the result. Conversely, it is also useful to understand what might be a dissatisfier or feature that isn't valuable to the end user so that additional money and time isn't wasted producing something that the customer doesn't want, need, or even like.

Be aware of different ways to utilize procurement contract types.   Because the scope of work is more flexible or malleable on Agile projects, it is important to have a procurement process that is as well. You won't get many questions on the exam about contract types specifically, just the need for scope flexibility and how different agreement types can accommodate that need. Having a good high-level understanding of procurement is also important in your day-to-day procurement endeavors, should your organizations utilize the use of sellers or suppliers.

Review Questions

You can find the answers to the review questions in Appendix B.

1. Who determines the process to prioritize value in an Agile project?

   A. The customer

   B. The Scrum Master

   C. The product owner

   D. The entire team

2. Misunderstandings of value, product, and customer needs can best be described as which one of the following?

   A. The gulf of constraints

   B. The gulf of Agile

   C. The gulf of misunderstanding

   D. The gulf value stream

3. You are coaching your Agile team in different ways to prioritize value. Which one of the following would not be a way to prioritize?

   A. Dot voting

   B. Value stream analysis

   C. MoSCoW

   D. Monopoly Money

4. During a prioritization exercise with your Agile team, you give each of the stakeholders 100 points. How will they determine priority with those points?

   A. They will put 100 points on the main feature they want.

   B. They will break the 100 points into 25-point increments for their top four values.

   C. They will put the points they want next to the options that they like, and they may place any number of points on any number of the options.

   D. The 100-point method isn't a prioritization method.

5. Your customer is describing items they want on the next release of their corporate software program. During discussions of valuable features, they ask if the software can include a new and innovative feature they read their competition may be creating. Your team performs Kano Analysis and determines this feature request falls under the category of:

   A. Satisfier

   B. Exciters

   C. Dissatisfiers

   D. Indifferent

6. Agile contracts differ from Waterfall projects in which of the following ways?

  A. They are longer term to accommodate iterations.

  B. They can use a fix and switch contract to allow for changes in scope.

  C. They can be adapted at any time.

  D. The can be updated for scope changes that have been approved through change control systems.

7. Your sponsor has asked you for a review of the scope, time, and cost performance so they can present the information to the shareholders. You have determined that the cost variance is –$3,000 and the schedule variance is $1,000. How is this project progressing?

  A. The project is over budget and behind schedule.

  B. The project is under budget and ahead of schedule.

  C. The project is over budget and ahead of schedule.

  D. There isn't enough information to determine project progress.

8. Your organization is using a mix of Waterfall and Agile techniques on its project and is very focused on reaching the return on investment level that it has determined the project should meet. Your sponsor is asking for the cost performance index information. What technique can you use to provide that information?

  A. Earned value technique

  B. Benefit cost measurements

  C. Monopoly Money

  D. Return on investment calculations

9. The planned value on your current project at this point in the schedule is $10,000, and the earned value is $9,600. What is the schedule variance?

  A. $400.00

  B. 0.96

  C. –($400.00)

  D. 1.04

10. Your customer has been adamant about a certain feature being a part of the finished increment. You have explained time and again that the feature they are looking for will interfere with the rest of the result and cause it not to work as well. What could be the reason for this confusion?

  A. The gulf of misunderstanding has occurred.

  B. Kano analysis wasn't performed.

  C. The customer is confusing exciters with satisfiers.

  D. The team isn't understanding the requirements.

11. You are being tasked by your organization to create a statement of work that will be utilized in the procurement process. The legal department explains to you that they want to make sure that all terms and conditions are negotiated and agreed to up front. Then, when scope needs to be changed, there is more flexibility in the process. To what type of agreement is the legal department referring?

    A. Fixed-price contract

    B. Cost-reimbursable contract

    C. Time and materials contract

    D. Master service level agreement

12. Bill is the sponsor on your project and is especially nervous about the budget and meeting the expected ROI. He asks you on a regular basis what things are costing and if you are spending money in the right areas. You suggest to Bill that he come to the team area and explain where he would spend the money if it were his decision and he had the entire project budget to work with. What are you suggesting Bill do?

    A. Use Monopoly Money to create his budget.

    B. Use Monopoly Money to show what he values and where he would spend the money.

    C. He is going to dot vote with the team to determine priority.

    D. Bill will be performing a Kano analysis on the budget.

13. Your customer is working very closely with your team on prioritization of value for their product. There are certain items that must be in the final product no matter what and others that won't be included unless different information is presented at a later date. Which of the following prioritization techniques does it look like they used?

    A. Dot voting

    B. Kano analysis

    C. MoSCoW

    D. Monopoly Money

14. You are delivering a performance report to your sponsor on the project and have put together an earned value report. Your cost performance index is 1.25. What does that information tell your sponsor?

    A. The project is over budget.

    B. The project is under budget.

    C. The project is getting one dollar's worth of work done and spending $1.25 on that work.

    D. The project is getting 1.25 dollars' worth of work done and spending one dollar on that work.

15. Your organization has entered into a contract that can best be described as good for the organization, and the budget requirements are known or stable. What kind of contract did your organization enter into?

    A. The fix and switch

    B. A service level agreement

    C. Fixed price

    D. Time and materials

16. Your project sponsor is asking for performance information on how your team is working in a new Agile environment, and you explain to them that your team is performing well together, that they have a good grasp on estimation techniques, and that their velocity has stabilized. These are all examples of what type of performance measurement?

    A. Key performance indicators

    B. Performance reporting

    C. Earned value reports

    D. Burn down charts

17. Brenda is sitting down with you for some one-on-one coaching because she is having trouble setting goals that she can meet. You are working through the goals that she has set and notice that they seem rather vague, and it's hard to determine what the end result should be. What would you recommend to Brenda?

    A. That she makes her goals more specific

    B. That she should be working with her team on goals and goal planning

    C. That Brenda needs some training on goal setting

    D. That she needs to work a little harder at achieving her goals

18. The mnemonic acronym SMART applies to which of the following project areas?

    A. Schedule improvement

    B. Cost improvement

    C. Goal setting improvement

    D. Team performance improvement

19. Jamal is the Agile project manager in charge of a new development project to create an app that can track how many times employees go to websites that are non–work related. Jamal is reporting to the sponsor that they have gone a bit over budget in the last iteration. Which of the following figures would show an over budget project?

    A. 1.6

    B. 1.1

    C. 1.0

    D. .80

20. Carol is writing down a goal she wants to meet. She starts with a very specific road map of what the result should be. She knows that she can get it done and has tracking mechanisms documented. Carol knows the goal is realistic as well. Which of the following is missing from her goal setting approach?

A. Specific

B. Measurable

C. Attainable

D. Time-based

21. If you were going to calculate the schedule performance index for your sponsor, which of the following variables would you need to do that?

A. Earned value and actual cost

B. Planned value and earned value

C. Planned value and actual cost

D. None of the above

22. According to Kano analysis, what do exciters typically become once substantial time has passed?

A. They become demotivators.

B. They become satisfiers.

C. The become dissatisfiers.

D. They remain exciters.

23. When you're reviewing constraints on an Agile project, which of the following are considered not as flexible as others?

A. Scope and quality

B. Time and quality

C. Cost and scope

D. Cost and time

24. When determining return on investment (ROI) at the beginning of a project, most organizations use which of the following techniques to help build a business case?

A. Earned value

B. Net present value

C. Monopoly Money

D. Cost performance index

25. Your team is holding a facilitated event in which the entire team will be given red and green stickers. The team will place red stickers on features that they don't want or like and green stickers on what they do want and like. This type of team event for decision making could be called which of the following?

A. A dotmocracy

B. A key performance indicator

C. A decision-making meeting

D. Backlog refinement

Chapter

9

Detecting Problems and Working Through Changes

THE FOLLOWING PMI-ACP® EXAM TOPICS ARE COVERED IN THIS CHAPTER:

✓ **Domain VI: Problem Detection and Resolution**

- Task 1: Create an open and safe environment by encouraging conversation and experimentation, in order to surface problems and impediments that are slowing the team down or preventing its ability to deliver value.

- Task 2: Identify threats and issues by educating and engaging the team at various points in the project in order to resolve them at the appropriate time and improve processes that caused issues.

- Task 3: Ensure issues are resolved by appropriate team members and/or reset expectations in light of issues that cannot be resolved in order to maximize the value delivered.

- Task 4: Maintain a visible, monitored, and prioritized list of threats and issues in order to elevate accountability, encourage action, and track ownership and resolution status.

- Task 5: Communicate status of threats and issues by maintaining threat list and incorporating activities into backlog of work in order to provide transparency.

In this chapter, you will work through the tasks for *Domain VI: Problem Detection and Resolution* of the exam content outline. The tasks directly relate to the team's ability to work in an uncertain environment and adapt to changing scope of work while maintaining focus on preventing risk events. The tasks include encouraging the team to experiment and learn in an open environment while identifying threats and issues. Because risk events can cause or create changes, you will also cover some information on managing changes that may come about due to progressive elaboration, changes in value, and how to avoid risk by processing changes as needed. This will address the preparation that is necessary to identify threats and issues and manage them accordingly while still embracing an open and communicative learning environment.

The Cost of Changes

In Chapter 8, "Agile Execution and Tracking of Iterations," you reviewed the earned value technique to keep track of the cost performance on a project. Although the chapter didn't specifically focus on the costs of changes, those costs are certain to affect the project's bottom line. You also reviewed how projects are selected to obtain return on investment from a corporate standpoint and how financial decisions are made during pre-project initiation.

In this chapter, you'll review how changes can be costly even when they are expected. Agile projects walk a very fine line between focused, set budgets and expectations of fluctuating scope of work.

In predictive Waterfall environments, there is a heavy focus on preplanning, working the plan, and then if a change is necessary, it is processed through a *formal change control system*. That system allows for a careful assessment of the impact of the change on the costs as well as the schedule and scope of work.

In an Agile environment, the sooner the need for change can be detected the less costly the changes will be over time. The assumption made regarding changes in Agile frameworks is that changes are always acceptable and always welcomed no matter what. Indeed, changes *are* welcome and acceptable to a point. Once changes occur due to a need to fix something or due to a lack of transparent communication of requirements, *that* is when changes become the costliest.

Regardless of the framework you choose, there is a continuous feedback loop between what is in the backlog, what is considered valuable, and what information is determined in reviews with the customer. Change is being managed quickly and iteratively without the need for formal change control. Change control in an Agile environment is, in a sense, formal because reviews and planning are timeboxed and scheduled and communication is transparent and constant. The difference is that Agile projects don't have to go through the steps of processing a change request and then formally send it up the chain of command; that is, unless you are working with a tailored project that incorporates some aspects of Waterfall and some aspects of Agile and your organizational process requires a formal system for changes. In Chapter 10, "Tailoring, Quality Management and Improving Project Processes," you'll review some different approaches that are tailored for better implementation on some types of projects as needed, and any combination of best practices could result in more static formal processes. For now, we'll go with the assumption that you are using an Agile framework specific to change acceptance, iterative reviews, and adjustments specific to the scope of work.

What about changes that occur due to mistakes, defects, or problems in the result? The longer it takes to identify a defect or a problem, the more it will cost to fix in both time and money.

The other consideration is that in large Agile projects, where it takes multiple iterations to produce a feature, the precise location of problems may be less obvious from iteration to iteration. The requirements may be course-grained at the start and then fine-grained as time passes and more information is known. Think about a large piece of salt in a salt grinder. You know that it's salt but it's too big to put on your food, so you have to take the extra steps needed to grind it down to a finer grain so that it works for your needs. The same thing goes for requirements.

Rolling Wave Planning

You've seen the term *progressive elaboration* as it pertains to adaptive planning and how we utilize information to help us implement our plans: We elaborate progressively on what we know today and use that information for planning for tomorrow.

Rolling wave planning, on the other hand, is waiting for the next *wave* of information to come rolling in and using that strategy to update our plans in an iterative nature as information becomes clearer. Using the strategy of rolling wave planning in Agile environments involves a conscious decision, knowing full well that we don't know everything in the beginning.

The strategy of rolling wave planning incorporates the model of replanning multiple times and waiting until the last responsible moment to put together those plans. As waves of information roll in, we can then plan accordingly.

Rolling wave planning is a term that comes from the Project Management Body of Knowledge (the *PMBOK® Guide*), and it appears on the PMP and CAPM exams. *Rolling wave planning* and *progressive elaboration* may also be terms that you'll see on your PMI-ACP exams. An easy way to remember the difference between the two is that rolling wave planning is the strategy of consistently replanning, knowing more information will reveal itself, while progressive elaboration is the act of using that information to plan further.

Because planning is done progressively and in waves, it's difficult for the team to see the finish line. In many cases, this is why heavy documentation isn't a *thing* in Agile environments. Can you imagine creating a bulky plan approved by everyone, and when all is said and done it looks nothing like what you thought it would look like due to all of the changes? That is precisely why Agile teams don't do that. Instead, Agile teams use a *value-based analysis* strategy and plan for the work to be done based on the results of that analysis.

It's all fun and games until someone does the work incorrectly, doesn't understand requirements, or produces defects in the increment. These and many other reasons are influencing factors that contribute to increasing costs.

There may be a preemptive strike to assure that the quality of the product is met. This would then be considered the *cost of quality*, where money is spent on the front end to produce an increment that works or after the fact to repair defects.

The development team may be attempting to do the simplest thing that works, except that it doesn't work as well as it could or should work. If a defect is created, and it isn't caught right away, the costs to fix that defect will be greater than budgeting to do it right the first time. The faster you find the defect, the less it costs to fix.

The reasoning behind this is that performing additional work on top of a single defect compounds the problem. It's like making one mistake on an Excel spreadsheet and then that mistake throws off the rest in a list. You may not notice until you have entered a ton of additional information, and then fixing the problem becomes very time consuming. If the mistake is not caught at all, it can create a real problem in the future and could be costlier for your organization over the long term than had the mistake been caught and remedied from the start. This is a pay for it now or pay more for it later type situation.

If you are just looking strictly at the monetary impact of changes on a project, whether it is to fix defects or to change direction, the further into the iteration you get, the costlier it can be.

Technical Debt

You know the word *debt*—we all do. It's what happens when you spend money that you don't actually have, and when you pay it back you are paying it down plus interest. It's the interest that makes it increasingly more difficult to get ahead. Unless you can get in front of the payments with a lower interest rate or a windfall occurs and you pay off all of your debt, the debt undoubtedly will accumulate.

What then is technical debt, or *tech debt*? In the software development arena, it is what happens when a development team writes code that is easy to implement in the short term instead of attempting to apply the best overall solution up front. Many times, the mantra of *create the simplest thing that works* holds true; however, simple doesn't mean lacking structure. If the code works in the short term and passes testing but it will not integrate well with the next increment, tech debt can arise and create extra development work at some other point in the project.

Just like any other type of debt, if technical debt is not repaid, it can accumulate interest, making it harder to implement changes later. There is a fine line between creating something that works today but maybe not tomorrow versus releasing something usable and minimal at the end of the iteration.

In most cases, tech debt is not necessarily a bad thing, and sometimes technical debt is required to create better solutions later or allow for better quality in the result. Knowing this in advance allows the team to create the simplest thing that works today, fully aware that they will have to allot time and energy to pay back that debt later in the project. In most cases, technical debt refers to *fixing* the code or finding a better way to accomplish the same result. On other types of projects, tech debt could refer to documentation, testing. or other items that have fallen by the wayside. Either way, the debt will need to be repaid.

As the team determines the amount of work they can accomplish in an iteration, it will also account for any tech debt to be repaid. As you'll see later in the chapter, the team also needs to account for risk. The team will allot time for removing technical debt and use a process called *refactoring* to do so.

Refactoring

Let's assume that your team took some shortcuts in the development of the code; the entire system may or may not work the way it is supposed to work. Obviously, operating this way wouldn't be sustainable in the long term. At that point, you and your team may meet with the customer and explain what has occurred and why it is important to stop what you are doing and spend the time needed to refactor the code.

Refactoring is the process of restructuring existing internal computer code without changing its external behaviors. The team will use an iterative cycle of making small changes, testing the result to ensure correctness, and making another small change or transform the code somehow. If at any point that code fails a test, the last small change is undone and tried again in a different way.

In eXtreme Programming (XP), the concept of integrated testing is part of the framework to make sure that the code passes necessary tests for increment approval. Testing can also point to the need to refactor. Tests are usually written in advance, and the increment is expected to fail the tests in the beginning. When they pass, they may or may not be ready. Maybe the test is passed but there is a better way to do it, or there is a way to improve the output with refactoring. You'll sometimes see this referred to as "red, green, refactor." Red indicates that the test has failed. Green shows that the test has passed. Refactor means that it's time to update the code.

Refactoring When You Don't Code Software

There are many people who do not code software for a living, much less understand the language of code. They still practice Agile. Marketing companies, sales companies, training companies, and so on can practice Agile.

To understand the need for refactoring without having to understand software development is to take the concept into our day-to-day work lives. If you have ever recorded a macro in any Microsoft program, you know that it's a process by which your clicks and movements are logged like a DVR records television shows. The object is to make life easier and your workflow more efficient.

Let's say that you record a macro in Microsoft Excel that selects a couple of ranges of cells, highlights them, and bolds them so that they're easier to see in a large spreadsheet.

The macro is stored and can be "played back" whenever you want to run it. That macro is written in Visual Basic for Applications, or VBA, code.

Now let's say that you wanted the macro to highlight certain cell ranges, make the contents of the cells bold, and highlight those cells with the yellow fill color. When you record the macro, you select the cells that you want, bold them, and then select the highlight color. However, what if you did the same task three times in a row just to be sure that the macro worked as you wanted it to work. Could you live with it? Sure, the end result is the same result you wanted, but now the code is messier and the macro is looping through the process three times. The result is still the same—select, bold, and highlight—but the process is not as efficient.

You have two options: You can delete the macro and record it again, or you could refactor the code to the way that you want it to be. Deleting and rerecording can be more time consuming in large, complex macros and it could affect your productivity. Or, you could just open VBA and delete the other two instances in the language of the code. You can even adapt the code as needed. If you don't know what that code is off the top of your head, you can ask Google—I totally do!

You have just refactored the code using a small change to transform it to be what you want it to be. You would then test the code to see if it worked. If the macro runs but doesn't bold the text, then your change didn't pass the test. Then you would hit my favorite button, undo, and try a different method and test it again until it passes. That's it. By taking small steps, you can fix the overall output.

Refactoring must be done on a regular basis, lest additional tech debt be created. In Figure 9.1, you can see a very simple string of code that applies to the example of the macro and how making one small change can affect the complexity of the code. The example on the left is the macro looping three times through the processes and the example of the refactored code is on the right. It's simpler, cleaner, and it does what you need it to do. That's refactoring for the non-technical!

FIGURE 9.1 Macro refactor

```
Range("A3:B3").Select
With Selection.Interior
    .Pattern = xlSolid
    .PatternColorIndex = xlAutomatic
    .ThemeColor = xlThemeColorAccent4
    .TintAndShade = 0
    .PatternTintAndShade = 0
End With
Range("A9:B9").Select
With Selection.Interior
    .Pattern = xlSolid
    .PatternColorIndex = xlAutomatic
    .ThemeColor = xlThemeColorAccent4
    .TintAndShade = 0
    .PatternTintAndShade = 0
End With
Range("A3:B3").Select
With Selection.Interior
    .Pattern = xlSolid
    .PatternColorIndex = xlAutomatic
    .ThemeColor = xlThemeColorAccent4
    .TintAndShade = 0
    .PatternTintAndShade = 0
End With
Selection.Font.Bold = True
Range("A9:B9").Select
Selection.Font.Bold = True
With Selection.Interior
    .Pattern = xlSolid
    .PatternColorIndex = xlAutomatic
    .ThemeColor = xlThemeColorAccent4
    .TintAndShade = 0
    .PatternTintAndShade = 0
End With
End Sub
```

```
Range("A2:B2").Select
Selection.Font.Bold = True
With Selection.Interior
    .Pattern = xlSolid
    .PatternColorIndex = xlAutomatic
    .Color = 65535
    .TintAndShade = 0
    .PatternTintAndShade = 0
End With
Range("A9:B9").Select
Selection.Font.Bold = True
With Selection.Interior
    .Pattern = xlSolid
    .PatternColorIndex = xlAutomatic
    .Color = 65535
    .TintAndShade = 0
    .PatternTintAndShade = 0
End With
End Sub
```

It takes a lot of courage to delete long strings of code completely and start over from scratch. It's also time consuming and costly. Many times, refactoring will happen on a small scale, fixing small items as you go rather than having to go back and start from the beginning. You may also determine that the priority of the code is low enough that, hey, if it works, why bother? The practicality of refactoring is done on a case-by-case basis. Either way, you are going back to work that is either in progress or is completed. It's a decision that needs to be made during iteration planning, so there is time to accommodate the refactoring tasks. Many developers see the value in refactoring some things, and for other developers, there may be the concern that if they update or streamline one aspect they could break another string somewhere else. Many Agile frameworks have a collective code ownership philosophy, meaning that anyone on the team may decide that refactoring is necessary and work to make the code easier to manage, cleaner, and more succinct and efficient in the future.

These changes, updates, and refactoring or fixing of defects cost time and money. The longer it takes to pay the debt off or to fix a defect, the more challenging it becomes to keep costs low and manage a set iteration length while still producing something usable. Those variables amp up risk and costs and ultimately affect the team's *throughput*. In project management, *throughput* is the term used for the average amount of time it takes the team to complete work within a specific time frame. Remember, ideal time isn't feasible. Nobody is working 40 hours a week every single week on project work. This is not to be confused with work in progress (WIP) or cycle time. *Cycle time* is how long it takes the team to run or cycle through the development and testing of the increment.

Remember, it is important to limit work in progress (WIP) because otherwise your team could experience a bottleneck in progress and have to stop work altogether to remove it. Bottlenecks create risk, which increases costs. Much like the triple constraints, the metrics of work in progress, cycle time, and throughput are linked and adapt when one changes. You'll learn more about cycle time and increasing the value stream as well as process efficiency in Chapter 10. For now, it's just important to realize that so many individual pieces of a project can influence change and cost.

The biggest offenders of cost increases are clearly defects: too much technical debt and risk events that impact the budget and the result. If the team stays ahead of the curve and allots time to refactor on a regular basis, repair defects when discovered, and reduce the amount of debt on the technical side, the impact on overall costs will not be as great, thus keeping things within budget as much as possible.

Determining Defects

If defects are one of the biggest offenders of cost increases, they are also one of the biggest reasons the increment isn't accepted as done and deployable. Defects do happen, though. It could be because of human error, machinery malfunctions, poor processes, poor implementation of a process, and frankly, flat-out surprises as well. Either way, the faster you recognize a defect and fix it, the faster the defect is fixed. That's easier said than done, right?

Think about any company suffering through recalls, which you have seen on the news recently. Not only are they losing millions of dollars to fix the defects, they are also being splashed all over the news, their stocks are plummeting, and consumers will think twice before they buy that product any time soon. Cha-ching, cha-ching—and not in a good way. How does this happen in today's world? We have people in charge who oversee work using state-of-the art technology. So why do defects still occur?

There are two main categories of the causes of defects: common causes and special causes. These main causes or categories of defects were defined in the statistical thinking and methods of Dr. Walter A. Shewhart and W. Edwards Deming.

Shewhart is credited with pushing statistical quality control to the forefront of best practices in the industrial age. He got his start at Bell Telephone, the precursor of AT&T, and worked to improve the reliability of the transmission systems that were in use at the time. In many cases, not just at Bell Telephone, but many organizations were building products and services and then inspecting them for defects or trying to improve their systems approach after the fact. At that point in the project, it's a bit too little, too late, and thus statistical quality control was born.

Shewhart believed that even with set processes in place, there were still variations in results. Not to oversimplify his efforts, but a lot of work and study went into the classification of causes. For our purposes, however, we'll keep it simple. He called the categories that he observed at that time *assignable cause* and *chance cause*. *Assignable*, because you could point your finger directly at the cause of the problem or defect, and thus this fell into the category of common causes, whereas chance causes were coincidental and often a surprise. Therefore, these could be categorized as special causes.

Shewart's work was quickly recognized by Deming, and their collaboration led to influencing the *Plan-Do-Check-Act* cycle of continuous improvement. This work directly helped repair the Japanese economy after World War II.

Even though Deming is often credited with the implementation of the Plan-Do-Check-Act cycle, he always referred to it as the Shewhart cycle. Why does this all matter? Because these two founders of quality management and their statistical analysis of why defects occur still influence how you can spot defects on your own projects today. You can use this information for lessons learned and continuous improvement whether you are working in a Waterfall or Agile environment. Even outside the sphere of manufacturing projects, these variables still hold up and can cause defects no matter the project type.

Common Causes

Common causes are sometimes referred to as *natural patterns*. These include things that we can identify and point to as the main offender and creator of defects. This is typically because there is tacit knowledge, lessons learned, or historical information that is presently known, or *common* information.

The good news about common causes is that we are aware of them and usually have some kind of workaround to fix them. Typically, these common causes have some level of predictability because they are actively influencing our projects: We know what to expect and the history is provable and well documented. It is one of those things where the cause impacts your project, and you shake your head and think, "Yeah, it's one of *those* days," and then move on to fix it. It's noise in the system.

According to Deming and Shewhart, the categories or the actual causes of the causes can include a lack of clearly defined procedures (because that *never* happens, I think sarcastically to myself), poor design, human errors in measurement, poor-quality control functions, or inadequate inspections. It can also be caused by normal wear and tear in machinery, or a variation in the settings of that machinery.

If you have ever sat in front of your computer and watched it spin for way longer than it should have before it launches your programs or web pages, that is a common cause. It's annoying but not uncommon. Almost everything that you can think of that throws a wrench into your project on a regular basis, but that is expected to occur at some point, could be called a *common cause.*

Printers commonly get jammed with paper, and in an attempt to fix the defect I usually end up walking away with toner all over my hands (hoping no one saw me wrestling wads of paper out of the printer). You win printer...until next time.

> No, not again. I... why does it say paper jam when there is no paper jam?
>
> *Office Space (1999)*

Special Causes

These days, special causes are things like faulty controllers, raw materials that are of mediocre quality, or even your computer crashing. Nobody wants to see the blue screen of death (BSoD), but it happens. Is it a surprise when it does occur? Yes, but you know that it's a random occurrence, and you know how to fix it, or you know how to pick up the phone and call the IT department.

Special causes happen outside the norm of historical experience: They are the surprises—the unpredictable events that nobody saw coming. It could be that a special cause is created because something wasn't set up correctly in the beginning, a system that needs updating was neglected, or in most cases, something completely new. Surprise!

The only way to prevent a special cause from happening in the future is to conduct frequent reviews of work products. Perform inspections, reviews, and/or testing, and identify and incorporate improvements into the overall process and product/service. That will help mitigate the surprises that cause risk, defects, and increased costs and create low team morale. Once a special cause occurs (usually on a Monday), you are now armed with new information, and if you can solve the root cause of the problem, then you can lower the probability of it happening again.

Risk Management

Risk management is a large topic, no matter what framework you are using. Anything that can pose a threat to your project, your result, or your organization is something about which you must be aware and for which you must plan. The hard part is getting to the point where you can identify the risk events that carry some probability and some impact without entering into analysis-paralysis mode.

There are three levels of uncertainty where risk is involved. There is the *known* level, as in it happens every single time you run a project. There is the *unknown/unknown* level, which is always a surprise, and the *known/unknown* level. The latter is the level at which you are working most of the time. You know that there is a probability and an impact, but it is unknown whether the risk will actually occur or not and if you are correct in your assumptions about the event.

Many Waterfall projects focus on the opportunity side of risk as well as the threat side. This is because so much is planned upfront and the projects tend to be longer. There is always something good to be found in the ether somewhere.

In Agile frameworks, there isn't a lot of time for daydreaming about the future; the focus is on the here and now, and how the project will affect the future will be revealed over time. If you are being optimistic, the reality is that on Agile projects, opportunities show themselves on a regular basis due to frequent interactions with the customer or product owner, reviews, and planning meetings.

In Agile and Waterfall projects, the threats and issues is what can really affect the short and long term. A known/unknown threat event can stop the iteration or the entire project in its tracks. In some cases, during a risk assessment, it may even be determined that the cost of the threats are more than the cost of the project. If that is the case, the project would reach *fast failure*, which means that the plug is pulled on the project because it's too risky or costly to move forward. It is also important to understand your stakeholder tolerance levels for risk.

 Real World Scenario

How Risk Tolerances Affect Your Assessments

Different people experience risk differently. For example, I would consider you a risk taker if you jump out of a perfectly good airplane or go swimming with sharks. If I entered the ocean (part of the food chain) and saw a shark, I would swim in circles hyperventilating (easy prey). Therefore, I am a risk averter. The craziest thing I've done lately is get on the Batman ride at Great Adventure theme park, and I hated all 3 minutes and 15 seconds of it.

Some stakeholders are risk neutral. They could go one way or the other, depending on the situation. For example, sharks no, skydiving yes. Why is this important? Because when you and your entire team sit down with your customer, your sponsor, and your product owner and discuss the probability of something happening and the impact of the risk to the iteration, what they think about it will depend on how they see risk. Typically, red, yellow, and green or high, medium, and low are used to describe a probability and impact score. Or, an actual probability percentage and the impact score in money or time may be considered. If I'm risk averse, I may think that the impact is red, while a risk taker may see it as yellow. The first step is understanding stakeholder tolerance levels for risk and then constructing a scoring model that everyone can agree on. I find it is best if you use specifics: Plus or minus 10 percent over budget is a yellow, over by 20 percent is red, and so on. I work with the big constraints first since they tend to impact everything else. The domino effect of risk is a very real thing. Once you have your strategy in place for risk assessment, it is easier to reach consensus on how to handle it. The problem is that nobody is ever really sure until the event occurs. If you were wrong, you'll need a work-around. I call this the "fire extinguisher method." Knowing tolerance levels can help keep risk front and center and allow you to create a system that will work for your projects.

Once your team has a system, the goal is to systematically reduce or mitigate risk on the project and the iteration level, not after it happens but before it occurs. As a worst case, you'll have to work on a response and implement it when the risk happens and hope that it works. Otherwise, it's a good best practice to attempt to stop risk in its tracks.

Issues, on the other hand, are risks that have been realized, meaning that they have occurred and you didn't see them coming. Typically, issues are less impactful than a full-blown risk event. It's the difference between having a massive defect in your product (risk) versus five people calling in sick with the flu (issue). You have to deal with both situations and both affect the project, but clearly a massive defect has a major impact and sick employees are a fact of life at some point.

It's always a good idea to question your assumptions no matter what. You know what assumptions are, right? Things that we think are true without any proof. Assumptions analysis is an excellent way to determine what risks could occur and what would be their root cause.

Another way to practice good risk management (short of being a catastrophic thinker) is to conduct frequent reviews of work products; to perform inspections, reviews, and/or testing; and to identify and incorporate improvements into the overall process and product/service.

Easier said than done, right?

Spikes

There are two types of spikes that can be performed on a project to help mitigate risk and to prove a strategy. The first type of spike is an *architectural spike* and the second is a *risk-based spike*. Both types are designed to support the project and to help mitigate the risk that could occur.

Architectural Spikes   Originally created in the eXtreme Programming framework, an architectural spike *typically* happens between iterations or sprints to reduce the risk of a technical problem occurring later. This is especially true when the developers aren't exactly sure how to work the user story or are working with innovative technology and need to prove that the direction they are planning to take will work. A spike also increases the reliability of a user story's estimate. Spikes aren't going to happen on every single iteration, and sometimes it takes a good sales job to convince the product owner that it is necessary to take the time and effort to perform a spike.

No matter what, it is a group decision as to what the duration of a spike will be and the objective(s) of the spike. Both the product owner and the team need to agree on those variables of time and objectives before a spike occurs. The other thing to consider is that it doesn't take an entire development team to perform a spike. Usually two team members work on the spike together. The rest of the team goes about their work. The duration of the spike is also *typically* about four to eight hours in length and not an entire iteration.

The spike may not result in an entire solution in the end, but at least there is more information and a strategy to attempt, or the result may include a *proof of concept*. This can lead to better estimates of what the story or work will entail and a close eye can be kept on any potential risk events that could affect the work as well.

Risk-Based Spikes   These spikes are special stories that are created and designed to remove or reduce risk from the iteration. A risk could very well come from the fact that the team doesn't understand the technology or the direction, and those unknowns can create risk. Risk can live at any level, from an epic to a user story, and oftentimes there are decision delays to assess potential risks or uncertainty. Typically, those decision delays are regarding implementation decisions or specific product details that are pushed out until the *last responsible moment* in order to mitigate risks, adapt to changes, and implement solutions based on the most *up-to-date* information, or based on taking *course-grained* requirements to the *fine-grained* level. If the spike fails to eliminate a severe risk event and mitigation techniques aren't working, then a project could reach fast failure mode. The project just isn't worth the risk.

You can think of risk-based spikes like a mitigation technique in any project management framework. Solving risk takes time and implementing a response takes effort, and without accommodating those variables when the team plans for the iteration, the risk will be compounded and not be managed.

Risk-Adjusted Backlog

Determining risks and issues early and often can help the team prioritize the risks to avoid and mitigate first. This is a process of determining the priority of the risks much like prioritizing any other story in the backlog. Much of that priority is based on the probability of occurrence and the financial impact to the scope and schedule. How do you prioritize something that can't be proven in the moment? You can use expert judgment and something called *expected monetary value (EMV)* to apply a *price tag* to the identified risks. Based on the expected monetary (money) price tag and assessed impact, your team can then determine priority more accurately. I think of it as objective/subjective analysis, and for some reason whenever you attach math and money to an assumption, the higher-ups tend to believe you more. This fascinating observation has been proven more times than not.

The bigger the fiscal impact, the greater priority the risk event and the risk response have. This would mean that the backlog is adjusted to accommodate the responses or mitigation strategies sooner instead of later.

Keep in mind that some assessed risks are near term and others are far term. You wouldn't be working to solve a far-term risk in Iteration 1 unless you could really nip it at the source and avoid it completely. Most risk identification and assessment of its probability and impacts will relate to the timing of the solution needing to be implemented. Not always, but then that is the risk with risk. Responses also need to be prioritized along with features for maximum positive impact.

Expected Monetary Value

The expected monetary value method allows you to apply objective analysis to subjective information. The formula calculates the average outcome of threats and assumptions based on probability and impact. It makes sense that threats cost money and/or time, but exactly how much remains to be seen. All you can do is assess impact at 100 percent and then, based on the probability of occurrence, determine what the price tag is now for the risk. This process will allow the team to adjust the risk backlog accordingly and that helps determine prioritization. There is a very simple formula for expected monetary value, and that is probability multiplied by impact. Probability, in this case, is represented by a percentage and the impact is in monetary terms, but you could use time as well if needed.

For your PMI-ACP exam, you will be asked to calculate expected monetary values based on the information provided in the question. You will also be asked to determine the risk-adjusted backlog based on the expected monetary value. Once you review the formula and the concept, you'll need to assess how the backlog is adjusted between feature stories and risk mitigation stories in order of importance. This is all based on the financial impact of the features and risks.

Your team may also decide to use another scoring system and predetermine what that is before the project begins. Many Agile teams prefer to use a 1–5 scaling system to assess probability and impact. When you multiply probability by impact, you still get a scalable scoring system that can help address priority.

 Real World Scenario

How a Risk-Adjusted Backlog Works with Expected Monetary Value

If your team identified four risk events and calculated the financial impact and expected monetary value of the potential risk events and the true monetary worth of the features themselves, it would be easy to see how the priority would work.

If I have a threat that has a 25 percent probability of occurring, and if it occurred at 100 percent, it would cost the project $20,000; then its expected monetary value at its assessed probability would be $5,000. This means that we don't expect the risk to happen at 100 percent (because if it did, it would cost $20,000); instead we are looking at how to prioritize based on its current probability and impact. It's an objective/subjective technique.

For example, on your current project, you have identified four risk events and calculated their expected monetary value. The result of the analysis is as follows:

Risk A: $3,000 EMV

Risk B: $7,500 EMV

Risk C: $2,700 EMV

Risk D: $9,200 EMV

Then you looked at the financial worth of the features that you are planning to develop and it breaks out like this:

Feature 1: $5,000

Feature 2: $2,500

Feature 3: $8,000

Feature 4: $12,000

How would you adjust your backlog accordingly? You would have to sort everything by financial impact, and if that is the case, then your risk adjusted backlog would look something like this:

Feature 4: $12,000

Risk D: $9,200

Feature 3: $8,000

Risk B: $7,500

Feature 1: $5,000

Risk A: $3,000

Risk C: $2,700

Feature 2: $2,500

Obviously, this is a very simple overview of very important and detailed stuff that you will be dealing with in your day-to-day work. Certainly, it is up to your organization or your team on how risk is managed. The goal of any risk assessment is to see trouble on the horizon and try to get in front of it.

Real World Scenario

Expected Monetary Value and the Believability of Math

My experience with expected monetary value lies in the art of convincing my sponsor that one seller/supplier/vendor is less risky than another. Of course, we always want to hire someone externally that will provide the best price for the contract and also deliver effectively on what we need to run the project. In one such case, we were reviewing bids from sellers that could provide the same materials. The short list included one bid for $102,000 and another bid for $105,000. When I asked my sponsor which bid we should accept, of course he said the lowest one. I was concerned that the lower-bidding company may have a shady record when it came to delivering on time, and I had heard grumblings from other project managers about that exact problem.

I did some research and talked to other people who had worked with both sellers in the past, and I found out that the lower-bidding company had delayed deliveries about 30 percent of the time. The late deliveries sparked a chain reaction on the project, and they ended up costing the other projects anywhere from an additional $10,000–$15,000, plus the cost of the contract. The higher-bidding company was much better and only delivered late about 5 percent of the time. This cost some projects around $5,000 additional dollars plus the contract price.

I know what you are thinking, "Why didn't you negotiate terms and conditions so that if they were late, they would then pay the overage price?" You are correct in your thoughts, but at that point we hadn't yet chosen a vendor to negotiate with. I proceeded to run expected monetary value analysis with my sponsor. I handed him a calculator and let him run the numbers.

Vendor 1: $102,000

Late deliveries: 30 percent

Costs of late deliveries at max: $15,000

Expected monetary value: $4,500 additional (30% × $15,000)

Total: $4,500 + $102,000 (for contract costs) = $106,500

Vendor 2: $105,000

Late deliveries: 5 percent

Costs of late deliveries at max: $5,000

Expected monetary value: $250 additional (5% × $5,000)

Total: $250 + $105,000 (for contract costs) = $105,250

Objective/Subjective Analysis

We went with Vendor 2. Here's the thing: Sometimes time is as important as money, and even though we knew if something went horribly wrong, for example, this could be the one time in history that Vendor 2 delivered late 30 percent of the time, it's the risk you take. We chose to limit the risk as much as possible and put our faith in historical information. Once the contract was negotiated, there were terms and conditions in place for late deliveries. The vendor worked out well, and because of that they became our preferred vendor going forward. It's all in how you analyze the risk and the expected monetary value. This is what allowed my sponsor to see that it was much riskier to go with a vendor that charged less and cost more in the long run.

If you've been in the software business for any time at all, you know that there are certain common problems that plague one project after another. Missed schedules and creeping requirements are not things that just happen to you once and then go away, never to appear again. Rather, they are part of the territory. We all know that. What's odd is that we don't plan our projects as if we knew it. Instead, we plan as if our past problems are locked in the past and will never rear their ugly heads again. Of course, you know that isn't a reasonable expectation.

Waltzing with Bears: Managing Risk on Software Projects *by Tom DeMarco and Timothy Lister (Dorset House Publishing, 2003)*

Assessing Risk

Many times, I revert to Waterfall best practices to manage risk and use a bit of tailoring practices to make sure my team detects risk on a regular basis and identifies categories of risk that are standard in any organization—technical risk, external risk, and scope risk to name just a few.

I also find that it is a best practice to use those categories of risk to focus the identification to specific elements of the project by using prompt lists. According to the *Project Management Institute's Practice Standard for Project Risk Management*, there are three *prompt lists* that can be helpful in any project environment. Each list *prompts* the team to brainstorm on specific categories rather than strength and weaknesses.

In Figure 9.2, you can see the three main prompt lists that your team can use to identify risks based on categories. The lists that work best for your team depend on the type of projects on which they are working. Many Agile projects benefit the most from the acronym *SPECTRUM*, shown in the figure, since it covers a wider gamut of categories. You could even make up your own categories as needed. Prompt lists are just a way to focus the conversation and label the risks that you identify.

FIGURE 9.2   Standard prompt lists

PESTLE	TECOP	SPECTRUM
Political	Technical	Sociocultural
Economic	Environmental	Political
Social	Commercial	Economic
Technological	Operational	Competitive
Legal	Political	Technology
Environmental		Regulatory/legal
		Uncertainty/risk
		Market

One of the best ways to identify risks on a regular basis is during the daily stand-up meetings. The question of what impediments are in your way today is crucial for identifying potential bumps in the road. Even though the problem won't get solved during the 15 minutes that you meet, everyone is now aware of the situation and can work toward a solution for it.

Also, as I revert to my Waterfall days for risk, I like to pull in another brainstorming technique called *SWOT*. SWOT is an acronym for strength, weaknesses, opportunities, and threats. A SWOT diagram is shown in Figure 9.3. The origin of SWOT is foggy at best, but what we do know is that SWOT was used at Stanford University by Albert Humphrey. Humphrey led a research project in the 1960s and 1970s to study data and surveys from many of the Fortune 500 companies at the time. The goal was to identify why certain corporate planning efforts failed as well as to help with the planning efforts of organizations going forward. Today, SWOT is most commonly used for risk assessment, and it is a very popular brainstorming technique.

FIGURE 9.3   SWOT

The key to using this as a brainstorming technique is to focus on each quadrant individually. Strengths are identified by answering the following questions: What do we have going for us now? Do we have a good customer base, a great product, or something completely new?

Next, what are our weaknesses now? Not enough time or money? Do we have a lot of defects to fix? The opportunities are obviously items that we want to leverage to produce opportunities for tomorrow, and the weaknesses are items to keep an eye on because they could cause threats in the future.

I also like to look at brainstorming on the diagonal as well. What if we don't take advantage of the opportunities? Could we create a threat in the future? Conversely, what if we overcome the weaknesses and challenges today and potentially produce an opportunity for the future. It's focused subjective analysis of what *could* happen so that we can plan for it just in case. It's also a great way to get your team to dig a bit deeper and help prevent risk events before they occur. But occur they shall!

Mitigation is a definitive buzz word for risk responses. It refers not just to the response, but to the main response. *Contingency* is also a good word for risk responses, and it is useful at parties when discussing what you do for a living.

You could work to remove the risk completely and avoid the threat. You can make it sound like you narrowly escaped something bad, but in fact you changed direction to avoid the risk. Just like swerving on the highway to avoid a pothole or a tire in the road, you may decide to change direction on the project. Your product owner may decide that the ripple effect of not avoiding one risk is too great to other activities and create adjustments to the backlog.

You could transfer the threat to a third party. For example, your health insurance, car insurance, pet insurance, or whatever kind you have is a way to transfer the impact to a third party. You see this in terms and conditions when using subcontractors or other vendors on projects through procurement.

You could also just accept the threat if it is of minimal impact to the project. It may cause a few headaches, but acceptance may be less disruptive than a full-blown response.

Always work with your team on spikes to affect the risk as needed, and if it can't be removed, then at least it can be prioritized and managed and a mitigation strategy can be discussed and agreed upon. A lot of the discussion will revolve around root cause analysis and determining what the actual cause for the risk could be so that you can figure out the best solution. Sometimes, the most obvious reason isn't the correct reason.

I like the technique of the *5 whys* to get to the root cause of a risk or any issue. I also like it because you get to act like a two-year-old. "Why is the sky blue?" "Why do horses have hooves instead of feet?" "Why is Bobby always on the swing set when I want to use it?" "Why do I have to take a nap?" You get my drift. Why are we going off on this tangent? Oh yeah, the 5 whys!

The practice of asking *why* five times in a row allows for the discussion to move away from the most obvious reason or cause of an identified risk event and look a bit deeper. We have identified a cybersecurity risk. Why do we have concerns about cybersecurity? Why have we determined that this risk is present in our current project? Why is security at risk? Why isn't our current virus protection enough? Why haven't we investigated other software for protection?

Without pushing the questions out to the team, you may very well miss something. Will the most obvious or proximate cause be the most likely? Yes, probably. That is until it isn't. There may be a deeper cause hiding that isn't identified. Then, when your team goes to implement the response, you create a *secondary risk* that you didn't see coming or a *residual risk*. Secondary risks are when you implement a risk response for one thing and create a whole other risk event. It's sort of like pouring water on an electrical fire—it never ends well. Therefore, you will have to create a workaround. Fire extinguisher time.

Residual risk is leftover risk after a response has been implemented and it doesn't get it all. Ring around the risk tub. The residual risk is usually not at an acceptable level as well, and you will need a workaround of some kind to mitigate the risk left behind.

So, how do we then document the risks, and how do we display our mitigation efforts? Just like most of the documentation in Agile, the data will be visible, front, and center.

Risk Burn Down Charts

Many charts and graphs are used in an Agile environment to keep communication transparent. Communicating risk isn't any different, and in fact it is as important as keeping your other project stats front and center, including your velocity, story points, and Kanban boards. The other reason charts and graphs are used extensively in an Agile environment, other than transparency, is to keep track of your mitigation efforts, and to do so you use a *risk burn down chart*. These charts effectively and transparently show that what you are doing with your mitigation or contingency strategies is reducing the probability and impact of the risk, removing it completely, or not handling it well at all.

Much like any chart or graph, risk burn down charts can be in depth or very simple, depending on the need for documentation. A typical risk burn down chart is used to show the project's exposure to risk and its trajectory up or down depending on whether your responses are working or not. The goal is to trend downward, or to *burn down*. That would show that your efforts are chipping away at the risk on the project in a progressive manner.

To avoid the analysis-paralysis that often occurs in risk management, and to keep a focus on the most impactful risks, I like to keep a top 10 list and use it to plot out project risk. Of course, I use this for the 10 most impactful risks, as of this iteration.

Remember, you are actively attempting to alleviate the project of its risk, and as new work is identified, new risks will surface as well. Every iteration will reflect the identified risks and the risks that carry over to multiple iterations. It may be that a *risk-based spike* is necessary to help with story point estimations, proof of concept, or simply to work on eliminating a risk event or at least minimizing the risk. That is easier said than done. The purpose of keeping the results of these efforts front and center is that it is motivating to see the risk trend downward. It's a graphical pat on the back. Or, it is a significant wakeup call if things aren't trending in the right direction.

In some organizations, time is more important than money, while in other organizations, the almighty dollar, yen, euro, or whatever currency is being used is most important. Whichever constraint is more important may drive how you construct your risk burn down chart.

The same formula of *probability × impact* holds true here, except in cases involving time, where it would be the total amount of time you would lose should the risk happen at 100 percent and the assessed percentage of probability. Otherwise, expected monetary value would be used and impact would be represented monetarily.

There are also very different charts that you can use. Some may use a simple line graph that shows the risk exposure based on days lost across iterations; others may use a very colorful chart and graph that shows red, yellow, and green to represent risk impacts; and still others may combine all of the risks across a total project and represent the individual risks with their own color coding so that the trends are more obvious for multiple identified risks. How you construct yours will depend on what information you are using it for.

For your PMI-ACP exam, you will need to know the differences between a burn up chart, a burn down chart, and a risk burn down chart. Here's a quick, easy way to keep them straight.

Burn Up Charts   Used to track the project's progress by comparing total scope against completed work over time. One line is scope and the other is completed work. Can also help track scope changes.

Burn Down Charts   Compare how much work is left to do with the timeline and help the team predict when they will complete the work.

Risk Burn Down Charts   Show risk exposure over time. The lines should be trending down as risk is mitigated; if not, the team will have to allocate some time to mitigate the risks.

In Figure 9.4, you'll see a very basic selection of burn down charts to give you a visual idea as to the different kinds of charts that are out there. Some teams will use an Excel spreadsheet to keep track of the other identified risk events above the big 10 and then chart those out as well. It's totally up to you!

FIGURE 9.4   Risk burn down charts

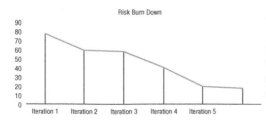

Risk is something that happens on *every single project*, whether we see it coming or not. Issues are always present and need to be accounted for. Whether your team uses an issue log and risk burn down charts or keeps everything on one big risk spreadsheet, the only wrong way to manage risk is to not manage risk at all.

Summary

This chapter started with information on the cost of changes on Agile projects. While change is acceptable, it can be costly—especially when the changes occur due to defects or feature changes late in a project.

In the next section, I discussed technical debt and the need to refactor code. Technical debt is something that accrues over time, and it must be repaid. Refactoring is making small improvements over time in order to simplify aspects of a project, or the process of restructuring existing internal computer code without changing its external behaviors.

Next I reviewed the different kinds of defects that can occur. Some are due to common causes that we can expect on every project, and others are due to special causes that create defects that will incur costs to fix and may influence your schedules as well. Time is money!

In the next section, I reviewed some of the aspects of creating spikes in order to help the project and to work through risk effectively. The first type of spike is an *architectural spike* and the second type is a *risk-based spike*. Both types of spikes are designed to support the project and to help mitigate the risk that could occur.

We then continued through risk and discussed the risk-adjusted backlog and expected monetary value (EMV). EMV is an excellent way to assess the probability and impact as it concerns money, but it can be used for time as well. Assessing risk is important on any project, so I reviewed ways to brainstorm using SWOT analysis, the 5 whys, and other aspects of risk responses.

Finally, I reviewed a different way to plot out risk mitigation strategies using risk burn down charts so that the team can keep an eye on mitigation efforts from iteration to iteration.

Exam Essentials

Understand how changes increase project costs.   Understand why it is important to know that changes that are necessary and identified early minimize the cost risk. In an Agile environment, the sooner that the need for change can be detected, the less costly the changes will be over time. Continuous feedback and rolling wave planning as a strategy can help with cost risk.

Understand the concept of refactoring and defects.   Refactoring is the process of restructuring existing internal computer code without changing its external behaviors. The team will use an iterative cycle of making small changes, testing the result to ensure correctness, and making another small change or transforming the code somehow. Defects can occur due to common causes or special causes, and they create risk and increased costs.

Be able to explain the different kinds of spikes used.   There are two types of spikes that can be done on a project to help mitigate risk and to prove a strategy could work before implementation of the chosen strategy. The first type of spike is an architectural spike, and the second type of spike is a risk-based spike, both of which are designed to support the project and to help mitigate the risk that could occur.

Be aware of the risk-adjusted backlog and how it's created.   You will be tested on your ability to run the expected monetary value formula in order to determine the cost impacts due to risk. That will then allow you to have a backlog that is adjusted to accommodate risk that needs to be mitigated while still accomplishing work on the features.

Be aware of different ways to assess and display risk.   Standard prompt lists, SWOT, and the 5 whys are just a few ways that risk can be assessed so that the team can determine the best way to mitigate the identified risks. Using a risk burn down chart is a transparent way to communicate mitigation efforts and to keep track of risk throughout each iteration. Be aware of the differences between burn up and burn down charts, including the risk burn down chart and its uses.

Review Questions

You can find the answers to the review questions in Appendix B.

1. Which of the following best describes progressive elaboration?

    A. It allows teams to pull new information into plans when it becomes available.

    B. It engages stakeholders in project decisions.

    C. It determines expectations.

    D. It allows documentation of all stakeholder needs across the project.

2. Agile teams incorporate rolling wave planning to do which one of the following?

    A. Schedule activities.

    B. Incorporate high-level plans with the knowledge that they will be updated.

    C. Assign tasks.

    D. Complete the personas for the project.

3. Utilizing decision delays in an Agile environment allows teams to do all of the following except _____.

    A. Mitigate risks

    B. Adapt to changes

    C. Implement based on the most up-to-date information

    D. Have "fine-grained requirements" until they can become "course-grained"

4. A risk has been identified in the first iteration. It's expected monetary value is projected at $45,000, and the value of the first feature is $23,000. If the risk can't be mitigated effectively and for less money, what could occur on the project?

    A. A risk meeting to determine what to do next.

    B. Update the risk-adjusted backlog to handle the risk before building the feature.

    C. The project may reach fast failure.

    D. Determine solutions in the sprint planning meeting.

5. A key stakeholder is asking what the overall risk situation is for the iteration. Which of the following will you show them to help answer that question?

    A. Risk burn down chart

    B. Burn up chart

    C. Burn down chart

    D. Velocity tracking charts

6. Jim is new to your Agile team, and he is interested in how your team will be tracking scope of work completed and risk on the project. Which of the following type of chart or graph will you explain that you are using for both?

   A. Velocity charts

   B. Cumulative-flow diagrams

   C. Kanban board

   D. Burn down charts

7. A risk event has been identified that will affect your current iteration. To investigate and determine ways to mitigate the risk, what will your team do?

   A. Perform expected monetary value assessments.

   B. Discuss the risk in their stand-up meeting and try to find a solution.

   C. Discuss it with the product owner and see if there is a way to remove the feature containing the risk.

   D. Perform a risk-based spike.

8. During your daily stand-up meeting, Karen has pointed out a new impediment that is in her way. She is concerned that it may evolve into a risk event. After the meeting, Karen works with Peter to develop a story to reduce the impact of the risk event and wants to perform a risk-based spike. Which of the following represents the correct way to do the spike?

   A. Identify problems and describe what has been accomplished since the last meeting in the next day's stand-up meeting.

   B. Describe the risk and the need for a spike with the product owner who will approve it, and Karen and Peter will allot time to work on it.

   C. Coordinate discussions on problems, and work on solutions with the entire team.

   D. Identify additional risks that can be managed in the same spike.

9. During a meeting with your sponsor, they bring up the fact that on your new Agile project your reporting has dropped off to the point where they barely have any information compared to Waterfall projects. How will you explain this to your sponsor?

   A. You will spend time doing the reports since they asked for them. Your team is self-directed and doesn't need you for a while.

   B. Explain that until the product owner prioritizes, you don't have the information to give them.

   C. Explain progressive elaboration and last responsible moment Agile philosophies to the sponsor.

   D. Ask your team to detail the work they have done so that you can process a report.

10. Your current project has both value and risks to consider. In what order would the risk compared to value be placed to have a completed risk-adjusted backlog?

    A. Highest-impact risk first

    B. Highest-value items first

    C. A review of both risk and value would be considered, and the one with the highest financial impact would be chosen to be accomplished first.

    D. A review of both risk and value would be considered, and the one with the lowest financial impact would be chosen to be accomplished first.

11. You are working with your team on a complicated software design. You really aren't sure if it is going to work, and at this point you aren't even sure if you can work it out in time to prove that you've determined the fix. What would be the best thing that you could suggest as their Agile PM?

    A. Talk to the product owner, and see if you can get better clarification of the scope of work.

    B. The project has reached fast failure, and the product owner needs to close the project.

    C. Have a meeting with the customer, and attempt to see if there are other features that they can use instead.

    D. Perform an architectural spike to determine whether the current approach can work or if another one is needed.

12. Chris identified a new risk early in the first iteration. This is due to the use of the newest technologies and not much is known about how to solve it. What is the best thing for Chris to suggest in order to manage the situation?

    A. Document the risk in the risk-adjusted backlog, and wait for the product owner to review.

    B. Perform a risk-based spike.

    C. Update the backlog.

    D. Move the risk affected work into the backlog for future iterations.

13. Jamal is writing code that is easy to implement in the short run instead of applying the best overall solution at the time to get the code completed in time. What could be the outcome of this technique?

    A. Jamal is getting the work done quickly and creatively meeting deadlines.

    B. Jamal may be inadvertently creating tech debt that will have to be paid later in the project.

    C. Jamal is creating source code that can be worked out using an architectural spike.

    D. Jamal is running tests so that they fail.

14. Gail is in the process of restructuring existing computer code without changing its behavior. Peter asks her what she is working on. How will Gail answer that question?

    A. I'm cleaning up tech debt.

    B. I'm trying to build in lead time.

    C. I'm refactoring the code.

    D. I'm building software.

15. Your team is analyzing risk events and trying to determine what the "price tag" is going to be based on probability and impact. Which of the following techniques will provide that information?

    A. Expected money value

    B. Expected monetary value

    C. Expected severity value

    D. Expected priority cost

16. Your Agile team is working on the fifth iteration of their project, and the sponsor is reviewing their risk burn down chart. How will the sponsor know if risk is being managed on the project?

A. As the team mitigates or avoids risk, the chart should trend up.

B. As the team mitigates or avoids risk, the chart should trend down.

C. As the team mitigates or avoids risk, the chart should have less information.

D. As the team mitigates or avoids risk, the chart should be distributed to the sponsor.

17. Which of the following is a brainstorming technique designed to get to the bottom of something and provide a clearer solution to the issue?

A. Ishikawa diagram

B. The 5 whys

C. Sailboat

D. Triple Nickels

18. As a product owner, you are reviewing the expected monetary value of identified risks and determining how to place the mitigation efforts into the backlog. Which of the following would go at the top of the list in a risk-adjusted backlog?

A. Feature A: $15,000

B. Risk B: $5,000

C. Feature C: $11,000

D. Risk D: $16,000

19. Sally is performing expected monetary value analysis on a newly identified risk. She has determined the probability is 30 percent and the impact is $10,000. What is the expected monetary value?

A. $3,000

B. $10,000

C. $300,000

D. $30,000

20. Three new risk events have been identified in your current iteration. Your analysis shows that two of the risk events' expected monetary value are higher than the features on which you are working, and one is not very impactful at all. What should you do if you are the product owner?

A. Perform a risk-based spike to determine the impact.

B. Put the two highly impactful risk events at the top of the risk-adjusted backlog.

C. Work with the team on mitigation efforts.

D. Place it on the risk burn down chart for tracking purposes.

21. Your team is working together to brainstorm potential risk events on a project, and they are using a technique that allows them to focus on what is going well now versus what isn't going so well now. Which of the following tools are they using?

    A. The 5 whys

    B. Risk burn down charts

    C. SWOT

    D. Delphi technique

22. At the end of the day on Friday, you are attempting to wrap up your work and head home. Right in the middle of finishing a string of code, your computer crashes without saving all of your work. This is considered to be which one of the following?

    A. A common cause; it happens.

    B. A special cause; it's a surprise.

    C. A common cause, it never happens.

    D. A special cause; it's just noise in the system.

23. You've just finished working on a long string of code, and as you review it, you realize that you have created the simplest thing that works but not necessarily the best solution. What are you creating for yourself?

    A. Tech debt

    B. Refactoring

    C. Risk

    D. Scope creep

24. A defect has been identified in the program you have worked on for the past three iterations. You aren't sure when the defect was created, but you know that the influencing factor was that someone else worked on earlier strings of the code while you were gone on vacation, which is a very common practice. What is the reason for the defect?

    A. Common cause

    B. Special cause

    C. Risk event

    D. Poor implementation of refactoring

25. A risk event has just happened on your project. You work to implement the agreed-upon solution for mitigation and create a whole other risk event. This is known as which one of the following?

    A. Residual risk

    B. Secondary risk

    C. Risk avoidance

    D. Risk backlog adjustment

21. Your team is working together to brainstorm out
   the names of items that allow them to focus on
   gaps as well now. Which of the following tools is the best choice?

   A. The Values
   B. Risk Breakdown chart
   C. SWOT
   D. Brainstorming

Chapter

10

Tailoring, Quality Management, and Improving Project Processes

---

THE FOLLOWING PMI-ACP® EXAM TOPICS ARE COVERED IN THIS CHAPTER:

✓ **Domain VII: Continuous Improvement (Product, Process, People)**

- Task 1: Tailor and adapt the project process by periodically reviewing and integrating team practices, organizational culture, and delivery goals in order to ensure team effectiveness within established organizational guidelines and norms.

- Task 2: Improve team processes by conducting frequent retrospectives and improvement experiments in order to continually enhance the effectiveness of the team, project, and organization.

- Task 3: Seek feedback on the product by incremental delivery and frequent demonstrations in order to improve the value of the product.

- Task 4: Create an environment of continued learning by providing opportunities for people to develop their skills in order to develop a more productive team of generalizing specialists.

- Task 5: Challenge existing process elements by performing a value stream analysis and removing waste in order to increase individual efficiency and team effectiveness.

- Task 6: Create systemic improvements by disseminating knowledge and practices across projects and organizational boundaries in order to avoid re-occurrence of identified problems and improve the effectiveness of the organization as a whole.

In this chapter, you will work through the tasks found in Domain VII: Continuous Improvement (Product, Process, People). The tasks directly relate to understanding that Agile frameworks are not one size fits all and that tailoring your projects and utilizing best practices that complement your current project is an important skill to have and to understand. Obtaining feedback during a product review and having retrospectives as a team will increase your ability to work together to learn, grow, and increase value across the projects on which you are working.

Continuous improvements are a major tenet of Agile project management, so this domain takes everything that we have reviewed so far and focuses on improving your skill sets. This will, in turn, improve the products you create, the processes you use, and your team. Some of the information on tailoring can be found in the *Agile Practice Guide* (Project Management Institute, 2017), and it aligns with updates found in the *PMBOK® Guide, Sixth edition*, released in September 2017. This overlap of best practices allows tailoring needs to pull from both Agile best practices and predictive best practices in a way that is most relevant for your project's needs.

Tailoring

Not every single project is going to gain value from a specific Agile framework. For some, Scrum is too rigid and focused on software development; meanwhile you are working in a hardware installation environment. Maybe you come from a Waterfall background and your organization isn't too keen to change anytime soon, and therefore you can only improve best practices in short bursts by pulling in one or two things that can help.

In fact, most tailoring will coincide with a Waterfall team's expansion into different industries. The amount of certified PMP professionals in the world are well over seven hundred thousand to date: that means a lot of professional project managers practicing Waterfall and needing variety to keep up with the technology. There is now a need to have experience or knowledge in multiple models or frameworks to determine how your unique projects can benefit from a different approach.

The selection of the best practice to utilize on a unique project is called *tailoring*, and it will involve the project manager collaborating with the project team, sponsor, and organizational management in order to make sure that the chosen approach is the best one to meet the organizational needs and the business intent for the project.

The sixth edition of the *PMBOK® Guide* references tailoring and Agile at the beginning of every chapter and knowledge area, and the *Agile Practice Guide* recently published by the Project Management Institute (in partnership with the Agile Alliance) shows that having the best of both worlds is possible as long as you select the best approach for the project on which you are working.

A lot of items trending now in the Waterfall space are visual management tools like Kanban boards and an expansion of the project manager's responsibilities in business case development and determining whether a hybrid approach to the project may be needed. Updates may need to be made to how a *project management office (PMO)* might be run to accommodate a multitude of disciplines rather than trying to work with a one-size-fits-all approach to overseeing projects on the organizational level. The PMO may have to adapt and shift to changing needs or unique projects and may become the *voice* for best practices from the top down. This can help the organization get through the chaos much more quickly if done correctly.

Hybrid frameworks have also become a necessity when one framework isn't scalable or even remotely applicable. Hybrids could include *ScrumBan* (Scrum and Kanban), Waterfall with aspects of Scrum, Scrum with aspects of XP, and others that have evolved due to the actual practice of new ways of performing similar tasks.

The following will be not an exhaustive list of tailoring or hybrid approaches, but it is comprehensive enough to understand where they came from and why they are important to review.

Scaled Agile Framework   *Scaled Agile framework (SAFe)* was designed as a response to some current challenges in Agile frameworks that included a limited number of team members in order for the process framework to work. That is unrealistic for many organizations, so SAFe created a way for alignment, collaboration, and delivery for large numbers of Agile teams ranging from 50 to 125 to several thousand members and was created from Agile development, systems thinking, and Lean product development.

Like Crystal methods, which use a scalable model, there are several SAFe configurations, as follows:

1. **Essential SAFe:** Basic Level
2. **Large Solution SAFE:** Enterprise-level and complex system (aerospace, defense, government)
3. **Portfolio SAFe:** Enterprise for multiple solution creation
4. **Full SAFe:** Large enterprise projects using hundreds to thousands of people

The elements of SAFe mirror many of the elements that you have reviewed in many other Agile frameworks, but they are appropriate for the tailoring of this framework, including metrics, road maps, shared services, vision, community of practice (CoP), a system team, milestones, and Lean UX (User eXperience).

The SAFe foundational elements reflect aspects of both Lean and Agile and are recommended experience for leadership. Some of the core values include built-in quality, transparency, program execution, and implementation road maps, as well as SAFe-specific principles and recommended consultants.

Large Scale Scrum   *Large Scale Scrum (LeSS)* is a product development framework that extends some of the confines of Scrum and allows for scaling guidelines without losing the original purpose or flavor of Scrum. LeSS was created by Bas Vodde and Craig Larman based on experiments in large-scale environments as simpler ways of working on larger projects, without devaluing the Scrum framework. There are two levels of LeSS:

LeSS Huge   This level has additional scaling elements of development added to accommodate hundreds of developers all working on the same project. That's a far cry from the original recommendation of no more than nine team members who are all colocated!

LeSS Level   This level began in the telecom and finance industry, and it can accommodate scaling up to eight teams.

LeSS utilizes core competencies that include ways to combat the organizational complexity experienced by many industries when attempting to implement Scrum-specific projects.

There are LeSS Roles, LeSS Management, and LeSS organizational structures. That sounds a lot like Scrum, except it is much larger!

Enterprise Scrum   Created by Mike Beedle, *Enterprise Scrum* was designed to allow for faster, more efficient, and customer-driven innovation for higher profits and revenue. Enterprise Scrum allows for scalable models and empirical project management. The framework includes multiple levels of planning and improvement cycles as well as reviews for business value and for the increment. Value list items are refined, much like backlog refinement before the cycle continues. Value includes cultural value, which embraces Scrum values and business analysis. A value list is created similar to a product backlog, and each has a *definition of ready (DOR)* and a definition of done (DOD).

The team roles are similar to Scrum in the sense that there are three key roles—the business owner (instead of product owner), Scrum Master, and team—as are the reporting techniques. Scrum boards, burn down charts, and tracking metrics are the same.

Enterprise Unified Process   *Enterprise Unified Process (EUP)* is a customizable framework that is iterative and incremental, architecture-centric, and risk focused. EUP can be compared interchangeably with the *Rational Unified Process (RUP)*, which is a tailorable process that allows for development guidance and automated tools and services, which allow both the processes and tools to be utilized and adopted quickly.

Agile Unified Process   *Agile Unified Process (AgileUP)* features accelerated cycles and less heavyweight processes than the Unified Process (UP) or (EUP) on the enterprise level. AgileUP contains seven key disciplines, which include modeling, implementation, testing, deployment, configuration management, project management, and environment- or situationally specific decision making.

Disciplined Agile Delivery   Developed by Scott Ambler at IBM to incorporate using networks of cross-functional teams, *Disciplined Agile Delivery (DAD)* was designed to scale key best practices in order to fill the gaps left by other frameworks in enterprise solution environments. DAD utilizes the best of the best from Scrum, XP, Agile Modeling (AM), Enterprise Unified Process (EUP), Kanban, and other approaches. The model also embraces a people-first approach, is learning oriented, incorporates a full delivery cycle and process-driven goals, and is solution focused and enterprise aware.

Agile Modeling   *Agile Modeling* (AM) is a collection of values and principles that can be applied to software development and may be considered an add-on tailoring approach for Scrum and XP as well as DAD. The focus is on documentation throughout the life cycle but documented as late as possible and stored in one place to prevent versioning confusion. Its requirements are specific to customer tests. Much like Scrum and XP, Agile Modeling is tough to implement on larger teams. Any team with fewer than 30 people is about the maximum capacity for this framework.

Tailoring and the *PMBOK® Guide*

Due to the necessity of different approaches for different project types, the Project Management Institute worked closely with the Agile Alliance to publish the *Agile Practice Guide*, mentioned at the beginning of this chapter. This collaboration resulted in updates to best practices in the Waterfall dynamic as well.

Each knowledge-area chapter like Scope, Time, Cost, and others has information on tailoring approaches and considerations for Agile. These considerations map to the *Agile Practice Guide* and allow discussions and training on other ways of performing the same tasks as needed.

Figure 10.1 shows an overview of all of the knowledge areas and how they map to Agile considerations. All of the information shown is from *A Guide to the Project Management Body of Knowledge (PMBOK® Guide), Sixth Edition* (Project Management Institute, 2017).

It's easy to see that tailoring considerations and Agile hybrids are becoming frontrunners in new and better ways of managing projects. In a way, it's freeing to be able to cherry pick what will work with your unique projects.

My advice is twofold: both for and against tailoring. If you are planning to incorporate new processes or tools on your current projects, make sure that you and your team understand those processes and tools and work to keep improving the implementation of them and checking the results. Be vigilant about stakeholder communication, and provide explanations if they aren't familiar with Agile or your chosen best practices. Practice servant leadership rather than project management, and communicate, collaborate, and congratulate.

Here's just a tiny bit of advice about tailoring, *especially if your team or organization is new to Agile*. It is better to use a proven method of best practices than to try to create a hybrid approach right out of the gate.

Learn the techniques before throwing a methodology out as not working. Remember, there will be some initial chaos, and typically that is the precise point when it's often determined that Agile isn't working. Keep practicing! Based on the criticality of your projects and the weight of method, you may need to adjust your framework based on team size and project length.

FIGURE 10.1   Mapping Agile to the *PMBOK Guide, Sixth Edition*

Knowledge Area	Agile Considerations
Stakeholder Management	• Regular interactions with stakeholders • Aggressive transparent communication • High degree of change; active engagement and participation with stakeholders by the team • Inviting stakeholders to project meetings and reviews and posting project artifacts in public spaces
Scope Management	• Spend less time defining requirements • Spend more time establishing the process for ongoing discovery • Keep their backlog updated based on customer or business value with reassessments per iteration
Time Management	• The theory of constraints (the study of bottlenecks) • A pull system moves work through the process instead of planning sprints or time boxes • One completed item triggers the "pull" of another
Cost Management	• High degrees of uncertainty in agile projects create more difficulty in detailed costs calculations • Lightweight estimates provide forecasted estimates • Many agile projects are held to strict budgets and if so scope and schedule would need to be adjusted accordingly
Quality Management	• Retrospectives • Time-boxed (two to three hours) • Meet with the team after the iteration reviews
Resource Management	• Generalized specialists • Self-organized teams • Lean management • Just-in-time (JIT) manufacturing • Kaizen • Total productive management (TPM) approach to eliminate waste associated with production equipment and machinery • Theory of constraints (TOC)
Communication Management	• Streamlining access to information • Frequent team check-points • Posting artifacts transparently • Regular stakeholder reviews
Risk Management	• Frequent reviews of incremental work products and cross-functional teams • Accelerates knowledge sharing • Each iteration considers risk when determining scope of work • Risk is identified, analyzed and managed during the iteration
Procurement	• Collaborative working environment • Sellers may be used to extend the team • Both buyer and seller may share the risk • Adaptive contracting like a master services agreement (MSA) • Allows for flexibility with scope changes

Because I personally love being able to pick and choose the how and why of my projects, it all is very exciting to see. My PMP brain and my PMI-ACP brain can fire in all directions, and where I see gaps or challenges in one, I find the answer in the other. You have a lot of options now, and training, mentoring, and coaching is highly recommended, so use them all accordingly. Agile and tailoring are the new face of project management, and having skills in many areas is to your benefit for sure!

Lead Time and Cycle Time

Like many project management terms and jargon, there is some overlap depending on what frameworks you use. In this case, the terms *cycle time* and *lead time* may have some overlap in their usage. I bring this up because there are some differences between the two, but they can often be used interchangeably depending on your chosen framework or organizational *lingo*.

According to the Agile Alliance, which helped coauthor the PMI *Agile Practice Guide*, *lead time* originated in the Toyota Production System (TPS) and was a part of their Lean manufacturing processes. In this context, lead time is the amount of elapsed time between when your customer orders an increment to the time of completion and the order being received by the customer—basically, from start to finish of the project itself. This may be very relevant to those of you who are working in a Waterfall or hybrid/tailored environment, since the assumption is that something tangible will be produced.

In a software development or Agile environment, it may very well be an internal project designed to provide a new product or service, be first to market, develop a bug fix, or perform an internal upgrade. If that is the case, then lead time may reflect the time between when the team determines a requirement is needed, a user is story created, and the point at which that increment is being utilized by an end user.

Lead time isn't actual effort either. *Lead time* is simply the time from start to finish. It could take the team five days from the request to the actual execution of the request. The actual execution could be considered effort, whereas the timeline is lead time.

In continuous improvement endeavors, reducing your lead time shows that improvements have been made.

Lead Time versus Velocity

The Agile Alliance's website (www.agilealliance.org) states that many teams who prefer the Kanban framework tend to work with lead time rather than velocity as a way to track performance and improvement efforts. Teams that use velocity to track performance want to *increase* velocity, and conversely, teams that use a Kanban approach want to *decrease* their lead time.

Cycle time, on the other hand, can be defined from the development side as the starting point of execution on a feature and getting that feature into the done column and ready for deployment. If you choose to use both terms, one could generically view lead time as a customer timeline and cycle time as the team timeline.

In terms of organizational return on investment, the focus is on lead time, as it represents the start and finish of the work, rather than the cycle time, which is more of a tracking mechanism for the team. In Figure 10.2, it is easy to see how they work together in a visual manner.

No matter how you track time on your projects, there are several variables that may be considered, including cycle time (development and testing time), work in progress (WIP), and throughput (average amount of time that it takes the team to complete the work within a specific time frame).

It is important to understand the percentage of efficiency on the iteration by comparing value time versus cycle time and to determine the efficiency of your process. One way to do this is to divide the value-added time by the cycle time for the process.

FIGURE 10.2   Lead time and cycle time

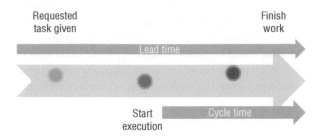

You may be asked on the exam to calculate the percentage of process efficiency. To do so, you would use basic math to calculate the information presented in the question. Don't worry, you will have access to a calculator, and even though the PMI-ACP exam isn't formula-focused, you may see a question like the following:

You have determined that you spend 45 minutes putting together a presentation that will last 10 minutes. What is the current calculated process cycle efficiency?

A.   55 minutes

B.   33%

C.   45 minutes

D.   18%

The correct way to determine this is to divide the valuable time of 10 minutes by the total cycle time of 55 minutes. The result will be 18 percent, meaning that your process efficiency is only 18 percent.

All results of process efficiency, value time and cycle time determination may be considered during a retrospective to effectively improve the value stream and the team's effectiveness. According to the PMI-ACP exam content outline, it is important for the team to challenge existing process elements by performing a value stream analysis and removing waste in order to increase individual efficiency and team effectiveness.

There are several variables to consider when looking at team progress and effectiveness of work to produce something that is considered valuable while at the same time attempting to increase your pace and output while producing something of quality.

The bigger focus on the PMI-ACP exam will be on cycle time and improving it as well as finding bottlenecks or issues in the work in progress (WIP) that may be causing issues or slowing down the cycle time. Also, you will not be asked to calculate cycle time on the exam, as there are very few formulas of which you must be aware.

Process Improvement

Because performance tracking and process improvements on Agile projects may be very different from a typical Waterfall project, it's important to define all of the variables that you may see on your Agile projects or on your exams. The following list will give you an idea of how they all contribute to the success of the project as well as how they can raise red flags for issues.

Throughput   Whether you use *throughput* or velocity on your projects depends on the Agile framework you elect to use and what your stakeholders want as far as information on time frames. Many people see *throughput* and *velocity* as interchangeable terms, whether you use Lean or Scum/XP. It is often difficult to explain the ideas of story points and velocity to those who are newer stakeholders to Agile environments. Velocity is more for the team's benefit when determining how much work they can take on in an iteration or sprint. Throughput is based more on duration estimates (the time work will take to complete), not calendar days *per se* but the number of backlog items that can be done in a given time period. This helps stakeholders who are used to duration estimates wrap their minds around the team's completed work. User stories are still included, but typically the team will pull the highest-priority stories from the backlog and complete them. They will keep track of when they started and finished those stories and summarize them monthly. Much of the calculation has to do with average amounts of work being completed based on the historical information of the current project.

Calculating Throughput

If you are using throughput to track performance, it is important to make sure that partial work isn't included in your calculations. The goal is to focus on finished or completed stories and how many have been accomplished. Let's say that your team has worked on stories over the course of the last six weeks/iterations.

    Week 1: 5 stories

    Week 2: 3 stories

    Week 3: 5 stories

    Week 4: 6 stories

    Week 5: 5 stories

    Week 6: 2 stories

The variations in completed stories may be because the story sizes are larger/smaller or the technicality is higher. Variations are to be expected over time. So, how do you then forecast or calculate? You create an average and use it as your guide as follows:

$$(5 + 3 + 5 + 6 + 5 + 2) / 6 = 4.33$$

Since partial work doesn't count, the team can choose to round up to five to be safe or to round down to four. Rounding up is recommended since many five- or six-story weeks have occurred. Basically, the average is four stories a week plus or minus one. Now that the team has that information, they can plan their next iteration knowing their average capabilities without needing to estimate individual story points, they can report on performance, and they can do a bit of forecasting for those stakeholders who are asking for it and looking for areas of improvement. The amount of work items that the team can complete in any given time period is contingent on keeping work in progress (WIP) limited to avoid bottlenecks and reduce a lot of unfinished work per iteration.

Takt Time   *Takt time* is the German phrase for pace or rhythm. To determine the team's pace or rhythm during an iteration is to determine the rate that the team needs to work to keep up with customer demands. Many times, this is seen in mass production manufacturing environments. If the customer wants a certain amount of mobile device batteries produced within a certain time frame, you can calculate how much time it takes per device by dividing the total amount of available time by the total amount of product demanded: time/demand. It's also a good indicator if the demand is unreasonable and it needs to be adjusted per your process and for quality purposes.

Work in Progress   By now, you probably have a good understanding of *work in progress (WIP)* and how important it is to limit WIP to avoid bottlenecks, unfinished work, or slow workflow. Much as it is difficult to truly multitask (that is, to do any one thing effectively when bouncing around from task to task), limiting WIP is a way to improve your process. It often takes a while for a team to find their groove and determine that there is a better way to doing things. A big part of a retrospective, however, is to look back and see what went well and what didn't. It's important to be aware of setting WIP limits as a way to improve your process flow continuously.

Cumulative Flow Diagrams (CFDs)   Another way to determine how your projects are progressing is to incorporate *cumulative flow diagrams (CFDs)* to represent visually the reality on your iteration. At a very high level, these diagrams can help your team track performance and forecast out by tracking features that are in progress, completed, or on deck to be worked on. Total features over time are addressed allowing the team to get a glimpse into their progress and see additional features added over time. Just like any diagram or visual representation of work, a cumulative flow diagram can show areas where issues have occurred or may occur, and it allows the team to adapt and adjust as needed.

Theory of Constraints   It is a foregone conclusion that project management is filled with constraints—scope, time, and cost being the big three offenders. The *Theory of Constraints (TOC)* is a management philosophy that looks at the speed bumps in a project and identifies the most influential constraint and then improves upon it until it no longer impacts the project in a negative way.

Constraints are often called *bottlenecks* in production systems: Once the bottlenecks are removed, the flow improves. Much as Pareto charts look at the most impactful reasons defects occur in quality, the Theory of Constraints focuses first on identifying the constraint, then determining how one could exploit the constraint, followed by subordinating all other processes in order to exploit the constraint. If that doesn't get it done, then more resources or capacity would have to be added to meet the need to attempt to elevate or remove the constraint.

Remember, TOC is a management philosophy, and your organization may have many ways in which constraints that impact the project are removed or worked around. One of the key aspects of an Agile team versus a Waterfall team is the Agile team's cross-functionality and self-direction. This allows for the team to decide exactly what the constraint is and how to manage it more effectively and in a timely manner. Waterfall teams may have to go through formal change control, update their documentation, or even implement a risk response if the constraint it too impactful.

While you may not be using all or any of these performance measurements on your current projects, it is always a good idea to know how performance is tracked outside of an earned value analysis for time and cost. It's very likely that you won't be using earned value analysis on an Agile project and that the team will look for waste in the system or the process instead, as well as determining how you can improve the value stream.

> Failure is only the opportunity to begin again more intelligently.
> *Henry Ford*

Value Stream Mapping

One of the coolest things about Agile frameworks is that some failure is expected. It would impossible to work in an environment of iterative and incremental development without taking a few extra steps along the way that cause you to stray from true performance. It is also a no-finger-pointing environment in which the team works together on solutions and the efforts to implement them. If that doesn't work, they try, try again.

Another aspect of Agile project management is the visual representation of performance in the team space. It's highly unlikely that something will squeak past without being noticed by somebody, and once noticed, it will be discussed and repaired.

The best-laid plans often go sideways; the goal is to not stay put and make the same mistakes over and over. Instead, the goal is to work through the processes that are being used and find the culprit causing the problems and remove it. This is where value stream maps can be a valuable asset in continuous improvement measures.

Value stream maps are designed to show a process visually from start to finish and to identify value and non-value-added time.

Real World Scenario

Time Doesn't Always Equal Value

An excellent representation of valuable time taken up and lost at the same time are status meetings. One of the tech companies for whom I worked in the early 2000s was famous for pulling management into meetings on a regular basis; so much so that actual work wasn't being accomplished. The organizer (sponsor) would schedule the meetings in different conference rooms spread out across a huge campus of buildings in an effort to be fair to all. The problem was that if you didn't work in the specific building for that week's meeting, it would take you 20 minutes just to find the kookaburra conference room as compared to the koala conference room in a totally different building.

On a side note: Why do large organizations always name their conference rooms with some crazy theme name? It makes it very difficult to find them when needed.

Anyhoo, people would filter into the correct room looking disheveled and apologizing profusely for being late to the meeting. Then the meeting would actually begin 30 minutes late and consist of a circular conversation that picked up right where the last meeting left off. Our one-hour meeting became two hours, and then it was necessary to schedule another meeting to discuss this meeting and on and on it went. If you were to plot out a value stream map of your cycle time and compare value-added time versus non-value-added time, it would be pretty evident how much time was lost and not valuable. Let's see how that plays out in lost time and poor process flow.

- 20 minutes to find the conference room (non-value-added time)

- 30 minutes of wasted time beginning the meeting and asking about the weekend and a variety of other inconsequential conversations (non-value-added time)

- 120 minutes of meeting (questionable, but considered value-added time)

The entire "one-hour" meeting that was supposed to occur cost the company almost three hours. One could argue that the 120 minutes spent in the meeting was valuable, and if that was the case, then 50 minutes of time was effectively wasted. Either way, our cycle time is exponentially longer than it needed to be. And that is just one meeting! Compound that number by four times a month or more and the value is lost in space.

Value stream mapping is used to identify process improvement opportunities and overall cycle time improvements, and when waste or non-value-added activities are discovered, the team works to remove those activities (if possible) and a new map is created. I say *if possible* because it isn't always possible to march into a meeting and explain to the sponsor that their meetings are a total waste of time. That tends to result in an RPE, or a resume-producing event! Where the team can make improvements, they will, and where they can't, they will work within those constraints to the best of their abilities. The steps for process improvements are a lot like the frameworks of Agile: easy to talk about and hard to do.

The most dangerous kind of waste is the waste we do not recognize.
Shigeo Shingo

A value stream map is a visual representation of the goal and the steps required to accomplish the goal. That may be the highest-value product or the highest-value process. Most of the maps I have seen are process oriented, but they affect the product or results. In manufacturing, identifying waste in the process flow includes delivery times, material flow, inventory, and so on, and the map will look at the current state of the process and then create an ideal state and a prediction for a future state. Thus, it involves the mapping of the current process steps using collected data about the process itself, the information flow, and the current cycle time. Much of wasted time involves waiting or lag time between deliveries or unnecessary movement of items, materials, or the team. The goal of the visual plotting out of the process is to identify what areas are causing the bottleneck in progress and which of those items may impact your timeline as the iteration progresses. Many times, the team will identify the pain points in the process and, if possible, work to include a *kaizen*, or continuous improvement effort.

If you are interested in a full-blown map for Lean manufacturing, you will see different icons that represent distinct aspects of the map and templates that you can use to create your own maps. For our purposes, it is a way to view value versus non-value.

Value stream mapping is something that you will see on your exams. However, you will not be asked to analyze a map for process improvements. Instead, you will be asked about cycle time improvements and why value stream maps help continuously improve the team's cycle time.

In Figure 10.3, you will see the difference between value stream mapping and process mapping. They are different items, but both are valuable for the long and short-term planning efforts in which your team will be engaged. Value stream mapping focuses on multiple processes versus a singular process that needs improvement.

FIGURE 10.3   Value stream and process mapping

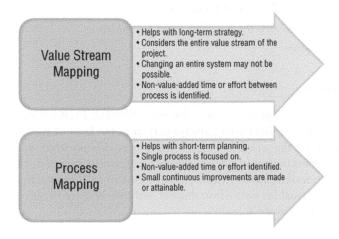

Value Stream Mapping
- Helps with long-term strategy.
- Considers the entire value stream of the project.
- Changing an entire system may not be possible.
- Non-value-added time or effort between process is identified.

Process Mapping
- Helps with short-term planning.
- Single process is focused on.
- Non-value-added time or effort identified.
- Small continuous improvements are made or attainable.

Continuous Product Improvement

The idea of continuous improvement in the context of project management typically involves a sharp focus on the product being made better. In a quality management arena, there are several ways that products are improved. Whether through pair programming in the eXtreme Programming environment, refactoring, inspections, reviews, or retrospectives, product improvement is a key aspect to many of the best practices found in Agile frameworks.

Earlier in the chapter, you reviewed some of the tailoring aspects of frameworks and how a *one-size-fits-all* approach isn't always the right answer. Many times, it is necessary to pull best practices from different methodologies and frameworks to create the better best practices needed for your industry. In short, Agile isn't just for software development anymore.

Instead, Agile frameworks come in a variety of combinations with other methods, or they are inclusive of Waterfall tools and techniques. Agile is becoming mainstream, as is the need for organizations to remain competitive in a global environment and produce the best products and services they can both internally and externally.

The necessity for understanding multiple ways to improve not only our processes but our products is driving organizations to find better solutions. Much of what drives continuous improvements are the efforts of the team and their management who are *in the trenches,* if you will. They are in the best position to identify needed improvements and to share those improvements transparently in a way that can be captured for later projects.

Improvements are difficult without growth, though, and the people who do the work and know the product or service therefore need to improve proactively as well through training, education, certifications, and coaching.

Much of the reason the number of PMI-ACP certified professionals is growing exponentially is a shift in the needs of project management. Current processes may need to be expanded and improved upon, and having the skills to do so are highly marketable and, moreover, highly necessary for continuous improvements and organizational growth. Proactive instead of reactive is the rising trend. There are several ways to do both and move forward with improved products and processes.

> Don't be afraid to give up the good to go for the great.
> *John D. Rockefeller*

Intraspectives

Sometimes things just aren't going the way the team planned. Even with the best of planning and communication, things aren't always perfect in the land of Agile. What is a team to do? Does it wait until the scheduled review meeting to discuss what went wrong? Not at all. In the case of something going sideways during a sprint or iteration, the team can call an ad hoc meeting to look inward with perspective, or call an *intraspectives* meeting. The meeting can be very casual (as needed) to discuss and review team practices openly and assess how the team is working together.

Continuous improvement doesn't take place only on the side of testing and reviews, it is also happens on the team level. Many times, just the act of recognizing that the team isn't working well together and that it may need a breather to review what has been happening and why is a good reason to practice introspection.

Even though the crux of an Agile team is open and honest communication, a focus on the iteration results doesn't mean that things are working the way they should theoretically. Often, when teams new to Agile are experiencing the pain of changing the new normal, intraspectives are needed to determine why the processes or framework isn't working out the way the team thought it would and to overcome any conflict that is occurring in the team dynamic.

Any one of the team members can suggest that a meeting of the minds might be necessary to switch gears in the middle of an iteration. Much as a quarterback calls an audible and changes the play at the last second, the team can change their tactics for the good of the result.

Premortem

What if you could see the future and determine if what you are working on will fail or be successful? What if your team talked about all of the ways the project could or would fail? It seems counterproductive and a bit negative to assume the worst and hope for the best. However, that is exactly what a premortem is.

As you may have guessed, a *premortem* is the opposite of a postmortem meeting, which typically takes place at the end of a project, and more likely at the end of a project that has failed. It's a case of too little, too late at that point, but it's good for future lessons learned.

A premortem meeting allows the team to discuss all of the ways the project could fail and discuss the reasons why, all in advance in a hypothetical way. This allows an open conversation with the team, who can express doubts about the project's direction or express realistic reasons why they personally feel the project won't work out as planned.

Premortems are much like risk assessments, where we catastrophic thinkers get together and talk about everything that can go wrong but don't know it for a fact: We just have guesses as to probability and impact—educated guesses, that is.

A premortem allows discovery of risk events, open conversation, rule setting to avoid problems, and a coordinated effort by the team to avoid any such downfalls going forward.

Retrospectives

Perhaps the biggest reflection meeting happens when the iteration is over and before the next iteration or sprint planning begins. *Retrospectives* are typically designated as a one-hour-long meeting of just the development team to analyze the development process, determine ways to improve productivity, and discuss what went well, what didn't go so well, and what improvements could be made immediately in the next iteration. Keep in mind that this isn't a finger-pointing meeting at all: It is a structured way to look back and determine what is needed moving forward.

There are many games that can help improve the flow of communication, and expressions of one's feelings is also encouraged. Whether the retrospective involves discussion or debate, it is important that everyone has a chance to express themselves. Some teams choose to provide their feelings anonymously—whether they are feeling mad, sad, or glad about certain aspects of the topics being discussed by writing their feelings down on a piece of paper and then having a facilitator count the number of each category. A rousing interactive discussion can be had on what helped the project, what hindered the project, and the team's hypothesis about this. Many teams will use flip charts to write out their ideas and then collaborate on them. Another type of discussion-based method to gain team insights is to simply use *plus/delta*. Plus/delta consists of two columns indicating what the team should do more of and what should be changed.

There are many ways in which the team can create an open and honest dialog, but no matter how the discussions occur or play out, it is important for the team to agree on what changes will be made going forward, prioritize them, and create an action plan to be implemented in the very next iteration. This is immediate, continuous team improvement.

The retrospective occurs directly after the review meeting, which is a demonstration of the increment to determine if the team is building the right thing and building the thing right. Armed with information on the result and having gathered feedback on the increment's performance, the team can use that information to broaden the retrospective to allow for improvements across the entire development cycle and make plans for improvements going forward into the next planning meeting.

It is up to the team how conducting the retrospective will be the most effective, and no matter how your team holds the retrospective, it isn't a free-for-all: It is a structured, facilitated meeting with an agenda. The Agile project manager will facilitate the discussions, coach as needed on the team level, and make sure that action plans are agreed upon and created.

All of these items that have been discussed in this chapter are designed to help your Agile teams improve their processes by tailoring as needed, improving the value stream by identifying waste in the process, and improving the team as a whole.

No matter what direction you choose or what best practices you take from this study guide, you are now armed with information to help you pass the exam and gain your PMI-ACP certification. More important (I hope), you walk away with some ideas on how to improve your current processes and results as well as your team dynamics.

Let me also be the first to congratulate you on sticking with it and improving your own processes and marketability by becoming certified.

Best of luck in all you do!

> If you can dream it, you can do it.
> *Walt Disney*

Summary

This chapter began with information on the different types of options one has for tailoring or adapting their current processes in a way that suits their industry or organization. Agile is not a one-size-fits-all approach, which is why tailoring is becoming a trend in the project management space. It is up to your organization and your teams to determine what best practices you can use and which ones simply will not work effectively.

In the next section, I discussed cycle time and value streams. Both are ways to see your process and whether it is working, or if there are areas of improvement that can be made. Speeding up the cycle time without losing quality allows for continuous improvement efforts toward the increment or result being built.

Then I reviewed value stream mapping and how the team can plot out visually all of the steps in the process and identify areas affecting their cycle time and productivity. By identifying unnecessary steps in a visual way, the team can identify necessary adaptations to the process and thereby improve upon it.

In the next section, I reviewed some of the aspects of continuous product improvement with a selected focus on the team dynamic. You have reviewed testing and other aspects of producing quality increments in other chapters. As this guide winds to a close, a focus on the team dynamic is worth mentioning. Training, coaching, and transparent communication is crucial to Agile team success.

Finally, I reviewed intraspectives, premortems, and retrospectives as specific meetings focused on continuous improvements across the entire project—from the product to the process to how the team works together—all designed to be an iterative way to maintain focus on the goal and better ways to attain it.

Exam Essentials

Understand how tailoring your process can help improve your projects.   Understand why it is important to know that one size doesn't fit all; and why, with the variety of project types globally, it is important to identify the need for a tailored approach when applicable.

Understand the concept of cycle time.   It's important to understand cycle time in order to be able to spot areas for improvement and utilize better best practices to improve your value stream.

Be able to explain value stream maps.   Value stream maps are visual representations of the flow of your process from the beginning to the end. This allows for the team to comprehend clearly the current state of the process flow, attempt to improve the future state, and develop a plan to implement the improvements.

Be aware of continuous product improvements.   Agile frameworks are designed for continuous improvements with very specific meetings and better best practices being implemented right away. Aside from integrated testing and quality management, which I discussed in other chapters, it was important to wrap up the last chapter with a core focus on the team's role in continuous improvements.

Be aware of intraspectives, premortems, and retrospectives.   Agile team interactions are by design excellent ways to look inward and determine the reasons an iteration isn't progressing the way it should. Intraspectives can be called at any moment when the team performance needs an immediate facelift. Premortems are designed to look into the future and discuss what could go wrong and to strike preemptively to remove future trouble. Finally, retrospectives are a way for the team to look at the performance of the last iteration and make a plan for the next iteration.

Review Questions

You can find the answers to the review questions in Appendix B.

1. After working through two iterations with your Agile team, you've noticed that velocity is a bit lower than anticipated. During a daily stand-up meeting, one of the impediments that your team identifies is that the process seems bulky and more time-consuming than it needs to be. What would you suggest as a good way for the team to analyze the team processes for areas of improvement?

    A. Wireframe

    B. Burn down chart

    C. Value stream map

    D. Replanning session

2. As an Agile project management expert, you know that the difference between lead time and cycle time is which one of the following?

    A. Lead time is the total amount of time that the process takes, and cycle time is the total amount of time that an iteration takes.

    B. Lead time is the total amount of time that the iteration takes, and cycle time is the total amount of time that the process takes.

    C. Lead time is the total amount of time that you get when fast-tracking your schedule, and cycle time is the total amount of time that an iteration takes.

    D. Lead time is the total amount of time that the process takes, and cycle time is the total amount of time that refactoring takes.

3. Your team is working on a visual representation of their current process to determine if there is a better way to perform the process. With which of the following visual items are they working?

    A. Value analysis

    B. Value maps

    C. Story maps

    D. Value stream maps

4. You are working on a Lean project. You have determined that you spend 50 minutes putting together a presentation that will last 20 minutes. What is the current calculated process cycle efficiency?

    A. 70 minutes

    B. 30 percent

    C. 50 minutes

    D. 28 percent

5. Your Agile team is in a scheduled timeboxed meeting and is asking questions like, "What *should* our product do?" "How could it fail?" "Why would it fail?" In what kind of meeting is your team participating?

    A. Retrospective

    B. Review

    C. Premortems

    D. Sprint planning

6. Which of the following is the best way to answer the following questions?

    What should we stop doing? Start doing? Keep doing?

    A. Introspective

    B. Reviews

    C. Iteration reviews

    D. Retrospectives

7. During the retrospective of your current sprint, your team seems to be all over the map in how they think things went. What is something that you can recommend to get to the bottom of the emotional reactions of the team?

    A. Brainstorming

    B. The 5 whys

    C. Mad, sad, glad

    D. Pair programming

8. What is the goal of a retrospective regardless of the techniques used?

    A. The goal of a retrospective is reflection.

    B. The goal of a retrospective is solutions.

    C. The goal of a retrospective is venting.

    D. The goal of a retrospective is formal closure of an iteration.

9. During your retrospective, what is the most important thing that you as a coach can do to help your team reflect on the iteration?

    A. The team is encouraged to express their negatives as well as their positives of the iteration if it is well facilitated.

    B. The team is encouraged to express their negatives but not their positives.

    C. If the retrospective is well facilitated, the team is encouraged to express the positives of the project only.

    D. The team is encouraged to learn from their mistakes and follow the lessons learned next time around.

10. Which of the following hybrid models of Agile is most common?

    A. Scrum and ASD

    B. XP and Crystal

    C. Scrum and Lean

    D. Scrum and XP

11. Your team is meeting during the early stages of the iteration to discuss some of the items that may go wrong in the iteration. Which of the following meetings are you conducting?

    A. Retrospective meeting

    B. Premortem meeting

    C. Kickoff meeting

    D. Sprint planning meeting

12. The Project Management Institute collaborated with which of the following organizations when developing its *Agile Practice Guide*?

    A. The Scrum Alliance

    B. The Agile Alliance

    C. The eXtreme Programming Alliance

    D. Project managers globally

13. Which of the following diagram types can show areas where issues have occurred, or may occur, and allow the team to adapt and adjust as needed?

    A. Cumulative diagram

    B. Kanban diagram

    C. Burn down diagram

    D. Cumulative flow diagram

14. Which of the following is the German term for pace or rhythm, and it is also used to help track performance on an Agile team?

    A. Lead time

    B. Velocity time

    C. Cycle time

    D. Takt time

15. Constraints are often called bottlenecks in production systems. Once the bottlenecks are removed, flow improves. This is an example of which of the following?

    A. The Theory of Constraints

    B. The theory of cumulative experience

    C. The theory of bottlenecks

    D. The theory of limiting WIP

16. Jim is new to your team of developers and has a small amount of Agile experience. You have been tasked with explaining how your team is using a process flow called ScrumBan. How might you explain ScrumBan to Jim?

  A. ScrumBan is more Scrum based.

  B. ScrumBan is a hybrid approach that incorporates aspects of both Scrum and Kanban.

  C. ScrumBan is a made-up term and isn't an actual framework.

  D. ScrumBan is a tailored approach using both Scrum and Kanban.

17. Any one of the team members can suggest that a meeting of the minds might be necessary to switch gears in the middle of an iteration. This is known as what type of meeting?

  A. Retrospective

  B. Review

  C. Stand-up meeting

  D. Intraspective(s)

18. Your team is attempting to calculate their throughput. So far, they have completed three iterations.

Iteration 1: 17 story points were completed.

Iteration 2: 15 story points were completed.

Iteration 3: 19 story points were completed.

What is your team's current throughput?

  A. 19

  B. 17

  C. 15

  D. 53

19. Your team practices a Kanban approach to project management and prefers to use lead time rather than velocity to track performance. You are explaining this to a key stakeholder who isn't well versed in Agile. How would you explain the difference between lead time tracking and velocity tracking?

  A. Teams that use velocity to track performance would want to *increase* velocity, and conversely, teams that use a Kanban approach would want to *decrease* their lead time.

  B. Teams that use velocity to track performance would want to *decrease* velocity, and conversely, teams that use a Kanban approach would want to *increase* their lead time.

  C. Teams that use velocity to track performance would want to *increase* velocity, and conversely, teams that use a Kanban approach would want to *increase* their lead time.

  D. Teams that use velocity to track performance would want to *decrease* velocity, and conversely, teams that use a Kanban approach would want to *decrease* their lead time.

20. Large Scale Scrum, or LeSS, can best be described as which one of the following?

    A. LeSS is a product development framework that extends some of the confines of Scrum but doesn't allow for scaling guidelines.

    B. LeSS is a product development framework that extends some of the confines of Scrum and allows for scaling guidelines without losing the original purpose of Scrum.

    C. LeSS is a hybrid of both Scrum and Systematic Systems thinking.

    D. LeSS is just another way of saying Scrum with less management.

Appendix A

Next Steps

The study guide is designed to help you take and pass your PMI-ACP exam. This appendix just contains some thoughts to help you on your way while preparing for your exam. The important thing about preparing for an exam like this is that not only will you have a new certification under your belt, you will also get a great overview of the different frameworks, tools and techniques, and best practices to be Agile in your own work environments.

It's always best to refer to the recently published *Agile Practice Guide*, which can be purchased at www.pmi.org, as well as other related materials that can help you successfully pass the exam. It is also important to mention that the exam may be updated several times, but the best practices remain the same.

PMI provides a reference list of numerous books that you can review and can be found here: www.pmi.org/-/media/pmi/documents/public/pdf/certifications/ agile-certified-practitioner-reference-materials.pdf?la=en.

Attempting to read through all of the 12+ additional books that are recommended can be a difficult endeavor while working full time and studying for an exam. The goal of this study guide is to help you navigate everything that you need to know to take and pass the exam. At the same time, this book is designed to ensure that you are engaging in new best practices or different ways of making whatever philosophies you follow a little bit better.

What Is the PMI-ACP Certification?

The Project Management Institute's goal in putting together the Agile Certified Practitioner exam is to call attention to the multiple frameworks and best practices involved in projects that utilize an Agile approach. There are many other certification types that are proprietary. For example, the Scrum Alliance (www.scrumalliance.org) has numerous certifications that are applicable to the framework of Scrum, but PMI-ACP is the first certification exam of its kind to combine many best practices across multiple frameworks. The content itself is not company specific or partial to any one framework over another. The content is based on numerous books and best practices surrounding Agile projects.

There are only about 12,000 people in the world to date who are certified in Agile through the Project Management Institute. Compare this to the 700,000+ people in the world who are PMP certified. I expect the number of Agile certified individuals to increase rapidly as soon as organizations recognize the benefits of Agile frameworks or of a hybrid approach that utilizes Waterfall project management with aspects of Agile.

A Guide to the Project Management Body of Knowledge (PMBOK® Guide), Sixth Edition (Project Management Institute, 2017), contains ways to

> tailor project management best practices to a predictive environment and aspects of Agile project management that may be necessary in knowledge-based types of projects.

I know that a lot of you might be Scrum (CSM) certified, or that you have gone through other types of training for different Agile best practices. The whole point of this guide is to get you prepared to take and pass an exam that incorporates a lot of different Agile approaches and best practices.

Maybe you have a PMP certification, or you're trying to get one, or you got the program management certification (PMPg) or a certified associate in project management (CAPM) certification. If you are already certified in something, then you've been on the Project Management Institute's website. If not, there is a wealth of information on all certifications and the included content outlines on the website.

When I took the PMI-ACP exam, I found that all four answers for each question were in some way, shape, or form correct. The key is about getting yourself into the right mindset and choosing the *best answer*. You can only do that by getting your Agile hats on and making sure that you understand what those frameworks include and what PMI looks at as best practices across multiple Agile frameworks.

To maintain your PMI-ACP® certification (much like a PMP® certification), you'll have to obtain 30 professional development units, or PDUs (basically 30 hours) every three years based on Agile topics. I read an article recently that basically said that the hybrid of both PMP® and Agile certification is going to be in *the top five* most-needed or necessary skills over the course of the next five years.

If you're not familiar with the professional development or PDU process, the best thing to do is to go to www.pmi.org and look at what counts as a professional development unit and how the Project Management Institute's talent triangle works for professional development.

Real-World Considerations

Simply passing an exam won't cause your organization suddenly to see the light if they are not currently using Agile approaches regularly. You may have to go through an analysis and design process to get the organization on board. This can be a more difficult prospect than learning the ins and outs of Agile itself as well as guiding your team to an understanding of what the Agile framework looks like.

The following questions are among those that may be applicable in this situation:

- What are the current guidelines and are they working?

- What are the processes that we can utilize to estimate how long things will take or how much work we can accomplish in a sprint or iteration?

- What interpersonal skills can we utilize to manage our team of individuals who are also self-directed?

- What different metrics are we closely following and how do we use those metrics to plan, monitor, and adapt our process?

The big dance is agility, and part of that dance is incorporating continuous improvement in the process by following the guidelines and best practices, and by keeping tabs on how the project is progressing. The *Agile Practice Guide*, published by PMI in collaboration with the Agile Alliance, addresses many of the concerns teams and organizations face when adapting strategies.

You help your organization by making sure the project and team produce something valuable with minimal defects, managing risk effectively, and mitigating risk using a risk-adjusted backlog, or even a risk register if you prefer. You also help your organization by having a backlog of work that is valuable to the customer and by being able to prioritize the work in such a way that provides value consistently through each sprint/iteration of the project.

Whether you're planning on getting certified or not, this is all valuable information if your organization is attempting to implement an Agile framework or if you're already using Agile in some capacity.

The results of an Agile project can be completely intangible, and the scope of work is expected to adapt and change with Agile, so we prepare ourselves for it. This means that continuous improvement is necessary. With Agile (think agility), be malleable in order to improve best practices, products, or services. You are self-driven, self-motivated, and self-managed for sure, but you are also coached in the best practices of the individual frameworks you choose or in a hybrid approach of several.

Work is planned at the *last responsible moment* with the expectation that things will change. What is interesting is that today more Waterfall or predictive types of projects are incorporating some Agile frameworks, and even the PMP® exam has adapted to accommodate more Agile types of approaches.

A Guide to the Project Management Body of Knowledge (PMBOK® Guide), Sixth Edition, is inclusive of Agile and tailoring approaches. This will make the PMI-ACP® certification more relevant than it is already. Soon, more people will get certified, and more organizations will be implementing the many best practices available. Agile will improve knowledge work globally.

Tools and Techniques Overview

There are many categories of tools and techniques that can be used across multiple Agile frameworks. Tools and techniques that you could see on the PMI-ACP exam fall under several categories and incorporate many best practices in most, if not all, Agile environments.

As an overview, we will go through all of the tools and techniques categories as well as the recommended best practices in those categories. As we move forward, I will address the "how to" of each as they appear within the context of the processes and best practices. This is a good checklist as well to make sure that you understand the content in the guide for exam purposes.

Agile Toolkit

An overview of the tools that are necessary to effectively manage an Agile project can be helpful in both your studies and your projects. The list below isn't exhaustive but it does represent the tools every Agile project manager needs to work on and improve upon:

- Agile analysis and design
- Agile estimation

- Communications
- Interpersonal skills
- Metrics
- Planning, monitoring, and adapting
- Process improvement
- Product quality
- Risk management
- Value-based prioritization

PMI Ethical Decision-Making Framework

In order to make the best decisions in a fair and ethical manner, it is best to follow the four "A"s:

- Assessment
- Alternatives
- Analysis
- Application

    Source: www.pmi.org/about/ethics/code

Code of Ethics and Professional Conduct

Any person who is in the process of certification or is certified will need to read, agree to, and abide by the code of ethics and professional conduct.

- The code has both aspirational and mandatory standards.
- It focuses on *responsibility, respect, fairness, and honesty.*

    The code applies to the following individuals:

- Nonmembers who hold a PMI certification
- Nonmembers who apply to commence a PMI certification process
- Nonmembers who serve PMI in a volunteer capacity

    Source: www.pmi.org/about/ethics/code

Task Overview

There are many best practices in an Agile environment that may be relevant to your current or future projects. Think of the following as a checklist, or high-level overview of tasks and best practices to consider. The following overview is also the exam content outline for review of all domains.

Source: PMI Agile Certified Practitioner (PMI-ACP®) Examination Content Outline© 2014. Project Management Institute, Inc. All rights reserved.

Agile Principles and Mindset Considerations

The principles and mindset considerations are important aspects to consider putting yourself in the right mindset for both the exam and when implementing Agile best practices.

- Explore, embrace, and apply Agile principles and the Agile mindset within the context of the project team and organization.

- Advocate for Agile principles by modeling those principles and discussing Agile values to develop a shared mindset across the team as well as between the customer and the team.

- Help ensure that everyone has a common understanding of the values and principles of Agile and a common knowledge around the Agile practices and terminology being used in order to work effectively.

- Support change at the system or organization level by educating the organization and influencing processes, behaviors, and people to make the organization more effective and efficient.

- Practice visualization by maintaining highly visible information radiators showing real progress and real team performance thereby enhancing transparency and trust.

- Contribute to a safe and trustful team environment by allowing everyone to experiment and make mistakes so that each individual can learn and continuously improve the way he or she works.

- Enhance creativity by experimenting with new techniques and process ideas and discover more efficient and effective ways of working.

- Encourage team members to share knowledge by collaborating and working together thereby lowering risks around knowledge silos and reduce bottlenecks.

- Encourage emergent leadership within the team by establishing a safe and respectful environment in which new approaches can be tried in order to make improvements and foster self-organization and empowerment.

- Practice servant leadership by supporting and encouraging others in their endeavors so that they can perform at their highest level and continue to improve.

Value-Driven Delivery

Deliver valuable results by producing high-value increments for review, early and often, based on stakeholder priorities. Have the stakeholders provide feedback on these increments, and use this feedback to prioritize and improve future increments.

Define Positive Value

The goal of any Agile project is to deliver value early and often so it is important to define positive value in a way that can be discussed and executed upon.

- Define deliverables by identifying units that can be produced incrementally to maximize their value to stakeholders while minimizing non-value-added work.

- Refine requirements by gaining consensus on the acceptance criteria for features on a just-in-time basis thereby delivering value.

- Select and tailor the team's process based on project and organizational characteristics as well as team experience to optimize value delivery.

Avoid Potential Downsides

Even the best plans don't always work out but if small releases are planned with effective feedback the downsides can be minimized.

- Plan for small, releasable increments by organizing requirements into minimally marketable features/minimally viable products to allow for the early recognition and delivery of value.

- Limit increment size and increase review frequency with appropriate stakeholders in order to identify and respond to risks early on and at minimal cost.

- Solicit customer and user feedback by reviewing increments often in order to confirm and enhance business value.

Prioritization

Performing valuable work means prioritizing what is most important to work on and what is considered valuable at the time.

- Prioritize the units of work through collaboration with stakeholders in order to optimize the value of the deliverables.

- Perform frequent review and maintenance of the work results by prioritizing and maintaining internal quality in order to reduce the overall cost of incremental development.

- Continuously identify and prioritize the environmental, operational, and infrastructure factors in order to improve the quality and value of the deliverables.

Incremental Development

Agile development is based on iterative and incremental development of a result. Rather than preplanning everything, small, incremental plans are created and executed upon with feedback in between.

- Conduct operational reviews and/or periodic checkpoints with stakeholders in order to obtain feedback and corrections to the work in progress and planned work.

- Balance development of deliverable units and risk-reduction efforts by incorporating both value-producing and risk-reducing work into the backlog in order to maximize the total value proposition over time.

- Reprioritize requirements periodically in order to reflect changes in the environment and stakeholder needs or preferences in order to maximize the value.

- Elicit and prioritize relevant nonfunctional requirements (such as operations and security) by considering the environment in which the solution will be used in order to minimize the probability of failure.

- Conduct frequent reviews of work products by performing inspections, reviews, and/or testing in order to identify and incorporate improvements into the overall process and product/service.

Stakeholder Engagement

Engage current and future interested parties by building a trusting environment that aligns their needs and expectations and balances their requests with an understanding of the cost/effort involved. Promote participation and collaboration throughout the project life cycle and provide the tools for effective and informed decision making.

Understand Stakeholder Needs

If your team understands the needs of the stakeholders, it is far easier to produce what it is they are asking for and helps engage them in the process.

- Identify and engage effective and empowered business stakeholder(s) through periodic reviews in order to ensure that the team is knowledgeable about stakeholders' interests, needs, and expectations.

- Identify and engage all stakeholders (current and future) by promoting knowledge sharing early and throughout the project to ensure the unimpeded flow of information and value throughout the life span of the project.

Ensure Stakeholder Involvement

Without the involvement of your stakeholders you would never know if you were building the increment correctly or building the increment they want. By involving the stakeholders at multiple points, your team can ensure they have the best information at the time.

- Establish stakeholder relationships by forming a working agreement among key stakeholders in order to promote participation and effective collaboration.

- Maintain proper stakeholder involvement by continually assessing changes in the project and organization in order to ensure that new stakeholders are appropriately engaged.

- Establish collaborative behaviors among the members of the organization by fostering group decision making and conflict resolution in order to improve decision quality and reduce the time required to make decisions.

Manage Stakeholder Expectations

Having a shared vision is an important aspect of providing value to the organization and to the stakeholders.

- Establish a shared vision of the various project increments (products, deliverables, releases, iterations) by developing a high-level vision and supporting objectives in order to align stakeholders' expectations and build trust.

- Establish and maintain a shared understanding of success criteria, deliverables, and acceptable trade-offs by facilitating awareness among stakeholders in order to align expectations and build trust.

- Provide transparency regarding work status by communicating team progress, work quality, impediments, and risks in order to help the primary stakeholders make informed decisions.

- Provide forecasts at a level of detail that balances the need for certainty and the benefits of adaptability in order to allow stakeholders to plan effectively.

Team Performance

Create an environment of trust, learning, collaboration, and conflict resolution that promotes team self-organization, enhances relationships among team members, and cultivates a culture of high performance.

Team Formation

Agile project management embraces self-directed and self-managed teams. That doesn't mean that the team arrives that way when they first begin to work on an Agile project.

- Cooperate with the other team members to devise ground rules and internal processes in order to foster team coherence and strengthen team members' commitment to shared outcomes.

- Help create a team that has the interpersonal and technical skills needed to achieve all known project objectives in order to create business value with minimal delay.

Team Empowerment

Empowering your team is necessary to be able to encourage self-direction and self-management.

- Encourage team members to become generalizing specialists in order to reduce team size and bottlenecks and to create a high-performing cross-functional team.

- Contribute to self-organizing the work by empowering others and encouraging emerging leadership in order to produce effective solutions and manage complexity.

- Continuously discover team and personal motivators and demotivators in order to ensure that team morale is high and team members are motivated and productive throughout the project.

Team Collaboration and Commitment

Collaboration and commitment are two of the keystones of Agile project management.

- Facilitate close communication within the team and with appropriate external stakeholders through colocation or the use of collaboration tools in order to reduce miscommunication and rework.

- Reduce distractions in order to establish a predictable outcome and optimize the value delivered.

- Participate in aligning project and team goals by sharing project vision in order to ensure that the team understands how their objectives fit into the overall goals of the project.

- Encourage the team to measure its velocity by tracking and measuring actual performance in previous iterations or releases in order for members to gain a better understanding of their capacity and create more accurate forecasts.

Adaptive Planning

Produce and maintain an evolving plan, from initiation to closure, based on goals, values, risks, constraints, stakeholder feedback, and review findings.

Levels of Planning

The ability to plan at multiple levels and adapt as needed is the crux of Agile project management.

- Plan at multiple levels (strategic, release, iteration, daily), creating appropriate detail by using rolling wave planning and progressive elaboration to balance predictability of outcomes with ability to exploit opportunities.

- Make planning activities visible and transparent by encouraging participation of key stakeholders and publishing planning results in order to increase commitment level and reduce uncertainty.

- As the project unfolds, set and manage stakeholder expectations by making increasingly specific levels of commitments in order to ensure common understanding of the expected deliverables.

Adaptation

Practicing agility allows the team to adapt to changing environments.

- Adapt the cadence and the planning process based on results of periodic retrospectives about characteristics and/or the size/complexity/criticality of the project deliverables in order to maximize the value.

- Inspect and adapt the project plan to reflect changes in requirements, schedule, and budget and to reflect shifting priorities based on team learning, delivery experience, stakeholder feedback, and defects in order to maximize business value delivered.

Agile Sizing and Estimation

Planning is different in an Agile project as compared to a Waterfall preplanned project, therefore estimation and sizing of work needs to be adaptable and relevant to the work itself.

- Size items by using progressive elaboration techniques in order to determine likely project size independent of team velocity and external variables.

- Adjust capacity by incorporating maintenance and operations demands and other factors in order to create or update the range estimate.

- Create initial scope, schedule, and cost range estimates that reflect current high-level understanding of the effort necessary to deliver the project in order to develop a starting point for managing the project.
- Refine scope, schedule, and cost range estimates that reflect the latest understanding of the effort necessary to deliver the project in order to manage the project.
- Continuously use data from changes in resource capacity, project size, and velocity metrics in order to evaluate the estimate to complete or ETC.

Problem Detection and Resolution

Every project will have risk events and problems. How the team identifies and works through those problems will determine whether the project was successful or not.

- Continuously identify problems, impediments, and risks; prioritize and resolve in a timely manner; monitor and communicate the problem resolution status; and implement process improvements to prevent them from occurring again.
- Create an open and safe environment by encouraging conversation and experimentation in order to surface problems and impediments that are slowing the team down or preventing its ability to deliver value.
- Identify threats and issues by educating and engaging the team at various points in the project in order to resolve them at the appropriate time and improve processes that caused issues.
- Ensure that issues are resolved by appropriate team members and/or reset expectations in light of issues that cannot be resolved in order to maximize the value delivered.
- Maintain a visible, monitored, and prioritized list of threats and issues in order to elevate accountability, encourage action, and track ownership and resolution status.
- Communicate status of threats and issues by maintaining a threat list and incorporating activities into a backlog of work in order to provide transparency.

Continuous Improvement

Learning and improving is part of practicing agility.

- Continuously improve the quality, effectiveness, and value of the product, the process, and the team.
- Tailor and adapt the project process by periodically reviewing and integrating team practices, organizational culture, and delivery goals in order to ensure team effectiveness within established organizational guidelines and norms.
- Improve team processes by conducting frequent retrospectives and improvement experiments in order to continually enhance the effectiveness of the team, project, and organization.

- Seek feedback on the product by incremental delivery and frequent demonstrations in order to improve the value of the product.

- Create an environment of continued learning by providing opportunities for people to develop their skills in order to develop a more productive team of generalizing specialists.

- Challenge existing process elements by performing a value stream analysis and removing waste in order to increase individual efficiency and team effectiveness.

- Create systemic improvements by disseminating knowledge and practices across projects and organizational boundaries in order to avoid reoccurrence of identified problems and improve the effectiveness of the organization as a whole.

Tools and Techniques Overview

You may be tested on all of the tools or techniques. The following is a good list of the tools and techniques to review to make sure that you understand them. These tools and techniques are found in the PMI-ACP Exam Content Outline.

Source: *PMI Agile Certified Practitioner (PMI-ACP®) Examination Content Outline©* 2014. Project Management Institute, Inc. All rights reserved.

Agile Analysis and Design, including but not limited to the following tools and techniques:

- Product road map
- User stories/backlog
- Story maps
- Progressive elaboration
- Wireframes
- Chartering
- Personas
- Agile modeling
- Workshops
- Learning cycle
- Collaboration games

Agile Estimation, including but not limited to the following tools and techniques:

- Relative sizing/story points/T-shirt sizing
- Wide-band Delphi/planning poker

- Affinity estimating
- Ideal time

Communications, including but not limited to the following tools and techniques:

- Information radiator
- Team space Agile tooling
- Osmotic communications for colocated and/or distributed teams
- Two-way communications (trustworthy, conversation driven)
- Social media-based communication
- Active listening
- Brainstorming
- Feedback methods

Interpersonal Skills, including but not limited to the following tools and techniques:

- Emotional intelligence
- Collaboration
- Adaptive leadership
- Servant leadership
- Negotiation
- Conflict resolution

Metrics, including but not limited to the following tools and techniques:

- Velocity/throughput/productivity
- Cycle time
- Lead time
- EVM for Agile projects
- Defect rate
- Approved iterations
- Work in progress

Planning, Monitoring, and Adapting, including but not limited to the following tools and techniques:

- Reviews
- Kanban board

- Task board
- Timeboxing
- Iteration and release planning
- Variance and trend analysis
- WIP limits
- Daily stand-ups
- Burn down/up charts
- Cumulative flow diagrams
- Backlog grooming/refinement
- Product-feedback loop

Process Improvement, including but not limited to the following tools and techniques:

- Kaizen
- The 5 whys
- Retrospectives, intraspectives
- Process tailoring/hybrid models
- Value stream mapping
- Control limits
- Premortem (rule setting, failure analysis)
- Fishbone diagram analysis

Product Quality, including but not limited to the following tools and techniques:

- Frequent verification and validation
- Definition of done
- Continuous integration
- Testing, including exploratory and usability

Risk Management, including but not limited to the following tools and techniques:

- Risk adjusted backlog
- Risk burn down graphs
- Risk-based spike
- Architectural spike

Value-Based Prioritization, including but not limited to the following tools and techniques:

- ROI/NPV/IRR
- Compliance

- Customer-valued prioritization
- Requirements reviews
- Minimal viable product (MVP)
- Minimal marketable feature (MMF)
- Relative prioritization/ranking
- MoSCoW
- Kano analysis

Knowledge and Skills

A large part of the effective management of Agile projects and the Agile tools and techniques is driven by knowledge and skills in a variety of areas. Part of the Project Management Institute's exam content outline defines knowledge and skills that are necessary to implement the tools and techniques effectively.

As an overview, you'll go through the knowledge and skills, and as you work through each chapter in this book, you will see that I have addressed the tools, techniques, and knowledge and skills not only to help you pass the exam, but to help you implement your current Agile projects as well.

Each statement is preceded implicitly by Knowledge of or Skill in the following areas:

- Agile values and principles
- Agile frameworks and terminology
- Agile methods and approaches
- Assessing and incorporating community and stakeholder values
- Stakeholder management
- Communication management
- Facilitation methods
- Knowledge sharing/written communication
- Leadership
- Building Agile teams
- Team motivation
- Physical and virtual colocation
- Global, cultural, and team diversity
- Training, coaching, and mentoring
- Developmental mastery models (for example, Tuckman, Dreyfus, Shu Ha Ri)
- Self-assessment tools and techniques

- Participatory decision models (for example, convergent, shared collaboration)
- Principles of systems thinking (for example, complex adaptive, chaos)
- Problem solving
- Prioritization
- Incremental delivery
- Agile discovery
- Agile sizing and estimation
- Value-based analysis and decomposition
- Process analysis
- Continuous improvement
- Agile hybrid models
- Managing with Agile KPIs
- Agile project chartering
- Agile contracting
- Agile project accounting principles
- Regulatory compliance
- PMI's Code of Ethics and Professional Conduct

Source: *PMI Agile Certified Practitioner (PMI-ACP®) Examination Content Outline*©
2014. Project Management Institute, Inc. All rights reserved.

Concluding Thoughts

Remember, this is more than about passing an exam: It is about learning best practices that you can take with you anywhere. Perfect practice makes perfect! As you gear up for your exam, always check out the latest information on www.pmi.org for any content updates, exam changes, and date adjustments. Take and retake the practice exams, read other books on the topics found here, and enjoy your agility!

Best of luck on your exam!

Appendix

B

Answers to Review Questions

Chapter 1

1. C. The first value points to focusing more on individuals and collaborations than on a set methodology or tools and techniques.

2. B. The Agile Alliance was created by a group of software developers who were looking for better ways to manage their projects with a sharper focus on software development.

3. D. Agile projects involve frequent changes and documentation at the last responsible moment. If a plan is followed to the letter, it doesn't allow for frequent changes.

4. D. All methods focus on ways to increase value for the customer by communicating and adapting to changing customer needs.

5. C. Even though there are specific frameworks like Scrum and XP that help manage projects more effectively, the main goal of Agile is to provide value and continuously learn and improve.

6. A. It's not uncommon that people new to Agile frameworks get confused about managing change over formal preplanning, but planning is a big part of Agile project management, just not long-term planning when you know things will change.

7. A. These pillars also support the Scrum framework and provide a good itemized list of the Agile mindset.

8. A. This is the biggest difference between Waterfall and Agile. Agile involves planning, but waiting until the last responsible moment to do so. The scope of work isn't fixed as it is with Waterfall projects.

9. B. Many organizations are too quick to say something doesn't work when they don't get immediate results. Agile is very different from many set processes that helped build out the industrial age, and it is open-ended and flexible. It takes practice and time to integrate.

10. A. It isn't recommended to try to create a hybrid approach until all best practices are well understood and have been used. This doesn't mean that you couldn't incorporate stand-up meetings on your next Waterfall project. It's just not recommended to combine full frameworks until everything is well accepted and understood.

11. B. The Agile Manifesto was the outcome of the meeting in Utah, which was held due to the frustration with current methods of software design and project management.

12. C. The Agile Manifesto isn't saying that you should choose one over the other; it is merely suggesting that you should place individuals and your interactions with them over sticking strictly to tools and processes that may or may not be working.

13. A. Because software design is about providing value to the customer quickly and that value can change frequently, Waterfall isn't the best method due to heavy preplanning and formal change control systems. While some software projects could be managed with Waterfall, depending on the nature of the project, Agile is better suited for rapid changes and planning at the last responsible moment.

14. D. Individuals and interactions over processes and tools is the first value of the Agile Manifesto.

15. A. Responding to change over following a plan is the fourth value in the Agile Manifesto.

16. B. Working software over comprehensive documentation is the second value in the Agile Manifesto.

17. C. Customer collaboration over contract negotiation is the third value in the Agile Manifesto.

18. C. The Declaration of Interdependence states, "We increase return on Investment by making continuous flow of value our focus."

19. D. Agile project teams are self-directed and self-managed, but they also have coaching from an Agile project manager to help them maintain the vision of the work and reach consensus as a team on next steps.

20. A. Agile project teams work best in a colocated environment. While that isn't always possible, it is suggested that the team colocates on a regular basis or at least for one iteration if they are remote/virtual team members.

Chapter 2

1. B. Scrum is a lightweight framework that is easy to learn and difficult to do.

2. A. A retrospective is the final meeting of a sprint, where the team discusses what went well and what didn't and makes plans for improvements. The other answers are actual outputs or artifacts of the Scrum framework.

3. D. Sprints are rarely canceled, and if they are it is because the product has become obsolete. Therefore, a sprint would not be canceled in the middle of a project for the other reasons given.

4. A. All of the other answers represent the core values of XP. Coaching is an important aspect of all Agile methods or frameworks, but it is not unique to core values.

5. D. Pair programming is a large part of XP, geared to maintain consistency, learning, and communication during programming. One programmer codes, the other oversees, and then they switch.

6. B. The daily Scrum allows the development team to discuss work in progress, work to be done, and impediments to their progress. The daily Scrum is timeboxed at 15 minutes.

7. D. Part of being a servant leader is to take on administrative work as needed to keep your team focused on the work in progress. You may also suggest to the stakeholders that asking for too many updates can hinder progress, but in this case option D is the best answer.

8. C. Daily Scrums are for informational purposes only, and the development team are the only ones to discuss what they have done, what they are doing, and what impediments are in their way. Any others attending the Scrum are silent observers. Other stakeholders can attend but not participate in the discussion. No solutions are generated during the meeting, only information.

9. C. The product owner's primary responsibility is to own the product backlog and communicate and redistribute the value as needed.

10. C. Regardless of the specific framework, all Agile teams are self-organized and self-managed.

11. A. Retrospectives allow the team to review what went well and what the challenges were during the sprint. This reflection point allows for discussions of continuous improvement for the next sprint.

12. D. Agile project managers are servants first to their team and practice leadership more so than management. Their job is to coach and support their team.

13. A. Understanding what "done" is allows the team to plan around the requirements and produce a usable increment at the end of each iteration/sprint.

14. D. The team is self-directed and self-managed so that they can make decisions about how they will go about creating the result. They communicate regularly to share knowledge.

15. A. Three questions in each daily Scrum or stand-up meeting are, What did we do yesterday? What we will do today? What impediments are in our way?

16. B. The product owner is responsible for the product backlog, but it is transparent and open to the entire team, who helps to determine what items of value will be delivered in the next iteration/sprint.

17. C. The daily Scrum or stand-up meeting is timeboxed for 15 minutes every day. This keeps it short and to the point while updating the entire development team on what is occurring during the iteration/sprint.

18. B. The grooming of the backlog process is done by the team, but the product owner is responsible for pushing items of value to the front. The team will select from the backlog work that can be accomplished in the iteration based on current value.

19. B. The sprint backlog represents the chosen items the development team will work on during the sprint. They will select what they believe they can accomplish and what they believe will produce a usable increment at the end.

20. A. The daily standup meetings or daily Scrums are designed to provide up-to-date information to the development team about work completed or in progress as well as anything that is preventing them from being totally successful right now.

Chapter 3

1. **D.** The MoSCoW approach to determining value is based on brainstorming what is the most important feature today and that it must be in the increment, following by what should be, what could be, and what won't be.

2. **C.** The Pareto principle was created by Vilfredo Pareto as a way to study distribution of wealth in Italy. It was adapted by Joseph Juran to determine what causes have the most effect on the results. Identify those causes and you can fix the defects.

3. **D.** In a Lean environment, determining waste in approach and result is the best way to remove it from the process. Waste is the opposite of value because it provides no value and instead produces problems in the increment and/or the process to create it.

4. **A.** In Lean, too many handoffs of pieces or parts of work create numerous problems regarding the quality and to the process, and it is considered one of the seven wastes of Lean.

5. **B.** A Kanban board is one of the most effective ways to show information and radiate it out to stakeholders. The Kanban board is a visual board displaying Kanban cards and using a pull system to replace work that has been deployed and pull more into the work in progress (WIP). Kanban boards are like Scrum boards, except in Scrum new work isn't added until the next sprint.

6. **A.** Limiting work in progress (WIP) allows the team to focus only on the work that is to be accomplished and not pull any additional work in until the team is ready to perform it.

7. **A.** Originally, Feature-Driven Development was created to counteract a more Waterfall type of methodology. Because larger teams were working on an increment or result, it was necessary to compartmentalize work by feature so that there wasn't any confusion or duplicate work occurring on larger teams.

8. **C.** Increasing criticality is the best way to manage projects that have a sliding scale of noncritical to critical work being accomplished. Larger projects with more intricate results need a heavier method than one that needs a lighter framework to produce to spec.

9. **D.** All frameworks and Agile methods are tolerant of changes and, in fact, expect changes to occur. This allows for flexibility in the design to best meet the needs of the client and to help the team adapt as needed to produce the increment.

10. **D.** Servant leadership is different from management in the sense that you will take on administrative work as needed to help your team be most successful. This could be anything from doing updates to status, or even coaching the other stakeholders in your Agile framework so that they don't inadvertently add more work to the team's plate.

11. **C.** Notice that the only answer that doesn't include *I* is the correct answer. Active listening as a servant leader is making sure that you are there for the team member, not thinking about yourself or what you need to do next. Once you have listened, you can then coach the team member through the issue.

12. D. Adaptive leadership is less about management and more about inspiration, active listening, coaching when needed, and helping your team to be more successful. This is a major trend in Agile projects and heavily tested on the PMI-ACP exam.

13. B. Colocation is highly important for Agile project teams. Even if the team is remote or virtual, it is recommended that the team be colocated for at least two iterations to build as a team and to focus on how to get the work accomplished as a team.

14. C. Osmotic communication is part of being colocated. It allows everyone to hear everything being communicated, and the individual can choose to listen if it relates to them or choose to ignore it if it serves no purpose. This communication method is highly regarded as one of the best knowledge transfer techniques.

15. A. Being a good leader is much more than seating your team together and having daily stand-up meetings. It's practicing motivating your team when needed, compensating and celebrating successes, and encouraging your team to be self-directed and self-managed while taking on administrative work as needed.

16. C. Even though this may not be the case in your current environment, it is important to note that Agile project managers spend most of their time communicating with their teams, product owners, customers, and other stakeholders.

17. A. Lean was created to help with the supply chain in Toyota manufacturing plants and was later adapted for Agile frameworks as a complementary process rather than an actual methodology.

18. C. The traditional cycle of Plan-Do-Check-Act in Waterfall was replaced by the ASD framework as a way to improve continuously in an adaptive way.

19. D. The Agile project manager's role is as a servant leader. The management tasks are done, but to a lesser degree than with Waterfall project managers. It is more important to serve your team as a leader. Your team is self-directed and self-managed. This concept is difficult for stakeholders new to Agile project management.

20. B. Using Kanban or Scrum boards is one of the best ways to show visually what work is in the backlog, what work is in progress, and what work has been done. Most progress is shown visually throughout the iterations in one form or another.

21. B. Much like the initiation phase in a Waterfall project, Iteration Zero allows the team to prepare for the iterations to come by creating a plan for the process and identifying the team roles and responsibilities and to determine officially the process that will be used.

Chapter 4

1. B. Osmotic communication is a way to absorb information even if you are not involved in the actual conversation. That information can be taken as important or not depending on the needs of the individual.

2. D. Wireframes allow the team to work through a type of prototyping in an easy and low-tech way by drawing or plotting out what the increment might look like.

3. C. Even though options B through D help organizations get to the point that a charter could be created, net present value is the only one that has all of the information in it and can provide the best overall determination of fiscal health when selecting a project.

4. A. Even though you could say that it is written in the format of a user story, the story itself is so vague that there isn't any way in which to direct the conversation. It's hard to negotiate features or really understand what the customer wants.

5. D. You are asking your customer for a very small, concise explanation of what success looks like. Even though elevator statements should be about 30 seconds long, a tweet cuts out all of the noise and gets to the bottom line in 140 characters or less.

6. C. The only answer that isn't self-focused is option C. The key to active listening is not thinking about what you are going to do or say next but to remind yourself to focus on the message you are receiving.

7. B. A user story that is too large isn't going to be effective. Even after it is broken down from the epic level, too much information in a user story doesn't follow the INVEST process of creating effective user stories.

8. C. In this case, all things have been calculated into the NPV equation, and if a decision needs to be made strictly on NPV, you would always choose the highest number with the most ROI.

9. A. A wireframe is a low-fidelity mock-up of what the user story represents or what success looks like.

10. B. Option B is the best answer because Agile project charters are more flexible in their approach and documentation by providing the who, what, where, when, and how as you know it today.

11. A. Emotional intelligence is the ability to recognize yourself in other people's experiences.

12. C. The correct format for user stories is:

As _____ I need _____ so that I can _____.

The format is important, but not as important as making sure the story is able to be tested, negotiated, and well understood.

13. A. User story workshops are a way to determine the user stories over the period of the project, but they are most important to engage stakeholders in what success looks like and to gain an understanding of what the customer wants through communication and collaboration.

14. A. Payback period tracks the amount of time outgoing expenditures are recouped before a profit is made. It isn't the most reliable selection technique, and it would need to be utilized in a net present value (NPV) formula with additional information to truly be relevant.

15. D. The project charter is an excellent jumping-off point, but it really is only describing things on a very high level. It isn't until you start working directly with the customer that your team can begin to figure out what success looks like.

16. C. Even though mirroring isn't something you'll likely see on the PMI-ACP exam, communication surely is. Mirroring it is an important aspect of effective communication. This study guide will prepare you for the exam, but there are other key points that are useful in your day-to-day work life, and mirroring is one of them.

17. A. An Agile project charter is more flexible in nature because the scope of work isn't set in the beginning, so determining full-blown schedules, budgets, and risk is much more difficult to accomplish. Therefore, Agile project charters wouldn't contain this amount of information.

18. C. A tweet can be created to gain an understanding of what the customer wants in a concise way.

19. A. Until your team knows the definition of done, it is virtually impossible to build a working or viable product or service because there isn't an end in sight.

20. C. A persona is a way to gain valuable insight into the customer's needs. It is sometimes developed around a fictitious character as a way to work through a similar situation and gain a better understanding of what the customer or end users want and need without yet knowing the customer very well. Or, it can be based on the customer themselves.

Chapter 5

1.   B. The gulf of misunderstanding occurs when the customer and the team misunderstand the requirements. It is often the cause of disagreement on direction and on features/functions of the increment.

2.   D. This is called "strategic avoidance." Many people have differing opinions about news stories, and the Agile project manager shouldn't get involved as it isn't relevant to project work.

3.   C. Even though this could describe an Agile team, all teams go through periods of adjustment before performing as a self-directed team. The Agile project manager is much more of a servant leader than a manager when a team is self-directed and self-managed.

4.   A. The product owner is using good negotiation techniques. It's important to be able to give value to the customer, but occasionally it's important to negotiate for the most important features and do away with the ones that don't serve a purpose.

5.   C. Obviously, which resolution strategy would work best in each scenario depends on the conflict situation. If, in general terms, you are asked what is the best or longest-lasting strategy, the correct answer would be confronting or collaboration.

6.   B. Since your team is in the performing phase of team development, they are working together and may only need coaching here and there, and only if they ask for it.

7.   B. Having your team be colocated is generally the best setup for team space. Even though it isn't always possible to do so, colocation is recommended as a best practice in Agile environments.

8. C. Having your team colocated in one team space improves communication and allows individuals to overhear information and choose to retain or discard it through osmotic communication. It also builds relationships and trust, but that only happens with improvement in communication.

9. C. Storming is a natural occurrence with newer teams. It is important for the coach/Scrum Master to coach the team through it.

10. D. Removing roadblocks and taking on administrative work is a key aspect to practicing adaptive leadership.

11. C. Engaging stakeholders in the definition of done and helping them determine what success looks like is a valuable way to manage stakeholder expectations.

12. D. Active listening is a large part of effective communication and stakeholder engagement. It's best to listen to what the stakeholder is saying rather than thinking about what you will do next or how to solve their problem.

13. D. In this situation, it is unnecessary to step in to help resolve the disagreement. Your team is collectively disagreeing, and it is working toward a solution. Unless you are asked to help, it's better to let them work through it on their own.

14. D. The Project Management Institute's Professional Code of Ethics and Professional Conduct describes mandatory skills, which include not breaking the law and not discriminating, and aspirational skills, such as communication, negotiation, and motivation.

15. D. Smoothing helps everyone focus on what things they have in common and what may be necessary to work on before any collaboration can occur. When used alone, smoothing is only a short-term fix, but it may be necessary in a heated exchange situation.

16. D. Even though questions about Maslow's theory aren't something you'll likely see on your PMI-ACP exam, having the ability to motivate effectively is important to servant and adaptive leadership. This study guide will prepare you for the exam, but there are other key points that are useful in your day-to-day work, and motivational theory is one of them.

17. B. Negotiations that are effective result in a win-win situation for all those involved. In this case, the team explained their side and the product owner explained why they thought their point was valid. In the end, the team determined that they could add one more story but not two. Both sides walked away with something in the exchange, and it was settled appropriately.

18. A. Good interpersonal skills are necessary to engage stakeholders and to have the emotional intelligence to work with them on determining value. Being an adaptive leader also involves interpersonal skill sets.

19. C. Engaging your stakeholders doesn't mean doing everything they say. In fact, a good servant leader would listen to their concerns but also explain how a self-directed team works together to estimate and protect the team from interruptions.

20. C. There are a couple of things going on here. First, the product owner is in charge of the backlog, and stakeholders should respect that. Next, adding a feature because the stakeholder finds it valuable may not match up with the customer's needs. Finally, in Scrum, no new user stories are added in the middle of a sprint.

Chapter 6

1. B. Velocity in the first several iterations/sprints will vary and then increase the amount of story points that can be accomplished as the team gets further into the project. Eventually, the velocity will plateau and then the team can most effectively forecast completion.

2. C. At this point, early in the iterations and with everything fluctuating, it's best to get an average and use that to forecast. In this case, the team would round up to 15 iterations, since partial credit isn't going to work.

3. D. This question includes the word *except*, meaning that everything is correct except option D. Decision delays are not applied to taking an epic and breaking it down to a user story level. Even if that were true, the correct order would be taking something that is course-grained and breaking it down to a fine-grained level.

4. C. Ideal time is basically a duration of time that something would take if you didn't have any distractions at all, meaning that in a 40-hour work week, you didn't do anything else except work on your project. Ideal time isn't an effective way to plan.

5. C. The format in which user stories are written include these three variables:
    As _____ I want/need _____ so that I can _____ .

6. D. Backlog grooming or refinement is the act of the product owner sorting the backlog by priority. The development team may be involved in this process, and it usually is, but it is the responsibility of the product owner to do so, and everyone else will respect their decisions.

7. C. For the most part, if you were to go hierarchically, that would be the order of decomposition. Just like anything in Agile, it depends on your team and how you decompose work, whether you work with themes or just epics. It is also the best answer from all the options, since many answers use the words *task* and/or *sequencing*.

8. D. A story map gives the team a visual representation of the work that they are going to do and what success looks like.

9. A. A definition of done is necessary so that everyone has a specific understanding of what the result will be so that they can create it and know when it has been created and is finished.

10. C. A persona is used by the team to understand the customer or end users in a way that makes them more relatable. Sometimes, a placeholder name or person is used to help describe what an end user might need from the deliverables.

11. C. Velocity is the amount of work a team can accomplish in an iteration. It is calculated by how many story points were selected and how many were achieved during an iteration.

12. D. When you divide 201 by the current velocity of 50, you get 4.02. The most logical way to calculate how many iterations are left in this case is to round up to five since partial work doesn't count and you have already attained a stabilized velocity.

13. C. It happens. Not everything will always be completed in every iteration, no matter how well you plan. If there is leftover work or there are story points, they will be put back into the backlog and sorted by priority. Typically, that work would be put into the next iteration.

14. A. Timeboxes are used for a variety of Agile activities, including the iteration length, planning meetings, backlog refinement, spikes, and stand-up meetings.

15. C. Iteration Zero, or sprint zero, allows a team that is perhaps newer to Agile and doesn't have a process intact yet to develop their process, or if a seasoned team determines that they need a discovery iteration to develop the best approach, they would use Iteration Zero.

16. B. Ideal time is time that is spent without interruptions and isn't an effective way to estimate.

17. D. The product owner will be the person responsible for the backlog. Even though the team may help with clarification or backlog refinement, the product owner owns the backlog and determines priority.

18. B. A master list of visible work is a backlog, and it is a living document that is reviewed, reorganized, and reprioritized by the product owner while grooming or refining the backlog.

19. A. Agile teams apply a certain amount of story points based on relative sizing to determine just how big the work is. They then use that information to plan how many points they can accomplish. *Lessons learned*, while not a key term in Agile, is an apt description of how teams learn from the past and apply it to the present. Velocity will eventually stabilize based on better estimates.

20. A. In this case, Bob may not understand the ins and outs of the technology, and because of the lack of knowledge about the work, it may seem bigger to Bob than to his teammates. In this case, Bob is an outlier and would need to explain why he chose 10 instead of 5. The team would then discuss and vote again.

21. C. If the team averages 10 points a sprint, and that is the maximum they can do, they would have three more sprints left to accommodate all of the work without partial work done in a sprint. The priority would be A and B, then C and E, and then D.

Chapter 7

1. A. Generalized specialists are excellent for Agile teamwork because the individual is an expert in their field but has additional skill sets and knowledge that can benefit the team.

2. B. If your team is performing, it is your role to be a servant leader, and if your team asks for or needs help, you provide it. Otherwise, you act as more of a facilitator.

3. A. The concept of Shu Ha Ri describes the progression from obeying the rules of new skills and then branching out a bit to something that suits you without breaking the rules. Finally, in Shu Ha Ri you achieve skill mastery where you can perform the skill in any way that it needs to be performed.

4. B. Colocation is highly recommended, if possible, for the team. Even if the team is virtual, it is recommended that they be colocated for planning and at least one if not two iterations.

5. C. Osmotic communication is the main reason. Obviously, some of the other reasons are relevant in colocation as well, but the main reason is to improve communication.

6. B. Since your team is in the performing phase of team development, they are working together and may only need coaching here and there as a team. Typically, the best time to do so is during planning and retrospectives.

7. C. Having your team be colocated is generally the best setup for team space, but even when the team is colocated someone may need privacy for a phone call or to work in silence when thinking through a difficult technical issue. Caves or common rooms can be provided for team members working on the same project(s).

8. B. The only guarantee in this model is the guarantee of safety rather than support. The support piece goes without saying, but having a safe environment in which to improve skills, ask questions, and learn allows for effective coaching.

9. B. Velocity fluctuates on any project, but typically the biggest fluctuations are in the beginning, and eventually the amount of work increases and levels off.

10. A. A burn down chart is used to show how much work has been completed, and it can help the team determine how much time the project will take. A burn up chart tracks work completed, but it also shows changes in scope and how that affects the ideal burn.

11. A. To determine how many iterations remain, the team would take an average of all of the iterations and divide it into the remaining points. In this case, the team would probably round up to 13.

12. B. Burn down, burn up, or velocity tracking charts are the best information radiators to present information on performance.

13. D. Most Agile projects do not use Gantt charts, unless they are using a tailored method that needs that type of reporting. In this case, reporting is best served in a highly visual way that is easy to understand.

14. A. Caves and common rooms are useful for colocated teams when they need a bit of privacy or need to work on something project-specific but need quiet to do so.

15. D. It's a best practice to try to colocate all team members for planning and at least one iteration, if possible.

16. B. This question pertains to actual virtual team members, and while video calls are great, the team is better suited for creating their own mission statements and ground rules in the beginning. That will make future video calls much easier.

17. C. Osmotic communication is realistic for colocated teams, and if the team space is set up correctly, this type of communication distribution and collaborative learning is easier.

18. B. Part of being a good coach is to provide a safe environment in which the team can make mistakes and learn from them. If the team asks for coaching, or if you see an opportunity or need for coaching during a retrospective, then it is perfectly within reason to provide it at that point.

19. C. Burn down charts provide a visual of iteration performance and allow the team to estimate when the project may be completed.

20. D. Burn up charts allow the team to track performance visually while also tracking changes in the scope of work that could affect their velocity or completion of stories in an iteration.

Chapter 8

1. D. The entire team includes the product owner, the development team, and the Agile project manager as well as other stakeholders—even the customer or sponsor. Inevitably, the product owner owns the backlog and needs to prioritize value. Nonetheless, they don't do that in a vacuum: There is much discussion and interaction when deciding how to determine what is valuable.

2. C. The gulf of misunderstanding can occur when value has not been clarified or either the customer or the team misunderstands what will be created on the project. To avoid this misunderstanding, the team will use a variety of techniques to reach consensus on what they are building and why.

3. A. Giving the team and other stakeholders colored dots and allowing them to vote on their choices of features and functions allows for discussion and consensus to be reached.

4. C. The 100-point method is designed to allow for prioritization in a facilitated way. This allows everyone to determine what they feel is most important and score it accordingly.

5. B. What this is describing is something new and innovative that hasn't been done before. That describes an exciter that the customer wants included in the next release.

6. B. Using a more flexible type of contract on Agile projects allows for updates or change in scope without any penalty or legal breach of contract.

7. C. This project is over budget because the cost variance is determined by comparing the earned value to the actual cost. Less work was done and you paid more for it. For the schedule variance, more work was done than planned, so the project is ahead of schedule.

8. A. The earned value technique will allow for a comparative approach between the scope of work planned to be accomplished and what it has cost to accomplish that in order to obtain the cost performance index, or CPI.

9. C. In this case, the question is asking for the schedule variance. The formula for that is earned value – planned value. Because less work was accomplished than planned, this project is behind schedule by $400.00, so the answer would be a negative value. The other answers are either positive numbers or indexes obtained by using the formulas incorrectly.

10. A. In this question, all answers could be, in some ways, correct. The best answer here is that the customer isn't understanding your technical jargon and/or why what they want will not be in the final increment. This is due to the gulf of misunderstanding. If Kano analysis had been performed, there would be a better understanding rather than misunderstanding.

11. D. A service level agreement allows for terms and conditions to be determined in the beginning so that future changes in scope won't result in renegotiations throughout the project.

12. B. Monopoly Money is a great way to see how a sponsor or customer would spend their money if given the entire budget to disperse.

13. C. In this case, the *must-haves* versus the *won't-haves* points to prioritization using the MoSCoW approach.

14. D. The cost performance index is a rating of efficiency on the project. Any result over a 1.0 shows that the project is under budget and essentially getting more work accomplished for less money.

15. C. A fixed-price contract is good for organizations that are trying to control costs and have a good understanding of the scope of work. There is less flexibility for scope changes, but cost risk is lower.

16. A. Key performance indicators will vary depending on what the return on investment looks like in an organization. Typically, KPIs relate to project and team performance.

17. A. Setting SMART goals is a large piece of improving all aspects of goal setting.

18. C. The SMART mnemonic acronym stands for specific, measurable, attainable/assignable, realistic, and time-based.

19. D. This response shows a cost performance index under 1.0; that is, the budget is only at 80 percent efficiency when Jamal expected 100 percent.

20. D. There isn't anything that points to a specific time frame for Carol to attain her goal.

21. B. You would need to obtain the planned value, or what you thought you would accomplish at this point in the schedule, and divide it into the earned value, which is how much was accomplished. The formula is EV / PV.

22. B. Over time and use, exciters become less exciting and fade into the satisfier area.

23. D. In an Agile project, it is typical that the cost and time would be more rigid and the scope of work would be more flexible. The opposite is true in a Waterfall type of project.

24. B. Net present value is used to help organizations make decisions based on the payback period, internal rate of return, and present values. The higher the net present value, the higher the expected return on investment.

25. A. Dot voting, or creating a dotmocracy, allows the team to express their opinions and vote on the options that they think are valuable. This allows for transparent communication and consensus to be reached.

Chapter 9

1. A. Progressive elaboration is the process by which information is learned and then added to the existing plan. Because changes are expected, the team will elaborate on the plan with new information when it is identified.

2. B. The strategy of rolling wave planning incorporates the model of replanning multiple times and waiting until the *last responsible moment* to put together those plans. As waves of information roll in, we can then plan accordingly.

3. D. Course-grained requirements are broken down to fine-grained requirements once more information is discovered, not the other way around.

4. C. If a risk event is more impactful financially than the ROI gain of a feature, the project may be cancelled.

5. A. A risk burn down chart will show the progression of mitigation efforts. If the project is going well, the chart will trend down.

6. D. Both sprint/iteration and risk information can be represented on a burn down chart. Risk burn down charts are typically separate, but for both, a burn down is what is represented to show the scope of work completed and risk mitigation efforts working.

7. D. Risk-based spikes are special stories that are created and designed to remove or reduce risk from the iteration.

8. B. The product owner would need to be made aware that a spike is needed and approve the spike to move forward. The entire team doesn't usually work on spikes. It is usually one or two developers.

9. C. Agile projects use progressive elaboration and the strategy of rolling wave planning rather than comprehensive upfront plans and documentation.

10. C. When you're creating your risk-adjusted backlog, the sequence would be determined by the financial values of both risk and features, and the one that is most impactful financially would be worked on first.

11. D. When needed, you may coach your team on the right direction to go. In this case, they may need to perform a spike to figure out their strategy or create a proof of concept.

12. B. Chris should discuss performing a risk-based spike with the product owner and move forward with approval to determine if the risk can be mitigated.

13. B. Tech debt would need to be paid later in the project because the easiest solution was implemented, but maybe it was not the best solution at the time.

14. C. Gail is refactoring the code to make the code easier to read and edit as well as to clean it up without impacting the actual performance of the code.

15. B. Expected monetary value allows for an analysis of risk events to determine the monetary value of risk at its current assessed probability and impact.

16. B. A risk burn down chart shows project or iteration risk. As steps are taken to mitigate or remove risk from the project, the risks should be burning out, and therefore the chart should trend down.

17. B. Asking "why" five times in a row allows the team to identify root causes of risk they might have missed otherwise without further discussion of the causes.

18. D. The most impactful financially would be placed at the top of a risk-adjusted backlog. In this case, Risk D is more financially impactful than the rest.

19. A. The formula is probability × impact. In this case, it would be 0.30 × 10,000 = $3,000.

20. B. The product owner would need to place the highest-impacting risks at the top of the risk-adjusted backlog since they are financially damaging and would need to be mitigated before working on the features currently on the backlog.

21. C. SWOT stands for strengths, weaknesses, opportunities, and threats. It allows for a specific focus on what is going well or not so well in the present that could impact the future.

22. B. Special causes are always a surprise and can lead to defects. Common causes are events that we expect in every project.

23. A. Tech debt is what happens when a development team writes code that is easy to implement in the short term instead of attempting to apply the best overall solution up front.

24. A. If it is a common practice to have more than one person work on a feature, then inevitable human error will create a defect at some point in the project.

25. B. A secondary risk is when you implement a response to a risk event and create a totally different risk. It is always a surprise, and it will require a workaround to manage it.

Chapter 10

1. C. Value stream maps are an excellent visual way to plot out the process and determine where there is waste that may need to be adjusted or removed.

2. A. Lead time reflects the total amount of time that it takes from a customer request until the customer reviews the final result, and cycle time is the development life cycle from a work request that the team receives up to the execution and completion of that specific request—the life cycle of the increment.

3. D. Value stream maps are a way to represent current processes visually and look for better ways to streamline those processes.

4. D. The way to calculate process cycle efficiency is to take the valuable time of 20 minutes and divide into it the total time of 70. That will give you a percentage of efficiency of 28 percent. 20/70 = 28% rounded down.

5. C. Premortems involve asking questions about how the product or project could fail in advance of the execution of the work in order to determine what problems could arise and to fix them before they occur.

6. D. Retrospectives are timeboxed events that the team attends to look back on the iteration that they just completed to determine if there are any improvements that can be made in the next iteration.

7. C. Mad, sad, glad is a way that the team can express their feelings on how the iteration went. This can be facilitated or anonymously submitted. Either way, it allows for the generation of conversation, and areas that may need improvement can be discussed.

8. A. The goal of a retrospective is reflecting on the previous iteration, how the team performed, how the work was executed, how the team's velocity was in the last iteration, and so on. This allows for transparent communication and action items to be discussed.

9. A. Addressing all aspects of the iteration helps the team focus on the good and the challenges the team is facing so that workable solutions can be created.

10. D. Scrum and XP have best practices that are the most compatible with each other, and many teams use a combination of best practices from each to tailor their projects.

11. B. A premortem meeting is a way that the team can discuss what may occur in the future and work to avoid any potential threats to the iteration.

12. B. The Agile Alliance is a group dedicated to best practices in Agile project management, and based on a collaboration with the Project Management Institute, the *Agile Practice Guide* was created.

13. D. Teams can use a cumulative flow diagram to review the flow of their process and determine where issues could occur or have already transpired. Its visual nature allows the team to make decisions on what to fix and how to fix it.

14. D. *Takt time* is used to determine the team's pace or rhythm during an iteration, and it is used to determine the rate at which the team needs to work to keep up with customer demands.

15. A. The Theory of Constraints, or TOC, is a way to look for any bottlenecks in the process, identify the cause, work to remove it.

16. B. ScrumBan is a hybrid approach that incorporates aspects of both Scrum and Kanban as needed, and it was originally created as a way to transition from Scrum to Kanban.

17. D. An intraspective meeting may be necessary when the team is experiencing a lack of cohesiveness or needing a different direction to go in on the iteration work. Anyone can suggest an intraspective meeting.

18. B. Your team can calculate their throughput by adding all of the story points together and then dividing by the amount of iterations. In this particular case, the throughput is equal to one of the total points completed in the iteration. It doesn't always work out that way.

19. A. When tracking velocity, a team would be working to increase the amount of story points they can accomplish in each iteration as a part of continuous improvements. Lead time, on the other hand, would need to decrease. If lead time decreases and velocity improves, this would show continuous improvements and better overall performance.

20. B. LeSS is a product development framework that extends some of the confines of Scrum and allows for scaling guidelines without losing the original purpose of Scrum. There are two levels of Large Scale Scrum: LeSS Huge and LeSS Level.

Index

Note to the Reader: Throughout this index **boldfaced** page numbers indicate primary discussions of a topic. *Italicized* page numbers indicate illustrations.

Comprehensive Online Learning Environment

Register on Sybex.com to gain one year of FREE access to the comprehensive online interactive learning environment and test bank to help you study for your PMI-ACP exam certification.

The online test bank includes:

- **Assessment Test** to help you focus your study to specific objectives
- **Chapter Tests** to reinforce what you've learned
- **Practice Exams** to test your knowledge of the material
- **Digital Flashcards** to reinforce your learning and provide last-minute test prep before the exam
- **Searchable Glossary** to define the key terms you'll need to know for the exam

Go to http://www.wiley.com/go/sybextestprep to register and gain access to this comprehensive study tool package.

Register and Access the Online Test Bank

To register your book and get access to the online test bank, follow these steps:

1. Go to bit.ly/SybexTest.
2. Select your book from the list.
3. Complete the required registration information including answering the security verification proving book ownership. You will be emailed a pin code.
4. Go to http://www.wiley.com/go/sybextestprep and find your book on that page and click the "Register or Login" link under your book.
5. If you already have an account at testbanks.wiley.com, login and then click the "Redeem Access Code" button to add your new book with the pin code you received. If you don't have an account already, create a new account and use the PIN code you received.

SYBEX®
A Wiley Brand

Printed and bound by CPI Group (UK) Ltd, Croydon, CR0 4YY

27/10/2024

14580321-0002